What, Then, Is Man?

GRADUATE STUDY NUMBER III

What, Then, Is Man?

A Symposium of Theology, Psychology, and Psychiatry

PAUL MEEHL, Ph.D.
Head of the Department of Psychology
University of Minnesota

RICHARD KLANN, Ph.D.
Professor of Systematic Theology, Concordia Seminary
St. Louis, Missouri

ALFRED SCHMIEDING, M.A., LL.D.
Professor of Psychology, Concordia Teachers College
River Forest, Illinois

KENNETH BREIMEIER, Ph.D.
Pastor-at-Large
St. Louis, Missouri

SOPHIE SCHROEDER-SLOMANN, M.D.
Practicing Psychiatrist
Oak Park, Illinois

Publishing House
St. Louis

BF
51
.W43
1958

37,631

Concordia Paperback Edition 1971

Copyright 1958 by
Concordia Publishing House
St. Louis, Missouri
Library of Congress Catalog Card No. 58-9438
Manufactured in the United States of America
ISBN 0-570-03125-7

Foreword

THE PRESENT GRADUATE STUDY was prepared by a special committee of experts under the direction of the School for Graduate Studies, Concordia Theological Seminary, St. Louis 5, Mo. It is the third in a series, of which the first two are titled *The Survival of the Historic Vestments in the Lutheran Church After 1555* and *Justification by Faith in Modern Theology*, the former by Arthur Carl Piepkorn of Concordia Seminary, St. Louis, the latter by Henry Hamann, Jr., of Concordia Seminary, Adelaide, Australia.

The primary intent of these studies is to serve as a means for helping to develop that quality of theological guidance and leadership which alone, under the blessing of the Head of the church, can adequately cope with the problems and opportunities of the church in a rapidly changing and deeply disturbed world. This age of the church's life calls for more than halfhearted devotion and haphazard information. These studies cannot supply personal dedication, but they can provide essential facts and necessary direction.

Graduate Study Number III is of particular significance to our day; for it seeks to grapple with one of the most crucial issues confronting theology, namely, what to make of the insights and concepts of psychology and psychiatry. Both have contributed too much to an understanding of human nature to be ignored; and yet both often proceed as though theology did not exist or as though it were a subject smacking of the superstition of a previous age.

v

Various attempts have been made to bring about some kind of understanding and reconciliation between theology and the newer disciplines of psychology and psychiatry. However, most of these efforts have resulted in selling theology short. They have for the most part been content to find some tenuous point of contact on little more than a humanistic basis. For that reason they are of little help to pastors and theologians who are seriously concerned with the truths of Biblical revelation.

Because of this deficiency the Committee for Scholarly Research of The Lutheran Church — Missouri Synod, on May 27, 1955, requested an allocation of funds from the church's Board of Directors to undertake a thorough study of the problem of man as he is viewed in theology, psychology, and psychiatry. Moreover, the Committee for Scholarly Research commissioned the following five persons to prepare this study under the direction of the School for Graduate Studies, Concordia Seminary: Dr. Paul Meehl, Head of the Department of Psychology, University of Minnesota, chairman of the symposium; Dr. Richard Klann, Lutheran campus pastor of the New York area and a graduate student who earned his doctorate under Reinhold Niebuhr and Paul Tillich; Dr. Alfred Schmieding, professor of psychology at Concordia Teachers College, River Forest, Ill., for the past three decades and now retired; Dr. Kenneth Breimeier, head of the field-work program at Concordia Seminary; and Dr. Sophie Schroeder-Sloman, a practicing psychiatrist in Oak Park, Ill.

This committee met for almost four solid weeks in July of 1956 and again for a week in January of 1957 to prepare the basic materials of this study. The final product is the result of reworking done by individual members of their respective assignments in the light of the detailed studies and discussions held in July 1956 and January 1957. As a consequence this study is without equal both for depth of thought and homogeneity of presentation in a most difficult area. The church is greatly indebted to the five members of the symposium both for their willingness to undertake this project and for the extraordinary skill each one has displayed in authoring portions of this study. The greatest contribution was made by the chairman of the special committee, Dr. Paul Meehl.

The School for Graduate Studies of Concordia Theological Seminary in St. Louis, Mo., is happy to release this particular document as Graduate Study III. It does so with the prayer that this book will prove to be of maximum assistance to professional theologians and parish pastors. Our hope is that its spirit and content may serve to glorify the Lord of the church, without whose benediction and guidance this volume could not have come into being.

MARTIN H. SCHARLEMANN
Director of Graduate Studies

Contents

I. Introduction

In RECENT YEARS increasing numbers of the clergy have come to realize that there is a high incidence of "psychological" problems among the members of their congregations who come to the pastor seeking personal and spiritual counsel. As a result, partly of this growing awareness among the clergy, but also because of the extreme shortage of trained secular practitioners of the psychological arts (psychiatrists, psychologists, and social workers), a trend has developed which is commonly referred to as the "pastoral counseling movement." Many books and articles have been written on the subject, and for some years there has even been published a periodical, *Pastoral Psychology*, devoted entirely to this field of endeavor.

Simultaneously with this trend, psychological practitioners outside the church have shown a somewhat greater interest in the religious life of their patients and in the role of religious belief and practice in mental health and illness. Conferences, round tables, symposia, joint committees, and the like, have begun to appear in abundance. There are now in existence several educational facilities where pastors may receive specialized didactic and practicum training in pastoral counseling and clinical psychiatry. Many feel that there is a healthy *rapprochement* beginning between two groups which for years not only have been separated by lack of mutual interest and communication but have in some instances shown suspicious, resentful, disdainful, or actively hostile attitudes to each other.

On the other hand, one can still find psychotherapists and pastors who take the view: "Those fellows are poaching on my territory"; and even when this extreme attitude is not present, there is often detectable a vague feeling of unease, together with a certain puzzlement as to just what these notions are that the other man seems to think so important. Even the desire to maintain amicable relations has at times inhibited effective communication. For example, a psychiatrist may recognize the pastor as a helpful and co-operative person who seems often to exert a salutary effect upon psychiatric patients; but he may simultaneously harbor the thought that the pastor has "some peculiar ideas about sin" which, if inquired into too closely, might lead to a disruption of the smooth working relationship.

Synod's Committee on Scholarly Research, in appointing and instructing the present working group, proceeded in true "Missourian" fashion by giving weight to scholarly aims and by focusing our attention primarily upon doctrinal questions. We were not commissioned to write yet another hand-me-down on pastoral counseling, of which there are many, some good and others not so good. The appointing committee took the position that what was most needed at this stage of development of the pastoral counseling movement, at least within the Missouri Synod, was an examination of the *concepts* employed by the psychological sciences in relation to the Christian doctrine of man as received within confessional Lutheranism. With the exception of a treatise or two written within the framework of Roman theology, insufficient attention has been paid to the doctrinal issues involved in pastoral counseling. A great deal has been said and written within Protestant circles about Freud and Christianity, largely in the fuzzy-minded and equivocating tradition with which so much of liberal Protestant writing is infected. A few loose identifications, a superficial parallel, a "modern"-sounding quote from Augustine, are offered in place of a serious attempt at rigorous theological analysis. These tactics, while they may engender a momentary feeling of safety, cannot provide the foundation for a healthy co-operation between psychology and theology *in the long run*, since they are essentially like neurotic defenses — they avoid the problem or gloss over it with a verbal trick instead

2

of facing it resolutely. As Freud pointed out, the repressed, when handled in this way, always returns to plague us, although perhaps in another guise.

If The Lutheran Church — Missouri Synod is to move constructively into a program of fostering and improving pastoral counseling, and helping its pastors to make more effective referrals to psychologists and psychiatrists, strong support from our theologians, teachers, and pastors will be necessary. A fundamental step in bringing about even the possibility of such support is the allaying of fears arising from uncertainty about the doctrinal issues involved. Perhaps it is not a cultural accident or ministerial overconservatism that many pastors are suspicious of the teachings of psychology and psychiatry. Perhaps there *is* some real ideological conflict in addition to the avoidable misunderstandings. What can be said about the relationship between the teachings of secular psychology and the Lutheran doctrine of man?

To answer the question in the general form in which we have just stated it would be a large order. It would have been grandiose indeed for any group of five people to take the responsibility of answering such a question. Our task was a more modest one, perhaps best described as the task of *approaching the problem to see how it might look upon a somewhat closer and longer inspection than it had hitherto received.* This is what we have tried to do. In brief, our aims were three: First, we wished to make available a brief exposition of the Christian doctrine of man which could at least constitute a starting point for inquiring non-Christian practitioners who wish to understand Christian patients and their pastors. Secondly, we have tried to set forth some of the basic facts and theories of psychology and psychiatry for the benefit of pastors and theologians who have had little or no technical training in these areas. Thirdly — *and this, it must be emphasized, was our chief task as set by Synod's Committee in its instructions* — we have attempted to make a beginning at the conceptual analysis of the relations between these two systems of ideas, especially at those points of contact where the likelihood of incompatibility appeared to be greatest.

Even assuming these three tasks were to have been reasonably well done, such a book will obviously make special demands upon our readers. The theologian will be dissatisfied by the condensed and partial exposition of Christian doctrine in Chapter II, while he will find that Chapter V on behavior shaping is technical and "rough sledding." For the psychologist this situation will simply be reversed. There was no way out of this difficulty, since we were under the necessity of explaining each of two sets of concepts to "beginners" before we could get on with the *chief* task, that of scrutinizing their relationships. Consequently, the reader who will get the most out of this book will be the rare one who is already fairly conversant with theology, psychology, and psychiatry (with a little analytic philosophy thrown in besides).

As part of the preparation for our work, we sent a letter of inquiry to a random sample of 50 pastors in the Missouri Synod as well as to all of Synod's pastors connected with secular universities, the District Presidents, and a special group of pastors and theologians known by our committee to be especially interested in the problem. In this letter we asked for their impressions of the psychiatrists and psychologists with whom they had had dealings, and also for any examples of practices or beliefs found among these professionals which appeared to be in conflict with Christian teachings.

To get a look at the other side of the coin, the 21 psychologists of professorial rank at a large secular university whose psychology department is of excellent repute were asked to write briefly on what beliefs they held, qua psychologists, that seemed to conflict with orthodox Christian teachings as understood by them.

No scientific pretensions are made for either of these preliminary surveys, and no statistical analysis was carried out upon them. We used the responses in a qualitative and impressionistic manner, trying to catch some of the flavor of thinking in the two groups. We hoped in this way to compensate at least partially for the inevitable biases and special interests of our committee. Fortunately it was easy to discern a core of problems which repeatedly recurred in these letters. Pastors were primarily concerned about the status of *Moral Law, objective guilt,* and *forgiveness* as dealt with — or ignored — in the psychologists' thinking about people. Psychologists were concerned more with the Christian system's apparent denial of *scientific determinism,* and

4

its acceptance of a *mind-body dualism*. Both pastors and psychologists saw sources of conflict over the concepts of *guilt, conversion,* and *original sin*. Certain special trends were also discernible, such as the tendency for pastors engaged in student work on secular campuses to be interested in the same kinds of "philosophical" problems voiced by the psychologists, no doubt because of these pastors' greater contact with non-Christian intellectual life as reflected in student questions and problems. Our selection of topics for more intensive treatment, which may appear arbitrary to some readers, was based upon a combination of criteria, in which the consensus of these letters and our own best discernment of what are doctrinally focal issues were happily in agreement. We are prepared to state firmly that *he who does not come to terms with such theoretical problems as determinism, guilt, original sin, materialist monism, conscience, and conversion cannot even begin to work out a cognitive* rapprochement *between Christian theology and the secular sciences of behavior*.

A strong disclaimer must also be made to avoid a possible serious misunderstanding. Neither the sciences of psychology and psychiatry nor the Christian doctrine of man are meant to be "established," "supported," or even "defended" in this volume. It would be absurd to try to "prove" to a skeptical preacher in a book of this kind the correctness of Freud's views of neurosis or the general theory of human and animal learning. It would be equally foolish to offer Chapter II on the Christian view of man as a kind of streamlined apologetics for influencing atheist psychologists. Inevitably, and quite properly, argumentative and even polemical statements occur in the course of such writing as this. But the reader will note that such statements almost always occur in a *context of possible criticism arising from an apparent conflict with the other discipline*. To do this much by way of controversy is, of course, implicit in the committee's assigned task. But the reader must not expect more than that. If a pastor asks: "Why should I begin by assuming that there is any truth to this 'unconscious' and 'neurosis' stuff to start with?" he will not find his answer in this volume. Similarly, if an atheist psychologist begins by asking: "Why should I give any credence to a system that deals with sin, since sin is an intrinsically theo-

5

logical concept, and there are no gods?" he will be disappointed. Insofar as we have occasion to go beyond exposition and enter upon trying to show or prove anything to the reader, we are trying to show that a relationship of contradiction, equivalence, compatibility, or independence obtains *between* an idea in theology and a related idea in psychology. If someone wants to learn why he should give any credence to the doctrines of psychologists or theologians in the first place, he must go to the appropriate sources.

Unless this methodological orientation is kept in mind, the reader will find himself unsympathetic to a good deal of our discussion. For example, a non-Christian psychiatrist will discover that what appears to him to be a simple, straightforward solution to a problem is summarily rejected on the ground that such-and-such Scripture texts rule it out of court. Here is an appeal to authority which has, for him, no evidential status whatsoever. Or, on the other side, a theologian finds us discussing the electrochemical state of Saul's brain on the road to Damascus, when all that we have had revealed to us is that conversion is God's work, not prepared for or earned by merits or works, and that election to it is a mystery. Are we not here committing the common error of trying by our speculative human reason to search out the divine secrets? Both kinds of readers can relieve their discomfort by keeping in mind the task here set. We simply take for granted the truth of revelation found in Scripture (as explicated by the Lutheran Confessions); we also take for granted the essential correctness of what is held, on experimental or clinical grounds, by students of physiology, psychology, and psychiatry. If these two belief systems are both true, we ask what possibilities are conceptually available for accommodating them to one another. Since we are particularly interested in canvassing conceptual *possibilities* wherever definitive resolutions of apparent conflict would be premature, in some respects we have, quite consciously, extended such speculations beyond where either scientific or theological caution would dictate. These speculations are admittedly in that no man's land between science, philosophy, and theology, where definite knowledge may permanently elude the human mind. However, to say, "These two systems of ideas are incompatible" (i. e., contradictory, incapable of being reconciled to each other) is a strong claim and one not infrequently heard where theology and psychology are under discussion. Even a speculative resolution, if not far-fetched, and if in accord with what *is* known at present, suffices to refute such an allegation. In a book devoted to the study of the conceptual relations obtaining between two incomplete systems, such daring speculation appeared to us to be justified.

It was naturally impossible for all five of us to come to agreement as to modes of expression, or, in some matters, even the substance to be conveyed. Our initial planning meeting (held in January 1956) resulted in the assignment of individual responsibility for the preparation of first drafts of chapters before and during the major work sessions, which were held in St. Paul during the following summer. Each chapter draft was subjected to detailed written and oral discussion, and its final form represents a group product. It was reassuring to discover that almost no major points of disagreement persisted throughout the group's discussion of any chapter, although in many instances the final form of expression represented a compromise with which no one was entirely happy. It is not possible under these circumstances to designate authorship above the separate chapters; we merely indicate here which members of the group had responsibility for preparing the initial drafts and final revisions. Where a second author contributed substantial portions of the first draft, or played a major part in writing insertions or revisions, his name is given also, the author having primary responsibility being indicated by italics: I, Meehl; II, Klann; III, Meehl; IV, *Schmieding*, Meehl; V, Meehl; VI, Sloman; VII–IX, Meehl; X, Breimeier; XI, *Breimeier*, Sloman; XII, Schmieding; XIII, Meehl. Appendix A, Breimeier; B, *Schmieding*, Meehl; C, Schmieding; D and E, Meehl.

To avoid the cumbersome and irritative repetition of the "psychology and psychiatry" doublet, we have ordinarily used the term "psychology" in contexts of a chiefly theoretical nature, psychology being the basic theoretical and experimental science and psychiatry a medical specialty. In other instances we use the neutral term "psychotherapist," where our primary emphasis

7

is upon verbal and gestural healing activity undertaken via the professional interview by either a physician or psychologist.

Quotations from Holy Scripture are from the Authorized Version unless otherwise indicated.

SUGGESTED READINGS

Feigl, Herbert. "Aims of Education for Our Age of Science," *Modern Philosophies and Education*, in Fifty-fourth Yearbook of the National Society for the Study of Education. Chicago: University of Chicago Press, 1955, I, 304—341.

Flew, Antony, and Alasdair Macintyre. *New Essays in Philosophical Theology*. New York: Macmillan, 1955.

Reichenbach, Hans. *The Rise of Scientific Philosophy*. Berkeley: University of California Press, 1951.

II. The Christian View of Man

SINCE A DISCUSSION of the relationship of theology and psychology must depend upon the meaning with which the terms are invested, this chapter will deal with major aspects of the meaning of Christian theology. We stress the fact that the discussion turns upon "Christian theology," not some form of philosophical or mystical theology.

1. *The Scope and Method of Christian Theology*

According to the Lutheran tradition, Christian theology is the logical analysis and pertinent application of the Word of God in terms of itself. The basic hermeneutical principle, Scripture interprets Scripture, is determinative.[1] Since the Scriptures constitute the written report of God's action and message to men, they are to be understood by man as fully as possible. The Christian theologian will, therefore, draw upon all available and useful tools in his attempt to set forth systematically the meaning of the Word of God. Christian theology as the logical analysis of the Word of God in terms of itself is a human effort, circumscribed by the limitations of language and knowledge of the subject matter. It is the systematization and interpretation of the spiritual, intellectual, and practical activity of the Christian.

---

[1] Most suggestive for this discussion of hermeneutics is a recent essay by Martin H. Scharlemann, "A Theology for Biblical Interpretation" in *Concordia Theological Monthly*, XXIX (1958), 38—45. The interested reader is urged to acquaint himself with this article because it elaborates a basic attitude of this section on the issue of Biblical interpretation.

However, the Christian theologian who is historically within the Lutheran tradition will carefully refuse to allow any one of his instruments to determine his systematic interpretations of the Scriptures. The historic method of Lutheran theology does not grant the theologian the right to use fashionable presuppositions of any particular philosophy, of the social sciences, or any other kind, to shape the logical analysis or interpretation of the Word of God. Otherwise the theologian's analysis will be indebted to his imagination for his facts and to his wit for his conclusions.

Christian theology as relevant logical analysis is exemplified by the Small Catechism which Luther wrote for children, the Confessions of the Lutheran Church, and the comprehensive and systematic works of Lutheran theologians. Their forms differ, but the method is consistently the same in all of them — the logical analysis, exposition, or synthesis of the meaning of the Word of God for man, and the Christian defense against erroneous interpretations. Theological analysis is a continuing activity because the Christian theologian has the obligation to interpret the meaning of the Scriptures against an ever-changing climate of human opinion, which is always in contradiction to the Word of God. This is essentially the reason why a theological "Summa" needs to be written for every generation.

Viewed in these terms, Christian theology is removed from the dim light of the speculative imagination into the noonday sun of a divinely communicated message. Modern theology also has been slowly retreating from its inordinate concern with speculative philosophy and the social sciences to the exegesis of the Word of God. While this movement is still very far from being complete, it appears that the direction is clearly set toward an exegetical method.

Logical analysis of the Word of God in terms of itself is not a mere collation of Aristotelian syllogisms, as though theology were hardly more than a series of pedantic logical exercises. Nor is it a mere dissecting of words and phrases, the diversion of subtle critics, and the sport of erudite philologists. Rather, it is the search for meaning in its ultimate and total sense. Hence the logical analysis of the Word of God in terms of itself is never mere diagnosis, but must continue with synthesis and pertinent application. It is the attempt of Christians to think the thoughts

10

of God after Him — thoughts which He has revealed to men. This God, the Christian theologian reminds himself at all times, is a God of order, not of confusion.

Christian theology is, therefore, the orderly consideration of all pertinent aspects of the human situation upon which the Word of God irradiates its light. It includes the proportionate contribution of every instrument in the orchestra of human communications. Drama and poetry, chronicle and prophecy, law and the creative spontaneity of a new being, enlist the comprehensive faculties of the professional or lay theologian. Christian theology will never be complete during human history, for each era gives rise to new problems which must be examined in the light of the "analogy of faith."

For the Christian the Word of God is several things. At its highest it is the Logos, the structure of intelligibility, that which is prior to all things, the creative and ultimate power. That Word is Jesus Christ, "who was made flesh and dwelt among us" (John 1:1-14). Here we find Logos, Word, Jesus Christ, and God totally identified.

The Word of God is also the message, communication, or revelation which God wanted men to know. As such it came to various individuals and in various forms. Lastly it was authoritatively declared by Christ and His apostles or representatives. This Word of God is also called the "Gospel," or "good news." In its comprehensive sense, "Gospel" includes all that God has revealed to men, both of judgment and of grace. More specifically, the term "Gospel," or "good news," refers to all that God has revealed to men regarding His grace (unmerited favor) toward man for the sake of His Son Jesus Christ, both in the Old and in the New Testament.

However, if it is to be of value to the addressee, a communication must be understood. It was therefore essential that the early witnesses of the great acts of God in Christ tell in their own terms what they had "seen and heard" and then relate it to the needs of their hearers. This is illustrated very well in the sermons of the apostles. They speak always with consideration of the background, attitudes, and needs of their audiences. The Gospels and Epistles of the New Testament also are written with close attention to the thought forms, cultural climate, and degree

11

of growth of the religious knowledge of the recipients. God's relationship with man has been truly dialectical, directly so with some men, and through them, with man collectively.

However presented, the teachings themselves never change. The doctrine of creation is the same in the New Testament as in the Old. The prophets bear the same witness to Christ as do the apostles. The apostles and evangelists agree totally on the meaning of the death of Jesus Christ for the world. The terms "doctrine" or "dogma" represent the "faith once delivered to the saints" (Jude 3).[2] Hence the content of dogmas or doctrines is not manufactured by the Christian Church; it was *given* to the church, and the church interprets it to the world, somewhat as *data* are the "given" with which a scientist deals in his particular field.

A communication must be presented within a frame of reference. Just as each science must establish its own categories, or frame of reference, and seek to explain the meaning or relevance of its content in terms of them — for example, the physical sciences employ verified measurements as the condition of their communication — so the Christian revelation has its own frame of reference. It makes assertions in terms of the events which the apostles called the "mighty acts of God" and which are recorded for us, at least in part and briefly, in the Scriptures. The Christian faith was not established by the church, but was *given to the church in the Word of God,* and it is the function of the church to declare these doctrines to the world.

But this Word of God which presents the Christian faith may be communicated variously, according to the requirements of particular situations. A missionary to the Eskimos will achieve his best results when he preaches the Gospel of Christ in terms of the cultural milieu of that people. His alternative is the danger of not being well understood. Some of the early Christian teachers sought to interpret the faith of the church in terms of

---

2 *Dogma* literally means opinion. The dogmas of the Christian Church are the "opinions" or "ordinances" of God. As such they are the teachings or doctrine of the Christian Church. The term *dogmatic* may mislead the nontheological reader by suggesting to him that it characterizes exclusively assertions or opinions made without sufficient warrant and the indisposition for further serious discussion.

the Hellenistic culture of their time. During the Middle Ages it became the vogue to interpret the Christian faith in terms of a rediscovered Greek philosophy. Many modern teachers believe that the message of Christ can be conveyed most effectively by borrowing some of the methods and terminology of modern science.

To present the Christian faith in the terms of a particular cultural climate is both necessary and risky. It is necessary if the Gospel is to be understood, because the church must meet people where they are. Both the example of the apostles and the dictates of common sense, not to mention Christ's own teaching, recommend this. It is risky, according to the history of the Christian Church, because the process of translating the Gospel into the terms of any particular culture is so delicate that most attempts have been partial or total failures.

Human language is far from being a perfect vehicle of communication, certainly in any form known to us. The choice of words or symbols, of sentence structure or forms of speech, is for every individual determined by factors which are not necessarily shared by another person. It is therefore imperative for the understanding of all human speech that particular statements or expressions be understood in the context of the entire discourse, or, better still, in the context of what is known of the history and character of the speaker. The Bible must be treated similarly. The alternative is a broken literalism.

When the Christian meets with different, or even conflicting, interpretations of the Word of God, his faith is by no means shaken by that encounter. It is axiomatic for the Christian that the Word of God is completely logical and consistent because it has the God of order for its source. If he meets with an interpretation of the Scriptures which conflicts with a more strongly grounded hypothesis regarding phenomena referred to in the Scriptures, the Christian, if he is consistent in his effort to understand the Scriptures, will re-examine his interpretation. His faith in the authoritative character of the Scriptures need not be disturbed at all, because that faith is a correlative of his faith in the person and work of Jesus Christ, the Logos who was made flesh. When, therefore, the Ptolemaic universe is supplanted by the Copernican picture, which, in turn, is modified by the Einsteinian space-time continuum, the Christian takes note of these changes in the picture of the universe and retains an open mind for the possibility that scientists may invent a still better interpretation of the world.

The Scriptures do not commit the Christian to a particular historical school, cosmology, system of chronology, or a fashionable methodology. The Christian theologian may find them useful in his effort to understand the Scriptures. But he does not feel bound by them; he will readily discard any one of these tools when he finds something better.

For the Christian, the Word of God is truth, as Christ also declared in His great prayer: "Thy Word is truth" (John 17:17). When Christians speak of Christian or Biblical truth, they do not speak in terms of a mathematical literalism. The attempt of philosophers to express literal truth in this sense has been a problem only since Descartes. It is indebted to the naive assumption that truth can be convincingly deduced, in imitation of mathematics and mathematical logic, from certain ultimate axioms, either in a straight line or circuitously. Cognitively, religious truth always represents a relation to an object different from itself. When we speak of truth, we mean an analogy through which a relation may be seen to be true. Of course, the same is true of any cognitive enterprise, such as philosophy and logic. Analogy is the vehicle for the expression of such truth.

2. *The Problem of Christian Assertion and Scientific Evidence*

A discussion of Christian theology (here, specifically, the Christian view of man) in its relations with modern psychology and psychiatry must reckon with the widespread assumption of modern philosophy and science that all statements about matters of fact are empirical and corrigible and require empirical confirmation.

Negatively stated, this axiom of modern science denies that any assertion is a statement about matters of fact if it is not subject to empirical confirmation or disconfirmation in the ordinary, "objective," sense of the term, because the methods of agreement and difference cannot be used.

Such demands would appear to make statements based on divine revelation rootless refugees in our modern scientific world.

14

Nonetheless, the Christian claims that his statements are factual and that they do not lose their hold despite evidence which may be asserted against them. In some respects their form resembles that of testable statements, as exemplified by John 1:1: "In the beginning was the Word, and the Word was with God, and the Word was God." More often they seem nonconfirmable and are given such labels as "presuppositions," "wishful thinking," "poetic myths," "wish fulfillments," "dogmas," or "articles of faith." The attitudes of the speaker or writer will usually furnish the overtones of derogation or respect.

Since it is a basic principle of modern philosophy and science that the human intellect is capable of understanding everything outside itself in the categories of its own thinking and acting, it is not at all astonishing that some modern thinkers find the paradoxical character of Christian statements annoying. They seem to violate the rules; in fact, there seems to be at least a shadow of duplicity about them. To summarize the complaint: the Christian appeals to evidence when it suits him, but he rejects evidence which can be used against him by asserting that God is compatible with all possibilities.

To this the Christian replies that there is a kind of empirical knowledge of God, as St. Paul explains it in Rom. 1:19-21,[3] and religious statements are intended to be a record of such experience.

It is inconceivable to Christians that anyone could have spoken about the wrath or the mercy of God if no one had experienced it. The disciples of Christ declared that He is God and Lord because they observed Him to posses the qualities or attributes which must be ascribed to God alone. If no one had experienced God, how could anyone assert that God is? Hence the Christian who accepts the Bible as a record of historical events is bound to say that at such and such points in history God revealed His being to men. Furthermore, if a Christian

---

3 "For what can be known about God is plain to them, because God has shown it to them. Ever since the creation of the world His invisible nature, namely, His eternal power and deity, has been clearly perceived in the things that have been made. So they are without excuse; for although they knew God, they did not honor Him as God or give thanks to Him, but they became futile in their thinking, and their senseless minds were darkened." (RSV)

appeals to the evidence of miracles, he certainly refers to observed events which addressed themselves directly to the senses.

Is the revelation of the Scriptures scientifically testable? For some modern thinkers, it would appear, Christian claims stand or fall at this point. It may be of some advantage to attempt to place the issue clearly in focus.

It is one of the first principles of science that no fact is considered valid unless it can be observed by any qualified worker in the field who is willing to make the effort to observe it. But how does this apply to historical data? If we insist on being consistent, the principle would render all experience incommunicable! Since the present is always the frontier of the past, and since the past tense applies to every form of human communication as soon as it has been made, it would seem that the criterion invalidates all statements, itself included.

Obviously, the principle asserts too much, and it is therefore not literally true. It applies to "things as they are," which lend themselves to scientific tests of repetition. But it is impossible to subject any area of history to the scientific test of repetition because history will not permit it to be done. We must use methods appropriate to the problems.

The Christian argument does follow the methods appropriate to the problem. Initially it was stated by the apostles of Christ: Did the key event of history, the resurrection of Christ, really happen? If so, then the rest of the divine revelation is confirmed. Hence the basic question which the *Christian* theologian incessantly asks himself is not whether the revelation is true, but whether his interpretation of the revelation is consistent and inclusive, adequate to deal with the issue which confronts him.

At this point it would also seem appropriate to question the validity of the inductive method of science for the purpose of making generalizations. Simply stated, it means that the scientist observes a series of events and formulates specific or general conclusions about the experience. However, the inductive method has implications beyond this, and unfortunately they are not always being given their due. In substance, the inductive method says that a thing which has happened a thousand or a million times will happen again and again. In effect, it will always

16

happen.[4] To illustrate: an apple has fallen on Newton's head. It has always been observed that apples fall, or tend to fall, toward the ground. This falling is accounted for by the law of gravitation. Hence we say that apples will always fall, or tend to fall, toward the earth. The law of gravitation is valid because "it works." That is another way of saying that induction is proved or justified by induction.

Science has no better foundation than that "it works." Without the inductive method the procedures of scientists would make no sense at all. However, it ought not to be forgotten that there is no logical necessity at all to this foundation of science. Consequently it would seem to follow that the apologists of science have exceedingly flimsy grounds for their refusal to take seriously the points of dissent of orthodox Christian theology. After all, the odds are very much against the former. Each experiment or observation favorable to any particular hypothesis is merely another stone added to an apparently enduring edifice. But a single adverse experiment or observation is an earthquake which lays the walls of the building even with the ground. This is pertinent especially when we confront the resurrection of Christ.

Because some non-Christian thinkers are acutely sensitive to the force of adverse evidence, they find it extremely difficult, if not impossible, to countenance the fact that the Christian does not react "objectively" to adverse evidence. That such evidence exists is undeniable. The story of Job illustrates the point very well. The completely scientific thinker, applying universally the assumptions indicated in this section, would join in the recommendation of Job's wife: "Curse God and die," instead of echoing Job's "Though He slay me, yet will I trust in Him." Surely, evil and suffering are adverse evidence and ought to weaken the Christian's claim that God is Love. But according to the Christian, God has it both ways: when the Christian suffers, God chastens him; when things go well, God takes care of him.

_____
4 All that scientists can justifiably mean by "necessity" is that they find uniformities in the course of events which they describe in "laws." However, these are not normative or prescriptive laws. Hence "necessity," as a scientific term, becomes much less formidable when it is understood in its literal Latin sense of "unceasing." A scientific law is merely a description of events which have been observed to recur "incessantly" and are therefore thought to be unexceptional on that basis.

17

Of course, such a response is altogether unscientific. But the Christian believer need not allow himself to be intimidated by that label. He refuses to accept the force of adverse evidence because his assurance or trust is more than the product of evidence. Adverse evidence cannot weaken the Christian's certainty regarding the truth of his religious statements because his certainty grows out of his faith that his God is a God of love and grace, not of caprice or moodiness, and that the character of God is consistent at all times and under all conditions regardless of the apparently contrary information or experiences which the Christian may encounter. In short, the Christian believes that God has been, is, and will remain God. As statements of faith the Christian's assertions remain incorrigible (but not logically so) because they also express his faith. At this point it becomes necessary to attempt a brief description of the nature of the Christian faith.

3. Pursuit and Confrontation

When St. Augustine prayed: "Thou hast made us for Thyself, and our hearts are restless until they rest in Thee," he indicated that man's ceaseless striving for certainties and securities is due to his need to find God. However, it is not true, according to the Christian revelation, to say that man seeks God, although man ought to do that. On the contrary, the natural desire of man is to escape from God — which cannot be done. Therefore God must always take the initiative and seek out and confront man.

He does this in remarkable ways on all levels of human existence. There is no possibility at all of avoiding Him, as the psalmist also writes:

> O Lord, Thou hast searched me and known me!
> Thou knowest when I sit down and when I rise up;
> Thou discernest my thoughts from afar.
> Thou searchest out my path and my lying down,
>   and art acquainted with all my ways.
> Even before a word is on my tongue,
>   lo, O Lord, Thou knowest it altogether.
> Thou dost beset me behind and before,
>   and layest Thy hand upon me.
> Such knowledge is too wonderful for me;
>   it is high, I cannot attain it.

18

Whither shall I go from Thy Spirit?
Or whither shall I flee from Thy presence?
If I ascend to heaven, Thou art there!
If I make my bed in Sheol, Thou art there!
If I take the wings of the morning
    and dwell in the uttermost parts of the sea,
    even there Thy hand shall lead me,
    and Thy right hand shall hold me.
If I say, "Let only darkness cover me,
    and the light about me be night,"
    even the darkness is not dark to Thee,
    the night is bright as the day;
    for darkness is as light with Thee.
                  (Psalm 139:1-12, RSV)

Some men have been confronted by God under highly dramatic circumstances. Moses met God in the desert at the burning bush which was not consumed (Ex. 3:3-6). While still a boy, Samuel heard the voice of the Lord at night near the ark of the covenant (1 Sam. 3:2-14). Isaiah saw the Lord in a vision of awesome splendor (Is. 6:1-9), and Jeremiah heard His stern injunctions (Jer. 1 and 2). The story of Jonah is undoubtedly one of the best-known illustrations of a man who desperately wanted to avoid his God. However, the lucid accounts of Paul's conversion serve our purposes best. His given name was Saul. Born of a prominent Jewish family of Tarsus, a city in Asia Minor, famous for its university, Saul had the distinction of having been educated both in Greek and in Hebrew culture. A Roman citizen by birth, reared in Jerusalem "at the feet of Gamaliel" in the strict Pharisaic tradition, he was marked early in life for a prominent place in the Jewish nation. He witnessed the death of Stephen, the first Christian martyr, and subsequently made it his business to extirpate the Christians among the Jewish people. Empowered by letters from the high priest, he journeyed to Damascus to arrest the Jewish Christians in that city and to bring them bound to Jerusalem. Near Damascus the astounding event took place. An unbearable, heavenly light shone about Saul and the little troop which accompanied him. His companions even heard a voice, but did not understand what was being said.

As we compare the three accounts in the Book of Acts (chs. 9; 22; 26), we note that each one, while dwelling on different inci-

19

dents, clearly points to the fact that Jesus confronted Saul in the most unexpected and extraordinary way: Saul and his company were in the pursuit of aims utterly opposed to what was about to happen; all were enveloped by the heavenly light; all heard a man's voice; only Saul understood what was being said to him. Hardly a situation conducive to hallucinations in the ordinary sense! The supernatural elements are simply there. The Christian theologian does not and cannot fit them into a naturalistic scheme of things. To do so would require stultification of the report.

4. The Logic of Faith

The scientist assumes that truth is unitary in character and that there is only one way of knowing it — not two ways or a dozen or any number of ways. To this the Christian theologian agrees. Behind all truth stands the Author of truth — God — whom the Christian worships in Jesus Christ. Since all facets of knowable truth radiate from the same source and are received by the perceptive means common to all human beings, the statement must stand. However, the fact is plain that human beings disagree widely about what they accept as truth. Obviously, the naturalistic or nontheistic scientist will want to know how Christian theology accounts for this.

Both the naturalistic scientist and the Christian theologian assert that truth must be objective in character, although it is subjectively received by human beings. To deny this leaves us with the alternative that truth exists relative to the observer or recipient. In that case, we may assert, human beings manufacture truths acceptable to the individual. If this were so, the validity of the scientific enterprise would have to be denied because it is based upon the assumption of the unitary character of truth. It is, therefore, impossible to affirm that truth is unitary and objective in one area of the scientific enterprise, but relative and plural in another.

If a proposition is affirmed by one and denied by another, it is obvious that the mere assertion of its character is not decisive. A psychoanalyst may assert with the utmost conviction that a particular patient has certain dynamics, while another psychoanalyst of equal competence contradicts him with equal conviction. The

20

arbiter of the presumed debate may affirm that the interpretation of dynamics is a relative matter, depending on the condition of the recipient's perceptive means. However, such a judgment reveals nothing more than that the arbiter knows of no universally compelling criterion of truth. The statement is true if the assumption is granted; but that there is no universally compelling criterion of truth is not true.

If the analysts have no compelling criteria for their judgment, they can do no more than to present their states of minds, emotions, or disposition as persuasively as possible to their audiences. Even a vote in favor of one or the other on the part of the audiences constitutes no final confirmation of either of the presumed assertions. But the physicist is able to present objective confirmation for his assertions. Anyone examining the atomic structure of the components of water under specified conditions will receive the same results. These illustrations do not indicate that the analysts and the physicists have their several ways of knowing, but rather that the capacity of the human perceptive apparatus varies greatly in the perception of truth in its manifold aspects.

One of the causes of this variability is the obvious fact that both of the psychoanalysts referred to above are subjective observers, whereas the physicist's involvement in his experiment is so minimal that he is said to be "objective." Furthermore, the physicist also seeks to control the conditions under which his experiment is conducted, while the psychoanalysts cannot control all the conditions which determine their observations and conclusions.

There is no compelling objective test of the Christian faith on the order of those available to the physicist. The spectator or observer of Christianity, regardless of his degree of methodological competence and determination to be objective, cannot find out whether the Christian faith is true or not. The man who has never been in love may be able to argue on rational grounds sufficient for him that love is an utter delusion, dangerous, debilitating, irrational, and a major cause of evil in this world (Nietzsche). But the fact is that he does not know the "truth" of love, never having been in that blissful state. Similarly, the

21

truth of the Christian faith cannot be "known" until a man has become a Christian, for only then can men "know the love of Christ, which passeth knowledge." (Eph. 3:19)

5. Faith and Scientific Certainty

For the scientist and the philosopher, certainty is a subjective term for necessity. For the Christian, faith is a sort of certainty; however, it is not the product of necessity or even of probability. "Faith is the substance of things hoped for, the evidence of things not seen" (Heb. 11:1). The believers mentioned in this chapter (Heb. 11) surely were possessed of an heroic certainty, but it was not grounded in necessity or probability. In fact, the scientist would say that they had no good reason to be certain about anything except that they had nothing to be certain about.

When St. Paul wrote, "I know whom I have believed and am persuaded" (2 Tim. 1:12), he expressed a kind of certainty and a form of knowing sufficient for him to stake his life on it. But his certainty and knowing was altogether different from the certainty and knowing of the modern scientist or philosopher, which is based on mathematical necessity or probability. For St. Paul's kind of faith certainty and knowledge was no necessary consequence even if the existence of God could have been proved by empirical confirmation according to the requirements of modern science.

Christian faith is therefore not to be equated with ordinary objective knowledge. The Christian does not believe "*that* there is one God." The devils, as St. James points out (2:19), also possess such objective knowledge "and tremble." Rather, the Christian believes "*in* God, the Father . . . and *in* Jesus Christ, His only Son, our Lord . . . *in* the Holy Ghost." This is an altogether different matter.

Faith, as Martin Luther translates Heb. 11:1, "is a sure confidence." It is knowledge, trust, assurance, and certainty. Christian faith is no mere assent to a cold and bare proposition, such as that the square of the hypotenuse in a right-angled triangle equals the squares of the other two sides. Nor is Christian faith simply the adherence to declaratory statements, such as "I believe that God exists" or "I believe that God is holy, righteous, and loving." When Christian faith is limited to this kind of knowl-

22

edge or propositional agreement, it is bound to be weakened, or even negated, in those situations which seem to constitute contrary evidence.

Dorothy Sayers illustrates the point very well, and Christian intellectuals would do well to remember it.[5] Taking dramatic license, she represents Judas as an intellectual who is the only one among the disciples to grasp the meaning of Isaiah 53 for Jesus Christ. But Judas' interpretation of events deceives him into concluding that Jesus had abandoned His divine mission in the interest of Jewish nationalism. Judas the intellectual had a firm "faith that," but not "faith in." He missed a stupendous opportunity because he would not trust the Son of God even when he saw Him!

The Christian believes *in* the Triune God. His faith is an attitude, or disposition, or commitment, or covenant. His faith is like a mountaintop from which he surveys the landscape around him. What he sees differs greatly from the view of the skeptic in the plains below. From this view the Christian believer admits contrary evidences and denies their apparently logical implications. Evil, pain, and suffering exist and must be taken seriously. But the Christian also sees beyond such adverse evidence. Every form of disorder is as bad as, or worse than, it appears to be. However, the Christian cannot admit defeat, because the ultimate issues have already been decided. Every one of his enemies has been measured and overcome by Him who said: "In the world ye shall have tribulation; but be of good cheer; I have overcome the world" (John 16:33). Christian faith is consequently unable to count that as evidence against it which has been overcome and whose total destruction is merely a matter of historical time. The Christian is somewhat in the position of a soldier in a victorious army who knows that he may yet have much to endure, perhaps even to die, before the enemy yields to unconditional surrender.

It is the fashion of contemporary theology to say that faith confronts contrary evidence dynamically. The power of God invests the Christian believer, enabling him continually to surmount

---

[5] *The Man Born to Be King* (New York: Harpers, 1943). Note especially Miss Sayers' psychological interpretation of Judas' character on pp. 199 f.

in triumph every adversity which confronts him. Obviously the Christian believer does not look at adverse evidence as it appears to be in isolation. To do so would most surely induce a sense of quiet or violent despair. But to confront such evidence dynamically in faith means that for the Christian it has already lost its force as adverse evidence. The argument is powerfully and movingly stated by St. Paul:

> If God be for us, who can be against us? He that spared not His own Son, but delivered Him up for us all, how shall He not with Him also freely give us all things? Who shall lay anything to the charge of God's elect? It is God that justifieth. Who is he that condemneth? It is Christ that died, yea rather, that is risen again, who is even at the right hand of God, who also maketh intercession for us. Who shall separate us from the love of Christ? Shall tribulation or distress or persecution or famine or nakedness or peril or sword? As it is written, For Thy sake we are killed all the day long; we are accounted as sheep for the slaughter. Nay, in all these things we are more than conquerors through Him that loved us. For I am persuaded that neither death, nor life; nor angels nor principalities nor powers; nor things present, nor things to come; nor height, nor depth; nor any other creature shall be able to separate us from the love of God, which is in Christ Jesus, our Lord. (Rom. 8:31-39)

6. Scientific Faith and Christian Faith

The Christian faith does not consist, as was said above, in the assertion that there is a God, but in confessing: "I believe in God the Father. . . . And in Jesus Christ, His Son . . . I believe in the Holy Ghost. . . ." The Christian faith, therefore, is the belief in specific Persons, not in some abstract conclusions of thought. Because Christians believe in the Father, Son, and Holy Spirit, they also believe what the Triune God has revealed about Himself. Hence what Christians believe about God is the consequence of their belief in God. When a man says of his wife that he believes in her, he is of course not speaking of her existence. That is assumed. He means that he trusts her and that he belongs to her.

The assertion that "God is" — rationally considered — does not constitute an act of faith different in kind from that of the physicist who infers that a physical world exists outside of his mind or that the behavior of physical objects is consistent. Without

24

a firm faith in such propositions scientists could not proceed with their work. Clearly, our answers depend proportionately more on what we already believe when we approach the questions concerning the ultimate meaning of things.

There is nothing greater by which men can attempt to demonstrate the existence of God. If there were, He would not be God or men's final answer to the questions regarding reality. That God *is*, while it can be rendered probable, cannot be demonstrated by empirical data and logic. If the possibility of demonstrating God's existence in the same sense that we demonstrate the existence of creatures were assumed, then God would cease to be Subject in His relation to creation [6] — "I AM THAT I AM" — and become an object among other objects.[7] The logical consequence of this would be the denial of meaning in anything whatever, because the very idea of meaning assumes an ultimate source, standard, criterion.

All human activity must implicitly or explicitly assume reality, and its character is beyond human explication. Hence all sciences, including psychology — using all the means of human perception for inquiries which are determined by the utmost methodological rigor — cannot possibly provide us with proofs or exhaustive explanations of God and faith. They cannot operate in a vacuum, but must start with an axiom or faith whether it is explicit or not.

Now, if a sincere and thoughtful person objects to the Christian Gospel because of the demand that he "accept things on faith," instead of on the basis of incontrovertible logic and reason, we must reply that this objection itself is based on the faith that there is a genuine meaning and answer to things. The alternative

---

[6] The unique is always beyond demonstration. *Is. 44:8* — "Is there a God beside Me? Yea, there is no God; I know not any." *Is. 45:22* — "Look unto Me, and be ye saved, all the ends of the earth; for I am God, and there is none else." *Is. 46:9* — "Remember the former things of old; for I am God, and there is none else; I am God, and there is none like Me."

When we say that God is uniquely "Subject," we mean that God does the acting entirely and exclusively; men and nature are "object" because they are acted upon. God is unchangeable; nothing ever "acts" upon Him.

[7] The reader who wishes to pursue the "subject-object" topic is referred to James Brown, *Subject and Object in Modern Theology* (New York: The Macmillan Co., 1955).

would be irrationality. If a man calls himself a materialist, believing that only physical things have reality, but that such phenomena of the spirit as the Christian faith are illusions, as Sigmund Freud has done,[8] he has no proof for such an assertion. In fact, he should remember that to classify someone else's faith as an illusion requires that he himself have faith in something. What has really happened is a decision, an act of the will, to believe and accept, or not to believe and accept, certain assertions. The materialist, e. g., must first decide that nothing but physical things exist. Materialism is therefore a faith, regardless of how much logical argument and inductive evidence is offered in its support. The same must be said of any other philosophical position. In fact, we may be excused for asserting the paradox that the real proof of God is the strenuous attempts to deny God!

Man cannot normally live or think in a vacuum. He does, in fact, begin with some belief. For the moment we shall call that a faith which makes more sense out of life than all other explanations. In contrast to all rival faiths, so Christians believe, the Christian faith is true because its answers to the questions which arise from human existence make sense. Reaching back to the creation of man, it irradiates an ultimately satisfying light upon all human problems. For example, the Christian therapist, believing that the universe is governed by moral principles, will be sensitive to his patient's emotional problems arising from a guilt feeling and other emotional realities, but his diagnosis will include the recognition that the patient, being a sinner, is genuinely guilty. His view of a cure and its limitations will include the resources of God's grace in Christ for the forgiveness of sins, whereas those with a narrower world view sometimes work, consciously or unconsciously, toward getting rid of the notion of sin.

---

[8] *The Future of an Illusion* (London: Hogarth Press, trans. W. D. Robson-Scott [International Psychoanalytical Library, No. 15], New York: Liveright Publishing Corporation [1928]). Incidentally, the criticism of Freud that God is an illusion was effectively answered a millennium ago by St. Anselm, when he sought to make it clear to the atheist that in the moment when he looks upon his idea of God as an idea produced by himself, he is thinking about his abstract conception of God. He is no longer thinking of God. Interesting for this point is Karl Barth's *Fides Quaerens Intellectum, Anselms Beweis der Existenz Gottes* (Munich, 1931).

7. "I Believe"

What happens when a person believes? Some of us cannot remember a time when we did not believe. Our attachment to the Christian faith occurred during the earliest days of childhood, and we developed spiritually as we also matured physically and intellectually. We were nourished on the affirmations of the Christian faith before we could understand their implications, and this experience made us what we are — as much as the fact that we were born into and reared in a particular family made us members of that family.

However, many Christians were not born into the "household of faith"; or, if born into it, never became a part of it until later in their lives. The number of these has noticeably increased. They become part of the "household of faith" after they discover that the Christian Gospel deals with and resolves the deepest and most urgent issues of human existence. From all strata of society they come — the wealthy and the poor, famous men and women as well as those whom life seems to have passed by, people of limited capacities and distinguished representatives of letters, the arts and sciences — people of all races have learned to confess with their hearts and minds the words "I believe."

Dramatic and spectacular events are most likely to engage our attention, with the result that the experiences of the Christian convert of maturer years appear as more significant than those of a Christian childhood. Consequently, it happens quite frequently that those who found the Christian faith and made it their own as adults are tempted to assign excessive importance to that fact, as though they were the only ones who really had the faith. This must be seen for what it is: a concession to human pride. Certainly, those who received the faith in childhood, gradually grew in grace, and with undramatic loyalty maintained their commitment throughout their lives are indisputably Christians, even though their response to the church's message of judgment and salvation was not made under the conditions of obvious emotional or intellectual storm and stress.

Can the process of becoming a Christian believer be analyzed? Attempts have been made, but beyond certain points we face an inscrutable mystery. Psychological explanations of conversion are failures because they have not bridged certain gaps. Efforts to understand the process of coming to faith by analysis of the reasoning process have not been successful either, for the latter is also a considerable mystery to us. However, both may afford us some help.

It must be plain that conversion to Christianity involves what the term "conversion" basically means: a change of mind. The man who becomes a Christian does not acquire a faith, but changes one faith for another faith. This is not done on the basis of reason and logic, even though the change may be defended by these means. It is a decision, an act of the will, brought about by the Holy Spirit through the Word and Sacrament.

The Holy Spirit is no moral influence, vague, impersonal, diffused; He is no general climate of opinion emanating from the Christian God; He is not to be equated — even remotely — with such a phenomenon as "the spirit of '76" or the *esprit de corps* of the military; He is not the common spirit pervading the members of a group, such as enthusiasm, devotion, or jealous regard for its honor. The Holy Spirit of the Scriptures is the Third Person of the Holy Trinity. He is God, equally with the Father and the Son, one divine Essence and three Persons. According to the Scriptures, the Holy Spirit is the Source of the spiritual life of all Christians.

All that is true and right in the world has its source in the Holy Spirit, as St. Ambrose also said long ago: "All truth wherever spoken is spoken by the Holy Ghost." His "chosen vessel" may be a heathen king, like Darius, who facilitated the return of the remnant of Israel from exile; or he may be a persecutor of the church, like Paul, who later became a zealous apostle. However, while we acknowledge that every virtue, all beauty, and all truth in the world has the Holy Spirit as the ultimate Author, we are concerned especially with His work as the Giver of spiritual life, and this is also the concern of the Scriptures.

We read that after Christ had made Himself known after His resurrection "by many infallible proofs" (Acts 1:3),[9] the early Christians remained in Jerusalem awaiting the day when they

---

[9] The nontheological reader is invited to study the context of this categorical assertion as it is presented in the last chapters of the Four Gospels and 1 Cor. 15.

28

would be endowed with "power from on high" (Luke 24:49), that is, until they received the Spirit in an extraordinary manner. Here is the record of that event: "And suddenly there came a sound from heaven as of a rushing mighty wind, and it filled all the house where they were sitting. And there appeared unto them cloven tongues like as of fire, and it sat upon each of them. And they were all filled with the Holy Ghost and began to speak with other tongues, as the Spirit gave them utterance." (Acts 2:2-4)

So compelling was the Presence, so personal in operation, so intense and overwhelming the enthusiasm which He created, that about three thousand souls gladly received and believed the first public sermon of the Christian Church. A very small band of naturally timid, uncertain, and unsophisticated men obtained power to persuade hostile crowds and to stand firm against the enticements and threats of the secular and spiritual rulers of their people. There was no doubt in the minds of the early Christians that it was the Holy Ghost who witnessed to Christ through them.

It is the work of the Holy Spirit to convey to the individual the salvation which Christ has obtained for all mankind. The Formula of Concord (Thor. Decl., Art. III, par. 41) states the matter thus: "First, faith is kindled in us in conversion by the Holy Ghost through the hearing of the Gospel. This faith lays hold of God's grace in Christ, by which the person is justified. Then, when the person is justified, he is also renewed and sanctified by the Holy Ghost, from which renewal and sanctification the fruits of good works follow."

To believe in Jesus Christ means far more than that Christ should be "something of an important influence in our lives." It is far more than the psychological description of faith by liberal Protestants as the "God-consciousness of the ego," or as the product of "historical impressions," or some other such absurdity. Nor is faith to be equated with mere intellectual knowledge of Christ, as has been done in the Roman Catholic confession of the Council of Trent, Session VI, Canon 15: "The faithful who are adulterers . . . thieves, etc." Lastly, faith in Christ is no mere blind trust in an institution or a body of dogma.

Over against such views the Lutheran Confessions state: "Faith is not only knowledge of the intellect, but also confidence of the will, i. e., it is to wish and to receive that which is offered in the promise, namely, reconciliation and remission of sins. Scripture thus uses the term 'faith'" (Apology, Art. III). In the exact sense of the term a person is converted when he turns from unbelief to faith in the Gospel or in Jesus Christ. As long as a man does not believe that Christ is *his* Savior from sin and that Christ bestows upon *him* eternal life itself, without any price or effort on his part, just so long that man is still unconverted, whether he be illiterate or highly educated, rich or poor, black or white, Jew or Gentile. Such men are still "without hope and without God" (Eph. 2:12). But in the moment that a person begins to believe in Jesus Christ, even though that faith be ever so faint and scarcely discernible, he begins to return to God. He is turning about: his conversion is taking place.

The human will or other faculties do not make the slightest contribution of their own toward the achievement of conversion. On the contrary, the mind of natural man is hostile toward God (Rom. 8:7). Faith in Jesus Christ is a gift (Phil. 1:29). "No man can say that Jesus is the Lord but by the Holy Ghost" (1 Cor. 12:3), and the prophet Jeremiah prayed: "Turn Thou me, and I shall be turned" (Jer. 31:18). For this reason the Formula of Concord (Thor. Decl., Art. II, par. 25) makes this uncompromising statement: "In this manner, too, the Holy Scriptures ascribe conversion, faith in Christ, regeneration, renewal, and all that belongs to their efficacious beginning and completion, not to the human powers of the natural free will, neither entirely, nor half, but *in solidum*, that is, entirely, solely, to the divine working and the Holy Ghost." Again: "On the other hand, it is correctly said that in conversion God, through the drawing of the Holy Ghost, makes out of stubborn and unwilling men willing ones, and that after such conversion in the daily exercise of repentance the regenerate will of man is not idle, but also co-operates in all the works of the Holy Ghost." (Epitome II, 17)

No one has ever been converted without hearing, reading, or in some way learning the message of the Word of God. The Holy Spirit will not work directly, but only through the means of grace. Christians are made by the Word of God (1 Peter 1:23). But the Word of God must come to man in its proper order. Here the conversion of the jailer at Philippi is an excellent illustration. His conscience awakened to the realization of his sinful condition, he asks Paul and Silas: "Sirs, what must I do to be saved?" It is a confession of his utter hopelessness; it is a total, unconditional surrender, caused by the terrors of his conscience. This condition is in every case produced by the application of the demands of God's Law to one's own condition. Then Paul and Silas spoke to his condition: "Believe on the Lord Jesus Christ, and thou shalt be saved and thy house. . . . And he took them the same hour of the night, and washed their stripes; and was baptized, he and all his, straightway. And when he had brought them into his house, he set meat before them, and rejoiced, believing in God with all his house" (Acts 16:31-34). It is similarly instructive to examine the record of David's sin and conversion. (2 Sam. 11 and 12)

When we affirm that it is necessary for a man to know the terrors of conscience, squarely to confront his own condition of utter hopelessness, we do not mean that the emotional reaction is the same in every person. For some this confrontation with themselves in the realization of their guilt and judgment under God may indeed result in violent and burdensome emotional distress, which becomes clearly apparent to their friends. But for others the terrors of conscience may be a relatively private and less violent experience, followed by a sure and calm confidence in God's mercy for the sake of Jesus Christ. No one may judge the genuineness or validity of a person's conversion by the emotional temperature which accompanies it. Obviously, people are not alike emotionally.

However, regardless of any incidental phenomena which may have come to our notice during the occasion of our conversion, these two things must have taken place: our evil, hostile will must have been broken by the Word of God, so that we know and confess ourselves as sinners before God, and we must have grasped in faith the promise of God's mercy through Christ's merit.

This leads us to the question of coercion in conversion. The therapist makes an extremely grave error if he allows himself to be persuaded that compulsion in any form whatever is a factor in the conversion of any Christian. God coerces no human being

31

in the process of conversion. Those who make the suggestion of some form of divine coercion do not understand the nature of God's love. By its very nature love cannot coerce. Furthermore, to say that a man is coerced when he is made aware of the perils of his predicament and offered a sure and entirely unmerited escape from it is to make an assertion which is peculiarly indebted to a perverse sort of logic. On all sides the Scriptures affirm that God the Holy Ghost alone converts us by His means of *grace;* nowhere can we find the slightest hint of an element of divine coercion. Nor does the suggestion honor God, who in His outgoing love created man to be man, not a thing or a puppet, and who redeemed him by the sacrifice of His only Son in order to restore man to that freedom which exists only in the presence of God. Hence the Formula of Concord firmly declines such a perverse charge: "Through this means, namely, the preaching and hearing of His Word, God works, and breaks our hearts, and draws man, so that through the preaching of the Law he comes to know his sins and God's wrath and experiences in his heart true terrors, contrition, and sorrow, and through the preaching and consideration of the Holy Ghost concerning the gracious forgiveness of sins in Christ a spark of faith is kindled in him, which accepts the forgiveness of sins for Christ's sake, and comforts itself with the promise of the Gospel." (Thor. Decl. II, 54)

Far from being the subject of God's alleged coercion, man can prevent his conversion. Christ wept over Jerusalem because His own people "would not" repent and believe His Gospel (Matt. 23:37). The martyr Stephen told his fellow Jews who were being wickedly stubborn in the face of the facts, "Ye do always resist the Holy Ghost" (Acts 7:51). Resistance to the truth is possible precisely because God will not coerce men to accept His grace in Christ. To insure that men are not reduced to the status of pawns or puppets, God works through means — the Gospel and the Sacraments — not directly, and under these conditions God can be opposed by men.

Here we must affirm the paradox — not a contradiction — that though God seriously wants all men to be saved, they are able to resist His gracious will; and though men can resist His grace, there is nothing whatever in the conduct of man during his conversion which can be referred to as his contribution to the final result. Only a logic which surreptitiously injects a concealed premise can come to the conclusion that a man's conversion is determined by the manner in which he "uses his liberty." Man has no spiritual liberty of any sort.

A man is either a believer, or he is not. There is no third position. Indifference, doubt, or the refusal to make a decision do not express his neutrality, but the fact that a man has declined the invitation of God. Apart from the illusory supposition that it is possible for man to be neutral toward God under certain circumstances, it also proposes the contradictory notion that man may, at the same time, be under God's grace and wrath, in death and life, an unbeliever and yet a believer.

The preparation for conversion may extend over a longer or shorter period of time, but conversion is always instantaneous, the matter of a moment. This does not mean that every Christian knows exactly when he was converted. Those who report their conversions in terms of a violent emotional upheaval undoubtedly very often do confuse their consequent joy of having become children of grace with the previous moment of conversion, which may not have been closely connected in time and may have escaped their notice. St. Paul could indeed point to the moment of his conversion, and so could the jailer of Philippi. But the Scriptures nowhere demand that a man know when he was converted, but rather that he be converted.

Conversion is not a once-in-a-lifetime event. Rather, it occurs again and again throughout the life of the Christian. The spiritual life of the Christian may be compared to the experience of a man who walks toward a certain destination, but who falls repeatedly and is raised again. Jesus speaks of those "which for a while believe and in time of temptation fall away" (Luke 8:13). Hymenaeus and Alexander made "shipwreck" of their faith (1 Tim. 1:19, 20), and there are the stories of the dramatic and calamitous lapses of David and Peter. However, there is always the possibility of another conversion, for it is written: "The Lord . . . is not willing that any should perish, but that all should come to repentance" (2 Peter 3:9); or: "God will have all men to be saved and to come unto the knowledge of the truth." (1 Tim. 2:4)

8. An Unrealistic Accommodation of Christian Faith and Scientific Method

Christian faith, as we have described it, is directed to the Triune God. He alone is able to elicit such faith, to sustain it, and to justify it. While faith cannot prove the existence of God, it must nonetheless assume it. Faith *in* Jesus Christ can say, I believe *that* God exists. God cannot be known redemptively except in Jesus Christ. "God was in Christ," the Christian repeats with St. Paul. Or with Luther: "I will know no other God except Him who was in Christ." This means, of course, that though the statements of Christian faith change with the contours of the factual world which it embraces, they do have their roots in objective facts.

It is important to affirm this. Many psychologists and psychiatrists have been willing to grant a gentlemanly form of accommodation to the Christian faith. Empiricists by stance and self-description, they have a difficult time with religious statements. Formerly empiricists spent a vast amount of time and energy to prove them untrue. Currently the shouting has given place to better manners. However, the objective is still the same: Christians must be prevented from getting a genuine hearing before the world.

The current gambit may be described as follows: Beyond the limits of science and philosophy we will grant the existence of the area of faith in which statements are incorrigible. However, they have no relevance to the empirical and corrigible statements which it is the function of philosophers and scientists to analyze and to confirm.

This permits the Christian philosopher, scientist, psychologist, and psychiatrist to live peaceably in two worlds (if he can) — a highly doubtful enterprise, because moments of crisis usually open the compartments in which such people seek to store their concerns. It is also agreeable to the analyst who has no interest in the Christian faith, because it permits him to ignore an awkward subject while continuing with the pursuit of his immediate interest.

But if the Christian faith is allowed to reach into the world which these people have staked out as their own preserve and upsets the congenial idea of a procession of "loose and separate" events, the non-Christian and irreligious analyst would quickly abandon his frosty courtesy for the most determined hostility, and the religious analyst who had decided to live cozily in two compartments of separate and sealed-off concerns would flounder in a most pathetic disorder of ideas. Both have the aim of suppressing the question of the truth or falsehood of religious statements. Both the religious (of the type under discussion) and the nonreligious analyst wish the Creator to remain securely in His heaven, the latter with tongue in cheek, the former with a devout concern for his own peace of mind.

The proposed accommodation will not work. The God whom the Christian worships will not allow Himself to be shut up in a remote heaven while scientific enterprise undertakes to govern the world below. The Creator is also the Preserver and Redeemer. He has reached into the world and will continue to do so.

For the Christian the contradictions between empirical evidence and the contents of his faith are constantly being overcome in the dialectic of action. Let us use a very ordinary illustration. A traveler badly rips his coat. The damage is real, and he has no means at hand to repair it. But he stirs about and finds a tailor who mends the coat. "He has no means at hand to repair it" is a true statement, but in the dialectic of action it becomes untrue as soon as he has found a tailor to do the job for him.

Similarly in the life of faith the contradictions of evil and suffering do not remain permanent obstacles, but are in the process of being overcome. The contemplative man surveys the damage and sees the contradiction. The man of faith grapples with the same, and at that moment the evidence against his faith, without changing its character as evidence, is in the process of being made irrelevant by a successful challenge.

Does the Christian faith merely make it possible to render a lifelong series of challenges irrelevant to his belief in his God? That would seem to be a dreary prospect. The Christian has much more to go on. He believes also that the whole situation is well in hand, and this conviction is based on his knowledge of the activity of God. This important point requires some discussion.

9. God's Activity Validates the Christian's Faith

Several millennia ago Carneades propounded a dilemma which is still being used by those who much prefer to leave God out of their consideration of events in the world (Hobbes, J. S. Mill, et al.). If God is good, He lacks power; if He has power, He lacks goodness. If the God in whom Christians believe were the purely contemplative deity of philosophy, not to mention the self-contemplative deity of Aristotle, the dilemma could not be overcome, and those who wish to live and act as though God *were* not, would be right. However, to lean on Dostoevski (who perhaps leaned on St. Anselm), the atheist never talks to the point.

If the above were no real dilemma, faith would have no function. But faith has the function of grasping the God whose activity is similar to ours in meeting obstacles to His purpose, but whose activity differs from ours because He is the Master of the entire situation, not merely of particular events and obstacles. For this purpose He entered the historical situation — "He came into the world" — He encountered obstacles, even death, the ultimate obstacle. But nothing could stop Him; He achieved a total triumph in His resurrection.

The Christian therefore trusts the God who is dialectically engaged in encounter and triumph with the same forces and obstacles which the nonbeliever tries to use as evidence against any kind of deity. Hence the proposed dilemma collapses utterly, along with its presuppositions. Its strength depended on the assumption that the God who rules this world had done nothing about the evidence which is cited against Him.

What force does such an argument have against a God who committed Himself to the removal of all contrary evidence and obstacles to His purpose? What power is there in the objections of the nonbeliever against a God who did this in the only way which leaves no traces behind which the scientist can explore "objectively"? What can be further said against a God who achieved His task by exposing Himself to the total force of evil, who let it do its worst to Him, and who triumphed totally over it?

10. Faith and Logical Necessity

We remind the philosophical and scientific reader that we impute no logical necessity to what we affirm in faith. Faith and necessity have no common area of discourse. We do not say that in the strict sense faith is logically grounded. The certainty of faith is not commensurable with its reasons, as far as we can state them. Yet faith is not without evidence, reason, or confirmation. The Christian *has* reasons for his faith and consequently for the statements which express it (1 Peter 3:15). He is also in possession of a form of confirmation, as Jesus explained it: "If any man will do His will, he shall know of the doctrine whether it be of God or whether I speak of Myself" (John 7:17). But since the statements of his faith are not logically grounded, the Christian does not say that they are *logically* incorrigible. Such a claim would introduce necessity, and where there is necessity, there can be no room for faith. Therefore the assurance of Christian faith is *logically* at all times compatible with contrary evidence, and it is so on all levels of historical existence. But not in the static sense, for the Christian does not have a static God. God has been at work and continues unceasingly to work: "My Father worketh hitherto, and I work" (John 5:17). Therefore the Christian asserts that God is dynamically compatible with all states of affairs, and in this dialectic the Christian continues to refuse to recognize evil as conclusive evidence against his claims, even though he admits its momentary or historical existence. The God in whom the Christian believes has been at work to overcome evil, and the process will continue until the end of time. Therefore the evidence which the nonbeliever uses has been made irrelevant as evidence.

11. Man as a Creature of God

Divine creation and human existence must be accepted as facts; they are the data of divine revelation and human experience, respectively. There is no coherent system of concepts which will reasonably explain them. Divine creation is a "mystery beyond both the natural and rational causalities" and hence must be expressed in the term "ex nihilo." [10]

---

[10] Reinhold Niebuhr, *Christian Realism and Political Problems* (New York: Charles Scribner's Sons, 1953), p. 181. Tillich's ontology of polar

The Scriptures are unanimous in their report that God created or made the world and all that it contains. This creation reveals the character of God as love. His art of willing the existence of other beings besides Himself is a demonstration of that fact. He needed no heaven, earth, and other living beings either "to fulfill Himself" or in any other way to make His situation complete and perfect. If we reverse our view, we can say that only such a God would be willing to grant existence or life. This God is the Holy Trinity — Father, Son, and Holy Spirit. No speculative inquiry will ever yield a rational explanation of the mysterious activity of the Holy Trinity in creation. The best we can do is to say with Luther: "It is the way of Scripture to say the world was made through Christ by the Father and in the Holy Spirit."

"And God said, Let Us make man in Our image, after Our

---

opposites, for which he asserts that it satisfies the claims both of the static and the dynamic aspects of being — freedom and destiny, self and the world, does not carry the conviction that God is more than the impersonal ground of being. Worse still, it does not allay the suspicion of the student that Tillich's ontology suggests a conception of being of which God is the product and that the self is only an aspect or expression of being as is freedom or necessity. It would seem appropriate to ask the question whether Tillich's ontology is a way of reducing the dynamic-dramatic history of creation, fall, salvation, and consummation into a static system ultimately determined by logical necessity. See Paul Tillich, *Systematic Theology* (Chicago: University of Chicago Press, 1951), I, 164 ff. A discussion of the argument between Niebuhr and Tillich is found in *The Theology of Reinhold Niebuhr* in *The Library of Living Theology*, ed. Charles W. Kegley and Robert Bretall (New York: The Macmillan Co., 1956), II, p. 36 ff. and 431 ff.

Modern philosophers like Whitehead have been moving toward a dynamic conception of being by stressing process or becoming. Others, like Bergson, have emphasized the freedom or creativity of the self. Personalists, like Charles Hartshorne, have worked toward a metaphysics for which the hope has been entertained that it might provide a better basis for Christian apologetics. However, the prospect of a solution for the problem does not appear to arise from these efforts.

It is probably true that things and events present aspects of uniqueness which are destroyed by attempts to establish any system of coherence. The venture, it seems, is bound to reveal itself as premature, especially if meaning is equated with rationality. An empirical naturalist like John Herman Randall, Jr., appears to be more discerning than the supporters of Tillich when he claims that Tillich's system is basically an enlarged naturalism which seeks also to account for the interests of religion, aesthetics, etc.

38

likeness; and let them have dominion . . ." (Gen. 1:26). What is the meaning of "image" or "likeness"? Does it perhaps refer to the "spark of divinity" in man, as has been suggested by some poets, philosophers, and theologians? Or is Shakespeare's laudatory enthusiasm in the well-known passage of *Hamlet* helpful? ("What a piece of work is man! How noble in reason! How infinite in faculty! In form and moving how express and admirable! In action how like an angel! In admiration how like a god!") The point is really beyond both the speculative reason and the poetic imagination.

The resemblance which man bears to God cannot be physical, for God is a spirit (John 4:24). Nor is the divine image to be thought of simply as man's unique endowment as a creature of mind and will. According to the Scriptures, man resembled God in the disposition of his intellect and will. In his original state man's intellect was perfect, though finite, and his will in every way agreed with the holy will of God. Therefore, within the limitations of his given faculties, man was as perfect, holy, and righteous as God, who made him, and he led a perfectly integrated existence.

Far from being merely the equal of beast — "a rational animal" — man was made to have dominion over the rest of the visible creation on earth. However, it was not a dominion based on brute force or technological compulsion, such as is the case now because his environment is basically hostile to him. Rather, his dominion was derived from, and patterned after, God's dominion over all creation, so that in this respect, too, man should exhibit the image and likeness of God in "knowledge" (Col. 3:10) and "righteousness and true holiness." (Eph. 4:24)

Divine revelation represents original man as an altogether wonderful being. He was intended to exist in perfect bliss, free from the slightest sin, without corruption of body and soul, and no distortion or contradiction of any kind in his intellect and will. His environment was utterly pleasant, and his time was spent in intimate association with God (Gen. 2:19 f.), in whose presence is "fullness of joy" and "pleasures forevermore" (Ps. 16:11). There was no suffering of any kind, and no haunting specter of death. Man as God's viceroy on earth — knowing, serving, and perfectly enjoying his Creator and King — presents a picture to us whose meaning or implications are far beyond our present grasp. We deal here with categories of tremendously transcendent dimension. Both our rational and our imaginative faculties are lamentably unequal to the task.

12. A Scientific View of Man's Beginnings

Scientists do not begin with an absolute beginning because science does not deal with concepts of this kind. Science begins with man as a part of nature and assumes that nature has been in a continuous process of development which resulted in increasingly complex forms of organization, the interplay of environmental stimulus and response.

Many thinkers of our time, exemplified by Whitehead and Alexander, speak of development as a series of emergent levels: matter, life, mind. The current popularity of this view may be due also to its indirect suggestion of the relation of the sciences: physics, biology, psychology. Alfred North Whitehead called this scheme "emergent realism," because "consciousness presupposes experience, and not experience consciousness." [11] "Emergent" has replaced "resultant," the term favored formerly, in order to allow for the conclusion that an evolutionary product is not predictable before its emergence.

Assumed as having emerged in the evolutionary process for the purpose of adjusting the organism to its environment, mind is sometimes thought of as a response to stimuli immediately present as well as to those still to be expected.[12] Mind is exhibited both by man and by animals which show a capacity for problem solving. However, this philosophy of pragmatism does not even attempt to explain large areas of mental behavior. Truth or validity would appear to be determined in terms of biological consequences. At this point a fatal weakness of pragmatism stands revealed: the ambiguities of its description of consequences.

---

[11] *Process and Reality* (New York: The Macmillan Co., 1929), p. 83.

[12] Ralph B. Perry, *General Theory of Value* (New York: Longmans, Green and Co., 1926), p. 177, § 72. *Prospicient Adjustment.* "However he may come by it, the animal is supposed at the moment of action to possess a capacity for *prospiciently* determined action," p. 178.

Against such a view, many scientists argue that although mind seems always to occur within a biological existence, and appears to be conditioned by that fact, there is much about mind which is not explained biologically. In recent thought much has been made of the distinctiveness of animal mind and human mind without denying a continuity between them. It is being emphasized that beyond the general awareness of other objects, which man shares with animals, he is also self-conscious, and that there appears to be no evidence of such self-transcendence in the animal world. This self-consciousness produces forms of behavior in man which differ sharply from anything found in animals. For example, man has language and symbols which he organizes in grammar and syntax intended as an objective means of communication. Animal life seems bound by the drive for self-preservation and self-perpetuation. Man has technology which requires a high degree of self-awareness. His religion heightens this faculty to an incomparable degree. These considerations would suggest a level of human freedom.

13. *Freedom and Determinism*

However, much of contemporary thinking in the sciences assumes freedom to be the obverse of determinism. The question becomes formulated in terms like these: Is man free to act as he will, or are his actions predetermined by external factors? If the scientific search is the search for causes or laws which explicate causes, then the scientist will proceed from the assumption that all events have their causes. The extraordinary scientific successes of our time have lent enormous force to this view.

Arguments have been developed against this view by those who felt that determinism forever catches man in the web of nature, so that there can be no human freedom worth the name. John MacMurray offers an analysis of the problem. The "inner antinomy" arises, he says, because our social behavior is not independent of our wills. If it were, how could science be considered a deliberate activity? "If sociology were a pure science, then the behavior of society must be represented as independent of human will and intention. Yet a society which can produce a scientific sociology is a society which proposes to control social behavior by human will and intention." [13]

His argument relates specifically to psychology: "If the psychologist gives a scientific account of his own behavior in producing psychology, he must consider his behavior as a set of processes which happen in accordance with objective laws. This means, however, that the idea of their being true or false is excluded" (p. 125). He continues: "If the belief that all beliefs are brought about in this way is true, then since it is a belief it cannot be true. For to say that a belief is the product of the operation of objective forces which necessitate its occurrence under certain conditions is clearly incompatible with holding that it is believed because it is true." (P. 129)

---

[13] *The Boundaries of Science: A Study in the Philosophy of Psychology* (London: Faber and Faber, Ltd., 1939), p. 124 f. The force of MacMurray's argument is suggested by the following:

"Now, when we are dealing with any part of human behavior which is theoretical in its aim, the intention which informs it is the intention to know something. Scientific activity is undertaken in order to achieve scientific knowledge. In terms of this intention the results of the activity, that is to say, the conclusions which are reached, may be true or false. If they are true, they have realized the intention of the activity which produced them. If they are false, they have not. In either case they can be true or false only because they are determined by the intention to achieve knowledge, and only with reference to this intention has the description of them as true or false any meaning. But if the psychologist gives a scientific account of his own behavior in producing psychology, he must consider his behavior as a set of processes which happen in accordance with objective laws. This means, however, that the idea of their being true or false is excluded. By making them the object of scientific research he has made it impossible to regard them as activities informed by an intention in terms of which they might be correct or incorrect. From the scientific point of view a scientific theory is simply a belief held that these people necessarily held these beliefs and could not, under the conditions obtaining, hold any others. In showing this, it would also show why certain other people necessarily refuse to accept these beliefs and could not do anything but reject them; just as a scientific account which shows that a stone must fall to the ground if it is free to do so will show also that a balloon must rise from the ground if it is free to do so. The question whether the beliefs are true or false cannot arise. Then we reach the paradoxical conclusion that the psychologists's account of psychology, if it is to be scientific, must exclude the possibility of considering it either true or false. His theory must be a theory such that, if it is true, it cannot be true." (See his discussion of "The Sociology of Science," particularly pp. 67—70)

42

If it were true that human actions are determined at all times by antecedent causes, so the argument runs, then the idea of human responsibility is destroyed. The fact is, however, that scientists, psychologists, and psychiatrists rarely fail to assume the existence of human responsibility in their professional and personal lives. The elimination of responsibility would eliminate *human* society.[14]

Thus briefly indicated, the scientific-philosophic view of man presents us with major problems which for many Christian theologians would seem seriously to raise the question whether it is really possible to develop an adequate metaphysics for psychology and psychiatry within the context of its ideas. The efforts of MacMurray will leave psychology unscathed. If "the history of the nervous system determines the present state of a person," a notable dogma relevant to this discussion, there is no way for MacMurray to win the argument. If we put this scientific doctrine into the form of an equation, we would say that (1) i believes p, (2) there is a function F $(x^1, x^2, x^3 \ldots x^n)$ such that its magnitude determines belief or disbelief, (3) p is true. This would include all intentions, actual reflections of any kind, and all religious conclusions. If this were true, Freud would be right in saying that the claims of the Christian religion are illusory.

The Lutheran theologian discovers a fundamental affinity in the nominalistic thinking of an important school of psychology. Methodologically these psychologists also use "Ockham's razor," that "entities must not be needlessly multiplied." This transfers the discussion to a different level. If there is agreement on the nominalistic program that reference to abstract entities is merely a convenient or "shorthand" manner of speaking, the debate must turn upon the question: Which are names asserting existence?

---

[14] The late Archbishop Temple has argued in behalf of freedom, which he calls "spiritual determination" in contrast to mechanical or even organic determination. Freedom is for him self-determination (William Temple, *Nature, Man and God,* pp. 229, 244). However, this term, borrowed from German idealism, which prefers "self-determined" to "not determined," is very misleading. Is "non-determination" another kind of determination? After all, determination is a two-term relation, meaning that a stands in a certain relationship to b. What meaning is there in saying that a stands in a certain relationship to itself?

The warp and woof of Christian argument inevitably is Jesus Christ, the Logos, who was made flesh and who is God. All else is preliminary to the main bout. The orthodox Christian theologian, as was stated previously, accepts both the existence and the claims of Jesus Christ as factual. This is his central point for his perspective. Consequently his view of the problem of determinism is also Christocentric.

The Christian is able to make a quick reply to this latter argument of the biophysicist and psychologist by placing against it his encounter with the historical facts regarding Jesus Christ. These objective events obviously produced stimuli in the nervous system of those who witnessed them, which led them to conclude that Jesus Christ indeed conformed to His claims. They asserted "many infallible proofs" (Acts 1:3) for this. Since these events are a part of history and therefore not repeatable for purposes of demonstration, the causal function previously mentioned (used as a criterion of relevance) is cognitively accounted for and at the same time superseded in the dynamic of divine action.

To be in creation means to be limited by "necessities." Another way of putting it theologically is to say that in the moment of His incarnation Jesus Christ refrained from using fully and constantly the unlimited, indeterminate possibilities open to Him in His divine freedom. The incarnation placed Christ "under the Law," both in the normative and in the descriptive sense.[15]

This is the same "law" under which all men have existed since the Fall. If we think of "law" in the normative, prescriptive sense, the liberation from "law" in its Judaic ceremonial and civil

_____

15 Gal. 4:3-5. Neither the Authorized Version nor the Revised Standard Version adequately render the Greek στοιχεῖα τοῦ κόσμου. In the Platonic sense στοιχεῖα refers to "the elements" out of which nature was constructed. The RSV is closer to the contextual sense of St. Paul when it translates the Greek phrase with "the elemental spirits of the universe." However, this is still not exactly what the apostle wrote. στοιχεῖα includes the notion of a serial order, e. g., military formations, the marks of the hours in a sundial. The verb form στοιχίζω means "to order, to arrange in system." Hence the following rendition of the passage is suggested: "So with us; when we were children, we were slaves to the system of the universe. But when the time had fully come, God sent forth His Son, born of woman, born under the Law, to redeem those who were under the Law, so that we might receive adoption as sons."

44

dimension has been consummated for the Christian; but the Christian is not yet free from "law" in its descriptive sense: he is still bound by the system, the uniformities, the order of the universe. The liberation of the Christian in this respect will be consummated, according to Christ's promise: "And when I go and prepare a place for you, I will come again and will take you to Myself, that where I am, you may be also." (John 14:3)

Existing as he does under the "system of the universe," the Christian unhesitatingly accepts determinism *in its function as a leading principle of inquiry into causes.* As such it functions as a criterion of relevance of conditions. It means that if we want to predict an event uniquely, we must know all relevant conditions. But if the prediction is not confirmed (assuming that we did not use the wrong laws), it follows that we must have failed to reckon with some relevant condition. In this function (as a criterion of relevance) it is impossible to refute determinism.[16]

Unfortunately, many people (including some who ought to know better) hold to the uncritical belief that human actions are never genuinely free. They have a sense of inevitability, which is indebted to the notions of the anthropological sciences that all of man's actions are determined by heredity and environment, to the point that they seem to speak of "fate." But "fatalism" is a thundering ambiguity built upon the term "free." An action is "free" when an agent has the choice of doing it or not. This is the sense in which "free" is used by the apostle Paul when he

---

[16] For example, it is impossible logically to show a contradiction in the principle of determinism *as a criterion of relevance* in the formulation cited before:

  (1) i believes p.
  (2) There is a function F $(x^1, x^2, x^3 \ldots x^n)$ such that its magnitude determines belief or disbelief.
  (3) p is true.

Practically, however, the value of the formulation is quite minimal for the psychoanalyst. Can he ever know *all* the relevant conditions of the function? To be specific: Can the psychoanalyst, employing this function, ever hope to understand why or how a logical positivist becomes a Christian? Applied to this area, it would seem quite certain that the predictions of the logical analyst (unless he entertains the delusion of having prospects to become an omniscient observer) are unlikely to exhibit a tendency toward uniqueness.

writes that the Christian is "free" from the Law. It is the sense in which Luther and the orthodox Lutheran theologians have employed it. It is also the sense in which Locke and Hume have used it.[17]

The term "choice" would be meaningless if some of our actions did not causally depend upon our choosing them instead of others. As Luther agreed in his argument against Erasmus, normal human beings are certainly able to choose to eat or not to eat, to walk, to stand or to sit down, as they may please. "Choice" is one of those singular psychological events known to every rational human being. To say that no one ever makes a genuine choice is as untrue as saying that no one ever experiences pain. If "choice" and "pain" do not exist, what on earth do we mean by those words? Obviously, "choice" and "pain" are psychological terms whose meaning we grasp through the experience of certain events which are given the designation of "choice" or "pain." The fact that we have and understand the term "choice" means that we sometimes have a choice.

For the morally important distinction between free and unfree actions the psychological meaning of "choice" alone is relevant. Therefore the Christian holds that an act is genuinely "free," according to the general meaning of the word, even though he believes that God, being eternal and omniscient, has a total and simultaneous knowledge of *all* factors which lead to an action as well as the action itself, so that He knows and is able to "predict" precisely which action a person will choose. But the action is free in this sense only if one of the determining antecedents was the person's decision to take this action and that it was possible for him to have acted otherwise, at least on the basis of the knowledge which may be presumed to be available to the ordinary person in such circumstances.

People who deny the reality of "choice" for human beings in this sense should (and often do) go on to say that it is improper

---

17 Unfortunately, this is not the sense in which other philosophers, such as Spinoza and Hegel, have used it, with the result that a fantastic amount of confusion was introduced into the theological literature which leaned on Hegelianism.

and illogical to hold men accountable for their decisions. It is from such conclusions that moral absolutes are denied.[18]

Moral evaluation is, of course, not justified if universal determinism is interpreted to mean that choices do not exist for persons. If this conditional statement is made, together with the categorical entailment, "he could have chosen differently, no matter what the factors or antecedents may have been," we assume a total set of conditions. This universal determinism, including both physical and mental events, does indeed remove the basis for the question of guilt and punishment for a defendant. It is as much as saying that "a man does what he does because he is what he is." Taken literally, this assumes that man is a thing, a pawn, a puppet. Praise or blame are fictitious notions which, together with the idea of human responsibility, have no genuine point of reference to the realities constituting man's nature.

But in ordinary discourse men do not speak in terms of a total set of conditions. We say, "Under the circumstances, he could have acted differently had he chosen to do so." If this were not so, no one could ever speak of any event as having been avoidable. It would mean to us that every evil in the world is devoid of moral meaning, that Hitler and Stalin did what they did because they were what they were; universal determinism relieves them of all responsibility, praise, or blame. Of course, such a practical application constitutes a misunderstanding and misuse of the idea of universal determinism, because the latter does not refer to refutable empirical statements; it is a criterion of relevance for research. This means that as long as the correlation between the conditions and the actual course of behavior seems to be one-many, the genetic psychologist will know that he does not yet completely understand all the relevant conditions.[19]

---

18 The late Chief Justice Vinson of the U. S. Supreme Court once declared officially that "there are no absolutes." If there are no absolutes which constitute a moral imperative, it is difficult to see why Mr. Vinson became a lawyer, served in Congress, and finally accepted the nomination to the bench of the highest court of the land. Logically, he should not have undertaken any form of juridical activity.

19 It might be added that the Lutheran theologian operates with a similar criterion of relevance: If the correlation between the interpretation of Biblical text and context appears to be one-many, the exegete will immediately conclude that he needs to have further knowledge of the subject.

With regard to any area of reality, physical events, or voluntary behavior, it is certainly both logical and commonsensical to assume that a difference in the result indicates a difference in the set of conditions. Consequently the completely deterministic scientist cannot be expected to grant that in a totally identical situation an agent might have acted differently from the way in which he acted. In short, if anyone could literally live part of his life over again, he would undoubtedly be both astonished and depressed by the experience. There isn't a thing he would do differently! [20]

Human moral evaluation is always justified by its fundamental purpose: the prevention or promotion of a desirable or undesirable result. It supplies the thinking agent with motives of conduct and thereby introduces new forces into the psychological field which may neutralize or modify the effects of the forces already at work. Stimuli, such as fines, imprisonment, execution, are certainly legitimate instruments of public law or rational legislation for the purpose of motivating actions intended to have desirable results.

Again, practically speaking, we refrain from moral evaluation when the action of an agent is said to be involuntary. For example, a man suddenly suffers a heart attack while driving a car. The result is a collision, involving the lives and health of several people. Here proximate moral judgments on our part would be pointless.

14. Man in Revolt Against God

Beginning with 18th-century "enlightenment," the philosophical idea of progress has served as an inspiration of the modern scientific endeavor. A good case can be made theologically for certain forms of progress. Man was assigned the task of subduing and using the earth, and if we speak of growth in any way, we do refer to a certain form of progress. However, the philosophical idea of progress is nontheistic, morally and ethically optimistic, and in several of its conclusions quite anti-Christian.

It is exceedingly difficult for a Christian theologian to think

---

[20] A classical expression of this is the statement of Heraclitus (Frag. 121): "Man's character is his fate." Schopenhauer's analysis of the point offers a similar conclusion, based upon the *post factum* of human experience.

of the philosophical idea of progress except as a demonic distortion of the clearly discernible record of man's history. The historical circumstances are, of course, always in movement; nevertheless, the record always reveals man as a killer and a healer. Man builds complex civilizations and at the same time brutalizes his neighbor and corrupts himself. His fabulous achievements in the arts and sciences have guaranteed him no happiness and no protection against the temptation to overreach and destroy himself. He is always in search of security against troubles and becomes their victim when he deems himself most secure. Endless discontent goes hand in hand with his fairest hopes and splendid triumphs. Lies and violence show the conflicts and depravities in his nature. Everywhere he is surrounded and bound by evil. Why is this so? On the basis of the Scriptures the Christian theologian answers: Man is God's creation, but he has revolted against his Maker.

Although God made man in His own image and likeness, so that there was no contradiction between God's holy will and man's will,[21] and man had every reason to be thankful for his exalted state relative to the created order, this happy condition did not long endure.

God exists in perfect freedom: His will and existence are in perfect congruence, so that we can say, God is what He wills and wills what He is. Not so with man. His freedom was a derived and finite freedom. God gave it to him. His creatureliness is clearly expressed in Gen. 1:26: "And God said, Let Us make man in Our image, after Our likeness." However, while it is necessary to emphasize man's total dependence upon God, the Creator, man's original state would be misrepresented unless it is understood that God did not create man as His puppet or mechanical toy. In this connection it is perhaps not inappropriate to repeat the affirmation that it is the character of God's love to will the existence of other beings besides Himself who will continue in *free* association with Him. The indeterminate character of this free association between man and God is suggested by Gen. 2:19: "And out of the ground the Lord God formed every beast of the field and every fowl of the air and brought them

---

[21] Perhaps notice should be given that here the term "will" denotes no isolated faculty but the total self-expression of a being.

unto Adam to see what he would call them; and whatsoever Adam called every living creature, that was the name thereof."

Man's perfect freedom within his creaturely limitations is especially clear from the fact that after God gave man all his requisite qualities, He also conferred upon man the opportunity freely to decide whether or not to continue his harmonious association with God. Specifically, he was given the freedom to decide whether or not to obey God, and the significance of disobedience is the assertion of a moral authority which is in contradiction to God's authority. The moral freedom of man consisted of his being able to sin and in being able not to sin. The latter is of considerable significance and should be borne in mind.

The image and likeness of God, according to which man was created, meant that man had a perfect apprehension of the good by virtue of his perfect creation. His will was always in total congruity with the will of God, and this was the measure of his equality with God. But disobedience to God's command suggested the prospect of an independent or autonomous moral equality with God. "For God doth know that in the day ye eat thereof, then your eyes shall be opened, and ye shall be as God, knowing good and evil." (Gen. 3:5, marginal note)

The initial assertion of independence, expressed in an act of disobedience, constituted man's revolt against the command or law of his Creator. It was a rejection of the status or condition of existence which the Creator had assigned to man. For this reason the Scriptures speak of sin as lawlessness (1 John 3:4) and rebellion (Deut. 9:23, 24). Ever since his first revolt against God (or his "fall" from the status initially assigned to him) man has continued to assert his moral independence of God by refusing to fulfill his obligation as the creature of God. (Rom. 1:18, 32)

When the Christian Church, on the basis of the Scriptures, speaks of sin, the meaning of the term is far more profound and comprehensive than its superficial usage in contemporary speech or literature.[22] The concept of "sin" presupposes a law or command of God (and, behind that, holiness as an inviolable quality

---

[22] Sin is no mere social offense or error which may be remedied by better training. A vastly deeper insight is offered by Martin Luther: "We are not sinners because we commit this or that sin, but we commit them

50

of God), for sin is above all else disobedience to God. This is vividly expressed in the penitential psalms, e. g.: "Against Thee, Thee only, have I sinned and done this evil in Thy sight" (Ps. 51:4). God alone has the prerogative of prescribing laws (James 4:12; Is. 51:4). Laws made by men are binding only when God has conferred such a right, as in the case of government (Rom. 13:1 f.) or parents (Col. 3:17-23), but always under the condition that such human laws or prescriptions do not conflict with God's Law and thereby become invalid. (Acts 5:29)

God's Law is violated by evil deeds (2 Sam. 12:13), and by evil thoughts and desires (James 1:15; Rom. 7:17; Matt. 5:28), regardless of whether they are expressed in words. These are sins. The lack of intent or awareness of the sinful act, thought, or word on the part of the person involved does not change its offensive quality (Rom. 7:19; 1 Tim. 1:13). Any kind or degree of distortion of the original image and likeness of God, conferred upon man at the time of his creation, is sin. This includes also the inherited corruption which attaches to the *Christian* against his will (Rom. 7:19, 20). Therefore sin is any transgression of the divine Moral Law, which the Lutheran Confessions describe as "the divine doctrine in which the righteous, immutable will of God is revealed, what is to be the quality of man in his nature, thoughts, words, and works in order that he may be pleasing and acceptable to God." (Formula of Concord, Thor. Decl., V, 17)

15. *Man Under Sin*

His original sin — his arrogant desire for autonomy, or independence from God — has had the most far-reaching consequences for man and for his environment.

As Adam and Eve, according to the story of the Fall (Gen. 3), immediately noticed their nakedness and thus revealed their preoccupation with themselves, so every human being always occupies the center of his world. To use an expression of Luther, the ego curves back upon itself. Each man is his own point of refer-

---

because we are sinners first." (*Luther's Works: Selected Psalms I,* American edition [St. Louis: Concordia Publishing House, 1955], 12, 348).

The Scriptures speak of sin as transgression (παράβασις) of God's Law, which results in a condition of deprivation — the consequences of having missed the mark of human existence (άμαρτία).

51

ence, and his horizon depends on where he stands. Like Professor Higgins in G. B. Shaw's *Pygmalion*, every man is astonished that other people are not more like him. He calls that good which pleases him, and what hurts him he judges to be evil. It is a disposition which exists at birth. Education may widen man's horizon of interests, but he still remains his own center and standard of reference, just as climbing a mountain will enlarge his field of vision without changing the point of reference — himself. In short, under the condition of sin each man is his own god instead of letting God be God.

This upside-down condition is the inheritance of each human being. Each baby is his own center of reference since his conception, as David confessed: "Behold, I was shapen in iniquity; and in sin did my mother conceive me" (Ps. 51:5). However, the origin of sin is not to be traced to the sexual relation but to the fact that the original parents of mankind became sinners and bequeathed their sinful condition to all their offspring down to the present time. Since the Fall, man is no longer able not to sin.

The Christian Church terms this inheritance "original sin." In the language of the Lutheran Confessions (Formula of Concord, Thor. Decl., I, 11, 12): "That original sin (in human nature) is not only this entire absence of all good in the spiritual, divine things, but that, instead of the lost image of God in man, it is at the same time also a deep, wicked, horrible, fathomless, inscrutable, and unspeakable corruption of the entire nature and all its powers, especially of the highest, principal powers of the soul in the understanding, heart, and will, so that now, since the Fall, man inherits an inborn wicked disposition and inward impurity of heart, evil lust and propensity; that we all by disposition and nature inherit from Adam such a heart, feeling, and thought as are, according to their highest powers and the light of reason, naturally inclined and disposed directly contrary to God and His chief commandments, yea, that they are enmity against God, especially as regards divine and spiritual things. For in other respects, as regards natural, external things which are subject to reason, man still has to a certain degree understanding, power, and ability, although very much weakened, all of which, however, has been so infected and contaminated by original sin that before God it is of no use."

The emphasis should also be made that man is an indivisible unity, according to the presentation of the Scriptures. He cannot be split into several parts. Total man is presented as a "living soul," and each bodily function is merely an aspect of the entire functioning person.[23] Biblical psychology speaks of the "breath" *(nephesh)* of man, of his "heart," his "bowels," his "mind," but only as aspects of the unity of personality (e. g., Deut. 6:5; Is. 1:4, 5; Rom. 8:7; 2 Cor. 6:12). (See also Ch. VIII and appendix on Dualism.) The Biblical view of "carnal man" does not confine sin to his body or his physical condition, but includes the total person. It does not grant any kind of dualistic conception of man, including the assumption that there is in man a separate entity (mind or soul) which observes and records without being involved in the process of change, growth, and corruption. The unity of man in anxiety expresses itself in amazingly various forms of illness — a headache, disorders of the stomach or intestines, or paralyzing fear.

Returning to a previous observation, the first sin of man involved the entire visible creation in his corruption, with the result that sinful man is born into a hostile environment. Now man must wrest his livelihood from nature and defend himself against the elements and other life. The fact that each man is a center of activity and meaning in competition with all others involves the corruption by this fundamental sin of the family as well as of all other social relationships in this life. As Cain murdered his younger brother, so the hand of every man is by his sinful nature raised against the welfare of every other man. Having renounced God as the true center of his life and standard of reference, Adam's anxiety (Gen. 3:10 — "I was afraid") is the ground of man's universal sense of anxiety, and his guilt is the source of all human guilt. His story is the story of all men of all ages, for the Hebrew name of the first man "Adam" means "man."

---

[23] An excellent monograph on the subject, though it deserves to be considered with reserve in parts, is John A. T. Robinson's *The Body* in *Studies in Biblical Theology*, No. 5 (Chicago: Alec R. Allenson, Inc., 1952).

16. Man in Anxiety

The Biblical view of man in anxiety is both comprehensive and unitary. When a psychologist like Rollo May,[24] a psychiatrist like Karl A. Menninger,[25] or an existentialist philosopher-theologian like Paul Tillich [26] offer descriptions of various forms of anxiety, the Christian would do well to remember that while these distinctions may have value to the clinical specialist, the Christian revelation does not make such distinctions. Anxiety is represented as a pervasive terror and dread with undertones of self-rejection and hostility. "For the thing that I fear comes upon me, and what I dread befalls me. I am not at ease, nor am I quiet; I have no rest; but trouble comes" (Job 3:25, 26, RSV). "I loathe my life; I would not live forever. Let me alone, for my days are a breath" (Job 7:16, RSV).[27] In his clinical encounters with forms of anxiety Sigmund Freud found the element of anxious expectation as an unfailing component: "We may perhaps say that there is here a *quantum of anxiety in a free-floating condition,* which in any state of expectation controls the selection of ideas, and is ever ready to attach itself to any suitable ideational content." [28] Anxiety, having its roots in the fact of man's alienation from his God, cannot be abstracted from an ethical and theological concern. According to the Scriptures, anxiety is the product of an uneasy conscience, e. g., Rom. 2:15.[29]

In his *The Courage to Be* Paul Tillich distinguishes three forms of anxiety: (1) The anxiety of death, (2) the anxiety of

---

24 *The Meaning of Anxiety* (New York: Ronald Press Co., 1950).

25 *Man Against Himself* (New York: Harcourt, Brace and Co., 1938).

26 *The Courage to Be* (New Haven: Yale University Press, 1952).

27 "Thus the fear of death is the one misery that makes us more miserable than all other creatures. Although these, too, are subject to change and death, they are not changed because of God's wrath as are we, who spend our lives in constant terror of divine wrath." *Luther's Works,* American Ed. (St. Louis: Concordia Publ. House, 1956), vol. 13, p. 116.

28 *Collected Papers I* (London: Hogarth Press, 1950), p. 80.

29 The study of the term *conscience* as used in the New Testament is recommended to the interested reader. E. g., C. A. Pierce, *Conscience in the New Testament* in *Studies in Biblical Theology,* No. 15 (Chicago: Alec R. Allenson, Inc., 1955), appears to offer stimulating insights.

meaninglessness, (3) the anxiety of condemnation (p. 41). He claims furthermore that these forms of anxiety "are immanent in each other but normally under the dominance of one of them" (p. 42). However, it is difficult to see, from the Christian theological point of view, how such distinctions have practical effects beyond that of an exercise.

Man's anxiety is the product of his sinfulness, that state of alienation or contradiction which exists between him and God, between man's will (taken as the expression of his being) and God's will. Because man's being is derived from God, as has been stated before, man in contradiction to God has good reason to feel himself threatened in his existence. It is the consequence of the threat upon his disobedience: "Thou shalt surely die" (Gen. 2:17). In the fulfillment of this ultimate threat man's anxiety takes various forms. In his analysis of the *Concept of Dread* Sören Kierkegaard speaks of the "comic" forms under which a man hides his real despair. However, no one can escape the consequences of anxiety in his life.[30] It will take its toll.

Since God is the source of ultimate meaning, man's alienation from God drives man continually to seek provisional meanings in his existence in order thereby to nullify the threat to his existence as man. His total alienation from God establishes the total measure of his guilt, and the consequent guilt and hostility will seek expression in his conscience. Operatively, in the unconscious, anxiety becomes a condition which distorts some basic intrapersonal relationship; and the person, because of his uncon-

---

[30] The reader may profit from the elaboration of this in Sören Kierkegaard's *Fear and Trembling* and *The Sickness unto Death* (Doubleday Anchor Books, 1954). He calls anxiety or dread "a sympathetic antipathy and an antipathetic sympathy" in *The Concept of Dread*, trans. Walter Lowrie (Princeton: Princeton University Press, 1946), p. 38. See also page vi: "As *Fear and Trembling* was the state of the man teleologically suspended when God tried him, so in dread the psychic state of the suspended is that desperate moment of exemption from realizing the ethical." (Quoted from *Concluding Unscientific Postscript*, p. 240)

Cf. also: "For dread is a desire for what one fears, a sympathetic antipathy; dread is an alien power which takes hold of the individual, and yet one cannot extricate oneself from it, does not wish to, because one is afraid, but what one fears attracts one." W. H. Auden, *Kierkegaard*, The Living Thoughts Library, ed. Alfred O. Mendel (New York: David McKay Co., Inc., 1952), p. 158.

scious sense of guilt and hostility, seeks to continue this distortion by manipulative control; and the psychotherapist confronts a case of neurotic anxiety.

However, Christian theology does not make the clinical distinctions of anxiety, because all anxiety is of one kind, though its manifestations may differ in form and intensity. Under psychotherapeutic treatment, neurotic anxiety *may* be relieved by means of a greater self-knowledge; however, an attempt to relieve existential or primary anxiety certainly remains unfinished unless the basic cause of anxiety is dealt with in the terms of the Christian insights of Law and Gospel. Hence there is a genuine understanding reflected in Shakespeare's physician who was called in to treat Lady Macbeth:

> This disease is beyond my practice: . . .
> Foul whisperings are abroad: unnatural deeds
> Do breed unnatural troubles; infected minds
> To their deaf pillows will discharge their secrets.
> More needs she the divine than the physician.
> God, God forgive us all! (*Macbeth*, V, i)

Anxiety is capable of a fantastic variety and elaboration. It may find expression in the pride of one man and the humility of another, in the rectitude of the upright as well as the confession of the sinner. It acts as a restriction upon every man in all his relationships. It begins at birth and stays with man in the hour of his death: man is anxious because he is afraid of his God. He needs to appeal to God for a clear conscience. (1 Peter 3:21, RSV)

17. *The Mind and Will of Man Under Sin*

In the consideration of the human situation special attention must be given to the consequences of sin upon the mind and will of man, because the estimate of these capacities becomes of fundamental importance in the consideration of the activities of God to secure man's salvation by the work of Christ. If theologians speak of the mind and will of man as capacities or faculties, the significance placed upon them is nonetheless in terms of the expression of total man. It may bear repetition that the Christian theologian always speaks of the entire human being when he treats particular aspects of expression, because the Scriptures do not present man in any abstraction.

Mention was made in a previous section of this chapter that the mind and will of man was free before the Fall. Of course, God alone is free in the absolute sense; however, man shared God's freedom within the limitations of his creatureliness. Consequently man's mind possessed a clear apprehension of the good, and his will desired nothing but the good. Man's fall radically changed his condition in this respect also. However, when the Christian Church speaks of the mind and will of man under sin, the meaning is not that sin has substantively changed man; the change in the mind and will of man is a qualitative change. Under the condition of sin man is completely unable to apprehend spiritual truths,[31] such as are conveyed in the message of the Gospel, nor is man disposed willingly to accept them (1 Cor. 2:14). When natural or historical man is confronted with spiritual truth, he will judge it both rashly and falsely (Acts 2:13; 17:18, 32) and harden himself in opposition to it (Acts 7:51).

The Lutheran Confessions (Formula of Concord, Thor. Decl., II, 9, 11, 12, 20, 26) state the matter as follows:

Although man's reason or natural intellect indeed has still a dim spark of the knowledge that there is a God, as also of the doctrine of the Law (Rom. 1:19 ff.), yet it is so ignorant, blind, and perverted that when even the most ingenious and learned men upon earth read or hear the Gospel of the Son of God and the promise of eternal salvation, they cannot from their own powers perceive, apprehend, understand, or believe and regard it as true, but the more diligence and earnestness they employ, wishing to comprehend these spiritual things with their reason, the less they understand or believe, and before they become enlightened and are taught by the Holy Ghost, they regard all this only as foolishness or fictions. . . . Now, just as a man who is physically dead cannot of his own powers prepare or adapt himself to obtain temporal life again, so the man who is spiritually dead in sins cannot of his own strength adapt or apply himself to the acquisition of spiritual and heavenly righteousness and life, unless he is delivered and quickened by the Son of God from the death of sin. . . . Therefore the Scriptures deny to the intellect, heart, and will of the natural man all aptness, skill, capacity, and ability to think, to understand, to be able to do, to begin, to will, to undertake, to act, to work or to concur in working anything good and right in spiritual things as of himself. . . . For, as Doctor Luther says on Ps. 90: "In worldly and external affairs, which pertain to the

---

[31] This term, as well as similar ones, e. g., "spiritual matters," "spiritual things," refers to those things which the Holy Spirit works in man.

57

livelihood and maintenance of the body, man is cunning, intelligent, and quite active." . . . Reason and free will are able to a certain extent to live an outwardly decent life, but to be born anew, and to obtain inwardly another heart, mind, and disposition, this only the Holy Ghost effects.[32]

Man has no free will *in spiritual matters* [33] precisely because

[32] *Luther's Works: Selected Psalms II,* American edition (St. Louis: Concordia Publishing House, 1956), vol. 13, pp. 75 ff. The reader who may wish to pursue the matter further is directed especially to Article XVIII of the Apology to the Augsburg Confession and to Article II of the Thorough Declaration of the Formula of Concord. All of these are contained in *Concordia Triglotta,* or *The Book of Concord.*

[33] Theologically we have, broadly speaking, at least four views in historical Christianity on the subject of free will.

The Pelagian opinion (opposed by St. Augustine) became dominant in Roman Catholic theology in its "Semi-Pelagian" forms. The major conclusion is that man is able to make a substantial contribution to his own salvation. The sacramental office of the church conveys to him a *gratia infusa,* i. e., divine powers are literally poured into him by the operation of the sacramental administration itself. The view argues that a man is free to co-operate with God spiritually even before he becomes a Christian.

Related to this view are various forms of Arminian humanism, which have been current in Protestant theology since the Reformation. The most subtle of these is the argument that the principle of man's residual spiritual freedom stands by virtue of the claim that some men resist the Holy Spirit less stubbornly in conversion than others. It is therefore essentially a negative spiritual freedom.

The Calvinist view, in its classical forms of expression, is rigorously determinative. Not only does man have no spiritual freedom of any kind whatever, but God in His sovereignty, before creation, ordained at random both whom He would convert and save and whom He would reject. The redemptive work of Christ is in principle merely incidental to this divine eternal decree.

The classical Lutheran view asserts that men must not speculate about the "hidden things of God." There is no information available to us regarding the *deus absconditus,* the God who hides Himself. Redemptively we can know only the God who has revealed Himself in Jesus Christ. Since the Christian cannot know the total situation, he cannot accept the rigorous determinism of Calvinism in the realm of the spirit. For the sake of Christ, God is gracious to all men, and it is His serious desire that all men be saved and come to the knowledge of the truth. On the other hand, the Lutheran view denies man any spiritual powers whereby he can co-operate in his own salvation. If a man becomes a Christian, it is due *totally* to God's grace in Christ. If a man is lost, it is totally his own fault and responsibility. Spiritually man is bound by sin and therefore not free. If he is converted and obtains salvation, this is entirely the unmerited gift of God. In the Fall, man collectively became responsible for his sin. God has the credit *in toto* when man is saved; man has the responsibility *in toto* when he is lost. A close examination will show that this is the affirmation of a paradox, not a logical contradiction.

he stands in revolt against the source of divine freedom — God. The holy will of God, expressed in His Law, puts man under constraint by its demand for perfection which he cannot attain. This, in turn, reveals man's sin (Rom. 7:7), for it is the nature of fallen man to love his own sin and to take delight in observing the sins of others. This love of sin is the chief sin of man. Psychiatry and psychology have yet to give serious and exhaustive attention to this fact.

According to the Scriptures, Satan seduced original man to sin, with the consequence that man became subject to the devil's tyranny, a realm of existence which is utterly separated from God, who is the source of all that is good. Death is the nature of Satan's tyranny, so that all men are born spiritually dead, eventually die a natural death, and lastly enter the state of eternal death, unless God intervenes. Death in any form is not the annihilation of man, but separation from the goodness of God, who is also the source of life. This separation is a condition so dreadful and beyond imagination that in its final stage man would prefer extinction if he could have his way.

In the consideration of the relationship of theology to psychology and psychiatry man's total lack of *spiritual* freedom (as opposed to historical freedom expressed in various forms of choice) is of vast importance. The discerning psychiatrist will want to reckon with this fact in the treatment of certain types of patients. The psychologist who is willing to reckon with spiritual insights must give weight to the doctrine of the bondage of the will in his examination of behavior and learning problems.

However, the Christian Church also holds to the view that indeterminate possibilities attach to man in his historical existence: there are no categories whereby these possibilities can be predicted for the individual with any precision.

18. *The Person and Work of Christ*

The Christian assertions regarding Jesus Christ involve categories with which science is unable to cope and which, consequently, it does not recognize. However, in his treatment of Christians, the therapist needs to understand the faith of his patients regarding Jesus Christ. The alternative would be an unscientific and deliberate refusal to consider a determinative

59

factor or series of factors which are constitutive elements of such a case.

But the reminder is surely appropriate that Jesus Christ is a mystery also for the Christian, and it is for these reasons that the Christian will insist upon placing limits upon his thinking about Christ. According to the Scriptures, the mystery of the Redeemer is of such a surpassing character that even "the angels desire to look into" it (1 Peter 1:12), and for nearly two millennia the Christian Church has sung with St. Paul: "And without controversy great is the mystery of our religion: God was manifest in the flesh, justified in the Spirit, seen of angels, preached unto the Gentiles, believed on in the world, received up into glory." (1 Tim. 3:16)

According to the Creed of Athanasius, par. 27 ff., *Concordia Triglotta*, the Christian Church, on the basis of the Scriptures, has maintained three assertions about Jesus Christ: (a) He is truly God; (b) He is truly man; (c) the two natures, divine and human, are uniquely united in His one Person.

The implications of these assertions are so far-reaching that the very content of the Christian religion is destroyed unless all three of them are entirely maintained in the way that the Scriptures present them to the world. For unless Jesus Christ is truly the Lord God Himself, there can be no salvation for the human race — only God can save. Equally so, Christ must be truly and fully a human being; otherwise He could not have made a vicarious atonement for mankind. The unique union of the divine and the human nature in His person enabled Jesus Christ to be the Redeemer, which was His office in this world.

The Christian Church believes Jesus Christ to be God because He disclosed Himself as such: "I and the Father are one" (John 10:30). That this was recognized as a fact is borne out by the record: He is given the name of God (John 1:1) or Son of God (Matt. 16:16). Even the essential and incommunicable name of God (Yahweh — I AM THAT I AM) is clearly ascribed to Jesus Christ (cp. Heb. 1:6 with Ps. 97:1, 7). Characteristics or qualities of God are ascribed to Jesus Christ — omnipotence (John 10: 20-30); eternity (John 8:58; 17:5; 1:1); omniscience (John 21:17). Only God can do the work which Jesus Christ has done and still does — creation and preservation (Col. 1:16, 17; John 5:17-19);

the resurrection of the dead (John 5:21, 28, 29); the performance of miracles by His own power (John 2:11). He is worshiped as God is worshiped (John 20:28; 5:23; Phil. 2:9 f.), and the majesty, glory, and honor of God are His. (Phil. 2:6)

Equally, according to the Scriptures, the Christian Church asserts that Jesus Christ is true man: "There is one God and one Mediator between God and men, the Man Christ Jesus" (1 Tim. 2:5), or His own words: "But now ye seek to kill Me, a man that hath told you the truth" (John 8:40). Through His mother He had human ancestors, and He grew up like any other human being of His time (Luke 2:52). He had human emotions and physical wants, and He died like a human being. (Matt. 27:46; John 19:30)

Jesus spoke of Himself as the "Son of Man" and represented Himself as "the Christ, the Son of the living God" (Matt. 16: 13-17). Both the Old and the New Testament know Jesus, the Son of Man, as the God-Man (cp. Dan. 7:13, 14; 1 John 3:8). On this basis Luther explains the Second Article of the Apostles' Creed: "I believe that Jesus Christ, true God, begotten of the Father from eternity, and also true man, born of the Virgin Mary, is my Lord, who has redeemed me . . ."

We have indicated before that Christ is man in a unique sense. There are aspects of His humanity which we find in no other human being. His conception was supernatural — "conceived by the Holy Ghost" in the womb of Mary, His virgin mother (Matt. 1:20). Among men He alone was conceived and born without sin. (Is. 53:9; Luke 1:35; John 8:46; 2 Cor. 5:21; 1 Peter 1:19 and 2:22)

Consequently Jesus Christ was not the acme of some evolutionary development, either physically or ethically. Neither is He unique because of the mistaken notion that He inherited this quality from His mother Mary. Like every other human being, Mary was conceived and born of sinful parents and remained a sinner like the rest of us human beings. Jesus was also her Christ and Savior, as she sang in her Magnificat (Luke 1:46, 47). That the holy Son of God was born of sinful woman is an astounding miracle, which the Christian Church worshipfully accepts. The incarnation of God is the glory of the human race and proof of God's inexpressible mercy and condescension. Speculative explanations are neither offered nor possible.

The fact that Jesus Christ was sinless had important implications. It meant that He was immortal in His humanity, for death is the consequence of sin. He died on the cross voluntarily, not of necessity, and by His own power: "Therefore doth My Father love Me, because I lay down My life that I might take it again. No man taketh it from Me, but I lay it down of Myself. I have power to lay it down, and I have power to take it again" (John 10:17, 18). His voluntary death was the price which He paid for the life of all mankind. He who was "very God of very God" and a sinless, immortal man "gave Himself a ransom for all." (1 Tim. 2:6)

If the human mind staggers at these statements, it is not because they are untrue but rather because they are measured by the circumscribed logic of the sciences and, above all else, judged by the corrupted will of sinful man, who by nature will not receive spiritual truth. The paradox of Jesus Christ (from the human point of view) does not reduce God to the level of caricature, but reveals that men have too narrow, all too human, a conception of God. God cannot be known speculatively. Men must learn who God is by learning where and how God has revealed Himself. It will not do merely to assert that these statements about Jesus Christ are contradictory or meaningless. The historical fact still remains that "God was in Christ" (2 Cor. 5:19) and revealed Himself as such to men. "In Him dwelleth all the fullness of the Godhead bodily" (Col. 2:3, 9) — this is the record of the Scriptures and the message of the church.

Jesus Christ is the supreme offense for those who have insisted upon staking out the limits of reality to serve their own convenience. To be told that Jesus Christ actually resumed His life in His body while in the grave and that "He arose again from the dead" constitutes notice that the world, or "nature," is not absolutely closed and that God can and does breach the circle of His "fixed order" (Jer. 31:36, RSV). This is what we meant, among other things, when we stated in a previous section of this chapter that Christians do not have a static God, but Him who is at work in the world to accomplish His designs.

When we examine the record of the Scriptures concerning the

resurrection of Jesus Christ, the empirical or experiential evidence of the witnesses becomes compelling. It justifies the assertion of the Christian Church that Jesus Christ, by His own power — the same as that of the Father and the Holy Spirit — resumed life in His body in the tomb and emerged from the closed and sealed grave (an angel subsequently rolled away the stone, Matt. 28:1-6) to exhibit Himself in His glorified body to His disciples in proof of His victory and for the confirmation of the Gospel.

The body in which He rose to life again was the same which the Logos, the Son of God, assumed in the womb of Mary and in which He suffered and died on the cross (John 20:27). The apostle Paul writes that in the resurrection the natural body of this life acquires additional qualities so that it becomes a spiritual and glorified body. (Phil. 3:21; 1 Cor. 15:44)

The Scriptural record of His resurrection and subsequent appearances reveals that Christ's body assumed a different relation to the space-time continuum in which we exist, without being cut off from all relation to it. For example, He appears and disappears without regard to locked doors. He walks with two followers to the hamlet Emmaus, converses with them without being recognized until He presides at the meal where He allows them to identify Him. Immediately Cleopas and his companion returned to Jerusalem to report the event to the eleven apostles and other disciples of Jesus. While they made their report, Jesus appeared in their midst and identified Himself to the terrified group. They imagined they were seeing a spirit, and so He asks: "Why are ye troubled? And why do thoughts arise in your hearts? Behold My hands and My feet, that it is I Myself; handle Me and see, for a spirit hath not flesh and bones, as ye see Me have" (Luke 24:38, 39). But these apostles and disciples were in no mood to be easily persuaded, despite His vigorous assertion that He was quite corporeal. To remove any further doubt, He asks for food and eats broiled fish and a piece of honeycomb in front of them.

The apostle Thomas apparently had left the gathering before Jesus' appearance and identification. Upon being informed of the momentous event, he asserted that for his part he was unable to accept the conclusions of the rest of the group, but must make a "scientific" or "empirical" identification of his own before he could agree to their report of the resurrection of Jesus Christ. This exceptional privilege was conferred upon Thomas eight days later, when Jesus suddenly appeared again to the assembled disciples and invited Thomas to make the very investigation of His wounds which Thomas had previously asserted would convince him of the resurrection of Jesus Christ. (John 20:26-29)

It was necessary that the apostles should acquire an irreversible certainty of the resurrection of Jesus Christ, because it was to be their particular assignment to witness to the world the fact that He was the Savior of mankind. This necessitated their having known Jesus both before and after His death. Thus Peter could claim, on the occasion of the birthday of the Christian Church, when he preached the first Christian sermon to the world: "God raised Jesus, whereof we all [the assembled Christians] are witnesses." (Acts 2:32)

It should be made clear at this point that the disciples did not claim to have seen the event of the resurrection of Jesus. There is no evidence that any human being witnessed that. What the disciples uniformly asserted was that they had seen Jesus Christ alive after His death, sometimes alone, sometimes in groups — on one occasion as many as five hundred of them. Writing about A. D. 55 to the Corinthian Christians, some of whom had their doubts about the fact of the resurrection of Jesus, Saint Paul said that the majority of those five hundred were still alive (1 Cor. 15:6). From the very beginning the witness of the Christian Church was, and still is: "But in fact Christ has been raised from the dead, the first fruits of those who have fallen asleep." (1 Cor. 15:20, RSV)

At this point we must reckon with the strongest arguments ever advanced against miracles, specifically the resurrection of Christ. David Hume writes in his essay "Concerning Human Understanding": "But it is a miracle, that a dead man should come to life; because that has never been observed in any age or country. There must, therefore, be a uniform experience against every miraculous event, otherwise the event would not merit that appellation, and as a uniform experience amounts to a proof, there is here a direct and full *proof*, from the nature of the fact, against the existence of any miracle; nor can such a proof be destroyed, or the miracle rendered credible, but by an opposite proof, which is superior." [34]

Hume's argumentation falls to the ground because he is using for proof the point he intends to prove — an elementary error in logic, called *petitio principii*, or begging the question.

The Christian, while admitting that miracles in the attested sense are relatively rare, cannot logically grant that rarity is the equivalent of improbability. To do so would permit Hume to bring off a feat of sleight-of-hand logic. His argument "against the existence of any miracle" is essentially based on nothing more than his affirmation that miracles are impossible. The aggregate force of his listed objections to miracles, and especially the miracle of the resurrection of Jesus Christ, is a *tour de force* whose impact is chiefly psychological. Upon analysis it becomes apparent that the question is being begged throughout.

During the forty days between Christ's resurrection and ascension He appeared many times to do "signs . . . in the presence of His disciples" (John 20:30), the aim being to persuade them also empirically to the unshakable conviction that "Jesus is the Christ, the Son of God" (John 20:31). But the association was no longer on the previous level of human intimacy. When He identified Himself to Mary Magdalene in the garden of the sepulcher, she exclaimed in her joy: "My Master!" and wished to touch Him. But He declined such a demonstration of her devotion for the moment: "Jesus saith unto her, Touch Me not; for I am not yet ascended to My Father; but go to My brethren and say unto them, I ascend unto My father and your Father and to My God and your God" (John 20:17). Since she had no need to be further convinced of His identity, He reminded her gently that the old relationship to His followers was at an end, that she and all others must remember His impending ascension to God and the assumption of the full use of the properties of His divine majesty also according to His human nature.

Since heaven is not created space, Christ's ascension was not a movement from one space to another, but His visible withdrawal from the hitherto perceptible association with His fol-

---

[34] *The English Philosophers from Bacon to Mill*, edited with an introduction by Edwin A. Burtt (New York: Random House, 1939), pp. 656 to 657.

lowers to the undisguised assumption of His omnipotence and divine majesty by His human nature. That is the meaning of the statement in the Apostles' Creed "at the right hand of God." The resurrection of Jesus Christ (and all subsequent events of His exaltation) is the specific witness to men of God's forgiveness of the sins of the world. By their faith in the risen Son of God, Jesus Christ, all men receive what God's promise offers — forgiveness, divine acceptance, eternal life with God.

19. *The New Creation*

Among the many, powerful, and incisive statements of the fact and implications of the reconciliation of God and man which are in the Scriptures we find none which suits our immediate purpose better than that of St. Paul in 2 Cor. 5:14-21 (RSV):

> For the love of God controls us, because we are convinced that One has died for all; therefore all have died. And He died for all, that those who live might live no longer for themselves but for Him who for their sake died and was raised.
>
> From now on, therefore, we regard no one from a human point of view; even though we once regarded Christ from a human point of view, we regard Him thus no longer. Therefore, if anyone is in Christ, he is a new creation; the old has passed away, behold, the new has come. All this is from God, who through Christ reconciled us to Himself and gave us the ministry of reconciliation; that is, God was in Christ, reconciling the world to Himself, not counting their trespasses against them, and entrusting to us the message of reconciliation. So we are ambassadors for Christ, God making His appeal through us. We beseech you on behalf of Christ, be reconciled to God. For our sake He made Him to be sin who knew no sin, so that in Him we might become the righteousness of God.

In their actualities the dimensions of existence for the Christians as a "new creation" are radically different from his former state. In his relation to God the Christian has unreserved access to the mercies which sustain him. The sense of lostness or brokenness, that pervasive terror which is engendered by any form of despair, the feeling of futility which men must ultimately confront in their existence, these the Christian overcomes by an unfailing hope. Nothing matters to the Christian, as St. Paul writes, "but a new creation. Peace and mercy be upon all who walk by this rule, upon the Israel of God." (Gal. 6:15, 16, RSV)

66

These are the terms on which the Christian accepts himself and is accepted by God.

However, the Christian, as Luther said, is both righteous and a sinner. St. Paul delineates very sharply the contradictions which the Christian discerns in himself as the new being struggles against the old nature, which the apostle calls "flesh":

> We know that the Law is spiritual; but I am carnal, sold under sin. I do not understand my own actions. For I do not do what I want, but I do the very thing I hate. Now if I do what I do not want, I agree that the Law is good. So then it is no longer I that do it, but sin which dwells within me. For I know that nothing good dwells within me, that is, in my flesh. I can will what is right, but I cannot do it. For I do not do the good I want, but the evil I do not want is what I do. Now if I do what I do not want, it is no longer I that do it, but sin which dwells within me.
>
> So I find it to be a law that when I want to do right, evil lies close at hand. For I delight in the Law of God, in my inmost self, but I see in my members another law at war with the law of my mind and making me captive to the law of sin which dwells in my members. Wretched man that I am! Who will deliver me from this body of death? Thanks be to God through Jesus Christ, our Lord! So, then, I of myself serve the Law of God with my mind, but with my flesh I serve the law of sin. (Rom. 7:14-25, RSV)

Paul develops the argument further (Rom. 8). The Christian is a new being, because his mind is set at that which is spiritual. He knows that his old nature is hostile to God, seeking its own primary and immediate interest at all cost. But the fact that he can struggle against the normally invincible egocentric forces of his own old nature and be victorious is proof itself that his mind is set "on the things of the Spirit" (Rom. 8:5). The divine power of the Spirit of God works in such a person, and God adopts him as His child.[35]

The Christian as a new being is engaged in a monumental struggle, and he knows it. The degree of intensity varies considerably with individual Christians, but none is ever without it. If a Christian complacently declares that he no longer has such struggles, it is to be feared that he deceives himself or, worse

---

[35] Rom. 8:14: "For all who are led by the Spirit of God are sons of God." (RSV)

still, that he refuses penitently to acknowledge his defeats and, strengthened by the Spirit of God, resume the struggle against his old nature. This constant struggle involves the Christian in much suffering, but he agrees with St. Paul that the prize immeasurably outweighs the cost.[36]

The Christian gains his victory by what has been termed "self-surrender" to that which God wills. It is a "letting go" of the things which would ordinarily, according to his old nature, mean much or everything to him. For the sake of that which God has promised him and works in him the Christian will in extremity let go his own life on the principle that it is better to lose what one cannot keep in order to hold what cannot be lost. The new being has shifted the direction of his personality from the prudential and anxious efforts to prove his worth to himself, to others, and to God, to an inwardly serene and relaxed conviction regarding his true worth in the estimate of God. The beauty and happiness of such a condition is really quite beyond communication. Analogical verbalizations cannot do justice to actualities.

This self-surrender of the Christian in his daily self-examination and penitent confession of his sins to God and his injured fellow men readies him for further blessings, like the fertile, well-prepared soil upon which the good seed falls and bears a hundredfold. Psychologically we may say that in this surrender experience the Christian acquires a positive attitude, and since the experience of divine forgiveness is the ultimate spiritual experience in this life, he eventually becomes realistically oriented to his world. His tenseness, hostility, and sense of isolation pass. The Christian who is aware of his spiritual resources and blessing is a relaxed person.

One of the facets of confession which is often viewed superficially in pastoral practice, or even ignored, is the detailed or specific confession of actual sins. Many of the Lutheran clergy do not minister to the needs of their parishioners adequately because they are content when their people participate in general confessions instead of insisting upon the health-giving function of specific confessions, as the Lutheran Catechism and stand-

---

[36] Rom. 8:18 (RSV): "I consider that the sufferings of this present time are not worth comparing with the glory that is to be revealed to us."

ard works in Lutheran pastoral theology recommend.[37] The result has been that the act of confession has become secularized. Educated people especially seem more often to feel that their needs are better met by psychoanalysis than the Word of God. Our pastors ought to re-examine both the healing power of the Gospel and the apparent self-sufficiency of their parishioners.

If the non-Christian psychotherapeutic effort has become vastly greater in our society and has obtained enormous recognition among our own people, it is in part the consequence of superficial pastoral care. Though it must not become exaggerated, so that it confers upon the pastor the role of grand inquisitor, there is nonetheless such a thing as penitential discipline to which *all* Christians ought regularly to submit. Self-knowledge really exists only to the extent that one does, or is able to, communicate it in speech to another person. The psychotherapeutic value of making specific, or even detailed, confessions is therefore very great.

Perhaps the difficulties in this respect arise altogether too often from the fact that the pressures of circumstances require the clergyman of today to be an executive too much of the time, instead of being pre-eminently the shepherd of his flock. However, the man who is the pastor of his people does by far the more valuable work. Modern man will seek self-understanding, forgiveness, restitution. The tragedy is that he often wrongly thinks the Christian Church has no more than opiates for his condition and that secular agencies offer an ultimate means of self-acceptance. The secular psychotherapist will undoubtedly invite him to understand himself and to accept himself within the limited context of a therapeutic relation, but the patient will not find forgiveness there. The peace of God which passes understanding is certainly beyond the secular level of understanding.[38]

---

37 E. g., John H. C. Fritz, *Pastoral Theology* (St. Louis: Concordia Publishing House, 1932), which is a revision of C. F. W. Walther's *Pastorale*, writes, p. 132: "Since private confession is no longer a common practice in our church. . . ." Also see his discussion of "Private Absolution and the Confessional (Preparatory) Service," p. 137.

38 The meaning here is not that secular psychotherapeutic efforts are without beneficial results. Quite the contrary: the Christian would not patronize the secular psychotherapist without a certain expectation of help from him. This is decidedly true of those cases which require a high degree

20. The Nurture of the New Being

The new creation, or new being, lives by faith. It is not a multiplicity of good works which makes a person acceptable to himself or to God, because no one is able to conclusively prove his worth by that means either to himself or to anyone else. However, the Christian faith does not relieve a person of the obligation to do good works, but from false motivations for them. Instead of compulsively proving his worth by them, he does them out of gratitude to God and because he is a new being in Christ. The Christian faith is not a "reaction formation," as Erich Fromm has falsely judged the faith of Martin Luther,[39] but living in the Spirit of Christ.[40]

---

of specialized treatment. Rather, we mean that there are large areas of the psychotherapeutic field where the discerning Christian pastor can offer the ultimate remedies of the Christian Gospel.

[39] The amazing superficialities of the secular psychotherapist are nowhere more clearly revealed than in his analyses of Christian insights, especially when he really means to carve ideological clubs out of them. In his *Escape from Freedom* (New York: Farrar and Reinhart, 1941), pp. 77, 78, Erich Fromm describes Luther's faith as a "compulsive quest for certainty," "a reaction formation against a fundamental feeling of doubt." Fostering this kind of faith, the Reformation taught people to submit to a tyrannical God, and presumably this eventually prepared the way for Hitler!

[40] In view of the general ignorance of psychologists like Erich Fromm regarding the true nature of Christian faith, as Luther expressed it, we append the following quotation from Luther's "Preface to the Epistle to the Romans": "Faith, however, is a divine work in us. It changes us and makes us to be born anew of God (John 1); it kills the old Adam and makes altogether different men, in heart and spirit and mind and powers, and it brings with it the Holy Ghost. Oh, it is a living, busy, active, mighty thing, this faith; and so it is impossible for it not to do good works incessantly. It does not ask whether there are good works to do, but before the question arises, it has already done them, and is always doing them. He who does not these works is a faithless man. He gropes and looks about after faith and good works and knows neither what faith is nor what good works are, though he talks and talks, with many words, about faith and good works.

"Faith is a living, daring confidence in God's grace, so sure and certain that a man would stake his life on it a thousand times. This confidence in God's grace and knowledge of it makes men glad and bold and happy in dealing with God and with all His creatures; and this is the work of the Holy Ghost in faith. Hence a man is really glad, without compulsion, to do good to everyone, to serve everyone, to suffer everything, in love and praise of God, who has shown him this grace; and thus it is impossible to separate works from faith, quite as impossible as to separate heat and light from fire." *Works of Martin Luther*, Philadelphia edition (Philadelphia: Muhlenberg Press, 1932), VI, 451, 452.

However, the Christian does not live in isolation. Above all else, his life is a grateful act of witnessing the grace of God which made him a new creation. This is done in the community or fellowship of other Christians — the church. Without the church the Christian would not have received the "Word of reconciliation," the means whereby he shared the grace of God in Christ Jesus. In the Christian community he first received Holy Baptism, instruction or discipline, and Holy Communion.

The means of grace are the Word of God and the Sacraments. The former is the Christian Gospel in its specific sense as the "good news" of God's grace in Jesus Christ. Believing it, the Christian has what the "good news" offers — God's unmerited forgiveness. However, the Christian is also part of the "new Israel of God" and as such shares in the "new covenant," or "new testament," which God has made for the sake of Christ. When a Christian is baptized, he joins this new covenant. God guarantees to him in Baptism that He will accept him. The Sacrament of Baptism is, therefore, no mere rite in which water is applied to an individual while the celebrant speaks a few appropriate words, but a genuine "washing of regeneration and renewal in the Holy Spirit" (Titus 3:5, RSV), it is "an appeal to God for a clear conscience" (1 Peter 3:21, RSV). By the command of God an outward or visible means, such as water in Baptism (or bread and wine in the Lord's Supper, or Eucharist), is used in combination with the divine promise to signify, seal, pledge, and guarantee to the person baptized "in the name of the Father and of the Son and of the Holy Ghost" (Matt. 28:19) that God is gracious to him and accepts him.

While the Sacrament of Baptism is to be received only once by the Christian, it has extremely important implications which are valid during his lifetime. Having been accepted into the body of Christ, which is the church, the child or adult begins his Christian growth. His nurture as a new creation continues in the terms of the baptismal covenant. At every stage in his life he can and ought to remind himself of the surpassingly high honor conferred upon him and of the responsibilities which his new status as a child of God demand of him. He can face anxiety in any form with the assurance, confidence, and certainty that

71

God will never nullify the covenant which He has made with him in Baptism. Therapeutically, Baptism is able to confer upon the believing Christian an unshakable sense of integration, of belonging, of ultimate security.

The Christian, as St. Paul pointed out (Rom. 7:23), discovers another law in his members, which is at war with the law of his mind and which makes him captive to the law of sin. Destructive attitudes and Christian living too easily associate in the same man. One of the true insights of the psychotherapeutic science is the fact that unresolved guilt and anxiety demand their own forms of retribution. The individual is caught in fruitless activities.[41] His guilty conscience will not permit him to apply himself fully and constructively to the tasks which lie before him. The degree of personality disintegration caused by guilt and anxiety varies enormously according to the individual and his circumstances. But in all cases the Christian Church offers the repentant Christian the consolation and spiritual renewal of the Lord's Supper.

This is to be received as often as the Christian is aware of his need for it. The ancient Christian community celebrated the Eucharist whenever the congregation met for worship. Many Lutheran congregations now offer the Christian an opportunity to receive benefits of the Lord's Supper at least once each week, not that every member is expected to present himself at the altar on each occasion of the celebration of the Eucharist, but in order to meet the needs of spiritually sensitive Christians.

Like Baptism, the Sacrament of the Last Supper joins visible elements — bread and wine — and the promise of God in order to confer, seal, or guarantee to the believing recipient the forgiveness of his sins. Not only that, but in the process of receiving the bread and wine the Christian also receives the very body and blood of Christ in a real (though supernatural) manner. He

---

[41] Shakespeare reflects this insight in his *Macbeth*, V, i: DOCTOR: "What is it she does now? Look how she rubs her hands." GENTLEWOMAN: "It is an accustomed action with her, to seem thus washing her hands: I have known her to continue in this a quarter of an hour." Other actions, arising from the same source, may be an unusual or excessive form of personal grooming, floor pacing, or any unconsciously motivated activity arising from a restless conscience.

becomes united with his Lord and Savior in the most intimate manner imaginable.[42]

In his participation of the Eucharist the Christian is also united with all other Christians. The action embraces him in a fellowship which reaches beyond time and place. It is both individual and collective in character: the Christian is most intimately made a part of the household of God, indeed, of the Son of God — he affirms himself and is affirmed in the most solemn manner a part of the body of Christ. Neither the Word nor the Sacraments operate magically, that is, by the mere performance of the act or expression of the formulas. In every case and under all circumstances the individual himself must be committed. Believing the promises of God, he also has what God has promised. Therapeutically, the means of grace are the spiritual healing par excellence.

The spiritual life of the Christian is one of constant joy if he will but grasp the joy which is offered him. It is an inner peace and rejoicing which reveals itself not in Stoic forms of tranquillity or disengagement from the world but in the most active possible forms of participation.[43] "Rejoice always, pray constantly, give thanks in all circumstances; for this is the will of God in Christ Jesus for you" (1 Thess. 5:16-18, RSV). One of the great consequences of the Christian's joy in God is his life of prayer. Spiritually he is constantly in the attitude of prayer, regardless of what he may be doing. His moments are spent in the presence of his God and Lord, and he has the privilege of constant conversation with Him. The subject of prayer is every concern of the Christian, trivial or great. Like a child beloved of his parent, the Christian knows that he can confidently present any matter to his heavenly Father and expect a hearing because God has promised that to Christians.

But why ask for anything if God is a loving heavenly Father

---

[42] It should be understood that Lutheran Christians do not believe that they ingest the physical substance of the body and blood of Christ according to the ordinary natural categories. On the contrary, they consider such a view a gross sort of perversion of the exalted mystery of the Eucharist. It is for that reason that Lutheran theologians have sought to guard the transcendent reality of the presence of Christ's body and blood by the terms "in, with, and under the bread and wine."

[43] Loc. cit. (n. 38, above).

who knows in advance what we need or want? Prayer would seem to be unnecessary. There have been psychotherapists who consider prayer at best a beneficial form of pep talk which devout people give themselves. Again, from the Christian point of view, this constitutes an extremely superficial and naïve interpretation of the meaning of Christian prayer.

Of course, the Christian is convinced that God knows what is best for him and that He would like him to have it. But God will not force His goodness upon men. He respects His handiwork. To do otherwise would require God to violate the freedom which He gave man in creation. The moment God applied His omnipotence in the interest of man's welfare, but in violation of man's created status as a human being, two cataclysmic events would happen: the lesser of the two being that man would be reduced to a thing, a pawn, a puppet in his relation to God. The second is of infinitely greater magnitude: God would become inconsistent or contradictory within Himself and in that instant cease to be God.

Prayer makes good sense to the Christian because it enables God to give him all good things without destroying the status which belongs to man. "You do not have, because you do not ask. You ask and do not receive, because you ask wrongly, to spend it on your passions" (James 4:2, 3, RSV). Again: "This is the confidence which we have in Him, that if we ask anything according to His will, He hears us" (1 John 5:14, RSV). One major objection to prayer has been the notion that answering every prayer would entail a change in God's mind to accommodate our needs. But it is merely a conventional and superficial error, voiced chiefly by the theologically uninformed. God does not live in time. He knew about the prayers of the Christians before the universe was made, so that He does not find it necessary to rearrange the universe every time a Christian prays. However, from this and from the quotations cited Christians make the obvious inference that their prayers are literally answered in proportion to their congruity with His will or purposes. A miraculous answer to prayer is given when God approves so thoroughly of what Christians request that He applies criteria which they did not know existed in order to grant the petition.

Not to take prayer with the utmost seriousness would imply

a damaging distortion of the picture which God gives us of Himself. If He is the God who has disclosed Himself to man, according to the Scriptures, it is altogether right and proper that Christians should want to address themselves in the most intimate terms to Him who has invited them to say "Abba" — Father.

21. *The Christian Hope*

The Christian life continues in hope. Hope is one of the very great words in human language, but it has suffered grievously from an unwarranted inflation due to excessive and thoughtless use. However, taken in its elementary sense, it can be said that every human being lives in terms of his expectations. He expects that the order of nature will continue; he hopes to prolong his life day by day, from childhood to old age; he looks for a reasonable number of opportunities to play his role in the society of which he is a member. But if he is a Christian, he also hopes, above all else, for the life eternal promised to him by God. His hope is therefore no vague expectation of "a pie in the sky by and by." Hope is illusory only when there are no grounds for it. In that eventuality Christians would really be the most pathetic people on earth. This was indeed well recognized, for Paul writes incisively on this very point (1 Cor. 15:19, RSV): "If in this life only we have hoped in Christ, we are of all men most to be pitied." But he does not stop here, because he cannot ignore the central fact of the Christian Gospel (v. 20): "But in fact Christ has been raised from the dead, the First Fruits of those who have fallen asleep." Each Christian, like the apostle Paul, hopes to "attain the resurrection from the dead" (Phil. 3:11, RSV). It is a hope which rests on the firmest possible foundation: the living God, who pledged Himself to this in Jesus Christ.

The nature of God's guarantee is such that hope becomes the certainty of faith. It begins with the incarnation of His divine Son. Jesus Christ became man in our place. God's promises to the human race were fulfilled in Christ. He became the pivot upon whom all of God's actions turn. What the first man rejected, this Christ fulfilled in obedient humility — not for Himself, since He had no need of doing that, but for us. He was not the example but the replacement of sinful men. He did not die on the cross because He had been defeated by His enemies. His death

75

was a voluntary act of substitution because all men had received the verdict: death for sin. But Jesus Christ was our replacement not merely in death but also for life. He arose from His grave in triumph and lives in everlasting glory. He is the new Man, the second Adam, who retrieved for the human race what the first Adam lost.

This hope has no subjective roots. It would be valid even if no man believed it. In God's dealing with men the main action centers exclusively in the Substitute. We are no longer a factor in this cosmic event except as we identify ourselves with the Man who acts in our stead. He has lived in righteousness and holiness — for us. He was judged and executed — for us. He rose from the dead — for us. Only as we identify ourselves with Him in repentance and faith, in obedience and hope, do we become members of the body of which He is the Head. By hope we now live in the new Being, which is Christ.

Hope implies a consummation. God promised this, but not at our pleasure. This means that the Christian hopes in patience, not because the victory is not won, nor for the reason that God's "timetable" is being awkwardly delayed! The consummation of the Christian hope is being achieved in mercy. As the parable of the great feast (Matt. 22:4) typifies, "all things are ready." The delay is for the sake of the guests who have not yet arrived, and the situation demands patience on the part of those who are already there.

Patience must be joined to hope. As others had to wait for us, so we wait for the consummation of all things for the sake of others. But this patience of the Christian is no passive, indolent waiting. The Christian begins in this life to live his life in Christ. It is a life of love and of work.

Our Substitute became what we are that we might become what He is. As He loved and worked on earth, so we love Him and all men and faithfully work at the stewardship assigned to us according to the talents which He gave.

There is no higher task for any man. There can be no greater reward.

The Christian view of man is not anthropocentric but theocentric. Ultimately it never matters what man thinks of himself, but what God thinks of him. If man is to be genuinely under-

76

stood, so the Christian affirms, the attempt must never be self-limited by the refusal seriously to entertain the claims which assert that man exists both in nature and beyond nature. He is a sinner before God and is involved in all the guilt which men owe one another. He is discerned to be a "rational animal" and observed to live subject to thoroughly irrational forms of anxiety and fear. God has reached down to his level, but man perversely rejects God. In his self-esteem he is both inordinately exalted and diminished. Man contradicts his own true self in every moment that God leaves him to himself. Man is a sinner and a rebel, but beloved and sought of God. And those who will be found of Him shall inherit the kingdom of His Son, the only and universal Savior, Jesus Christ.

SUGGESTED READINGS

The Holy Scriptures. Authorized Version and Revised Standard Version.

Concordia Triglotta. The Symbolical Books of the Ev. Lutheran Church, German-Latin-English edition. St. Louis: Concordia Publishing House, 1921.

To the reader who wishes to acquaint himself more extensively with the theology of the clergy of The Lutheran Church — Missouri Synod we suggest:

Pieper, Francis. *Christian Dogmatics,* translated from the German by Theo. Engelder et al, 3 vols. St. Louis: Concordia Publishing House, 1950–53.

Mueller, John T. *Christian Dogmatics: A Handbook of Doctrinal Theology for Pastors, Teachers, and Laymen.* St. Louis: Concordia Publishing House, 1934.

III. Philosophical Presuppositions of Psychologists

IN THIS SECTION we shall try to set forth the views of man, of the world, and of knowledge itself which the psychologist takes pretty much as rock bottom to his whole scientific pursuit. It is difficult to give a generic name to these pervasive ideas, without prejudging, by the very act of naming them, some technical and controversial issues in a field which is neither psychology nor theology — namely, philosophy. As an example of one of these rock-bottom ideas consider that called *determinism*. Critics of contemporary secular psychology sometimes say that it "makes the metaphysical assumption of determinism." Now, there is no gainsaying that an important bit of truth about psychologists lies behind this statement; nevertheless it is a misleading and even dangerous remark as it stands. There is an important difference between what may perhaps best be called a "working orientation toward the world" and an inflexible, absolute ontological presupposition. Practically all scientific psychologists are determinists (or near-determinists) in the "working orientation" sense. That is, they make their observations and construct their theories with the hope of finding regularities in human behavior which will enable them to explain it, to predict it, and to control it. If a psychologist did not hope (and expect!) that such regularities would be discernible in the facts of behavior, his whole enterprise would be pointless. There would be very little sense in performing an experiment on how school children learn to do

78

fractions, or on the effect of a certain drug on the efficiency of industrial workers, or concerning which of two types of psychotherapy is more beneficial, if the experimenter supposed these kinds of events to be intrinsically capricious; for the "laws" exhibited in the experiment would not then really be laws at all. The results of the experiment would not be applicable to further cases of the same kind of situation as they arose.

It is obvious from a consideration of this simple truth that the psychologist is not proceeding differently from the way we all proceed in daily life. The predictability of human behavior, at least in a crude, over-all sense, is such a universal and familiar fact that we are likely to be unaware of the extent to which we all take it for granted. If you ask yourself how much of what you did and said during the past 24 hours was predicated upon the unquestioned assumption that human behavior is, in the main at least, predictable, you will see that psychological determinism as a general orientation is not some kind of special pet prejudice held by atheist materialist psychologists, but is rather an implicit working assumption that we all hold pretty much as a matter of course. Why, for example, would the congregation make every effort to run a pleasant, attractive Sunday school (or, for that matter, to have a Sunday school at all) unless they took it for granted that the laws of learning, such as the effectiveness of teaching in certain ways rather than others, applied to the indoctrination of their children?

Determinism as a working orientation amounts to taking the attitude: "Human behavior seems to exhibit regularities (laws), to be susceptible of rational causal explanations (theories), and to be largely controllable by the use of these laws and theories; let us therefore set up as our research program the aim to push this program to the limit. Let us operate provisionally on the working assumption that any behavior domain (whether it be learning fractions, drinking beer, being psychoanalyzed, composing symphonies, falling in love, translating Aramaic, or whatever) is orderly, predictable, 'lawful' (in the scientific sense). If a bit of behavior appears to be capricious, we will not accept it as really being so, but we will subject it to careful study, hoping to find the obscure laws which we expect really underlie it." It is difficult to see how a Christian theologian, or indeed any rational person, could find fault with such a statement of policy. It amounts to almost no more than the philosopher Hans Reichenbach's view of induction: He who wants to catch fish, while he has no assurance of success, must at least cast his net![1] This kind of determinism may be called *methodological determinism* and is shared by psychologists with the practitioners of all natural and biological sciences, as well as artisans, businessmen, schoolteachers, and preachers.

But suppose the psychologist were to go beyond this research strategy and pronounce some such proposition as the following: "All human thoughts and acts occur in accordance with psychological laws." Or, in a "materialist" form popular a half century ago but now largely eschewed (without being thereby denied): "All human acts are instantializations [2] of the laws of physics and chemistry." This is, of course, a much more inclusive pronouncement. It is an extrapolation, and a somewhat rash one, from the admitted fact that our ability to explain and predict behavior has increased steadily as we have learned more about it. No psychologist can prove any such universal propositions as the two just stated. The predictability that we can attain in practice, or even in the experimental laboratory, is largely of a "probabilistic" type. That is to say, by suitable manipulations of the organism's history and of its momentary state and external situation, we can render certain responses highly probable. If a sanguine psychologist wishes to envisage an idealization of the situation, in which he would possess exhaustive and exact knowledge of all the conditions prevailing at a given moment and possess unlimited instantaneous calculational powers, he is at liberty to do so. But he must remember that this is his idealization, and that the existing body of scientific knowledge, however suggestive it may be of such an extrapolation, does not suffice to coerce all rational men to accept it.

---

[1] *Experience and Prediction* (Chicago: University of Chicago Press, 1938). Ch. V, especially pp. 339 ff.

[2] When the events occurring at a particular place and time satisfy the equation stating a general law, these events are said to instantialize the law, i. e., they are realized instances of it.

Following up this line of thought, we find it important to distinguish between three forms which the determinist thesis may take:

1. *Methodological determinism:* "Let us seek pertinaciously for the laws which we hope, and expect, will be exhibited by any given domain of behavior. If these laws hold strictly, well and good; if they are at best probabilistic, we will settle for that, since they will still be very useful."

2. *Empirical determinism:* "Since the quest proposed in (1) has been fairly successful thus far, it seems likely that all behavior domains do, *in fact,* follow such exceptionless regularities. Apparent exceptions are very probably due to incomplete information and, pending further investigation, will be assumed to be such."

3. *Metaphysical determinism:* "All human psychological events instantialize universal laws, and we hold this thesis as an absolute ontological presupposition which no empirical evidence could be permitted to gainsay."

Now, as has been said above, all (or nearly all) psychologists hold (1). Most psychologists seem to hold (2). It is impossible to say how many hold (3); since logical positivism, with its repudiation of metaphysics, dominates contemporary psychology, probably most do not.

The Christian theologian must be careful to distinguish between what is actually part of the *corpus* of scientific knowledge and what happens, by virtue of historical and cultural forces, to be the prevailing climate of opinion on extrascientific or meta-scientific matters among a certain body of scientists. For example, the best available statistics show that the great majority of American psychologists are atheists and that their unbelief is stronger than that of physicists or chemists as a group. But obviously "There is no God" could not occur as a scientific proposition in a psychology text, any more than such statements are to be found in a treatise on theoretical physics. Similarly, the metaphysical thesis of determinism is very congenial to the dominant *Weltanschauung* of American scientific psychologists, even exhibiting itself at times in scholars who would not assert it explicitly be-

81

cause they eschew all "metaphysical" contentions as a matter of (positivist) principle.

In setting forth the basic epistemological and substantive assumptions within whose frame the psychologist operates, we shall therefore endeavor wherever possible to distinguish among those views which are in some sense included in the corpus of scientific knowledge, those which are of a "procedural" or task-setting character, and finally those *Weltanschauung* components which, while partially inspired by the science and more or less characteristic of its practitioners as a group, are nevertheless neither procedural nor substantive in nature. At times, of course, these three categories will shade imperceptibly into one another.

The first philosophical assumption, that of determinism, has just been considered, and we saw that it has a procedural, a (broadly) empirical, and a metaphysical form. Certain of the more abstruse issues involving determinism, particularly in its theological aspects, will be discussed in Chapter VIII. Here we shall confine our further discussion to two substantive examples of the sort of scientific evidence that supports empirical determinism (thesis 2 above) and in turn encourages psychologists in their scientific policy of methodological determinism (thesis 1). These two examples are taken from the fields of criminology and psychiatry. Sociologists have studied the lives, characteristics, and background environments of criminal and delinquent individuals with great care. The result of these investigations has been an impressive mass of evidence regarding certain family and neighborhood factors which strongly predispose a person to become delinquent. Statistical studies of the incidence of crime over the geographical areas of large cities reveal a depressing predictability in the number and nature of crimes that will occur in each section of the city in the course of a year. It is known that certain unfavorable characteristics of a child's home environment, particularly when present in adverse patterns of combination, may increase by a factor of 15 or 20 to 1 the probability of that child becoming involved in delinquency. When a criminal is paroled, mathematical methods have been devised which combine certain objective facts about his history and traits to yield a number expressing the probability of parole violation. Such equations, while very far from perfect, seem to be fairly effective in predicting the course of events and often predict more accurately than other widely used methods such as opinion of experts. As the sociologists have accumulated more evidence and become more ingenious in combining this evidence mathematically for predictive purposes, their confidence that criminal behavior is understandable in causal terms has of course increased.

In psychiatry, the greatest support to the substantive component of determinism came from Sigmund Freud, the founder of psychoanalysis. He brought observations to support the view that neurotic symptoms, minor mistakes in writing or speaking (so-called "Freudian slips"), seemingly random or arbitrary choices of words or metaphors in ordinary speech, automatic gestures and patterns of bodily expression, and even the fantastic events of our dreams, are not capricious or "senseless" but exhibit lawfulness, if we will only take the trouble to study them thoroughly and in context.[3] To the psychotherapist since Freud, "nothing is accidental, everything is a symptom." If a patient who has ordinarily begun his interview without preliminaries makes a remark about the weather or comments that the therapist is wearing a pretty necktie, the therapist makes a mental note of this fragment of behavior and expects that the ensuing interview will make clear what special factor caused this minor variation to occur. It is of course impossible to present here the evidence which led Freud and others to these views; and there are special features about the psychoanalytic field that make it unwise to try for something less than a solid documentation. Suffice it to say that even psychologists and psychiatrists who are "non-Freudian" in their views are universally convinced that this portion of his contribution is valid and important.

Many other kinds of evidence, from very diverse sources, contribute to the psychologist's conviction of substantive determinism. They range from laboratory experiments, in which specific little habits are formed and eliminated during the course of an hour, to large-scale statistical surveys of the characteristics of so-called primitive cultures, by means of which anthropologists

[3] A General Introduction to Psychoanalysis (New York: Liveright Publishing Corporation, 1945).

have discerned relationships between such factors as the child-rearing practices of these societies and the modal "personality type" found in the adult products of these practices. Impressed with many lines of evidence such as these, and no doubt influenced as well by his scientific hopes and his world philosophy, the psychologist conceives of each person at a moment in time as the inevitable outcome of the myriads of forces and events which have converged to produce him. These forces include such varied factors as his inherited musical capacity, the kind of neighborhood he was raised in, his father's political views, and the chemical constitution of the fried eggs he had for breakfast an hour ago.

A second basic assumption which appears to be shared by almost all psychologists is materialist monism. The materialist monist holds that there are no substances, forces, or events in human thought or behavior which are of an irreducibly "mental," "psychic," or "spiritual" nature. Thus, for example, the idea of a substantive soul, or of a nonmaterial personal agency such as an angel, could not be included in the materialist monist's framework. All functions of the human person are held to be complexes of events which could, in principle, be formulated in physico-chemical terms. It must not be supposed that the materialist monist denies that distinctively psychological events *occur*, or asserts that they are less "real" than their physical component events. His thesis merely states that, given adequate knowledge, descriptive and causal statements in the familiar psychological language could be translated *without residue* into statements in the physiological language. It is admitted by sophisticated monists that a "psychological" statement such as "Jones laughed when he perceived the logical fallacy" cannot be completely rendered in physiological language, inasmuch as the term *fallacy* designates a logical (normative) concept rather than a physiological state. But the original statement to be translated was in itself not purely causal or descriptive. All that the materialist monist claims is that the purely descriptive components of psychological assertions, not themselves involving logical or ethical modalities, can be translated without causal residue into physiological language. A materialist may, therefore, quite readily concede the irreducibility of logical or ethical categories to descriptive ones.

Here again we must emphasize that most contemporary psychologists are really uninterested in materialism as an ontological thesis, and would on antimetaphysical grounds avoid labeling themselves as "materialist monists." However, this studied avoidance of the traditional labels should not mislead the theologian in his thinking about the psychologist. The latter, when pressed, shows that he firmly believes in the same kind of world that the traditional materialist monist believed in, whether he is philosophically prone to apply the old label or not.

Intersubjective confirmability: A third orientation shared by almost all psychologists is the restriction of discourse to propositions that can be confirmed or disconfirmed ("proved" or "refuted" is too strong) by appeal to empirical evidence which we can all obtain at will. In laying down this requirement, the psychologist is merely following the universal practice of the more advanced sciences. A scientific experiment involves setting up certain conditions which can be satisfactorily described in language and in reporting what observations were then made of what took place. Theoretically any normal observer should be able to bring about the same sensory experiences in himself by putting himself in the described conditions. When a new experiment is performed and reported in a scientific journal, other investigators then undertake to repeat the procedure as described. If the same results cannot be obtained, the experiment is not given a place in the body of scientific knowledge, but is left in an indeterminate position. If nobody seems able to repeat it successfully, it is quietly buried. It may not be possible to decide what went wrong, and the integrity and skill of the original investigator may not be seriously questioned. The point is simply that "nonrepeatability," if it persists, bars an honest-appearing finding from acceptance. This means that what might be "evidence" to one person or group of persons might not be evidence at all for a psychologist.

So far as we can see, these three ideas — determinism, materialist monism, intersubjective confirmability — exhaust the list of notions which, in some form or other, are well-nigh universal among scientific psychologists. There are numerous associated beliefs that either preponderate or are held by sizable minorities, but are far from being universal. For example, many — perhaps most — psychologists hold a position which may be called *biological reductionism* with repect to drives. That is, they hold that the basic biological wants, such as hunger, thirst, sex, and so on, which we share with other living creatures, constitute the basis for all so-called "higher-order" motives, such as curiosity, social interest, familial devotion, self-esteem, art, music, and religion. Other psychologists deny this and consider the development of the latter tendencies to be fundamental to our nature and not based upon the association of early life experiences with biological gratifications. The experimental and clinical evidence on this question is scanty and inconclusive, so that no consensus exists among qualified scholars.

Another example of a scientifically "open question" is the precise evidential status which should be accorded to reports of subjective experience. For almost half a century the backbone of scientific psychology was the introspective method, in which the conscious experience of persons was taken as the basic domain of data to be investigated. Between the two World Wars this approach was largely abandoned (in the United States) in favor of an exclusive preoccupation with *behavior*. The importance of subjective experience was minimized, and even when verbal reports were utilized in the course of experimentation, these utterances were treated somewhat differently than before. They were rejected as "observations" by the speaker, but included along with the (preferred) nonverbal performances as merely additional behavior, albeit verbal in nature. In recent times there has been a revival of interest in conscious experience as such, with a more sophisticated re-examination of the epistemological problems of the introspective method. Here again, however, in spite of some strong swings in the scientific pendulum over the last half century, it has never been possible to state a generalization regarding the evidential status of introspective reports which could command the universal assent of psychologists.

IV. Man's Biological Nature

1. *Distinctive Features of Man's Biological Nature*

As WE VIEW man's dominant position in the world, his versatile mind, and the quality of his intellectual, emotional, aesthetic, and religious life, we naturally ask: Can these be accounted for in his biological nature? Whether we take the position that they can or cannot, we must admit that all of them become effective and observable through man's physical and biological self. The second question which occurs to us, since there are such vast differences between the behavior of man and animal, is: Are there also notable differences between the biological structures?

While we cannot at the present state of scientific knowledge account for all of man's gifts in his biological nature and physical structure, we can point to certain distinctions between his biological organism, its development and function, and that of the animals.

The miracle of human life begins when the sperm of the male merges with the ovum of the female. It is estimated that the small fertilized egg increases two hundred million times by the time of birth, that is, in a period of 265 days.[1] Within the fertilized cell, smaller than an "i" dot, are already contained all the basic elements which will make up the body as it grows and develops into adult stature.

---

[1] *The Miracle of Growth* (Urbana: University of Illinois Press, 1950), pp. 3 f.

The rate of growth of the human body and its long life span are significant. The human being has a longer period of growth and development than animals. While this may have some disadvantages, since it makes the child and youth dependent on others for a longer period of time, the advantages for a fuller development and a higher level of achievement are significant for the individual as well as for the human family. Man's relatively longer life span also contributes toward a higher level of achievement.

There are other differences. M. F. Ashley Montagu lists fifty differences from an anthropological point of view.[2] He does not consider this a complete list by any means, and in addition points to certain qualitative features, such as man's educability, his capacity for complex symbolism, his speech to express his thoughts, and his whole distinctive way of life.

Together with others he points to the size and complexity of man's brain, his bipedal and erect posture, and the remarkable ability of his hands as significantly important in human life and culture.

While the entire organism is important in human behavior, the nervous system, particularly the complex brain, has the vital function of making life integrated and rational. Man is more than a collection of different cells and cell fields. He is an integrated being, an organized system. Brain size, for example, is not the only factor. Man does not have the largest brain. With rare exceptions his brain is the largest in relation to his total body weight.[3] In the study of human intelligence in relation to brain size little or no correlation has, within set limits, been found.

The complexity of the brain, particularly of the cerebral cortex, is more important than size and weight. The individual cells and cell fields, the millions of connections possible, the many folds or convolutions, are all intimately related to man's activity as a rational being.

While the nature of the changes in the brain cells and fibers due to learning and education has not been determined as yet,

[2] *An Introduction to Physical Anthropology* (Springfield, Ill.: Charles C. Thomas, 1951), pp. 84—86.

[3] John W. Klotz, *Genes, Genesis, and Evolution* (St. Louis: Concordia Publishing House, 1955), pp. 342 f.

the brain centers for some specific functions have been located. Among these are the sensory and motor-control areas and possibly the speech area and the association areas. Experimentation with animals has also demonstrated that the thalamic area of the midbrain is directly involved in emotional behavior. It may be inferred that this also holds true in human behavior, but we may also assume that the cerebrum plays an important part in the individual control of human emotions. The frontal and parietal areas of the cerebrum appear to be particularly significant in mental life.

Other areas of man's biological equipment, such as the division of the neural system into somatic and autonomic stems and branches, the endocrine system, and the vascular system are all vital to human life physically and mentally. Man is a complex being biologically, and there must be maintained in him a synchronized balance of functions if life is to be maintained.

2. Drives and Needs

Drives and needs have received frequent attention in psychological, psychiatric, and biological literature. They have been under investigation in much laboratory work as well as in clinical theory and procedure. Under the concept of motivation, interrelated systems of primary and secondary drives, urges, needs, and motives have been brought together to lead to theories of personality, or at least to an explanation of a more specific behavior phenomenon in a given instance.

A particular drive, such as hunger for food, for example, cannot easily be isolated as though it existed by itself as an island. Any drive must finally be interpreted in relation to the whole field of physical, social, ethical, intellectual, and religious motives. It is not the purpose here, however, to develop a theory of motivation, but merely to discuss the basic biological drives which enter into human behavior.

The human body is a delicate arrangement of balances in fluids, blood, lymph, and chemical elements, together with a synchronized, rhythmic, largely automatic functioning of the various organs. This process of the living organism, known as homeo-

89

stasis, has been aptly called the "wisdom of the body."[4] Interference with this balance and rhythm results in rapid deterioration and eventually in death.

The body likewise has numerous protective and corrective devices and functions which help to safeguard the balance and rhythm of the living organism. To mention a few, there is the process of eliminating waste materials. In case of a wound, the blood tends to coagulate. The blood has the tendency to maintain its chemical balance in case of thirst or an oversupply of water in the body. A number of important organs come in pairs. When a foreign body lodges in the nasal passage, sneezing is automatic. Skin subject to constant wear becomes callous. These are but a few illustrations.

An appreciation of the homeostatic process as well as of the protective devices of the body helps in understanding the need and purpose of such basic and more conscious drives as oxygen hunger, food hunger, thirst, sex, pain avoidance, the maintenance of body temperature and comfort, and the necessary balance in rest and activity. It would be more in keeping with the purpose of these drives if they were defined as needs. Their primary purpose is to serve the body in the maintenance of life.

In the sense of needs we can say, then, that they are God-given for the maintenance of life. Food hunger, for example, serves as a warning that the body is in need of certain chemical elements. Fatigue, leading to rest, helps to re-establish a chemical balance and tends to give the entire organism a needed lower level of rhythmic action. Activity, mental and muscular, tends to renew and to invigorate the living organism.

It is also a part of the wisdom of the body that the Creator has made the satisfaction of the biological needs of man enjoyable and pleasurable. Unfortunately, in man's depraved and anxiety-laden state, the biological needs may take on distortions and exaggerations which may give a temporary satisfaction, but will, if persisted in, surely lead to psychological, psychiatric, social, or religious difficulties in the personality. Overeating as a substitute for emotional needs, or alcoholism to escape from stark reality, serve as stock examples.

---

[4] Walter B. Cannon, *The Wisdom of the Body* (New York: W. W. Norton and Company, Inc., 1939).

The sex drive or need has been singled out for special emphasis in pietistic thought and, in fact, in our entire culture. The secretiveness often surrounding it has tended to make sex a forbidden area for instruction and counsel. The very fact of having a sex urge has been thought of by some as being a sin in itself, and this notion resulted in wholly unnecessary emotional problems. The remarkable extent to which pietistic mores have mistakenly made sexual behavior the core of morality can be illustrated by the religious housewife who speaks with horror over the back fence about the rumors of the Joneses' adultery, apparently feeling that God is more concerned about the Sixth than the Eighth Commandment.[5]

The person who adheres to a Christian view of life will earnestly endeavor to keep his biological drives in control, to exercise moderation in keeping with the laws of God and man, and to strive to have them serve their primary purpose. In this no one will attain perfection. Nevertheless, Paul says: "For ye are bought with a price; therefore glorify God in your body and in your spirit, which are God's." (1 Cor. 6:20)

The body needs and deficiencies will, of course, always be given the required attention for the physical and mental welfare of the individual. Glandular imbalances, reversals in blood count, asymmetrical brain waves, brain lesions, organic defects, nutritional deficiencies, and injuries are illustrative of the conditions which may need attention for physical and mental health. The hope is that the condition may be corrected. If this cannot be done and the situation is serious, the individual faces new and grave problems of emotional and religious adjustment.

Such drives as hunger and thirst have their origin in tissue needs of the body. Depletion of body fluids, for example, is reflected directly in the blood chemistry and also produces a local dryness of mouth and throat surfaces, and these conditions in turn produce their characteristic representations in the brain; at this stage the body's *need* has given rise to a *drive*. The term "drive" has a psychological (i. e., behavior-controlling, but not necessarily conscious) implication which the term "need" does not. Not all tissue needs produce drives, if by a drive one means

---

[5] Lutheran numbering; Seventh and Ninth in the Reformed system.

a brain state capable of controlling behavior. A person may, for example, have a severe deficiency of certain vitamins or minerals without having a corresponding drive state which guides his food-seeking behavior.

Because of their prevailing evolutionary orientation, the concentration of drive research upon animal subjects, and the great difficulties in experimenting upon complex human behavior, psychologists have learned more about these tissue-need drives than they have about other motives, such as curiosity, affection, philanthropy, power, prestige, security, group identification, or money. The only drives not based upon tissue depletion which have been investigated in any detail, even with animal subjects, are sex and fear; and even these "simple" drives are incompletely understood at present. For example, the extent to which the sexual drive in animals is based upon local conditions in the genitals (e. g., accumulation of seminal fluid in males) is still unknown. External stimulation and sex hormones in the bloodstream acting directly upon brain centers seem to be more important factors. Fear in animals is elicitable by pain, by certain kinds of novelty or strangeness, and by certain other stimulus patterns characteristic of the particular species.

Some psychologists believe that all drives have their origin, during the course of an individual's development, in tissue needs or tissue injury (including painful stimulation). Efforts have been made to explain such drives as the desire for affection, security, achievement, or knowledge as derivatives of hunger, thirst, warmth, erotic tension, and pain avoidance. It is probable that these efforts were based more upon the psychologists' "simplicity drive" than upon an unbiased look at the behavior of humans or animals, and much of the current research and theorizing about animals has cast doubt upon the idea of tissue need and pain as basic to all drive. For example, "curiosity," "manipulation," and "activity" are three drives which many experimenters do not believe are aroused by tissue needs (i. e., they originate centrally, the brain being the kind of mechanism it is, when certain conditions of stimulus input to eyes and ears are provided by the environment).

In the human species very little is known experimentally about these non-tissue-need drives. (For an excellent study in which an entire book deals with research on one such drive, the achievement motive, see the work of David C. McClelland and John W. Atkinson.[6]) Drives for achievement, affection, knowledge, and the like are commonly called "secondary" by psychologists, a term which is unfortunate because it surreptitiously prejudges an experimental question by suggesting that such drives originate from (and depend upon) so-called "primary" drives, such as hunger, thirst, evacuation, sex tension, and pain avoidance. Since there is no clear-cut (or even impressive) experimental or clinical evidence to show that children are curious, manipulative, prideful, or aggressive on any more "secondary" basis than they are hungry or thirsty or pain-avoidant, such a terminology should be dropped until we know the facts. If "primary" means "arising from inherited structure," there is as much reason to call curiosity primary as there is to call hunger or fear primary. If the facts that the *form, arousability,* and *goal-object* of a drive are modified by experience justify us in calling it "secondary," then hunger, thirst, and sex are all secondary. Similarly the term "biological" is misleading as applied to a subclass of drives. The living brain is as "biological" as the stomach, and a child's or chimpanzee's manipulation of a toy is an overt behavior by a biological organism. H. A. Murray[7] uses the distinction between *viscerogenic* and *psychogenic* drives, but at least two of the twelve drives he lists as viscerogenic (sex and sentience) are not known to be based primarily upon tissue "lacks, distentions, or harms." There is actually no good evidence for attributing the sexual behavior of a female ape (or of an erotically active prepubescent human male) to a local "visceral" condition, while attributing a child's drive for cuddling, manipulation, or dominance over a sibling to "psychogenic" sources.

The best terminology in the light of present evidence would perhaps be between "unlearned" and "learned" drives, leaving entirely open the questions of tissue need or bodily locus.

---

[6] *The Achievement Motive* (New York: Appleton-Century-Crofts, 1953).

[7] *Explorations in Personality* (New York: Oxford University Press, 1938), p. 79.

Besides, from the methodological standpoint the fundamental characteristic which defines a drive is neither its tissue basis nor its inherited origin, but its being a *variable state* of the organism which controls the activation of available habits, and expectancies, so that by manipulating the drive intensity (e. g., by starving a rat) one can manipulate the expression of habits and cognitions in overt behavior. This "functional" criterion for identifying a drive, based jointly upon its causal role in behavior activation and the conditions which arouse it, is experimentally more fruitful and leaves the questions of innateness and tissue need for further scientific research. (See Chapter V for further discussion of this point.)

On present evidence it is already clear that some drives are innate and others have to be learned. Obviously no one is born with a drive for money, nor would such a drive develop spontaneously through maturation. It is the experiences with money, provided by the culture, that create this drive in people. The thirst drive, on the other hand, is unlearned. It is also based upon a tissue need. The curiosity drive is probably unlearned, although this is not definitely established; but even if unlearned, it is presumably not aroused by a tissue need. It is well known that even unlearned, tissue-based drives are modified by the individual's experience, so that their arousal and satisfaction in the adult shows considerable variability from one individual to another. From our knowledge that hunger is an unlearned and tissue-based drive, we cannot infer what foods a man will prefer to eat, whether he dawdles or gobbles at meals, whether he is a gourmet or a gourmand, how much time he spends thinking about food, or many other such facts about his "hunger drive."

Even when a motive is originally acquired in the course of the infant's or child's experiences with tissue needs and their gratification, or with pain and its avoidance, does such a motive subsequently "depend upon" the original drive and its natural reward, or does it come to have a life of its own, so to speak? For example, it seems plausible that the child's desire to know the names of things is initially inculcated by a combination of more basic drive-reward systems. Thus, the child learns that he is rewarded with approval for correctly naming objects, and also that he can often bring about the presence of an object by speaking its name. ("Milk" brings milk, and hence reduces hunger. Saying the word correctly also gets a smile or a pat from mamma.) Does this history of motivation-for-naming imply that when a seminarian looks in the dictionary to check up on the name of an obscure heresy, he is in some sense, at some level, "really" motivated by hunger and by the approval motive (or the unworded expectation that these drives might otherwise be thwarted)? This is one of the most difficult theoretical questions in psychology and has been studied without a definitive outcome for many years. The problem, which Allport christened "the functional autonomy of motives," and the related questions concerning innateness and tissue need, have considerable theological relevance, but the interested reader must go to the sources for an adequate presentation.[8—15]

3. Heredity and Individuality

"Jimmy can't read. His father can't read. Neither could his grandfather." With this statement the parents express their belief that Jimmy has been born short. They express resentment that nothing can be done about it. This makes it easier for Jimmy. Why should he try to learn to read if "it isn't in him"?

All indications, on the other hand, are that James has limited mental ability. Tests, observation, and his inability to do simple

---

[8] Gordon W. Allport, *Personality* (New York: Henry Holt and Co., 1937), Ch. VII, pp. 190—212.

[9] Judson S. Brown, "Pleasure-Seeking Behavior and the Drive-Reduction Hypothesis," *Psychol. Rev.*, 1955, 62, pp. 169—179.

[10] John Dollard and Neal E. Miller, *Personality and Psychotherapy* (New York: McGraw-Hill Book Co., 1950), pp. 50, 71—74, 79.

[11] Calvin S. Hall and Gardner Lindzey, *Theories of Personality* (New York: John Wiley and Sons, Inc., 1957), pp. 269—273 and references cited therein.

[12] Harry F. Harlow, "Mice, Monkeys, Men, and Motives," *Psychol. Rev.*, 1953, 60, pp. 23—32.

[13] David C. McClelland, *Personality* (New York: William Sloane Associates, 1951), pp. 217—220, 234, 403, 404, 434.

[14] Neal E. Miller, "Learnable Drives and Rewards," in S. S. Stevens, ed., *Handbook of Experimental Psychology* (New York: John Wiley and Sons, Inc., 1951), pp. 435—472.

[15] B. F. Skinner, *Science and Human Behavior* (New York: The Macmillan Co., 1953), Ch. 9, especially pp. 150, 151.

school tasks testify to his limitations, which he probably has inherited. But the father does not accept the verdict, saying: "James can do it if he wants to. He merely lets his sense of humor run away with him."

These illustrations from actual experience are indicative of the divergent position that people may take toward heredity. Neither position is tenable in view of the actual situation. Given a normal general intelligence, Jimmy can probably improve his reading skills, whereas James is not likely ever to perform skills requiring a higher degree of intelligence.

Fortunately the debates about heredity versus environment have now largely subsided. We realize that nature does set limitations and that parents cannot always attain in actuality the aspiring plans they may have for the life and career of their child. But we also realize that what appears to be heredity is sometimes no more than role playing and that heredity usually sets a potential limit which makes it possible for a stimulating environment to achieve worthy results. At times nature may indeed set a severely restricted limit as, for example, in the case of amaurotic idiocy.

Human inheritance is so complex that any typing and classification can do no more than set gross and generalized categories. Genetics has a sound basis for saying that the chances for two individuals (with the possible exception of cell twins) to be duplicates are virtually nil. It follows, then, that genetically each person is an individual different from every other person.

Modern genetics bases its theories of heredity on the chromosome-gene arrangement found in the fertilized ovum. When the sperm of the male penetrates the wall of the ovum, each parent contributes twenty-three pairs of chromosomes. By a process of reduction the fertilized ovum contains not forty-six pairs of chromosomes but twenty-three. Although millions of male sperms surround the ovum, only one merges with it. The actual carriers of heredity are the genes which make up the chromosomes. While the chromosomes may be seen under the microscope, in both the ovum and the sperm, the genes cannot. Since hundreds, even thousands, of inherited traits and characteristics come from the chromosomes, it is entirely reasonable to assume that there must be many smaller bodies within the chromosomes. Whether we call these smaller bodies genes or by some other name makes little difference.

While the fertilized ovum attaches itself to the wall of the uterus, there are no nerve connections between the mother and the growing embryo. Thus it is clear that from the very beginning the embryo is individual in its own right, although it receives its nourishment from the mother through the placenta via the umbilical cord.

It is a miracle of miracles that all the inherited biological characteristics which make physical and psychological functioning possible stem from the tiny pairs of chromosomes and the even smaller genes within them.

Actually only those traits are inherited which can be led back to the reproductive germ cell. Syphilis and gonorrhea, for example, are not inherited. These and other congenital infections may have a damaging effect on the unborn child through the mother's blood stream and thereby interfere with the potential inheritance.

Probably all human beings carry some faulty genes which may not be manifested in their own lives. It is possible, and it happens, that two intellectually gifted parents may have a mentally deficient child. But in considering the transmission of adverse and atypical traits, we must keep in mind that infections, damage during the period of pregnancy, injuries at birth or thereafter, and not genes may have been the contributing factor. Abraham Levinson points out that mental retardation and deficiency may have been caused more often by brain damage, malnutrition, premature birth, and infectious diseases than was formerly believed.[16] A further point to be kept in mind is that an individual may inherit a disposition toward a disease rather than the disease itself. In that case precautions may prevent the disease from ever taking a strong hold. Tuberculosis, which was at one time popularly believed to be hereditary, serves as an excellent illustration showing how a disposition toward a disease may be thwarted by environmental measures.

---

[16] *The Mentally Retarded Child* (New York: John Day Company, 1952), pp. 93—103.

Whether or not mental illness is inherited is a controversial question. Some students of heredity assume that a predisposition toward schizophrenia is inherited, since it "runs in families." It does not seem necessary to be completely fatalistic about inherited mental illness. When a member of a family, especially a parent, becomes mentally ill, the shocking and terrifying effect on children is observable. It is probable that the environment may furnish the irritant which, together with a hereditary susceptibility, is causative. With the advance of medicine and psychiatry and a growing understanding of the meaning of religion in the life of the individual, it is reasonable to hope that mental breakdowns may more often be prevented from becoming permanently disabling even though there may be a hereditary susceptibility toward them.

There are, of course, innumerable physical, biological, and systemic differences which are inherited. Among them are facial features, shapes of noses, eyes, and ears, physiques, tallness, shortness, glandular differences, the amount of pigment in the skin and other racial features, brain and neurological differences, baldness, and many more, some known, some unknown.

Modern methods of testing and measuring biological, physical, and psychological differences have been developed. Anthropometric measurement, measurement of blood pressure, the basal metabolism test, the cardiogram, the electro-encephalogram, a number of chemical tests, together with others, have all served useful purposes in physical and mental diagnosis. In psychology we have the intelligence test, special ability and interest tests, personality inventories, and similar devices. When a test has been developed under controlled conditions and when it is then administered to an adequate sample of persons, the test results generally appear in the form of a normal distribution. The administration of an intelligence test, for example, may result in the following classification:

A small percentage of mentally deficient persons ____ 5
A somewhat larger group below average ____ 20
A large average group ____ 50
A smaller group above average ____ 20
A still smaller group in the superior range ____ 5

The exact distribution is somewhat arbitrary, depending on the test as well as on the persons to whom the test was administered. Whether a person is classified in one group or another, he still remains an individual different from all other individuals in the world.

The relation of man's physique to his social and psychological nature is an age-old question of perennial interest. In its popular conception the assumptions are on an approximate level of the now discredited geographical map of the brain known as phrenology.

More serious students of the relation of physique to personality and character, such as Ernst Kretschmer [17] in Europe and W. H. Sheldon [18] in America, have set up intricate systems of measurement in order to arrive at empirical verification, but so far their findings remain controversial. One of the major difficulties arises from the condition that physical as well as psychological types are seldom found in a "pure" state.

The complicated nature of Sheldon's work as well as that of Kretschmer should thoroughly discourage the overconfident from judging character "at a glance."

Man's superior inheritance stands out when his achievements in learning and culture are compared with those of animals. While in early life the chimpanzee may attain behavior patterns equal to or exceeding those of children, gradually the child will develop qualitative superiorities which surpass anything the ape has to offer. In the recent Hayes experiment,[19] after three years of intensive effort, the ape was able to say three words, mamma, papa, and cup. The child's ability to use abstract symbolism and language far beyond that of the ape points to one of the major differences between man and ape. The considered opinion of the Hayeses, that if our culture were dependent on transmission by apes it would be lost, points to the superior human inheritance by contrast.

---

[17] *Körperbau und Charakter* (Berlin: Springer Verlag, 1944).

[18] *The Varieties of Temperament* (New York: Harper and Brothers, 1942).

[19] Cathy Hayes, *The Ape in Our House* (New York: Harper and Brothers, 1951).

Where human inheritance is faulty and defective, it is the business of all concerned with human welfare to recognize the condition as early as possible and to correct or meliorate it if this can be done. If this cannot be done, the provision for a wholesome and constructive milieu in keeping with the individuality of the person still remains for scientific and practical efforts and surely for the sake of Christian love.

Where nature has been liberal, the problem of conservation and development is of vital interest to science and religion.

SUGGESTED READINGS

Cannon, Walter B. *The Wisdom of the Body*. New York: W. W. Norton and Company, 1939.

Miracle of Growth. Urbana: University of Illinois Press, 1950.

Scheinfeld, Amram. *The New You and Heredity*. Philadelphia: J. B. Lippincott Company, 1950.

Sinnott, Edmund W. *The Biology of the Spirit*. New York: The Viking Press, 1955.

V. The Molding and Activating of Behavior[1]

A HUMAN INFANT at birth is strikingly different from an adult person. In fact, while the newborn is a "person" in the legal, theological, and census meanings of the word, he is hardly a "personality" in the usual sense. The infant has a limited set of *needs* (for example, it will die if not fed and protected from the elements), and most of these needs make themselves known as psychological states called *drives* (as when we say, "That child is hungry," or, "He is crying because he feels cold"). There are some ready-made reactions, some of which are called *reflexes*, to certain physical stimuli (e. g., babies will cry if stuck by a pin). Now the adult human individual, too, has needs, drives, and "reflex" actions. But what a vast array of properties the adult exhibits which the infant lacks! Of a particular grownup Smith we can meaningfully assert such varied things as the following:

1. Smith reads Greek.
2. Smith is a Republican.
3. Smith is fond of beer.
4. Smith collects stamps for a hobby.
5. Smith knows the rules of chess.

---

[1] I am greatly indebted to Professor Kenneth MacCorquodale of the University of Minnesota for his careful reading of this chapter. But I have not followed all of his suggestions, and he, of course, has no responsibility for the errors of content or infelicities of expression which remain.

6. Smith commits logical fallacies.
7. Smith is pious.
8. Smith's friends tend to be introverts.

None of these things can be said of any newborn child. How does this alteration from a squirming, inarticulate, poorly co-ordinated little organism to a thinking, perceiving, arguing, sacrificing, praying adult human person come about?

First of all, there occur certain changes in the structure of the body, and particularly of the nervous system, which depend minimally or not at all upon the particular experiences to which the organism is subjected. Given the bare necessities, such as warmth and nutrients, which are required to preserve life, it seems that there are progressive changes in the brain and other tissues which are determined by biological heredity. These developmental processes, which go on merely by virtue of our having been conceived by human parents rather than by fish or rabbits, alter both the behavior and the potentialities to acquire behavior. Behavior changes of this kind are referred to as *maturation*. For example, there are experiments indicating that the age at which walking begins is not appreciably influenced by opportunities or encouragement or "practice." Indian children whose limbs are almost continuously restrained develop the ability to walk when they have reached "walking age," an age which is the same in these tribes as in those who do not carry the infant in a limb-restraining fashion. Again, the sexual drive with its special tensions, reflexes, interests, and perceptual sensitizations develops at pubescence, over a dozen years after birth; the processes of ovulation and sperm production are accompanied by the release of chemical substances called *hormones* into the blood stream, which profoundly influence both appearance and behavior. These developments are determined by our biological heredity. (Incidentally, the maturation of the sexual function over a decade after birth shows that inherited behavioral determiners may begin to exert their effects relatively late. Such terms as "constitutional," "inborn," "hereditary," or "native" refer to the nature of the *causes* of behavior, and not to the question of whether the behavior is present at birth.)

102

Maturation, however, accounts for only a portion of the behavior changes that take place as the organism grows up. We all know that a child will not learn to speak English or play the piano merely by a passage of time during which the nervous system spontaneously undergoes the necessary changes. For such behavior to be acquired, the child must be exposed to the relevant experiences and must perform the relevant actions. If a child can say "cow" when he sees a cow, he does so because he has previously seen cows (or pictures of cows) concurrently with hearing the word "cow" spoken by someone else; has subsequently, by a gradual process of refining his own crude vocalizations of similar sounds, heard himself say "cow" in appropriate circumstances (a "self-rewarded" action); and has been noticed, praised, and smiled at for saying it properly.

The generic term used for the process of acquiring and modifying behavior as a result of suitably timed behavior-and-experience combinations is *learning*. It should be emphasized that when the psychologist speaks of "learning," he does not refer only to "formal learning" in the sense of indoctrination, tutelage, precept, deliberate practice, and the like. This kind of systematic learning, in which adults more or less consciously set up the conditions for acquiring new behavior, is only a subclass — a rather special and unusual subclass — of all the learning which goes on. Suppose a child discovers by himself that when grandfather goes to sleep on the sofa, coins often fall out of his pocket; and that one can retrieve this money and spend it for candy by not telling the grownups of it. This child's subsequent behavior is just as much a result of learning as the ability to say the multiplication table.

From the natural science point of view the most remarkable property of the human being is his great capacity to learn complex behavior. Some animals — particularly the insects — are marvelously adapted to their conditions of life by virtue of having inherited extremely complex but highly rigid behavior patterns. They require almost no previous experience with the crucial situations of their lives (food-seeking, nesting, mating, egg-laying) in order to be all set — by maturation alone — to perform them flawlessly. The human being's inborn behavior, taken by itself, would not suffice to enable him to maintain his adult existence,

103

even if he could somehow be kept alive during the period when maturation is completing itself. When we examine the great collection of behaviors which adult humans exhibit, we find that almost all (except the simplest reflexes, such as blinking when a foreign object approaches the eyeball) are at least modified and shaped by learning; and the great majority are entirely the results of learning.

The facts and laws of the learning process have been investigated by scientific psychologists in the nursery, the field, and the laboratory for over half a century, employing both human beings and animals as subjects of study. Many of the basic processes of learning can be fruitfully investigated by the use of animals, such as rats, dogs, chimpanzees, etc. As in medical research, we can exert greater experimental control over the animal and can subject him to psychological pressures not allowable with human subjects. Ultimately, of course, the tentative formulations based upon animal experiments have to be independently confirmed with human beings. Often the complexity of the human case requires that this confirmation be less direct than the original animal research; but some confidence in these extrapolations can be attained, as is shown in the book by Dollard and Miller in this chapter's suggested readings.

As is often true even in the exact sciences, it is easier to summarize the broad factual findings for practical purposes than it is to state precisely the "first principles" (i. e., the fundamental, rock-bottom postulates of an adequate scientific learning theory, from which the myriads of observations should theoretically be deducible). There are certain basic theoretical issues regarding the nature of the learning process itself which are still undergoing intensive study, and there are disagreements among the competent scientific workers as to which theoretical formulation is the best one. The issues involved in these disputes are extremely technical and cannot be treated here. Fortunately the differences in theoretical orientation do not make themselves acutely felt under most circumstances because the consequences drawn from the competing theories do not differ appreciably in the great majority of concrete learning situations. Even under the controlled conditions of the laboratory, with a deliberate attempt being made to set up experimental conditions which

104

will tease out the differences between theories, it turns out to be extraordinarily difficult to design crucial experiments; most of the observations can, with a little ingenuity, be fitted into alternative theoretical systems. This in itself, while intellectually frustrating to the theoretical psychologist, should help to reassure the reader that the resolution of these theoretical divergencies is not crucial for our present purposes. Accordingly, we shall adopt a somewhat eclectic point of view in the following presentation, realizing that such a policy will be safest in terms of the possible upsetting effect of subsequent scientific research. It goes without saying that many problems are still unsolved, and some have hardly been touched by research to date. Psychology is a young and poorly developed science (some would refuse it the honorific title of "science" at all), and it attempts to treat objectively with the most complex domain found in the created order, the behavior of living organisms. Certainly there is no material object known to any other science which even remotely compares with the human brain in complexity of structure and function. The demands of a brief and introductory presentation force us to oversimplifications and, where eclecticism is impossible, to a choice which may strike the expert as ill-advised. We can only say that the formulations offered represent the present consensus of the profession and seem to be the best-supported by the available evidence. If the pastor wants to know how most American psychologists think about their subject, we believe that he will find it here.

We may begin by inquiring, "*What* is learned?" and then, "*How* is it learned?" As a first approximation it will be convenient to assume that *what* is learned falls into one of four classes:

1. Habits   3. Cathexes
2. Expectancies   4. Perceptions

1. *Habits.* The term *habit* was taken over by the psychologist from the language of everyday life. We say, "He has the cigarette habit," or, "He habitually goes to the theater on Friday evenings." The important thing to see about a habit is that it is not an *action*, nor a *class of actions,* but rather it is *a disposition to a specified class of actions in a specified class of circumstances.* Thus a person may be properly said to "have a habit" even if he is not at

the moment manifesting it. The class of circumstances which will, *ceteris paribus*, lead the habit to manifest itself in an action which exemplifies it is called the *stimulus situation* (usually designated by the symbol S). By "stimulus" here we may mean something simple or atomistic, like a pinprick or a tone; or we may mean something complex and difficult to characterize physicalistically, as when we say that the stimulus for Jones's resentment is "a male person in a position of authority." (The configural character of stimuli was studied experimentally and emphasized theoretically by the *Gestalt* psychologists, whose influence became great in the 1920's and 30's. For readers who may be surprised to see no further discussion of this group, may we say that this is because the *Gestalt* concept has been assimilated by psychology so that this emphasis no longer defines a "position.") The class of actions which is the output term of a habit is called the *response* (designated R). This R, again, need not be a simple, segmental action like turning the head; it may be, for example, a complex utterance. A habit, then, is a *stimulus-response connection* (S.R), by which we mean that the individual tends or is disposed to emit the response R when the stimulus S is presented.

We know a good deal about the laws of habit, such as how habits are acquired, modified, weakened, and under what conditions, once acquired, they are manifested or "activated." The basic condition for the formation of an S.R connection is that the response R must occur in close temporal proximity to the stimulus S. This is admitted by all theorists to be the necessary condition for setting up a habit. Some theorists hold that it is also a *sufficient* condition, but most psychologists disagree and hold that a second necessary condition must also be fulfilled, namely, that the occurrence of the sequence S—R must be followed (immediately) by a third event, the presentation of a *reinforcer* (or "reward," to use the more colloquial synonym). For example, one teaches a dog to shake hands by saying "Shake" (= stimulus), following which the paw is lifted (= response), whereupon we give the dog a pat on the head or a bit of beef (= the reinforcement, denoted by symbol S*). With repeated occurrences of this simple sequence S—R—S* there is established a habit S.R which is the "disposition to emit R in the presence

106

of S." The dominant theoretical school in American psychology, known as the "S-R-reinforcement school," considers this process to be the paradigm of all animal and human learning.

The class of reinforcers is identified experimentally by finding out for each species what kinds of "consequences" will exert this strengthening effect upon the habits S.R whose elements (S–R) are terminated by them. For man, as for other mammals, there is first of all the usual class of biological reinforcers: food, sexual gratification, water, and the like. There are also so-called "high-order" (or "derived" or "secondary" or "psychogenic" or "socio-genic") reinforcers, such as money, praise, attention, affection, and deference. The relation of these latter to the former, and to the biological nature of the species, has been treated above in Chapter IV and will be further discussed in the section on *Cathexes* below.

If a response R is repeatedly elicited (by presentation of S) but without subsequent presentation of the reinforcer S^*, the S.R. disposition will undergo a weakening process which is called *extinction*. It is also known that when a habit has been momentarily extinguished to the point that presentation of S will no longer elicit R, a lapse of time without further training will ordinarily result in some considerable return in strength. This peculiar property of habits is known technically as *spontaneous recovery*. However, with successive re-extinctions and recoveries but no further reinforcement, recovery will cease to occur, and the habit then remains extinguished.

Except for rather simple manipulations of the immediate physical environment, an organism's S–R sequences are reinforced only on a probability basis. That is, the reinforcing event S^* occurs in less than 100% of the occasions on which S elicits R. Reaching for a pencil seen on one's desk is always "successful" (i. e., the sequence S:*visual pencil*–R:*reaching* is consistently terminated by S^*:*tactual pencil*). But such 100% contingencies between response and reward are unusual. Most of our everyday behavior, especially behavior which is acquired by interaction with other people and reinforced by "social" rewards, is maintained upon what psychologists call an *intermittent reinforcement schedule*. Not all our friendly gestures are returned; some of our jokes turn out to be unfunny; not all our thinking results in problem solution; we cannot even be certain of getting something when we put a penny into the gum-dispensing machine. An organism whose responses extinguished too quickly following nonreinforcement, or underwent marked and rapid fluctuations in strength in the short run, would be poorly adapted for survival in a world where probability must be the "guide of life" because there are so very few sure things. The birds and mammals which have been intensively studied are "wired" appropriately in this matter of intermittent reinforcement. For example, an increase in the objective probability of reinforcement produces a rise in the response probability; i. e., the organism adjusts its output to the payoff, often displaying a remarkable sensitivity to small changes in the reinforcement probability. On the other hand, intermittently reinforced habits, although their instantaneous *strength* is appropriately lower than that of comparable habits which have been given 100% reinforcement, are harder to extinguish than the latter. Behavior which has been intermittently reinforced shows what we might characterize as "calm persistence" even in the face of prolonged failure, while "failure" (i. e., nonreinforcement) of a consistently reinforced response is more likely to be followed by signs of emotional disruption: we are annoyed, surprised, and sometimes violent if the usually open door is now locked for the first time. A man will continue putting nickels into a gambling device without winning for a much longer time than the same man will put them into a nondelivering gumball dispenser! For a thorough theoretical understanding of the quantitative details of both normal and neurotic behavior, a consideration of this whole topic of *reinforcement scheduling* is unavoidable. We, of course, cannot develop the subject here, but it had to be briefly alluded to, lest the sharp-eyed reader might be bothered by such questions as, "Why aren't most of our responses rapidly extinguished?" The influence of reinforcement schedules is discussed in the recommended readings for this chapter,[2] and recently an entire book devoted to this subject has appeared.[3]

---

2 *See* Fred S. Keller and William N. Schoenfeld, *Principles of Psychology,* p. 130, below.

3 Charles B. Ferster and Burrhus F. Skinner, *Schedules of Reinforcement* (New York: Appleton-Century-Crofts, 1957).

It will be recalled that in introducing the habit concept we were careful to stress its *class* character. The notations "S" and "R" denote classes of individual, dated recurrences of stimulus and response, and the members of the class S may differ considerably among themselves. A child learns to say "dog" when he sees a poodle, a terrier, and a bulldog. If now we show him a dachshund for the first time, he will in all probability label it correctly as "dog" without specific training to this variety of canine. The advantage of this "spread" of stimulus equivalence, called *generalization,* is obvious. A living organism is rarely, if ever, presented repeatedly with exactly the same constellation of physical energies. If the forming of a habit is to be of any utility, the organism must be able to respond appropriately to all stimulus patterns which are sufficiently "similar." Thus, you have habits adequate to opening doors; on each single occasion of meeting a door and opening it, the precise pattern of light waves from the knob, wood, hinges, etc., which reaches your eyes and travels along the optic nerve to your brain, is unique — not an exact reproduction of any one of the thousands of visual patterns which have fallen on your retina in the past, even from the same physical door.

The nervous system is so constructed that this factor of stimulus variability is taken care of in the formation of habits. When an individual has been reinforced for making a response R in the presence of a stimulus S, we find that stimuli *similar* to S will also serve to elicit R. Sometimes the limits of generalization are very wide, as when a child sees a cat for the first time and calls it "doggie." An important aspect of children's learning, particularly of language, consists of the forming and restricting of such generalizations. The term generalization does not, of course, imply that the generalizing individual can *state the basis* on which he is reacting to the broad stimulus class. Nonspeaking organisms can also form generalizations. With sufficient training, a white rat can be made to generalize the visual form *triangle* to a triangular pattern of three circles, while appropriately avoiding an extension of the habit to a circle itself. A great deal of human neurotic behavior is based upon unworded generalization, particularly upon what the objective outsider sees are nonrelevant bases of similarity. For example, suppose a neurotic lay-

109

man is unable to get along with any pastor, almost independent of the pastor's personality characteristics. When we explore this person's intimate psychological processes, we find that he reacts to all pastors on the basis of the fact that his father was a stern, harsh, tyrannical man and that his father often read the Bible to the family. Our patient has an automatic reaction of resentment and fear toward all "authority figures," the mere fact that they are in a position of authority, respect, and instruction constituting them "father surrogates" in the psychologist's jargon. Add to this role similarity the specific stimulus overlap that pastor, like father, reads aloud from the Bible, and we can see that, try as he may, the unfortunate pastor has an uphill fight to meet with this neurotic's approval.

If a habit is generalized over one stimulus class but not over another, we say that the two stimulus classes are *discriminated*. A child says "doggie" to dogs but not to cats, for example. Commonly, the originally effective stimulus class is narrowed from S to a subclass S_1 by reinforcing R when emitted in the presence of S_2 (which is in S but not S_1). The child who says "doggie" to a cat is not reinforced, and after withholding reinforcement a number of times in the cat situation (and other dog-resembling quadrupeds), we find that the desired limits of generalization have been established — we have *set up a discrimination*.

Just as habits generalize over stimuli (hence giving the stimulus its class character), so, too, there is spread on the response side. No two instances of the "same response" are physically identical, although for some responses there is a remarkable resemblance among the several occurrences. The spreading of habit strength over similar reactions is called *induction*. The process of restriction, refinement, and alteration of the properties of an R-class (analogous to discrimination for stimuli) is called *differentiation* or *shaping*.

2. *Expectancies*. If a certain sequence of stimulus and response (S_1–R) is characteristically followed in time by a second stimulus S_2, there is some evidence for the notion that the organism comes to "expect" S_2 will be a consequence of performing R in the presence of S_1. In this case we find it convenient to speak of a disposition called an *expectancy*, designated by the

notation S_1RS_2. Some psychologists believe that all expectancies are really subtle habits (e. g., "expecting food" = making tiny chewing movements, salivating), while others deny this. At present the experimental evidence is inconclusive, so it seems safer for us here to speak of both habits and expectancies. If what are currently taken to be expectancies turn out in the course of scientific advance to be completely reducible to chains of "silent," inner habits, no harm will be done to the present formulation. Like habits, expectancies probably exhibit quantitative properties such as generalization, induction, and extinction. From the above brief remarks the reader can see that, crudely speaking, habits are involved with *doing* something while expectancies are involved with *knowing* something. Hence those learning theories which give a crucial role to the expectancy concept are sometimes referred to as "cognitive" theories, as contrasted with the S–R theories which are habit-oriented.

3. *Cathexes.* If a hungry white rat, dog, ape, or human child is presented with a piece of food immediately following the performance of some action (say, pressing a lever), the lever-pressing habit will, *ceteris paribus,* receive an increment in its strength. The food presentation which strengthens the S.R. connection we have called above a *reinforcement,* and a pellet of food S^* is said to be a *reinforcer* (or, to *possess the reinforcing property*). Similarly, the building up of an expectancy (S_1RS_2) by the running off of the sequence S_1–R–S_2 depends upon the temporal contiguity of the last portion of this chain of events with presentation of a reinforcer S^*. (Whether it is true that *no* growth of habits or expectancies can occur in the absence of reinforcement, as alleged by many theorists, is still unsettled; but that reinforcement facilitates their acquisition is shown by a great body of evidence.) Now it is obvious from common observation, and borne out quantitatively by laboratory research, that stimulus patterns differ in their possession of the reinforcing property. It is probable that the vast majority of stimuli to which an organism may be subjected do not, at least initially, possess this property to an appreciable degree. Such stimuli are called "neutral" stimuli. When a stimulus has the power to act as a reinforcer, it is also said to have a *cathexis,* or to be *cathected.* One of the most important kinds of learning manifested by both

111

animals and human beings is the *acquisition of cathexes by stimuli which did not initially have any.* For example, we cannot train a rat to press a lever by merely sounding a click whenever he presses. Repetition of the sequence (S_1:sight of lever—R:pressing lever—S_2:click) does not strengthen the habit S_1R because the sound of a click is not a reinforcer, has no cathexis. However, we can *confer* cathexis upon the click. Suppose we sound a click every time we deliver a food pellet (no lever-pressing being involved). After a number of such temporal pairings of S_2:*click* with S^*:*food,* it turns out that S_2:*click* alone, without food, has acquired the reinforcing property. It is now possible to strengthen the lever-pressing habit S_1R by following the occurrence of R by S_2:click. (Actually a white rat so trained can be made to press a lever a considerable number of times "merely to hear the click" — no food ever having been given him in conjunction with lever-pressing at any time in his life history.) In such cases we say that the click has an *acquired cathexis,* or has become a *secondary reinforcer.*

A very large portion of everyday behavior is maintained and controlled by the operation of such secondary reinforcers. In human life money is perhaps the most obvious and ubiquitous case of acquired cathexis. A dollar bill cannot be eaten, drunk, used as shelter, made love to, or whatever. But it has acquired powerful secondary cathexis. That this cathexis, overlearned though it is, can still be lost by extinction, is shown by the loss in behavior control by paper money in such a phenomenon as the post-World War I German inflation. This extinction consists, naturally enough, in the repeated presentation of the secondarily cathected object *without* the associated primary cathexis following. Organisms other than man also acquire secondary cathexes. In the more intelligent species of animals the *quantity* of a secondary cathexis can be varied by suitable experimental procedures, thus producing a situation similar to the human use of money. For example, apes can learn to work harder for a blue poker chip than for a red one if the blue chip will operate a food-vending machine which dispenses a preferred food.

If we study the moment-by-moment behavior of an adult human, it is apparent that it is largely maintained by the operation of secondary reinforcers. People perform actions and re-

112

ceive as immediate rewards (or punishments) smiles, frowns, money, praise, blame, attention, "security," "knowledge," and so on. None of these stimulus events is a primary reinforcer; all of them have originally "borrowed" their cathexis from other kinds of events with which they have been paired in the life history. If a mother consistently frowned at her baby when feeding or otherwise tending to his needs, and smiled sweetly whenever she spanked him or treated him roughly, a frown would presumably acquire positive cathexis. Such a baby would have "learned the language backwards." This may be partially what has happened in certain types of problem children, for whom adult disapproval, being the only kind of "attention" they ever got from rejective parents, has acquired the reinforcing property!

Whether a thoroughly stamped-in cathexis, having persisted over many years and become involved in a dense, ramified network of psychological connections, can be completely extinguished by repeatedly presenting it in the absence of any association with some primary reinforcer is a moot question. As pointed out in the preceding chapter, some psychologists (notably Allport) hold that strong, multiple-connected cathexes come after a time to "live a life of their own," no longer drawing strength from the physiological drives or demanding any further association with the primary rewards which were responsible for their origin. This theory is called *functional autonomy,* and the evaluation of evidence on what appears at first to be almost a truism turns out to be an extraordinarily technical and difficult matter.

4. *Perceptions.* Whether the formation of perceptions, as distinct from habits, expectancies, and cathexes, is fundamentally a separate kind of learning, we shall not examine here. Suffice it to say that what we have referred to as "stimulus patterns" in the preceding discussion possess considerable internal organization in the experienced adult organism. There is experimental and clinical evidence to indicate that before an organism can generalize over two simple visual forms (say, two black squares) as being somehow equivalent — i. e., before the S-class which enters into a habit can be, so to speak, *constituted* as a class, the individual must previously have experienced many (hundreds

113

or thousands) visual sensations of suitable diversity, intensity, repetitiousness, similarity, and distribution. Crudely, we might put it this way: Before an animal can learn to press a lever when it sees one (habit), or to anticipate that food follows pressing (expectancy), or value the mere sight of a lever by virtue of its food association (cathexis), he must first of all learn to see a lever, when there is one there, as a separate *thing* among the complex of sensations arising from his environment. The week-old infant not only doesn't discriminate between mother's face frowning and mother's face smiling, in the sense of not reacting differently; there is reason to think that he literally cannot *see* the configuration "smile" at that early stage in his history of visual experience. Since psychologists usually work with adult (or at least partially grown individuals), almost all of this per-ceptual groundwork has already been thoroughly laid in by the time they get hold of the subjects. Hence the brain's automatic classifying of nonidentical sights and sounds as equivalent (gen-eralizable) does not itself stand out as a dramatic and major result of the learning process. We have listed it here, in spite of some scientific disagreement on its exact status, for complete-ness' sake; it plays a lesser role in comparison with the other three so far as the religiously relevant questions of psychology are concerned.

Thus far we have considered habits and expectancies only with respect to how they are acquired, modified, or extinguished. Another question arises when we remind ourselves that habits are *dispositions,* so that a habit continues to exist during the time intervening between its concrete manifestations in particular acts. When we say, "Jones has the cigarette habit," we do not, of course, mean to assert that Jones smokes continuously. Since a habit is a disposition to respond with behavior R in situation S, one can be so disposed when he is not exhibiting R — namely, when S is lacking. (This, of course, is the nature of a disposition and distinguishes it from an *event* and a *thing.*) There is, how-ever, another and more complicated way in which a habit is "inactive," not manifested for a time. Sometimes we observe that the R does not occur *even when the S is presented,* and when we know, further, that a strong S-R connection has in fact been formed by the reinforcement history and has never been extin-

114

guished. Suppose I have a cat well trained to lift his paw when he hears the command "Shake," having in the past used bits of liver as a reinforcer to build up this paw-shaking habit. If I now say "Shake" and the cat fails to respond, I cannot conclude immediately that the habit has been extinguished (unlearned). Why not? Because, as any sensible person would point out, "perhaps he just isn't hungry." If that is the reason why the habit is not activated, why R fails even when S is presented, then we know what to do in order ·to strengthen the response. We let the cat go hungry — we withhold food for a time, and after such a period of deprivation the stimulus "Shake" again begins to elicit paw-lifting. Note that here we have modified the strength of certain behavior *without further learning,* i. e., by simply permitting time to elapse. Whereas, if the habit had been extinguished, we would have to put the cat through some more training in order to re-build it.

This familiar fact about behavior, that there is a variation in the strength of S-R dispositions other than that based upon learning and unlearning, is what gives rise scientifically to the notions of *drive* (or *motive*) and *emotion.* It appears that there are certain *states* or inner conditions of the organism which change over time and which exert a control over the activation of habits. We need not go to the animal laboratory to find support for such concepts. In everyday life we are accustomed to distinguishing between habits and drives and between habits and emotions. Thus if a clerk commits numerous errors in making change, we want to know whether she is "stupid" (i. e., can't learn the multiplication table), "uneducated" (i. e., could learn it but hasn't), "careless" (knows the multiplication table but doesn't try hard enough to make the right change), or "emotionally upset" (knows the table and tries hard, but some factor such as anxiety is interfering with her output). The first diagnosis, "stupid," refers to the defective *capacity* to form certain numerical habits (it is what psychologists call a learning parameter [4]). The second label, "uneducated," denotes a habit defect;

---

[4] One very important branch of psychological science which is not treated in this book is devoted to the study of such quantitative factors as rate of learning. For a brief introduction to this field, known as *differential psychology,* see Appendix D.

that is, we are saying that the previous history has not put the desired S-R connections into this individual's behavior repertory. The third and fourth, "careless" and "upset," make reference to the strength or quality of the *controlling state* (motive or emotion). One who has thoroughly learned the multiplication table may show errors if he is too excited, or bored, or anxious, or depressed, or resentful of the task. The reason we mentioned a cat instead of a dog in our previous example is that a dog, being a more social organism, would typically respond to "Shake" even though he wasn't momentarily hungry. Other drives, for affection, approval (a pat on the head, "Good Rover," etc.) are available to activate the paw-lifting response, even if the hunger drive is momentarily satiated. The cat, being a solitary beast, ordinarily shows much less manipulability by purely social forces. Hence arises the common (erroneous) notion that cats are too stupid to learn tricks. Most people try to teach cats to perform by employing mainly those social reinforcers, and the associated drives, which work well with dogs, and hence usually get poor results.

These inner conditions which exert a sort of superordinate control over habits we have called generically *states*. Since they usually exist in various degrees, they are also referred to as *state variables*. The following short list of common words is composed of the names of some important state variables: fear, rage, anxiety, thirst, hunger, lust, fatigue, curiosity, shame, guilt, elation. Obviously no account of human or animal behavior could be given which omitted consideration of such state variables.

A cursory examination of the preceding sample list of state variables indicates that they have certain interesting properties. First, each state variable tends to be associated with a characteristic reinforcer, or elicitor, or both. Thus "hunger" as a state variable is co-ordinated to "food" as a reinforcer. "Curiosity" as a state variable is co-ordinated to "examining a novel object" or "looking over a strange place" or "hearing a new fact" as reinforcers. "Fear" as a state variable is associated with "pain" and "threat of injury" as elicitors.

Secondly, the same state variable may exert an influence over a wide variety of habits. For example, a girl who is very angry with her suitor may perform such diverse actions as being over-friendly toward another man, tearing up the suitor's picture, and canceling a violin lesson because the suitor is fond of the violin. In general, we find that a state variable is likely to affect the manifestation of almost all habits, at least slightly; but that it exerts an especially strong control over *those habits which have been built up by reinforcing with its "proper" reinforcer.* By making a rat hungry we will, to be sure, activate many responses — the whole activity system of the organism is, so to speak, *energized* by the state of being hungry. Or, again, when a female rat has recently ovulated and would be sexually receptive to mates if available, she runs two to four times as far per day in a squirrel cage, even though running as such is not a sexual response. Countless other examples, both human and animal, could be given in illustration of the point that state variables influence many topographically unrelated behaviors. Nevertheless they ordinarily exert a special control over those habits which were (historically) acquired by the use of their associated reinforcers. If we make a rat hungry, the most pronounced effect upon habit activation will be upon those habits which were built up by food reward. If we make a person anxious, he tends to do those things which have allayed anxiety for him in the past. The adult, experienced organism can be conceptualized for most scientific purposes as the repository of a huge collection of habits, differentially activated by a (much smaller) collection of controlling states.

A third property of state variables is that their reduction or increase, as the case may be, acts as a reinforcement. Psychologists customarily reserve the term *drive* for a state variable whose reduction has the reinforcing effect upon habits; but, of course, the short-term effect of a reduction in drive will be to lower momentary response strength. By feeding a rat large amounts of food after each pressing of the lever, I strengthen the *long*-term disposition to press. That is, I reinforce the response and thereby build up the habit. Yet the *momentary* tendency to press may be progressively declining during the experimental hour, because the eating is meanwhile reducing the hunger drive, which acts transitorily as a controlling state variable. Thus the same reinforcement operation characteristically acts in opposing directions. It tends to lower response probability by virtue of its

117

drive-reducing property, and it tends to raise response probability by virtue of its habit-strengthening property. The precise interaction of these effects is too technical to develop here; but, as we have seen, the chief point lies in the distinction between a short-term and a long-term disposition. We are made less hungry by eating food, less sexually inclined by orgasm, less tired by sleeping, less curious about a novel object by examining it at length, and so forth. Some theorists hold that all cathexes, all reinforcing power attached to stimuli, are ultimately based upon their association with the occurrence of such decrements in a suitable state variable. (This is the so-called "drive-reduction" theory of reinforcement.) We need not come to a decision about that theory here.

There are other state variables, such as "joy," "elation," whose *increase* is reinforcing. These are not usually referred to as drives but as emotions. On the other hand, some emotions, notably fear and rage, act like drives in that their reduction reinforces. Some psychologists therefore consider such "negative" emotions to be drives, and in several important respects they behave analogously to hunger, thirst, and sexual desire. This is partly a terminological question, but there are also important substantive issues that bear upon the decision to use the word drive in this way. Again, the problems are too technical for present consideration.

A fourth, and very important, feature of state variables is that some states seem to be induced, or their intensity increased, spontaneously or endogenously. That is, by the mere lapse of time, certain of the organism's own inner processes suffice to build up the state. Hunger, thirst, and sleepiness are examples. Other state variables seem to be dependent mainly upon elicitation from outside stimuli (e. g., fear). Still others depend upon both (e. g., lust, acquisitiveness). There is a rough correspondence between this spontaneous-versus-elicited distinction and the distinction between motives and emotions. The states commonly called motives tend, on the whole, to be internally aroused, at least at first; whereas those states called emotions tend to be elicited by the external situation. A child becomes hungry pretty much independently of the context, provided a sufficient time elapses since food was last ingested. Whereas a child becomes

118

frightened or angry on the basis of what is happening to him; fear and rage are mainly *elicited* states. We do not ordinarily think of *hunger* as an emotion, and we rarely think of *sadness* as a motive. It turns out upon careful analysis that these distinctions, while reflecting a truth, are extremely difficult to draw so as to express exceptionless rules. Is lust, for example, a motive or an emotion? Both, as these words are ordinarily used. Is it externally aroused or time-dependent? Both, again. Even hunger is not a clear case. I may say that I am hungry for a chocolate sundae "because I haven't had one for months," implying that this subhunger grows by the mere lapse of time. But I may also say that I have been hungry for a chocolate sundae "ever since I saw that full-page ad with the big chocolate sundae depicted in such realistic colors," indicating that the chocolate-sundae drive can be aroused by external stimuli. Upon the present experimental and clinical evidence, both with humans and infrahuman animals, it appears that most, if not all, state variables are dependent upon both cumulative inner processes and external elicitors. Whether one calls a given state variable a "drive" or an "emotion" depends upon several considerations, of which the inner-outer control question is only one, and not always the determining one.

In infrahuman animals there is one state variable which is almost entirely controlled by external elicitation, namely, *fear*. Given a familiar environment, a white rat or a chimpanzee will not become frightened "on his own." The state of fear affects all habits in the repertory, decreasing the momentary strength of most and increasing that of a few. Very extreme values of this state variable ("terror") may completely inactivate the entire repertory in some mammalian species, as in so-called "freezing" behavior. A thoroughly frightened rat will not manifest any of the S-R dispositions he has acquired, even if other strong controlling drives might be expected to activate these habits. He may become immobilized, so that the only responses at high strength are those of a reflex nature. Some of these latter are innately connected with the fear state, such as squealing, hair-raising, urination, protrusion of eyeballs. Acquired responses based upon positive drives such as hunger, sex, thirst, or curiosity may be reduced to zero or near-zero strength by the state of fear. The innate elicitors of fear are somewhat variable from one species to another and also depend upon the developmental stage the individual has reached. *Pain* is the universally adequate elicitor. *Novelty*, especially in the forms of "unexpected" novelty (as when a familiar sequence is suddenly disrupted) or the presence of strange organisms, appears also to be a common elicitor. There is some evidence that highly specific stimulus patterns are innate fear-elicitors for certain species, especially stimulus patterns characteristically produced by members of hostile species (e. g., a moving hawk shadow for certain birds; a coiled snake for chimpanzees).

When the fear state is elicited by a class of external stimuli S^-, we find that we can set up a new habit S.R by the procedure of *removing* S^- as a reward for the emission of R. A stimulus whose removal acts as a reinforcer we call *aversive*, and its "negative," "to-be-avoided" character is indicated in our notation by the minus superscript. Examples of aversive stimuli for the white rat are: pain, a loud noise, being in a wide-open expanse, a bright light. Stimuli which organisms tend to avoid, whose presentation "punishes," and whose removal acts as a reward, are said to possess the *negative reinforcing property*. Contrasted with them are, of course, those stimuli, such as food, which have the *positive* reinforcing property.

If an aversive stimulus is repeatedly associated in time with a neutral stimulus, the latter becomes aversive also. That is, it begins to elicit the fear state, and it acquires the negative reinforcing property. For example, a rat will not normally acquire the habit of turning a wheel if the only consequence is that he can by so doing get from a white chamber into a black chamber. But if we first associate a painful electric shock with being in the white chamber, and escape or avoidance of shock with the black, then he will learn to turn a wheel if it opens the door between them. We say that "white wall" has become a *secondary negative reinforcer* and that the fear state has now become *conditioned* to the white wall. One definition of "anxiety" which is widespread among behavior scientists is based upon the facts we have just described. The definition runs: "Anxiety is the conditionable component of the innate response to pain." Whether this definition is adequate to cover the conditioned fear state as we know

120

it in adult humans, remains to be seen. A related definition, arrived at through the psychoanalysis of human neurotics rather than from the experimental study of animals, is Sigmund Freud's: Anxiety is the internal signal of anticipated danger.[5] The similarity of these two concepts of anxiety is obvious.

Anxiety is a state variable of supreme importance in the understanding of human behavior, particularly neurotic behavior. Some clinicians have gone so far as to say that the problem of neurosis *is* the problem of anxiety — how we acquire it, how we handle it, how we get rid of it. One of the striking features of the neurotic person is that a large part of his behavior seems primarily based upon the avoidance of aversive stimulation or the inner state produced by it. We get the impression that most of the neurotic's time and energy are expended not in seeking positive gratifications but in staving off the ever-present threat of the anxiety experience. He cannot give or accept love (sexual, filial, or other) because he is afraid of being rejected. He cannot achieve in his trade or profession because he is afraid that he will fail; or that if he succeeds, he will draw the envy and enmity of others upon him. He cannot enjoy the contemplation of nature's beauties because he is too busy worrying about whether the drive home will be safely completed; even the flavor of a good beefsteak is subtly poisoned by guilt about spending too much money.

The development of responses whose main function in the economy of behavior is anxiety avoidance (or anxiety reduction) proceeds in the acculturated human to the elaboration of extremely complex chains and structures. A very considerable part of this anxiety-based behavior is "normal," in the sense that it is not indicative of a psychiatric condition and is a routine part of adult human behavior control. It is inconceivable to most psychologists that a society could function if all behavior control (including self-control) were mediated solely by positive reinforcers and their associated appetitive drives, without the use of aversive stimulation ("punishment") at any point. When the alarm clock goes off and goads the average sleepy adult into abandoning his warm bed on a cold, dreary winter morning, it

---

[5] *Inhibitions, Symptoms, and Anxiety* (London: Hogarth Press, 1948).

is not the positive prospect of the day's activities which controls his behavior during those first ten reluctant minutes. The undercurrent theme — not even put into words, in many instances — which here controls behavior is, "If you don't get up, you'll be late," which for some people means, "The boss will be angry"; for others, "You'll be docked"; for others, "You'll feel cheap later," or whatever else it may be.

The psychologist does not, as this example shows, confine the word "anxiety" to extreme or intense states. These he calls by special names, such as "anxiety attack" or "panic state." The anxiety concept is a theoretical concept and may refer to minimal arousals of the state; so minimal that they are not even subjectively experienced or labeled as "fear." When the initial link, internal or external, of a learned chain acts as a *signal* of possible danger (pain, physical or social punishment), producing a response which successfully prevents the occurrence of the anxiety experience, we commonly speak of the anxiety as *bound*. A person is then said to *bind* his anxiety by the learned response which avoids it. Anxiety, in small doses and appropriately handled, is not, in and of itself, abnormal or unhealthy or even necessarily "bad." A modicum of anxiety is part and parcel of normal human life. The intrafamily civilizing of the young organism, a slow and sometimes painful process, as even the best parents know, proceeds by a suitable mixture of reward and punishment, of cultivation and restraint, of gratification and deprivation. Psychotherapists who try to treat the adult or adolescent products of a child-training philosophy based only upon the use of appetitive drives take a dim view of the results. To be civilized means not only to have acquired the usual appetitive habits and positive cathexes; it also means (as it has always meant, in all cultures) to have acquired a system of aversive conditionings capable of exerting restraint. Further, since the police cannot watch all of us all the time, the arousal of the appropriate negative state variable must be to a considerable extent under internal control. When external control preponderates in an adult's aversive conditionings, we have the scoundrel and the psychopath.

In terms of learning theory we could say that the neurotic differs from the normal individual in (a) the frequency and intensity of his anxiety responses; (b) the techniques by which he handles or avoids them; and, perhaps as a joint consequence of (a) and (b), (c) the over-all extent to which his behavior is anxiety-motivated rather than appetite-motivated. More detailed discussion of these matters will be found in Chapter VI.

The "internalization" of restraining aversive conditionings alluded to brings up one of the most striking contrasts between man and the infrahuman animals. We mentioned earlier that fear in other animals is elicited by outside stimulation, while thirst or the sex urge becomes strong by mere "deprivation time." In the acculturated human adult, a very important class of state-elicitors are *self*-produced, by the occurrence of certain inner events. We all know that anxiety can be produced in us by our own inner processes, once a complex chain of words, images, or postural adjustments has been acquired by the learning process. It is probable that in adult humans, both neurotic and healthy, there is more elicitation of the anxiety signal by self-produced stimuli than by gross external threat. After all, under all but the most extreme conditions of war, famine, or other catastrophe, very few people in civilized societies have any appreciable exposure to physical pain or the immediate threat of it. Even aversive social stimulation is pretty infrequent; we are rarely rebuffed, insulted, or rejected by others. Thus when we find a neurotic "introvert" for whom social stimulation in and of itself has acquired the negative reinforcing property, it turns out that this aversiveness (of what, for most of us, is a mildly positive stimulus class) is mediated by certain inner events. Such a person has, for example, thoughts about what others *might* think of him or what he *would* say if such and such *were* to happen, and the like.

Looked at purely from the naturalistic standpoint ("What is a healthy animal?"), it could be said that the human organism pays a certain price for the possession of his distinctively human powers. Rats, cats, and apes cannot plan for years ahead, elaborate theories, ponder the mysteries of life, form societies which accumulate and transmit culture, or worship their Creator. Such distinctively human powers as speech, discursive reasoning, moral feeling, self-induced recollection, systematic forecasting, and causal analysis by reference to complex inferred events — these require man's kind of brain. He who has this kind of brain becomes capable also of such peculiarly human phenomena as worry, scrupulosity, delusions of persecution, unresolvable guilt feeling, or fear of many things which cannot hurt him and are not even valid signals of objective hurtful events to come. Rats and cats can be trained to fear originally neutral stimuli, as we have discussed above. A naïve rat does not fear a faint buzzing sound, or quickly becomes accustomed to it. By temporally pairing it with electric shock we can confer the aversive property upon a buzzer, so that henceforth the buzzer will elicit the fear state (or, better, its conditionable component "anxiety"). Turning off the buzzer will then constitute a reinforcement. But we cannot train rat, cat, or ape to experience anxiety about the foreseen fact of inevitable death or about the loss of "meaning." Only man can be frightened or depressed by the realization that he will someday face death or that his long-held political philosophy is false, or that he is more selfish or hypocritical or hostile than he had permitted himself to believe. By virtue of his special powers man can invent such a thing as the stock market, whereby a large number of persons can co-operate in the sharing of a material risk; but these same natural powers bring about the absurdity that a stockbroker kills himself because he is down to his last half-million dollars and cannot face the "terrible consequences" of this. No ape could do such a thing.

The activation of habits by state variables has been discussed; a similar activation process applies to expectancies, perceptions, and cathexes. For example, if a person is presented with ambiguous pictures and asked to tell what he sees, visual perceptions of food will be more frequent if he is hungry. Given extreme intensity of certain state variables, the dependence of perception upon the objective facts of the outer world as reflected via stimulus input may be reduced to a negligible amount. Thus a person dying in the desert of thirst may "perceive" an oasis when there is none there. Here the great intensity of the drive has sufficed to determine the character of the perceptions. It is generally assumed that the hallucinations of mentally ill patients are brought about by virtue of the intense needs which are struggling for fulfillment, although in these cases there is probably some additional factor of breakdown of cognitive control which makes such reality distortions possible.

In the next chapter we shall examine some of the concrete forms of behavior to which these general processes give rise. The learning process as such will not be constantly alluded to, since it is taken for granted that the laws of learning underlie and explain the various psychological events and structures we meet in practice. Similarly, in Chapter XI the counseling process is discussed in terms appropriate to that level of discourse. The reader should not form a mistaken impression that these chapters present contradictory formulations. It is rather a matter of *levels of analysis,* each of which is consistent with the others but more suited than they are for its task. For example, a counselor may say: "Through acceptance by the therapist, this client became less rigid in his ways of perceiving and was able to examine new possibilities." The terminology of learning theory is entirely absent from this short sentence. But each of the succinct phrases making up this statement can be "unpacked" in the learning-theory language. Thus the phrase "acceptance by the therapist" seems simple to us because we are human beings with feelings, and we know what it means to be accepted by another person and to accept him. Yet this "simple" process is, after all, a subtle and complex one, if one begins to analyze its behavioral components. The therapist's voice does not sound shocked when he responds to a confession by the client, he does not frown or look critically, he smiles a little, he permits the client to talk about what he wants to talk about, and thus, via several different kinds of overt behavior, his "acceptance" is communicated. A learning-theory account of this process would break it up into literally hundreds of *episodes* in the client-therapist interaction and would reformulate the events in terms of such concepts as extinction, generalization, spontaneous recovery, and the like.

The client has to learn that not everyone is as unforgiving as his harsh father was (discrimination). He has to verbalize and reimage certain painful experiences in the "safe" context of the therapy until, by such repetition, they lose some of their sting (extinction). He comes to expect that, since the therapist can accept him in spite of his defects, perhaps other people can like him too (generalization). As he becomes more successful in his interpersonal relations (reinforcement, drive reduction) his overall load of frustration decreases; he feels less chronic anger (a state variable). Being less angry, he has less need to be afraid of his own impulses (anxiety, another state variable, is reduced). Since the rigidity of perceptions is known to be increased by anxiety, anxiety reduction makes it possible for other marginal perceptions to occur at times in competition with the dominant neurotic ones.

The recasting of familiar statements in the learning-theory language is useful in thinking about the underlying causal relations involved and in seeing why a certain healing procedure works (or fails). Many examples of how the application of learning principles stimulates and clarifies thinking about neurosis and its treatment can be found in the suggested readings for this chapter, especially the books by John Dollard and Neal Miller,[6] and by O. H. Mowrer.[7] But it would be too cumbersome to carry out such a translation every time we wanted to express a human fact. And it would be pointless, just as it would be pointless to avoid saying, "I started my car," by substituting each time a detailed account of the motions of the driver's hands and feet and of the electrical and mechanical events taking place under the hood. To test his understanding of the concepts, however, the reader may find it an interesting exercise to try such translations into the learning-theory language from time to time.

THEOLOGICAL NOTE

If this system of concepts is put forward by the psychologist as adequate to cover all human activity, can the Christian accept such a claim? We must avoid jumping to "obvious" conclusions about this question. It appears, for example, that there is no room among these concepts for such characteristically theological notions as sin, grace, regeneration, and the like. Learning theory is a closed system, a machine with no "play" in its parts. But the dissimilarity of the two languages does not tell us how their concepts are related; and to "explain" an event is not the same thing as to "explain it away." The terms in theology which refer to

---

[6] *Personality and Psychotherapy* (New York: McGraw-Hill Book Co., 1950).

[7] *Learning Theory and Personality Dynamics* (New York: Ronald Press, 1950).

human actions and dispositions direct attention to their religiously relevant properties — this language "slices the pie" in a different way. Whether the total structure of the two languages is such that theological discourse runs afoul of learning-theory discourse could be determined only by a detailed logical analysis of concrete psychological events as formulated in each. To our knowledge, this task has not been seriously attempted by anyone to date, and we shall make no attempt at it in this volume. Our tentative opinion is that the most likely focus of disagreement, if any exists, is in the determinist and materialist presuppositions underlying the psychologist's use of his language, rather than in substantive incompatibilities between learning-theory formulations and religious accounts of a particular state or action.

Of course, the concepts of theology cannot be expressed within the language of learning theory and psychoanalysis. That simple and unexciting linguistic fact has misled some psychologists into thinking that they had overthrown theology and has made theologians suspicious of the psychologist's formulations. The thing to see, of course, is that the psychologist's language is deliberately and systematically impoverished, as is all good scientific language. Moral predicates, for example, are not to be found in it any more than such evaluative ideas as "the circle is the perfect figure" occur in astronomy. The scientific language is a *sublanguage* of the total language which men speak, and it includes only those predicates which are relevant to the scientific task, namely, causal analysis. Scientists have learned, often by painful experience, that certain categories are simply not relevant to this task of causal analysis. In order to develop a respectable physics, it was necessary to eliminate such concepts as "perfection," the "natural end" of a body, the "higher substances," and the like from scientific discourse. After we have sterilized a language for scientific purposes, however, we ought not to be surprised to find that we want to say things which we cannot say with the tools it provides; nor should we draw any earth-shaking conclusions from this fact. That a conception cannot be expressed within an impoverished language is one thing; that statements in the wider language must therefore *contradict* any true statements in the impoverished language is another, and it does not follow. (In fact, unless some special logical relations are set up, such a contradiction cannot occur because the contradictory of a statement in the richer language cannot even be *formulated* in the sublanguage and a fortiori cannot be proved therein.)

Consider, for example, such a statement as the following: "Raskolnikov, having committed a fallacy in his ethical reasoning, perpetrated a murder in the first degree; in so doing, he sinned." This rather simple, everyday account of a behavioral sequence cannot be expressed in psychologese. The phrase "committed murder" may perhaps be adequately translated as "struck the old lady with an axe, and she died as an immediate result. This outcome was among his expectancies, and his action was motivated by his cathexis of her money." "Murder in the first degree" is a legal conception; possibly it is adequately rendered by the translation in terms of the action and its motivation. The phrase "an ethical fallacy" involves ethical categories and also logical modalities, neither of which occur in psychologese. "Sin" is a theological category, and it also transcends the impoverished language. But it does not follow that our original statement *contradicts* any statement, or class of statements, which can be made and confirmed in psychologese. A complete learning-theory account of Raskolnikov's behavior would deal with his acquisition of the perceptual and motor skills involved in directing the hatchet blow; it would perhaps make use of "avarice" and "guilt" as state variables; possibly it would include certain theoretical assertions concerning unconscious mental processes. Given the idealized state of a "complete" learning theory, and the further idealization involved in assuming an exact knowledge of all of Raskolnikov's state variables and reinforcement history, the killing would be derivable as a consequence of the behavioral laws together with the momentary psychological conditions. This account would constitute attainment of the scientist's theoretical task, which is to show how a unique behavioral event instantializes the law network. The complete set of descriptive sentences does not, however, suffice to express the fallaciousness of Raskolnikov's ethical reasoning or his theological situation, because these concepts are not formulable in the purely descriptive, factual-causal language of psychologese.

But perhaps there is a still wider language, whose terms are co-ordinated in definite ways with terms or expressions in each of the two sublanguages, in such a manner that contradictions can be developed? This is conceivable. Consider a nontheological example involving ethical modalities. Suppose we have the following two propositions:

A. A ruler *ought* always to take those steps which maximize the state power.

B. Nobody *ought* to be punished for his thoughts.

Neither of these can be expressed in psychologese, because the word "ought" denotes an ethical (i. e., nonfactual) relation. Both of them are expressions in English, of which psychologese is a (technical) sublanguage, systematically impoverished by the elimination of ethical modalities. As the two stand, they are not contradictory. But if we now combine them with the large class of descriptive (empirical) statements which can be gleaned from textbooks of social psychology and political science, a contradiction emerges. It turns out that the nature of man and of his *de facto* political organizations is such that punishing people for their thoughts tends, on the whole, to maximize the state power. Hence the ruler is required to violate either prescription A or prescription B. Thus we see that a system of nondescriptive propositions, involving ethical categories not represented within an impoverished sublanguage, can *as a system* be "contradicted" by the empirical facts, in the sense that an ethical agent may find himself confronted with a reality situation for which the application of the ethical "rules" leads to incompatible obligation statements. (This, incidentally, is one easy refutation of the claim of classical Vienna positivism that ethical assertions are devoid of factual content.)

Returning to Raskolnikov, we are led to wonder whether the exhaustive psychological description of his behavior and its causes might, when juxtaposed with a theological account of the same facts, develop contradictions in some more encompassing language which includes propositions *relating* theological and psychological discourse. One such overarching proposition might be, "No one is guilty of sin if he acted predictably," where "predictably" = "instantializing natural laws" = "of necessity" = "by coercion." Conservative theology would of course deny this statement in its first form and would be joined by most non-Christian logical analysts in denying the final equality between "necessity" and "coercion." But having disposed of these initial too-easy equalities, we are then confronted with a problem in unscrambling conceptual relations so complex as to require a long treatise in itself.

This example perhaps suffices to illustrate our contention in the first paragraph of this note, that the compatibility of learning theory and theological formulations of the same behavioral event could be properly investigated only by means of detailed and rigorous logical analysis.

(I am greatly indebted to the Reverend Woodard Ching for many stimulating discussions, in the course of which this and related problems in co-ordinating psychological and theological discourse have been greatly clarified. — P. E. M.)

SUGGESTED READINGS

Bugelski, B. R. *The Psychology of Learning.* New York: Henry Holt and Company, 1956.

Dollard, John, and Neal E. Miller. *Personality and Psychotherapy.* New York: McGraw-Hill Book Co., 1950.

Keller, Fred S., and William N. Schoenfeld. *Principles of Psychology.* New York: Appleton-Century-Crofts, 1950.

Mowrer, O. H. *Learning Theory and Personality Dynamics.* New York: Ronald Press, 1950.

Skinner, Burrhus F. *Science and Human Behavior.* New York: Macmillan, 1953.

VI. Psychodynamics and Psychopathology

CONSIDERATION OF the emotional problems of human beings involves an almost unlimited number of factors. The same basic problem is presented by different persons in different forms, depending on their background, personality, and environment. Attempting to help resolve these problems presents further considerations which involve not only the person with the problem but also the person attempting to help, as well as the environment.

In this chapter we will attempt to classify and clarify the types of problems and their causes in order to indicate the function of those called on to help.

To many people not in the field of psychology or psychiatry the terminology used in discussing mental and emotional problems is confusing and often misleading. Actually, of course, this is a specialty which has its own specific terminology just as any other highly developed field, such as law, theology, and others. We will, however, attempt to clarify this terminology so as to give a basic knowledge of the broader aspects of the field.

There are several reasons for the confusion which exists in this field. One is the recent and rapid development of the study of mental and emotional problems and the heightened interest of the general public in these problems. In the early years of the century the psychiatrist worked almost exclusively in institutions for the insane. At the present time he is found in these institutions as well as in out-patient adult mental-hygiene and child-guidance clinics, in the Armed Forces, in schools, various

131

types of institutions, medical, surgical, and pediatric wards, with social agencies; in fact, the scope seems almost unlimited. With this increased scope and our increasing knowledge there have developed differences of opinion in the field, which are gradually being resolved. There has also appeared a fringe consisting of those who, even though not professionally trained, write articles merely to take advantage of the universal interest in this comparatively new and, to many people, mysterious field. Books, both fiction and nonfiction, which have as their basis some psychological problem, are assured of a good circulation. The same applies to plays and moving pictures.

There is grave danger in dealing with people's mental and emotional problems when one is not equipped with accurate knowledge of the subject and the factors involved. The solution is not a simple matter of advice and admonition. This chapter will attempt to clarify those things which are known and accepted at the present time as professionally accurate.

For our purposes we will consider primarily four chief types of mental illness, the four which comprise by far the majority of situations with which we have to deal. These are

1. Mental Deficiency
2. Psychoses
3. Psychoneuroses
4. Sociopathic Personality (formerly called Psychopathic Personality)

1. *Mental Deficiency* is that condition presenting an intellectual defect existing from birth. This defect includes all the mental functions — learning ability, reasoning, memory, and judgment, although not always in equal degrees. These patients are divided into subgroups, according to the extent of their deficiency, called Mild, Moderate, or Severe.

The diagnosis of mental deficiency and its degree is confirmed by intelligence tests. These tests are at present our most accurate gauges for measuring the mental age, which age, divided by the chronological age, will yield the "intelligence quotient," or I. Q. Thus a 10-year-old whose mental age is 7 has an I. Q. of 70. The average I. Q. at any age therefore is around 100. A person with the Mild type of mental deficiency cannot be expected ever to reach a mental level beyond that of a 12-year-old, the Moderate a mental age between 8 and 12, and the Severe a mental age of no more than 8 and sometimes much lower. Much research and study has been done on this condition, but we have as yet no clear answer as to its cause in many cases.

This condition is not amenable to any type of treatment that has been attempted up to this time, though study still goes on. The Severe type usually requires custodial care in an institution. The other types can sometimes be handled within the family, with understanding, supervision, and training. The parents usually need help in accepting this condition and planning for the future.

It must be realized that it is a severe blow to parents' pride as well as their hopes for the future to be confronted with the fact that their child is a mental defective. If no history of injury or other physical reason can be found, they frequently develop strong guilt feelings and regard this as punishment. They may recall that they did not want this child, or they may bring out some misdeed of theirs in the past for which they feel they are being punished. For instance, it may be the mother who had an affair with another man before marriage, or the father who had to be treated for a venereal disease at some time in the past. Any one of a number of factors can cause such severe guilt that it may even result in a complete mental breakdown. This must be handled on a realistic basis — that none of these is the causative factor, that the condition is biological, as was noted in Chapter IV. Then the guilt feelings need to be dealt with in a reassuring, positive way. This presents an opportunity for the pastor and the psychologist or psychiatrist to work together, and there should be no hesitation in arranging consultations to exchange knowledge and ideas.

2. *Psychoses* are those types of mental illness, formerly classed under the heading of "insanity," in which the person loses control over his action and in most cases is institutionalized, at least for a period of treatment. The psychoses are classified into specific categories:

        A. Schizophrenic Reaction
        B. Manic-Depressive Reaction
        C. Paranoid Reaction
        D. Involutional Psychotic Reaction

A. *Schizophrenic Reaction.* — This term is synonymous with the formerly used term "dementia praecox." This old term was applied because the disorder tends to make its first appearance in the late teens or early twenties, although it is not always diagnosed early. This illness is characterized by fundamental disturbances in reality relationships and concept formations and with emotional and behavioral disturbances in varying degrees. Most marked is a strong tendency to *retreat from reality*, a reality which has become too painful for the patient to face. These patients are divided into subgroups according to their specific symptoms.

In the *Simple Schizophrenic* there is little interest in the environment or in the persons around him. The chief characteristic is indifference and apathy, inability to carry through on any plans, and finally deterioration. These are the people who have no goal in life, who go from job to job, who have few or no friends, and who, unless they are institutionalized or supported by relatives, may end by eking out an existence on skid row for the men and prostitution for the women. In the early stages of the illness they do not as a rule exhibit severe symptoms and are often undiagnosed until deterioration sets in. They are recognized at first only as misfits. If they are diagnosed, there is a reluctance on the part of crowded mental hospitals to give them custodial care, since they are not considered a danger in the community. This is the group which some psychiatrists have referred to as ambulatory schizophrenics.

In the *Hebephrenic* type of schizophrenia the characteristics are inappropriate emotional reactions to situations, foolish conversation and behavior, delusions, and hallucinations, and often childish behavior, with a need usually for custodial care. A *delusion* is a belief which has no basis in fact, such as the unfounded paranoid belief that one is being poisoned, or the grandiose belief that one is Napoleon or some other famous person. A *hallucination* is a sensory or perceptual experience which has no basis in reality. There are visual hallucinations in which the person thinks he is seeing certain things which are actually not there, such as an animal who may be getting ready to attack him. Auditory hallucinations, which are more common, are the hearing of voices which are saying things to the patient, again when no one is speaking to him. They may be calling him bad names, or may be giving him instructions to do certain things. These delusions and hallucinations need to be recognized as such, since they make the patient potentially dangerous and they cannot be dealt with by reasoning.

In the *Catatonic* type, which is the least common, we find one of two characteristic types of behavior — stupor, mutism, and negativism, or excessive motor activity and excitement. These patients need institutional care.

The *Paranoid* type of schizophrenia is characterized by unrealistic thinking, chiefly with delusions of persecution and delusions of grandeur, often accompanied by hallucinations. There is an attitude of hostility and aggression, and the patient shows unpredictable behavior. These are the patients who make unprovoked attacks on other persons and can be a danger to their family and the community. The pastor should be alert to the possibility of this dangerous condition whenever a parishioner begins to speak of people talking about him, "having it in for him," following or plotting against him. These are grave danger signals. Psychiatric advice should be sought without delay in cases of this kind. One needs only to read the newspapers to see examples of innocent people, sometimes even unknown to the patient, who are attacked, often with serious results.

B. *Manic-Depressive Reaction.* — This type of psychosis is characterized by severe mood swings, with a tendency to recovery and then recurrence. In the manic phase the reaction is one of elation or irritability, with overtalkativeness, flight of ideas, and increased physical activity. In the depressive phase there is an outstanding mood of depression with inhibition of mental and physical activity and frequently uneasiness and apprehension. These patients sometimes recover from an attack spontaneously, but frequently have to be hospitalized. In all cases of depression one needs to be aware of the danger of suicide. The depressed patient should be referred to a psychiatrist for evaluation and treatment.

C. *Paranoid Reaction.* — This is the group which shows persistent delusions, either delusions of persecution or of grandeur or both. The emotional responses and behavior are consistent with the ideas held. Intelligence, however, is often well preserved for some time, and the person is able to function to a certain extent until deterioration sets in. In general the personality is preserved more intact than in the paranoid form of schizophrenia. These are the cases, for instance, in which the person can hold a position and do the work adequately, but is convinced, without foundation in fact, that he is unfairly treated by his immediate superior or by the company. Some of these people can be very convincing in their reasoning until all the facts are known. It is desirable when possible to obtain information from independent sources.

D. *Involutional Reaction.* — These are the symptoms which occasionally occur in the involutional (change of life) period. The chief symptom is severe depression in a person who has not previously been subject to it. Other symptoms commonly found are worry, insomnia, strong guilt feelings (often about insignificant things or things which happened in the past), anxiety, agitation, delusions, and preoccupation with physical symptoms. This type of illness is most common in persons with a compulsive personality (perfectionists). It occurs in men as well as in women, though it is less common in men and comes at a somewhat later age, usually at the end of the sixth decade. Here also, as in the manic-depressive depressions, there is grave danger of suicide, particularly because these patients are characteristically not "slowed down" and can therefore take resolute and clever steps to carry out their self-destructive impulses.

3. *Psychoneuroses* (also called neuroses). — Included in this term are a number of symptoms — anxieties, conversion reactions (displacement of one symptom for another, as in psychosomatic illness), phobias, obsessive compulsion reactions (the overpowering urge to do certain things and to do them in a certain way), depressions. In contrast with the psychoses these patients have a good sense of reality and no disorganization of the personality. They may function well until some particular stress arouses their anxiety and results in severe symptoms which make it difficult for them to carry on, but they are well aware of their difficulties. As a matter of fact, it is felt that most persons have some of these reactions in a mild form (various phobias, such as the common

136

fear of height, compulsions, such as the need always to be a little ahead of time for an appointment, or perfectionism in housekeeping). Unless, however, these reactions develop to such an extent as to interfere with adequate functioning in everyday life, no particular attention is paid to them.

We have gone into some detail in giving symptoms, especially in the psychoses, since it is important to be able to evaluate a person's mental condition in terms of his own best interest and that of the community. We have also attempted to point out that there are gradations of emotional illness. One cannot simply call a person normal or abnormal. The psychotic should be referred to a psychiatrically trained physician, and if he resists this, it should be done through his family.

In addition to the conditions described above, there are others, not so commonly encountered and not lending themselves to counseling. These include the mental illnesses found in connection with certain diseases, as well as the mental deterioration which comes with senility. There is also an increasing awareness of the problem of sexual perversions, particularly attacks on children and homosexuality. These are due to deeply rooted emotional problems and require expert evaluation and advice as to handling. The same is true of the serious and apparently increasing problem of alcoholism and other forms of addiction. Many persons, both pastors and psychotherapists, feel that the answer to alcoholic addiction has been found in the group called Alcoholics Anonymous. Actually this does seem to work out better than the usually accepted forms of psychotherapy or counseling, which do not seem to fill the need of the alcoholic or perhaps do not provide the needed acceptance. An attempt is being made to organize similar groups for drug addicts.

4. *Sociopathic Personality.* — This type was formerly classified under the term Psychopathic Personality. It is an inclusive term, which designates those persons who are unable to adjust to society on what might be termed a "moral" level. They have no evidence of possessing a conscience or of being able to develop one. In fact, they usually seem markedly free of anxiety. This is the classification under which one is likely to find the habitual criminal, the pathological and convincing liar, the confidence man. He is often difficult to identify for what he is, since

137

he has excellent powers of rationalization. He is found at every economic and educational level. He is generally thought to be beyond help, since he shows no guilt or anxiety and seems satisfied with his way of living. The only regret he may have is in being stupid enough to get caught in his transgressions when he is caught. Being caught may deter him, at least for a short time, but he returns to his ways with the determination to be cleverer next time. These people have an inability to delay their gratifications and to work toward distant goals. In school they often fail to achieve their potential. They react poorly to routine, resent discipline or authority, and like to "stir up some excitement." In spite of their superficial sociability, they are basically cold, unable to form deep emotional relationships to others, and they characteristically exploit those about them. These people may be highly intelligent, with a misleading "charm" which leads people into believing their stories.

5. *Behavior Problems of Children.* — The fact that children have always presented problems in their behavior is certainly one that must be accepted. However, it seems that in our present-day culture this has presented itself as a major problem. Many schools and children's institutions employ psychologists and psychiatrists to help them cope with the numerous and varied problems presented, both in the academic learning and in the adjustment areas. Parents, too, come for help in dealing with their children who "have got out of hand." In fact, the entire country is now covered with child-guidance clinics, whose function is to help children, their parents, and others dealing with children, through the use of psychiatrically trained social workers, psychologists, and psychiatrists.

The forerunner of the present-day child-guidance clinic was a clinic set up in the Juvenile Court of Cook County in Chicago to study the children who were in difficulty, to try to determine the factors operating in each case, and thus to find out if there were some common factors which might be eliminated. In the hope of preventing serious delinquency, this clinic was gradually extended to include those children who presented problems but had not yet been in difficulty with the law. Eventually the clinic was taken over by the State of Illinois and became one of the original child-guidance clinics. Then a national organization of persons interested in mental hygiene set up pilot clinics in various communities, and thus the movement was started. Today all these clinics have long waiting lists and cannot begin to fill the need which exists.

What is a problem child? A simple definition seems to be that it is a child who causes concern or discomfort to any of the adults in his environment. Thus a child may present problems at home but not in school or with his peers. Another may present problems at school but not in the home. Another child may be considered a problem by someone not acquainted with the expected behavior of children, when he is only reacting normally to an expected situation. For example, the 10-year-old boy who came home with a bloody nose because he was in a fight with another boy who called him a bad name; or the teen-age girl who argues with her mother about the clothes she should wear. To the girl it is extremely important that she dress like the other girls in order to maintain her status, while her mother has preconceived ideas of what a girl this age should wear. The mother is not aware that she herself changes her styles from time to time in order to fit in with the changing styles of her own group. One girl was brought in because she had had a temper tantrum when she found that her mother had beautifully cleaned her saddle shoes. In her particular group saddle shoes were supposed to be dirty and to look disreputable. In other words, before a child is considered a problem, one must take into consideration the normal aspects of children's behavior. Many parents have become so frightened at the specter of the "problem child" that they lose their perspective in dealing with their children. In its simplest terms from the point of view of psychiatry one might say that a problem child is one who shows behavior unacceptable in his own culture according to the standards set by his family and the community.

Why is a problem child? In this connection it should be mentioned that some psychiatrists and psychologists, including Freud, put considerable emphasis upon hereditary or "constitutional" factors, which produce a differential *readiness* to develop personality difficulties under comparable conditions. The quantitative importance of the hereditary factor is a matter of disagreement among qualified experts and is not resolvable on the basis

139

of present evidence. To the extent that it is operative, the "responsibility" of parents for the child's maladjustment would be lessened. The tendency at the present time, however, is to place the blame for problem children on the parents. This has basic validity, but the mere statement that parents are responsible for the fact that their children are problems is an oversimplification. In other words, merely placing the blame is not even the beginning of the solution. One must go much further and inquire into the problems of the parents. Intellectual limitations, resentment at the responsibilities involved, indifference, immaturity with its poor judgment and dependence on the advice of others — these are just a few of the problems with which parents need help. Very few parents are consciously resentful of, or indifferent to, their children. However, the husband or wife who has had all the attention of the spouse may resent, possibly unconsciously, having to share this with a child. In the same way parents frequently resent the intense interest their parents show in the grandchildren and may even express this with: "You never fussed over me or spoiled me that way."

A bad neighborhood will increase the tendency to delinquency. Why do parents stay in these neighborhoods? This is a complex social and individual problem.

Another factor which operates is one for which the professional psychologists and psychiatrists themselves have been responsible. Some thirty years ago, when psychotherapy and psychoanalysis began to have great impetus, it was felt that many problems were due to the repression made necessary by the rigid discipline and standards which had been imposed. It seemed obvious that to help establish good mental health these standards should be relaxed, and thus the cult of "permissiveness" was advanced. Actually it did not take long for the therapists to become aware that the answer was not so simple. Children brought up in a permissive atmosphere had problems, too, although of a different type. The pendulum then swung to a middle ground, where it is felt that children must have direction and discipline and that limits must definitely be set on their behavior, though with understanding and affection. However, many parents still cling to the idea of permissiveness, chiefly because it relieves them of the responsibility of enforcing discipline. Many immature or indifferent parents also tend to depend on outside agencies to help in the training and discipline of their children. This often begins in nursery school and goes through elementary and high school and includes camps, boy or girl scouts, YMCA and YWCA, and the Sunday school and church. None of these agencies can replace the parents, who have the guidance of the child from the moment of birth.

In any case where we are dealing with a problem in a child's behavior, there must be an evaluation of the feelings of the child, the feeling of both parents toward him and their own problems, which may be reflected in their treatment of him. For instance, we have the "self-made man," brought up in poverty, who gets a vicarious satisfaction in seeing that his son does not lack for any of the material things, a big allowance, a car of his own, etc. Or we may get the opposite reaction of the father who is successful and resents his son's comparatively easy life and therefore deprives him of the things his peers have. Then there is the mother who may have a serious and studious daughter but insists on many clothes and a full social life for the girl so that the mother herself can enjoy the things she longed for and never had. Examples of the problems of parents being expressed through their children are as numerous as the problems of the children.

What is the answer? The answer is a simple statement, but its implementation is frequently difficult. All parents make what might be considered mistakes in the bringing up of their children. They sometimes punish unjustly without knowing it, and in other ways hurt their children. Some parents are too strict, some too lenient. However, after years of study of parents and children we have come to a simple conclusion. Good behavior is not dependent on the fear of punishment or the hope of a reward. A child does what pleases the parent because of love of the parent and identification with him, a love which he gives because the parent first loved him. In a mutual love relationship neither will knowingly hurt the other, though there are certain to be incidents when there will be a fall from grace. But with love there is true forgiveness. Therefore our objective in dealing with children who are behavior problems is to foster a mutual love by giving both child and parents an understanding of their under-

141

lying problems with a hope that a recognition of these will solve the problems. Sometimes this will even have to be done by providing a substitute parent, such as a foster parent.

This fits in with the concept of the Christian doctrine, in which one leads a Christian life because of a love of God and confidence in His love for us, rather than from a fear of punishment or reward in the hereafter.

In order to help us understand our own thinking and that of others we should spend some time in the study of *mental mechanisms.* These are certain processes of thought in which everyone indulges, but one needs to be able to recognize an exaggeration which is causing trouble or may be the symptom of a severe emotional illness or psychosis. A knowledge of these devices will deepen one's understanding of both normal and psychotic behavior.

Mental mechanisms are those methods by which persons strive to protect the personality, satisfy its emotional needs, solve conflicting tendencies, maintain the self-image, and alleviate anxiety. They help to preserve self-esteem by an unconscious denial of unacceptable thoughts or tendencies. They are not indulged in deliberately but are unconscious reactions to certain situations. They are acquired by the processes of learning, of reward and punishment, which have been set forth in Chapter V. *Repression,* for example, is acquired by repeated experiences of disapproval and punishment for actions *and for verbalized tendencies to actions.* At first we merely hide our forbidden impulses from our parents; later we become so skilled at this hiding process that we deceive ourselves as well. The reward (reinforcement) for this intrapsychic tactic is the immediate goal of lessened anxiety. So with the other mental mechanisms to be described. While they may be inefficient or even (as in the neurotic) harmful in the long run, in the short run they are effective in protecting us from dread, conscious guilt feeling, and loss of self-esteem. The following are the commonest types:

Repression. — The process by which the individual excludes from his consciousness desires, impulses, thoughts, and strivings which are contrary to the ideal which he has set up for himself.

142

For instance, hatred of a parent, which is unacceptable both from a cultural and from a religious standpoint, is repressed so that the individual is unaware of it. This illustration will serve to show that the mental mechanisms are able to serve a useful function, since the guilt engendered by the admission of such feelings could be the cause of a great deal of severe emotional conflict and even breakdown. The mechanism of repression should be distinguished from *suppression,* in which the attention of the individual is deliberately directed elsewhere when the undesired material appears in conscious thought.

Sublimation. — The substitution of an acceptable and useful form of activity for selfish and possibly destructive impulses. The soldier who is decorated for destroying a large number of the enemy may actually be sublimating his innate hostile, aggressive, and destructive impulses.

Rationalization. — The process by which we justify questionable actions by advancing a legitimate reason which provides a rational, intellectually acceptable explanation. This is not done consciously but arises from the need to maintain self-esteem or to salve our conscience. Thus when we have some task to do, we can convince ourselves that an afternoon of golf will help us to relax, and we will feel so much better that when we do approach the task, we will be more efficient.

Compensation. — An attempt to adjust to inadequacies in a way by which the person can obtain the recognition he craves. The student who is not popular with his classmates may make a special effort to excel in scholarship in order to satisfy his need for success.

Symbolization. — A mechanism whereby one idea or object is employed to represent some other idea or object. It is used to avoid direct expression of fears or other unacceptable thoughts. An example of this is the good-luck charm.

Displacement. — The mechanism by which an emotional feeling is transferred from some really important object or experience to a substitute and relatively unimportant object or experience. Thus a child who is forced to forgo some pleasure in order to care for a younger brother or sister will displace the resentment she feels against the mother, who imposed this upon her, to the child for whom she must care, since this is the more acceptable reaction.

Projection. — The process by which those deficiencies, wishes, and motives which one may not consciously acknowledge as his own are transferred to others. A basically dishonest person is likely to be suspicious of the honesty and motives of others.

Identification. — That mechanism by which we attach to ourselves certain qualities or elements associated with the personality of another. This may be found in the boy who admires his father and intends to follow his calling, or in the boy who admires an athlete, or pathologically in the psychotic with delusions of grandeur who imagines he is Napoleon.

Escape. — An effort to avoid the tensions and unpleasant realities of life by indulging in some activity which gives satisfaction. This is used at some time or other by everyone. It may be the busy executive who reads mystery stories, the bored housewife who watches TV, or pathologically, the unhappy child who does excessive daydreaming, the adult who becomes an alcoholic, or finally, the schizophrenic who rejects reality entirely and lives in a dream world of his own.

Reaction-Formation. — The familiar device in which a person unconsciously covers up an unacceptable impulse by working very hard at doing the opposite. We have all seen the hostess who is especially nice to the person she would really rather not have had at the party anyway. The mother who unconsciously rejects her child may be overprotective of him and make many sacrifices in order to give him material things.

Conversion. — An impulse is expressed, or the environment is unconsciously controlled, through the medium of a physical symptom. For example, a hysterical girl enacts an erotic fantasy in the form of a convulsion; a workman becomes "blind" after an industrial accident, even though his eyes were not organically injured. Such psychologically engendered symptoms, superficially mimicking organic disease, are called "functional." (The term *conversion* was originally chosen because of Freud's theory that sexual energy was somehow "converted" into the energy of the symptom and thereby indirectly expressed itself.)

144

In our consideration of the mental mechanisms we have mentioned the unconscious. This concept, frequently difficult for persons not trained in this field to understand and accept, needs further elaboration here. Experiences, thoughts, motivations, and memories which are unacceptable and painful to us are repressed into the unconscious. It is therefore helpful in letting us live our daily lives without the fears, doubts, and guilt feelings which would interfere with our satisfactory functioning. The existence of the unconscious is obvious in many aspects of our living without our conscious realization. The forgetting, the slips of the tongue, the associations we have with certain ideas, our use of mental mechanisms, all point to a part of our mind over which we have no control. Neurotic symptoms are alleviated by bringing out of the unconscious some material which has significance in terms of the symptom presented. In the psychotic the existence of the unconscious is indicated when one listens to the material which he brings out during his psychotic episodes. For instance, the formerly quiet, inhibited person may use profanity or express sexual thoughts and desires. The usually and normally friendly person will express all his repressed hatred and resentment. All these are bringing material from the unconscious because the defenses have been broken down by some strain with which the personality could not cope.

TREATMENT

A discussion of present-day mental and emotional problems needs to include some clarification of the many types of treatment available and in use.

Psychotherapy. — This is a type of treatment conducted by interviews in which an attempt is made to help the patient solve his problems by reassurance, suggestion, clarification of feelings, uncovering of the presence of various mental mechanisms which are operating, and help in substituting positive values for the negatives in the patient's attitudes. This type of treatment is administered by psychiatrists, clinical psychologists, and social workers who have had specialized training in the concepts of psychiatry. This is at present the type of treatment most in use.

Psychoanalysis. — This is a highly specialized type of therapy, administered by psychiatrists who, in addition to their prescribed psychiatric training, have taken several years of work in the theory and practice of psychoanalysis. They also undergo a personal analysis, since it is felt that one is better equipped to help other people if one first can solve one's own problems. Psychoanalysis is a long process, involving a minimum of three one-hour sessions weekly and continued for two or more years. It is used in those cases in which the neurotic is so incapacitated by his neurosis that he is unable to function adequately or to adjust to his environment. These are the persons who cannot respond to the usual psychotherapy.

Shock Therapy. — Insulin or electrical stimulation sufficient to produce unconsciousness and convulsions are used in certain severe mental conditions, where the patient needs to be helped quickly to overcome serious illness. This form of treatment, called "shock therapy," is less used than formerly, since it has been found that some conditions are not alleviated and may even become worse, because it is a frightening experience for many patients. It is usually used in institutions because of the need for close supervision during its use. Ideally it is accompanied by psychotherapy so that an effort can be made to determine the cause of the breakdown which made the therapy necessary and to prevent a recurrence. In most instances shock therapy is now limited to the treatment of the symptom of psychotic depressions.

Medication. — There are now available to physicians an almost unlimited number of drugs with which to treat symptoms, even in some of the psychoses, though the result here is variable and lasts only as long as the patient continues the drug. The extravagant claims recently made for drug therapy have not been entirely substantiated. In any case medication is only a palliative, and unless the underlying problem is resolved, there is a recurrence or the medication loses its effect. Therefore the administration of these drugs is ideally accompanied by psychotherapy.

Surgery. — Within the last two decades an attempt has been made to alleviate some of the symptoms of mental illness by a surgical procedure called lobotomy. In simple terms, this involves cutting into the brain and severing nerve paths which are

146

thought to control behavior. Much work has been done on all types of patients. The present status of this type of treatment is that it is confined to the treatment of severely disturbed, unmanageable patients in institutions, since it does quiet them and make them more tractable in most instances.

It would seem helpful at this point to clarify some of the ideas and particularly misconceptions concerning the profession and practice of psychiatry. It is not a mystical, mysterious type of thinking which attempts to break down all of a person's previous concepts and ideals. It is most helpful to think of it as what it really is, a branch of medicine which has developed as a result of exhaustive studies on the part of psychologists and psychiatrists. It might be likened to surgery, which received its first real impetus with the discovery of anaesthetics and still continues to develop and progress, helped by constant research and study of new techniques and new anaesthetics.

As in other fields of medicine, there is first a study of the history, the symptoms and their duration, and their possible or probable cause. Then treatment is prescribed, according to the experience and convictions of the physician. One should not be too much concerned if there is not always agreement among the physicians or if different physicians use different treatment for what is seemingly the same condition. This occurs in all branches of medicine and surgery and is based on the honest opinion of the diagnostician and his experience with previous similar cases.

Many of the resistances to, and misunderstandings of, present-day psychiatry stem from the fact that it is equated with the teachings of Freud and the feeling that he placed an overemphasis on sex and its conflicts. Many persons manifest their own conflicts about this subject by their need to avoid any discussion of it and their overreaction to any reference to it. Actually the sex drive is one of the basic instincts for self-preservation and preservation of the race, and it is our own reactions which have made it unacceptable for discussion on a factual and rational basis. Ethical and well-trained psychiatrists do not advocate excessive sexuality. They realize, possibly better than anyone else, that sexual license creates problems rather than ameliorating them. An excess or perversion of *any* of the instincts (or appetites), such, for instance, as eating, gives rise to conflicts and problems. One should again refer to the whole field of medicine and realize that Freud made his pronouncements and advanced his theories in an age and culture different from ours and that subsequent studies have modified them, just as other medical teachings have changed. If one questions a theory or type of treatment used by a doctor, one has a right to challenge it.

The fact that emotional problems are so often based on sex conflicts is a reflection on our need to repress all thoughts, desires, and conversations concerning this subject. Stories concerning this subject are universal, but are thought of as "dirty" stories. Marriage is considered sacred, and it is felt that it should be performed in a religious setting, but the sexual implications of marriage are very likely to be the subject of jokes. Also, there is in many instances no preparation on the part of the pastor or the church for this very important aspect of a person's life. Some of those Christians who take their religion most seriously are most inhibited in this aspect and are only too glad to turn over to mass education in schools and the unsupervised use of sex-instruction booklets the problem of acquainting their children with an important aspect of their Christian life. It seems to follow that our obvious avoidance of discussion of this one particular subject will make it more mysterious and interesting to the children placed in our care, and the problems of repression in this area will continue to be present.

Addendum

There is frequently some confusion in the minds of persons not in the psychiatric field as to the qualifications and functions of the professions involved. The following descriptions are an attempt to clarify this confusion.

A *psychiatrist* is an M. D. who has had specialized training in the field of psychiatry. The American Psychiatric Association requires five years of work devoted exclusively to the study and practice of psychiatry for a doctor to be eligible for the examination which qualifies him as a specialist in psychiatry, competent to diagnose and treat mental and emotional illnesses.

A *psychologist* is a Ph. D. who has done his undergraduate and graduate study on the mental life and behavior of humans

148

and animals, with emphasis upon experimental methods, the other social sciences, and philosophy.

A *clinical psychologist*, in addition to these basic academic studies, must have done supervised clinical work in the diagnosis and psychotherapy of mental patients. To obtain the Diploma in Clinical Psychology as a practical specialty, he must present five years of clinical experience in a medical setting beyond the date of his doctorate and pass a further theoretical and practical examination. Clinical psychologists are not physicians and hence do not prescribe or carry out medical treatments (such as shock, drugs, or surgery). They are now certified or licensed under the laws of sixteen states.

A *psychiatric social worker* is a person with a degree in social work and several years of specialized courses and training in clinics associated with the specialty of psychiatry. The psychiatric social worker works in close collaboration with the psychiatrists and psychologists and sometimes does counseling under the supervision of a psychiatrist.

It is felt desirable that the people in this field should themselves experience some counseling, psychotherapy, or psychoanalysis in order to clear up any personal problems, since it is felt that adequate work in these areas is best done by persons who are themselves well adjusted.

SUGGESTED READINGS

Maslow, Abraham H., and Bela Mittelman. *Principles of Abnormal Psychology*. Revised Edition. New York: Harper and Brothers, 1951.

Menninger, Karl A. *The Human Mind*. 3d ed. New York: Knopf, 1945.

Munroe, Ruth. *Schools of Psychoanalytic Thought*. New York: Dryden Press, 1955.

Noyes, Arthur P. *Modern Clinical Psychiatry*. 4th ed. Baltimore: W. B. Saunders, 1953.

White, Robert W. *The Abnormal Personality*. 2d ed. New York: Ronald Press, 1956.

Josselyn, Irene M., M. D. *The Happy Child*. New York: Random House, 1955.

Levy, John, M. D., and Ruth Munroe. *The Happy Family*. New York: Alfred A. Knopf, 1938.

Preston, George H., M. D. *Psychiatry for the Curious*. New York: Farrar and Rinehart, 1940.

VII. Tensions Between Psychology and Theology

SOME OF THE PROBLEMS which arise when a psychotherapist tries to help a Christian patient, or when a pastor in the course of his ministry has occasion to deal with a parishioner who has personality difficulties, have their origin in doctrinal issues. Even though these issues arise in a practical context, and without taking the form of a theological or philosophical dispute, they nevertheless reflect doctrinal frictions or confusions at several levels and in various degrees of explicitness. When the aims and tactics of pastor and psychotherapist seem to be getting in each other's way, it is sometimes difficult to tease out the precise locus of a cognitive disagreement, because they use largely nonoverlapping terminologies. There are two opposite and extreme reactions which can be found among pastors and psychotherapists in dealing with the conflicts and anxieties that their interplay sometimes produces. One "solution" is to say: "There isn't any conflict, and there couldn't be any." (This approach can further be subdivided into two lines of thinking, one being: "The two are just talking about the same concepts but in different words," the other being: "They are talking about two completely separate and unrelated domains; therefore how can they be in conflict?") A second solution — fortunately rare nowadays — is to say: "There is a conflict, and it is of such a rock-bottom character that we'd better have nothing to do with those other fellows."

We believe that all three of these approaches are unsound

150

and not based upon an adequate analysis of the practical and conceptual situation. While we shall not pretend to resolve the problems, and may even raise some disturbing questions that the reader had not been bothered by up to now, this course has seemed to us wiser than that of seizing upon easy oversimplifications (such as, "Freud and St. Paul are really saying the same thing"), or trying to sidestep certain problems by ignoring them. The Missouri Synod is not historically given to glossing over doctrinal conflicts, but rather insists upon bringing them out into the open so that all may see what is being said by whom. Since psychology also teaches that real conflicts are not solved by repressing them, but that they return to plague us in devious ways, both pastors and psychotherapists should favor the "uncovering" orientation we have adopted.

Anyone who has talked or corresponded with a fair number of pastors and psychotherapists quickly discerns that one of the first conditions for two people to work together effectively — that of understanding each other's views and aims — is often lacking. Individual psychiatrists and psychologists are frequently products of essentially irreligious (or modernist Protestant) homes, and nothing in their social or educational history has given them even a superficial exposure to the perspectives and vocabulary of Christian orthodoxy. It is probable that if one were to ask a random number of clinical psychologists or psychiatrists what Luther's view of justification involved, the vast majority would not have any idea. Terms such as justification, sanctification, sacrament, original sin, remission, power of the keys, stewardship, election, salvation, and the like, either do not mean anything at all or have mainly a faint negative emotional quality. On the other side, very few pastors have had any formal instruction in the basic principles of psychology, child development, psychopathology, or mental hygiene. The mechanisms of defense (Chapter VI) which are the daily, routine stock-in-trade of psychology, are often a foreign language to the working pastor.

Even if there were no overt frictions, this situation of mutual ignorance would of itself tend to produce diffidence, hostility, and wariness. After all, both the pastor and the secular healer are working with *people;* and both are trying, in some sense,

151

to improve the "condition" of these people. Yet they seem to each other to think in a wholly different way and to use an esoteric jargon. It is hardly surprising that the feeling should arise, with varying degrees of self-insight: "That fellow is poaching on my territory and using secret weapons besides." Needless to say, one main purpose of this book is to clear up some of the mystery — at least that part of it which is due to lack of information. Even a non-Christian psychotherapist can at least come to know what his Christian patients or their pastors are talking about when they speak in the religious vocabulary. Similarly the pastor who studies this book should be able to follow most of what a co-operative psychotherapist conveys to him about a parishioner.

A special source of confusion, partly due to ignorance but deserving of special mention, is semantic in character. For example, there are cases in which the two vocabularies do overlap, in that they use the same word; but unfortunately the word is being used in two quite different ways. The word "guilt" provides a sorry example of this type of semantic problem. When a psychotherapist speaks about "guilt," it is almost always short for "guilt *feeling*," i. e., a psychological event or state. (Even so-called "unconscious guilt" is of this character, since a logical analysis of its technical usage shows that it is similar to bound anxiety, in that there is an inner signal which elicits a defensive response that avoids the fully developed conscious guilt experience.) Now when the pastor or theologian speaks of guilt, he does not intend to designate a *feeling;* he refers to an objective ethical or forensic relation between a man and God (or between a man and another man). To *feel* guilty and to *be* guilty are, quite obviously, not the same thing. Nor are these two (logically) distinguishable states found to exist in direct proportion. One man may feel terribly guilty because he played a game of checkers Sunday afternoon, while another may be remarkably lighthearted about having committed murder. Now it is one of the usual aims of psychotherapy to explore the patient's feelings of guilt, particularly those which are hooked up with matters of which the patient is unaware and about which, when he confronts them, he often sees less reason to feel currently guilty. As one secular therapist has put it: "The trouble with most neurotics is that they actually feel guilty about quite other things than the ones they *should* feel guilty about."

If, in the course of therapy, a neurotic individual improves, the therapist may say (with approval): "He is getting over some of his guilt." Suppose, for instance, that the patient constantly injured himself (fell downstairs, cut himself shaving, exposed himself needlessly to infections, had puzzling auto accidents) because of his unconscious need for punishment; and suppose that he needed to punish himself because as a small boy he resented his young brother, who died suddenly and left the patient with the unconscious notion: "I resented him; he died; so I killed him." Obviously the clearing up of this mess of psychological forces is a thing to be desired. No pastor would hold that it is religiously fitting or socially desirable for a 30-year-old man to drive his car dangerously because he (without knowing it) is trying to atone for a childhood fantasy that he murdered his little brother! But when the pastor, not knowing these details, hears simply the claim: "We are helping to free him from guilt," he naturally doesn't interpret it this way. He takes the psychotherapist to be saying either: "I am removing his guilt" (which the pastor knows that only Christ has done), or else: "I am convincing him that he *has* no objective guilt" (which the pastor rightly sees as counseling impenitence if done apart from the Gospel). So here the double use of the same word "guilt" as meaning both *objective guiltiness* and *guilt feeling* has led to a needless conflict.

The "lifting of repression" is a phrase often having a similar semantic fate. *Repression* is a technical term taken from psychoanalytic theory, and it means the *unconscious inhibiting of the (inner) expression of an impulse or idea in the interest of momentary anxiety avoidance.* When a therapist helps the patient to undo a repression, he is actually helping him to *confront,* as honestly as possible, the character of one of his own impulses or attitudes. There is no implication here that, once the hidden impulse is revealed and confronted, the patient must then go and act it out in order to be healed. Freud described three ways of handling our unacceptable impulses: to repress, to suppress, and to renounce. To repress is to "put out of mind" unconsciously;

153

when we repress, we do not know that we are doing it, even at the time. To suppress is to put out of mind consciously, but with a minimum of confrontation and in the interest of momentary anxiety reduction. We say: "I won't think of this; I will put it aside, I will think of something else; I will try to ignore this feeling and hope it will go away." This tactic is less dangerous to mental health than is repression. Finally, we may confront the impulse squarely, take a long look at it, examine it unblinkingly, and (for either moral or selfish reasons, or both) deliberately and consciously renounce it. In this case we have not hidden it from ourselves or fostered an erroneous self-picture. Freud, although an atheist, saw clearly that the maintenance of even our modicum of civil righteousness necessitated frequent and drastic acts of renunciation (see especially his *Civilization and Its Discontents*).[1] He once complained that certain of his critics, misunderstanding the therapeutic undoing of repressions to be the advocacy of license, seemed to think that psychoanalysis advised taking a can of wieners and sauerkraut into the opera house just in case one might be assailed by hunger pangs during the third act of *Lohengrin*.

We do not, of course, mean to deny that there are a few secular psychotherapists who do counsel impenitence and license. If a psychiatrist or psychologist is himself an atheist, he may have come to adopt a code of morality, especially of sexual morality, which is anti-Christian. Even if he intends to remain "ethically neutral" in his treatment of patients (a feat difficult, if not impossible, to accomplish), it is easy for his unconscious choice of words to reflect his own moral attitudes. There is some experimental evidence to show that patients in therapy tend to identify with their therapists' value orientation and to converge toward it, especially when the therapy is successful. But this is a matter which will vary with the individual therapist. The point is, that while a particular therapist may, in the course of uncovering and relieving neurotic guilt feelings, also indoctrinate an unchristian point of view of objective guilt, this is a personal failing on his part and not a consequence logically intrinsic to

---

[1] London: Hogarth Press, 1953.

154

the theoretical tactic of "alleviating neurotic guilt." Similarly, a physician treating a man for infection with gonorrhea might, in trying to relieve the patient's anxiety about his health, make remarks which convey the physician's personal point of view about sexual contact with prostitutes. But this is not a necessary consequence of either the penicillin injection or the medical reassurance that recovery will follow. And the same is true for the relation between lifting repressions and subtly counseling immoral conduct.

A third source of difficulty is in the general area of "open questions," theological or scientific. There are concepts in the two disciplines which seem as if they should have mutual implications and which are sometimes juxtaposed rather uncritically. Some of these will be examined at length in the latter part of this chapter. For present illustration we may choose the concept of determinism mentioned in Chapter III. One sometimes hears it said that Lutheranism is more compatible with the current scientific *Weltanschauung* than Romanism is, because the latter theology insists upon free will, which Lutherans repudiate. All the same, many Lutheran students find themselves in great conflict when they study psychology and sociology at secular universities, because they perceive (as do most of the professors) the doctrine of scientific determinism as there taught to be incompatible with any meaningful kind of moral accountability. Most secular psychologists see the belief in some kind of "choice," involving radical unpredictability, as a part of Christian teaching which is fundamental to it and which they repudiate in one of the three forms of determinism described in Chapter III. The article "II: Of Free Will" in the Formula of Concord lists as the first of the contrary false doctrines under this heading "The delirium of philosophers who are called Stoics, as also of the Manicheans, who taught that everything that happens must so happen, and cannot happen otherwise, and that everything that man does, even in outward things, he does by compulsion, and that he is coerced to evil works and deeds, as inchastity, robbery, murder, theft, and the like" (*Conc. Triglotta,* p. 789). Does this confessional statement deal with "scientific determinism"? The first half, referring to the idea that "everything that happens must so

155

happen," would be acceptable to most contemporary scientific determinists; the second half, which the confession seems to treat as merely another way of saying the same thing, or at least a consequence of it, speaks of men being "coerced," a way of speaking which many contemporary determinists would reject *even though holding the first*. This is not the place to develop the intricacies involved, since we are here only giving an illustration. The point is that such concepts as *determination, predictability, necessity, coercion, possibility, choice,* and *freedom* are all extremely complex ideas; their interrelations are still in need of logical clarification, quite apart from the theological mysteries which touch upon them.[2, 3, 4] It is surely rash, if not absurd, to identify Luther's thesis of *De servo arbitrio* or St. Paul's doctrine of election with contemporary scientific determinism! Yet, if "free will" is taken to be the contradictory of "determinism," the Scriptural and confessional denial of free will would automatically be an assertion of determinism. This in itself suffices to show that the problem is not a simple one and that one cannot begin by equating all concepts designated by the term "free will" in different writings.

There are mysteries of the faith which seem (to the rare psychologist who hears of them) to present scientific difficulties. One such is the doctrine of election, particularly as combined with the Lutheran denial of reprobation. We teach that those who are converted are moved by the Holy Spirit, and that the selection of some, the elect, to be so moved is not based upon any characteristic which they possess prior to conversion. The consistent denial of synergism by orthodox Lutherans suggests to the philosophical-minded psychologist that no advancement of his science could, in principle, ever enable him to predict who would be converted by even the most exhaustive scientific knowl-

---

[2] Antony Flew, "Divine Omnipotence and Human Freedom," in *New Essays in Philosophical Theology,* ed. Antony Flew and Alasdair Macintyre (New York: Macmillan, 1955), pp. 144—169.

[3] R. E. Hobart, "Free Will as Involving Determinism and Inconceivable Without It," *Mind,* XLIII (1934).

[4] University of California Associates. "The Freedom of the Will," in *Readings in Philosophical Analysis,* ed. H. Feigl and W. S. Sellars (New York: Appleton-Century-Crofts, 1949), pp. 594—615.

edge of the preconversion history of an individual.[5] At the same time he is told that God rejects no one and that those who are lost are lost by their own fault. Finally we inform him that while conversion occurs only by the action of the Holy Spirit and is not correlated with any merits or dispositions previously existent in the person; and while even the person's "passive co-operation" is not exercised; nevertheless we deny the Calvinist fourth point and we say that grace is resistible. He hears from us that no one can come to faith in Christ unless drawn, that who will be effectively called is known to God in eternity ("before the foundation of the world"), and yet that God's call to repentance is truly universal and that God wills that all men should be saved and come to the knowledge of the truth. We point out that all of these doctrines are the plain and explicit teaching of Scripture and that the theological problem they pose is a mystery. To the psychologist, accustomed to thinking in terms of explicitly stated laws, this "mystery" appears as a flat contradiction. Within the closed system of determinism, it may be. Scientific humanists do not find mysteries to their taste, and when a theologian deals with one of these problems by expounding Scripture and resting at that point, the insistent secular psychologist reacts to the resolution as being essentially obscurantist. It is likely that no amount of semantic clarification or mutual education will fully dispose of conflicts of this type, because the methodological premises differ. The Christian rests (sometimes uneasily if he is a philosopher!) when the plain teaching of Scripture has been elucidated; short of a flat logical contradiction, clearly discernible by juxtaposing two propositions of assured meaning, he will accept a puzzle, a paradox, or a mystery as "not having been revealed and not necessary for our salvation." The whole epistemological tradition of science, and of the science-centered man generally, finds such a stopping place intolerable.

---

[5] That predictability is synergistic is one of those "obvious" implications which must be carefully scrutinized. That a man cannot morally or religiously "prepare himself" for conversion does not imply unpredictability at all levels of analysis. It depends upon the nature of the co-ordination between the theological and microphysiological languages. We found the explication of this relationship far too formidable a task to be attempted within our time and powers.

Finally, it must be admitted that there are at times genuine disagreements between the substantive views of psychologists and theologians. For example, almost all psychologists hold that man has evolved from an apelike primate by the statistically selective cumulation of random heritable variations *and nothing else*, and must therefore not differ in any essential qualitative respect from the other animals. Such characteristically human powers and dispositions as reverence, conscience, or the "religious impulse" — which the theologian sees as stemming from man's having been originally formed in the image of God, together with God's present working in men in a unique manner different from the way He works in white rats — are viewed by the scientific naturalist as merely the resultant of randomly produced features of the body, such as the larger forebrain, more complex ramifications in the neural network, an opposable thumb, and the like. The theologian, of course, has no theological stake in denying the relevance, or even cruciality, of these anatomical features. Man is a biological organism, not only a spirit. But the theologian can hardly square with revelation either the view that these important anatomical features were randomly, "purposelessly," produced; or the associated view that the capacity of man for religious experience and behavior consists of *nothing but* these biological peculiarities.

Another example of genuine disagreement lies in the general area of ontological dualism. It is true that modern thinkers should beware of projecting into Scripture the philosophical views deriving from the pagan Greeks (and, more recently, from Descartes) with regard to the metaphysical dualism of "mind" and "body." Even Lutheran writers have sometimes been insufficiently critical in this respect and thereby have unwittingly put an additional stumbling block in the psychologist's path. It is now generally accepted that this kind of metaphysical dualism, in the form usually stated by post-Cartesian philosophers, was not natural to the thinking or idiom of the ancient Jews and New Testament writers (see Appendix C). It is worth noting that the *Book of Concord* indexes the word "soul" only four times, as contrasted, say, with the philosophically more neutral term "man," which requires a full index column for the mere listing of page

158

references! (The phrase *rational soul* is used four times in the Confessions, but a definition of it nowhere appears.)

Nevertheless we know from Scripture that a human person, albeit perhaps in some sense "incomplete," must be capable of surviving bodily death in some kind of state prior to the resurrection. For example, we have Jesus' saying to the penitent thief: "*Today* shalt thou be with Me in Paradise" (Luke 23:43). Furthermore, the doctrine of angels, or for that matter of God Himself, presupposes the possibility of personhood, and of cognitive and volitional powers, apart from matter. This notion is anathema to the very great majority of psychologists. It is important for pastors who come in contact with persons influenced by scientific naturalism as a world view to be sophisticated as to just *what* the scientific naturalist denies about dualism. A misunderstanding makes the pastor appear uninformed or even ludicrous, thus hampering his bringing of the Christian message. Scientific naturalism does not deny the existence of those properties and powers of man which have been traditionally tied to the soul concept. It is evident to all, believers and unbelievers alike, that man reasons, worships, writes music, feels conscience pangs, builds science, and what not. It is even becoming respectable again for psychologists in American universities to be interested in consciousness, in the subjective stream of experience, in the "phenomenal field." But the mental processes of man are conceived by the psychologist, first of all, as *events* (i. e., not *things*); and secondly, the "things" which participate in these events, the things whose interactions and actualized dispositions constitute (note, not "produce" or "underlie," but *constitute*) the mental events, are material entities. From the point of view of most psychologists, thought, passion, love, guilt, etc., are not produced by the body or "secreted" by the brain or "dependent upon" living tissue — rather they are all literally *activities* of living tissue. Thinking and willing are actions by the human machine. The human machine is made up of chemical elements put together in a certain way, and, adds the scientific naturalist, *nothing else.* Hence if you ask him, "Where does the mind go when the body dies?" this question cannot make any sense to him. From his point of view such a question is like asking, "Where does the timekeeping go when a watch is smashed?"

159

Answer: Nowhere, because timekeeping is not a thing but an event, and in this smashed watch, events of that kind no longer take place. The denier of dualism does not say that minds do not exist. What he says is that minds are successions of mental events, grouped on the basis of "whose brain they happen in." The *word* "mind" is, grammatically, a noun, but it refers to acts and dispositions. The monistic view can be succinctly expressed by the analogical equation Mind: Brain:: Timekeeping: Watch:: Function: Structure:: Event: Thing.

Some of the genuine disagreements between contemporary psychology and theology are, potentially at least, resolvable by the accumulation of further factual evidence. For example, there has recently been a revival of scientific interest in the question whether a materialist-monist conception of the human psyche is adequate to even the nonreligious facts. Experimental data, collected by the usual scientific means and by non-Christian investigators, indicate the reality of such phenomena as telepathy, clairvoyance, and even nonratiocinative foreknowledge in the human organism. There is nothing Christian, or even broadly "religious," about such [6] experimental findings or the crude sketches of theory that have been erected to explain them. Furthermore, only future developments will clarify the bearing that these so-called paranormal mental powers and processes have upon the scientific view of man. At present some scholars incline to the opinion that any adequate theory as to the explanation of these phenomena will involve some form of dualism. Others deny this. It is premature to judge the relative merits of these scientific views, and it would be a serious error for Christians to rely heavily in their apologetics upon such a disputed scientific matter. But it is appropriate to mention it here, as an example of the *kind* of evidence that could result in considerable alleviation of conflict. For, if the scientific developments in this area of research should continue along present lines, the plausibility of the materialist hypotheses as judged purely on scientific grounds would be considerably reduced. Another example would be the organic-evolution hypothesis. Assuming that the ensuing years

[6] S. G. Soal and F. Bateman, *Modern Experiments in Telepathy* (New Haven: Yale University Press, 1954).

of geological excavation continue to expose the lack of those transitional life forms required by the theory, and that the conspiracy of silence on this point is broken, a major source of intellectual difficulty — undoubtedly constituting the severest blow which the church as a social institution has received in modern times, if not in its entire history — would be ameliorated. The advances in Biblical archaeology during the last half century constitute a solid example of how the gathering of additional empirical evidence can reduce conflict between secular scholarship and the Christian claims. The substantial accuracy of the received texts in respect to those historical matters which are independently confirmable has been so well demonstrated by the findings that when competent and unprejudiced scholars experience difficulty in accepting the report of Scripture as to the historical happenings there set forth, they do so on extrahistorical (e. g., philosophical) grounds.

Developments in the logical analysis of concepts may also be expected to exert a beneficial effect upon psychological-religious frictions. Creedal, confessional, and synodical pronouncements have usually been produced in the course of controversy, their language being chosen from a current vocabulary so as to force certain distinctions and thus to smoke out the particular heresy momentarily dominating the scene. While there is such a thing as "weaseling out" of Scriptural and confessional formulations while pretending to retain them, there is also a valid and defensible type of language analysis which seeks to clarify further the conceptual content of a familiar and accepted theological expression. While the saving truths of Christianity are apprehended by faith and through revelation rather than by unaided reason, yet, insofar as "reason" includes the consistent and communicative use of language, reason is unavoidably utilized by the pastor or theologian. The advances in technical logic and epistemology in the last half century have proved themselves so powerful in the clarification of scientific concepts that the contemporary theologian would be unwise to remain ignorant of them. It is probable that there are disputed concepts and paradoxes of the faith which only *seem* to conflict with what the psychologist believes in his scientific capacity and which would be recognized as truly consistent after a sufficiently thorough linguistic analysis. Such

161

concepts as time and eternity, necessity and contingency, doubt and decision, causality and noncausal correlation, are much better understood since the rise of analytic philosophy; and these concepts, while not intrinsically religious concepts, are frequently invoked as ancillaries in the course of a discussion of certain theological matters. That the most important technical developments of secular philosophy have been achieved by analytic philosophers of predominantly irreligious stamp ought not to result in Christian thinkers' dismissing the powerful tools that have been forged or their being frightened by the widespread use of some of these tools for anti-Christian purposes.

We have discussed some of the potentially removable sources of conflict between secular psychology and the cognitive components of Christianity. Persistent, rigorous, and creative efforts along the indicated lines will do much to improve the relation between disciplines. It must be frankly admitted, however, that even if the factors of mutual ignorance, semantic confusion, dogmatism about open questions, incomplete empirical evidence, and philosophically unclear concepts were wholly eliminated, certain divergencies would exist between the attitude and belief systems of most secular psychologists and the Christian orientation. One dramatic example, actually the *fons et origo* of all such disagreements, will suffice. The Christian has made a certain kind of commitment, with a vigor and pervasiveness which is far out of proportion to what the empirical evidence warrants. Reason, working philosophically with the facts of science and history, and being confronted with the church's proclamation, might lead a man to some such grudging admission as the following: "Well, it does look interesting and appealing, what you say. It might be so, for all I know. I guess I will have to admit that the rational case for Christianity is somewhat stronger than I had been led to suppose. But it's too loose, and it has too many mysteries and paradoxes for my taste. It's a live option, all right. It's not intellectually a dead duck, as my more dogmatic atheist friends try to tell me. I can see how a sane man might opt for it. But it's far from rationally compelling, as you admit. So I won't buy it, although I admire the ingenuity of your defense."

Here we see reflected one of the basic procedural policies of the scientist, for which the word *skepticism* is perhaps as good

162

a word as can be found. A modern *locus classicus* is the passage in W. K. Clifford's *The Ethics of Belief*, where we read: "It is wrong always, everywhere, and for anyone, to believe anything whatsoever upon insufficient evidence." While all good scientists, in the practice of their research, are passionately committed to this position, there are two special features of the form it takes in psychologists. First, man and his beliefs are part of the proper domain of the psychologist. Hence he applies the usual scientific criteria in that domain; whereas a chemist may be extremely skeptical in his chemical laboratory but find no particular difficulty with his Christian convictions, because it does not occur to him (or seems inappropriate) to carry over his scientific habits into his thinking about himself and his fellow man. We see here that the psychological sciences do actually occupy a unique position with regard to the Christian claims. A devout mathematician may say: "I wouldn't think of approaching the question of conversion or sanctification in a detached, cold, scientific way." The non-Christian psychologist is baffled by such an attitude and wants to say, "Why not?" The psychologist takes man — St. Paul, Augustine, Luther, and the psychologist himself — as an object of scientific study; which means to him that all of man's works and ways must be approached, insofar as possible, in the same spirit in which the chemist approaches a lump of synthetic rubber or the zoologist an earthworm. To be sure, there is no logical contradiction involved in a shift of *attitude* as one leaves the laboratory or classroom for reimmersion in "real life"; a physicist's attitude when he hears Mozart played is quite unlike his attitude when delivering a lecture on acoustics. An attitude, not being an assertion (proposition), can hardly be "contradictory" to another nonpropositional state! However, the enjoyment of Mozart (taking the "musical attitude") does not involve the prior acceptance of any *cognitive elements*. One could adopt the musical attitude, quite unimpaired, even if he entertained grave doubts as to whether Mozart even wrote the piece being performed. The same is not true of the Christian. To take an extreme case, what "attitude" could a professor of history take while on his knees hearing the liturgical prayer for Easter Sunday if he were firmly persuaded (qua historian) of Reimarus' theory that the disciples stole the body and by means of this simple piece of fakery gave rise to the Christian Church?

This unique problem of the psychologist, having man as a scientific subject matter, is aggravated by a second factor. The skepticism of the psychologist has a special quality to it, in that his training generates a habitual suspiciousness and depreciation of the human mind as a truth-gathering instrument. A great body of experimental and clinical evidence convinces the psychologist that human beings cannot observe, record, retain, or report events with precise accuracy and that these defects are notably heightened by the presence of strong emotional forces. Miraculous narratives found in historical documents are therefore rejected as a matter of course, since it is assumed that the self-deceiving powers of the human observer — especially if not scientifically trained and if of a "religious" turn of mind — are almost without limit. The conviction born of personal experience in the lives of contemporary Christians is equally unimpressive, since the hidden forces of the mind are known to express themselves in devious ways and with remarkable subtlety. It is hard for a Christian who has not himself been thoroughly immersed in this intellectual climate really to understand it (just as it is hard for unbelievers to get a "feel" for what Christians are talking about). But there can be no doubt that the daily concern with human self-deception, wish-fulfillment, and distortion tends to develop in the psychologist a special brand of skepticism, if not cynicism, about human beliefs which is not so acutely felt by the practitioners of other sciences. We should also be just in recognizing that this skepticism, although often corrupted by pride, and always utilized by the powers of darkness, is in itself associated with one of the noblest passions to be found in the natural man: the passion to think straight, not to be fooled, and not to fool anybody else.

It appears to us that these conflicts, partly over what modern logicians call "decision policy," are genuine and that they are irresoluble. There will, for example, never be any scientific evidence showing that men are accurate and unbiased in their observations of emotionally significant events. The resurrection of Jesus was a unique historical event, and it will never be experimentally repeated so that scientists can "determine its causal conditions." If a scientific psychologist is a Christian, we know immediately that he has adopted (speaking cognitively) a standard of evidence in the religious realm which is different from that which he maintains in his scientific activity. He has made an "exception," because he has approached certain questions concerning man and his condition with a different attitude, and therefore with altered epistemological standards, not with those he applies to *other* questions concerning man (e. g., what is the nature of color blindness?). Nor does it seem possible to give any intrascientific justification for making such an exception. The scientific psychologist, confronted with the church's proclamation, is (we still speak epistemologically) invited to make a decision on special — he would say "biased" — standards of evidence. For anyone to do such a thing is of course not, primarily, an intellectual matter. This observation can hardly be expected to disturb Lutherans, who learn in the Small Catechism: "I believe that I cannot by my own reason or strength believe in Jesus Christ, my Lord, or come to Him; but the Holy Ghost has called me by the Gospel, enlightened me with His gifts, sanctified and kept me in the true faith."

We have now examined the major sources of conflict between psychology and theology. We saw that there are incompatibilities, both real and merely apparent, between the views of the typical psychologist and Christian doctrine. It is our opinion that the apparent incompatibilities preponderate over the real; and, as was pointed out in Chapter III, one must always be careful to distinguish those views which are held by psychologists as a group but are not logically implied by well-attested facts and theories of the science from views which are genuinely implied by the received scientific content itself. In the present section we shall consider briefly some relations, other than contradiction, which may obtain between psychological and theological teachings.

One type of relation is that of independence. An example of independence of categories would be the relation between the ethicotheological classification of an act as sinful, and the statistical or biological classification of the same act as "natural" (or, as some prefer to put it, "normal"). We are, of course, considering here only the designation of *actual sins,* not the dispo-

165

sitional concept of *sin* which the Lutheran tradition has always emphasized as more fundamental. Actual sin being a normative category, in which the existent is compared with the ideal (i. e., a *fact* with a *norm*), it represents a different kind of categorization from the purely descriptive or empirical classifications available to the scientist. When a social or biological scientist asserts that an action is "natural" or "normal," examination of his basis for saying this will reveal that he means that it is frequent, or that impulses to it are somehow rooted in man's nature, or both. Obviously the normative distinction of sinful-versus-licit cuts across the empirical-descriptive criterion of frequency. Murder is relatively infrequent, adultery is remarkably common; both are sinful. Risking one's life to save that of a stranger is rare (and "unnatural"?), making love to one's wife is common; neither is sinful. Whether a particular act is a sin cannot be determined by investigating its frequency of occurrence, or the intimacy of its causal connection with the urges of our biological nature. The philosophical superficiality of some social scientists is nowhere so crudely displayed as in the contention that the social sciences have, "by the study of different cultures," demonstrated that there are no absolute moral standards. This is a remarkable assertion, involving both an elementary philosophical error and the arrogant assumption that until the rise of modern social science, people had the delusion that moral standards were the same the world over! One wonders what these social scientists think the term "heathen" has designated in the church for the last two millennia, or to whom Christians have been sending missionaries. The famous Dr. Kinsey has been guilty of the same philosophical carelessness, contending to be "purely scientific" in his nonjudgmental, empirical-descriptive approach to the *facts* of sexual behavior, but simultaneously propagandizing on the hidden premise that *frequent* = "natural" = "normal" = *licit*.

Pastors are sometimes disturbed to hear of a psychologist having described something sinful as "natural" or "normal." When a psychotherapist says that it is natural for an adolescent girl to feel jealousy and resentment toward her brighter and more attractive sister, even to the extent of harboring unworded death wishes against this "competitor," he is merely describing a psychological truth about human nature as we find it. All of us have murderous impulses at times, of which we are variously aware, and the notion that the child is free of such impulses is a pleasant fantasy cherished by naïve adults. "For the imagination of man's heart is evil from his youth" (Genesis 8:21). Of course it may happen that a non-Christian therapist inadvertently or deliberately conveys the added idea ". . . and there's nothing wrong or sinful about it." But even this is only a bit of nonprofessional commentary, supplied *gratis* and worth the price. A properly instructed Christian should be able to make the distinction, perhaps with a little help from his pastor, provided that the latter sees the underlying logic of the situation.

Suppose that a Hard-Shell Baptist physician, in advising a Lutheran patient suffering from coronary heart disease to stop smoking, should go on to say: "And, anyway, using tobacco is a sinful practice." We do not believe that a Lutheran pastor would be greatly disturbed by this "medical" attack upon his parishioner's Christian liberty. By the same token, he need not be upset by any of the theological obiter dicta which may fall from the lips of secular psychotherapists. If this sort of thing can make deep inroads and lead the sheep astray, we had better take a critical look at our religious instruction. Other things equal, it is admittedly preferable for Christians to seek psychiatric or psychological help from Christian agencies or practitioners. Failing that, pastors having occasion to make referrals or to consult secular experts should try to ascertain which among the non-Christian professional workers are best informed about Christian doctrine and are most scrupulous in confining themselves to their own proper role and competence. Unfortunately there are many communities in which these religious criteria are difficult or impossible to meet. When this is so, the pastor may have to use the available resources, even though he knows them to be unbelievers with an unconscious need to "convert" believers. With proper safeguards, such as preparing the parishioner for what he may meet with, it is usually preferable to utilize the professional skills of a competent atheist than to proceed without him. The theological ignorance of most such practitioners should be sufficiently apparent to the Christian patient that he will find it

167

easy to discount unprofessional conversation if it should appear in the interviews.

Another type of relation that may exist between theological and psychological categories is one of partial overlap. In such cases, a subset of the criteria for applying a certain theological concept is shared with criteria used by the psychologist, but this overlap of criteria is incomplete. An example would be Freud's concept of the id and the Christian concept of original sin, or of the old Adam remaining in the converted. Some pastoral counselors, overeager to make the Freudian lion lie down with the Christian lamb, have made an incautious identification of the two. It is not hard to see how this comes about, because there are in reality certain common defining properties. Freud's id (das Es)[7] is the unconscious source of instinctive energy which is completely dominated by pleasure seeking and which retains certain primitive properties of the unformed or infantile mental life, such as illogicality, immorality, a kind of chaotic disunity, "timelessness," and the like. Now insofar as the imperious demand for impulse gratification is a property of the id, the id is like "the flesh" in New Testament language. Certain manifestations of the impulse life, given free expression by some of the unregenerate and constituting trials and imperfections of sanctification among Christians, are equatable with "derivatives of id impulses." But a complete identification of the concepts can certainly not be defended. For one thing the N. T. σάρξ, as is well known to Christian scholars, is not the same as σῶμα, but designates rather the entire class of ungodly impulses. Thus such a thing as spiritual pride is found in the natural man and is also a temptation of the Christian. Avarice, pride, and envy are works of the flesh, theologically speaking. From the Freudian point of view none of these could possibly be found in the id. Pride, for example, is a manifestation of the "ego's narcissism" in Freud's system and is therefore relegated to a different portion of the mental apparatus, the ego, which is contrasted with the id. Other reasons can readily be adduced to refute any notion that id = original sin (or old man in the regenerate), but the preceding,

---

[7] *The Ego and the Id* (London: Hogarth Press, 1927).

being so clear and simple an objection, will suffice for present purposes.

Pastors and psychotherapists should beware of such easy identifications as this. They are made in an irenic spirit and sometimes facilitate co-operation in the short run; but like all quick-and-easy solutions of abstruse problems, they are harmful in the long run. The well-meaning pastor who, in effect, says to the psychiatrist, "Sure, your 'id' corresponds to my 'flesh,'" will find sooner or later that he has to call a halt on some of the implications of this mistaken identification, and the pseudo harmony is then rudely dispelled. It would be far better to state frankly that while the two concepts exhibit important resemblances, yet they are not equivalent; that the fine details of their relationships are presumably complex, and as yet have been insufficiently studied by scholars competent in both disciplines.

We have considered relations of incompatibility, independence, and partial overlap between theological and psychological categories. Although the equation id = original sin had to be rejected upon closer scrutiny, one may ask whether *any* valid equations can be written between theological and psychological categories. Reversing the case considered at the beginning of this chapter, where the same word (guilt) is used by theologians and psychiatrists with two different meanings, are there genuine cases where the same concept is designated by different words? It would be rash to speak here with confidence, since we have not considered every possible candidate; but it seems very doubtful to us that any such complete concept identities exist between theology and psychology. This is presumably because theological terms, even when not denoting an attribute or action of God, are always referring to someone or something *in relation to God;* which of course is not true of secular psychology's vocabulary. Since the content of theoretical terms is given (ultimately) by their role in the systematic language of a given domain, the meaning of most, if not all, theological terms involves at least indirectly and implicitly a reference to God. With that intrasystemic reference excised or suppressed (as it is by the non-Christian psychologist) the term cannot have quite the same meaning as it does to the Christian.

Can the Freudian superego, for example, be equated with

the Christian conscience, as some overeager synthesizers have assumed? There are undeniable similarities between the concepts denoted by these two terms. Yet it is surely incorrect — and theologically dangerous — to make a simple identification of them. In classical Freudian theory, the superego is the "heir of the Oedipus complex," arising via an introjection of the parent image (with the associated prohibitions) following the partial resolution of the Oedipal situation. It is not possible to equate such a structure with the Christian conception of conscience. The relationship among the superego concept, the concept of a properly informed Christian conscience, and St. Paul's concept of the Law written on the heathens' hearts is exceedingly complex, and the theoretical difficulties are so great that we have reluctantly decided not to treat of the matter in any detail in this book. For a few hints about fruitful directions which an adequate discussion might pursue see Appendix B.

Even when a term is actually taken over from one discipline to the other, with the intention to designate the same concept, we find that an exact synonymy is lacking. Consider, for example, the word *conversion*, which is used by psychologists doing research on the psychology of religion. While Christians do not ordinarily permit themselves a judgment about the genuineness of another's conversion, the *theoretical* concept of conversion necessarily involves the assumption of the Holy Spirit's action as a *causa efficiens*. If a person were to undergo certain psychological experiences of remorse, trust, and resolution and to behave in a manner suggestive of specified kinds of attitudinal change, with all of this taking place in a "religious context," then he would be described *ipso facto* as "converted" by the secular psychologist. That is, to say these things about the person *is*, by (psychological) definition, to say, "He was converted." But theologically these experiences and behaviors could presumably occur without the operation of the Holy Spirit and hence without constituting an instance of conversion as the term is used theologically.

This is not to say that there is no connection of any kind between the psychological signs or manifestations of conversion and the theological concept, rendering the latter completely cut off from the empirical order. That this is not intended is shown

170

by the practice of the church since its inception with regard to admission, administration of the Sacraments, excommunication, and the like. Pastors and congregations do exercise judgment in these matters and are thought to do so properly as part of church discipline and the maintenance of good order. A conscientious pastor would obviously not commune a man who said that he had been reconverted after a long lapse if the man continued to live openly with a mistress and make his living as a pickpocket. These examples, in which the theologically postulated relation of conversion to sanctification is actually applied *in concreto*, show that the concept of conversion is not a transempirical one. In the language of contemporary philosophy we would say that "true conversion" is a *theoretical concept* of which behavior is an *indicator*. The indicator (like most indicators used in social science) is, however, probabilistic only. Hence we do not *identify* the behavior, or the behavior dispositions, with the presence of the construct. The action of the Holy Spirit is the dominant theoretical component in the theological conception of conversion, which it obviously cannot be when the "psychology of religion" is studied by an unbeliever. If even a term such as conversion, which the secular vocabulary deliberately imported from the theological in order to be able to talk about "the same thing," has undergone a conceptual modification in its passage, one can hardly expect that any two different words in the two technical vocabularies are likely to refer to precisely the same concept.

VIII. Determinism and Related Problems

THE CHRISTIAN who has been nurtured in a Christian environment, parochially educated throughout, and has continued to move within a Christian social and intellectual climate, finds it hard to understand the special significance that scientific determinism has for the thoughtful unbeliever.[1] As is true of all pervasive and subtle *Weltanschauungen*, one can appreciate the true spirit of "naturalism" only by being really immersed in it, and for a considerable period. Christians are fond of pointing out — and quite rightly — that one cannot fully grasp the character of the faith, even in its *cognitive* aspect, from without the fold. *Credo ut intellegam*, as Augustine has it. It is important for Christians to realize that the same is true *psychologically* (although not upon the basis of a supernatural grace) for the scientific naturalist world view. Only by frequent and sincere intercourse with the naturalist unbeliever can a Christian become capable of entering "provisionally" into the other's frame of reference. It must be frankly admitted that most of the attempts (thankfully, seldom Lutheran) to write "rational apologetics" upon the modern naturalist's own grounds could be most charitably characterized as irrelevant. To most naturalists they are merely ludicrous. They simply do not speak to the naturalist unbeliever's condition, with the result that this kind of approach is worse than none at all.

---

[1] See brief discussion in Chapter III.

We introduce the more technical discussion of determinism with these remarks because we realize that many of our Christian readers will feel that the topic is hardly deserving of such emphasis. Perhaps some will even feel that the members of the symposium, infected by a love of logomachy and a yen for the arcane and abstruse, have here permitted their idiosyncratic interests to guide the work, instead of being oriented to the "practical, down-to-earth" problems. In opposition to such an interpretation we are prepared to defend the following thesis: *Scientific naturalism (philosophically underpinned by logical empiricism), often in an unquestioned and even unstated form, is today the strongest intellectual enemy of the church and among educated people gives the most powerful no to the church's proclamation.* Anyone who has daily contact with college professors at the great secular universities (the majority of whom are either atheists or "liberal Protestants") knows that this is the case.

The impact of Freud, Marx, Bergson, and the like — while a great stir is made about them by talkative people who want to "keep up with the latest stuff" — is of minor importance when compared with the steady influence of that more subtle, silently working set of assumptions and attitudes called scientific naturalism. When intellectuals (or, in this case, more often pseudo intellectuals) ask, "How does the church come to grips with Sartre?" one is reminded that almost a half century ago Santayana (speaking momentarily for the Roman Church) answered a similar question involving Bergson, saying essentially that there was no reason to "come to grips" with Bergson at all, since he would shortly be forgotten. This cannot be said of scientific naturalism and its philosophic ally, logical empiricism. The former has held sway as the consensus of educated unbelievers for over 150 years; the latter provides the most rigorous and beautiful technical tools ever forged for its systematic explication and defense. It is extremely probable that this congenial pair, which we shall here marry verbally as "logical empiricist naturalism," will provide the dominant climate of opinion for the pagan intelligentsia (and hence of the great secular universities)

173

for the present and at least the next generation.[2] Since psychologists are among the most methodologically conscious of scientific workers, they are especially likely to be identified with this position. (That this is already true of the younger generation of psychologists can be readily discerned by even a cursory examination of the psychologists' theoretical journal, the *Psychological Review*.)

Assuming that these historical extrapolations are even approximately correct, any examination of the sources of conflict between theology and scientific psychology must devote a large share of attention to logical empiricist naturalism. The thesis of determinism, in one form or other, occupies a central place in this theoretical framework. Determinism and its (seeming) implications constitute for the psychologist both a *scientific* stumbling block in respect to miracles, conversion, and the action of God in history, and a *moral* stumbling block in regard to responsibility, choice, "freedom," election, and related concepts. Over the course of the last two generations the naturalist world view has gradually been disseminated "from the top down," so that today there are very many people (even within nominally Christian bodies) who hold it unquestioningly, even though they could not formulate their naturalist faith in technical language. The naturalist college professor teaches the journalism major or the secondary school teacher; over the years the naturalist philosophy percolates throughout the culture, molding even those whose serious reading is confined to the newspaper's Sunday Supplement Section. Hence the man on the street is normally a materialist and a determinist, though he may know neither of these words. In this way it has come to pass that "logical empiricist naturalism" is the great enemy of the church *even among people who have never heard of it.* We therefore felt justified in devoting special effort to the elucidation of this question.

The complexity of the determinism issue is so great that it seems best to approach it by first presenting a somewhat crude formulation of both the thesis itself and the theological difficulties

---

[2] Herbert Feigl, "Aims of Education for Our Age of Science," *Modern Philosophies of Education,* in Fifty-fourth Yearbook of the National Society for the Study of Education (Chicago: University of Chicago Press, 1955), I, 304—341.

it presents, so as to introduce both Christian and non-Christian readers to its essential character as taken *simpliciter* (Section 1). In Section 2 we shall introduce some important warnings against possible misunderstanding that can hopelessly becloud the issue and arouse needless antagonisms; and then we shall attempt (in Section 3) a more rigorous exposition of the position particularly in its intimate relation to scientific materialism. After these necessary preliminaries, the relationships between determinism and the doctrine of grace will be analyzed in some detail, utilizing an individual's conversion as a type specimen of the class of problems which arise. This long discussion (Section 4) will constitute the main body of the chapter.

1. *Preliminary Statement of the Problem*

Psychological determinism as a *thesis* (distinguished from the investigative policy called "methodological determinism" in Chapter III) asserts that all states and activities of the human person exemplify exceptionless causal regularities called *natural laws*. Some of these laws are presently known to mankind, while others remain to be discovered. Of course, the determinist does not claim that all of the laws are known; if they were, scientific research would no longer be carried on, since all the laws exhibited by human behavior would then have been discovered. The thesis itself, then, is a hypothesis; it might be viewed as the cognitive expectation that methodological determinism is a program capable, in principle, of achieving success.

Since natural laws are not statements regarding individual events but rather consist of *generalizations* about particulars, they are often represented in abstract form by such models as, "Every A is a B," or "Whenever A happens, B happens." Examples of these two forms are: "All crows are black" and "Whenever pure water is heated to 212° Fahrenheit under standard atmospheric pressure, it boils." The first "law" is false, the second true. In the advanced sciences the laws characteristically take a mathematical form, in which the numerical value of one quantity or "variable" is related to some other quantity by a certain mathematical equation. We say usually that y is a *function* of χ. Note that these hypothesized laws are of universal character. Thus we say *"Every χ is a y"*; or *"Whenever*

A happens, B happens"; or, "*For every* space-time point, the values of the variables χ and y satisfy the equation $y = f(\chi)$ [where f ( ) is the mathematical function expressing the law]." Since a particular individual or occurrence is an *instance* of the general law (a "particular" exemplifying a "universal"), philosophers of science speak of the unique, dated event as *instantializing* the law. One succinct formulation of empirical determinism is therefore simply, "All events are instantializations of natural laws."

We are not concerned here with the reasons for and against adopting this rather daring hypothesis about "all events,"[3] a question which is beyond the scope of this book. In the present section we wish merely to state the position and to sketch the theological questions posed prima facie by it.

What does such a view mean for our picture of the human individual? Consider Saul on the road to Damascus. According to the determinist, his experience and behavior as described in Acts 9:1-9 must all conform to the laws of psychology and physiology. Everything that he hears, sees, says, and does during those historically tremendous moments is an instantialization of the laws of mind and matter. (Here we avoid prejudging the relation between determinism and materialism.) If we imagine a superpsychologist who knew all these laws of the mental life and who also possessed an exhaustive knowledge of Saul's precise psychophysical state and of the incoming stimuli at the instant before his conversion, the determinist thesis asserts that this imagined psychologist could have predicted the conversion in all its particulars. Since in fact we never do know all there is to know about the laws and the momentary conditions, determinist philosophers are fond of invoking a fortunate manikin known as "Omniscient Jones," who does occupy, for purpose of theoretical discussion, this idealized epistemological position. Omniscient Jones would have foreseen Saul's Damascus experience in every detail.

It is obvious that for one who holds the determinist view, the Christian doctrine of man presents peculiar difficulties, in

---

[3] In his *The Continuum of Inductive Methods* Rudolf Carnap now holds that the probability attaching to a generalization of universal form is always zero.

both the causal and the ethical domains. Christians hold that while God acts in accordance with general law (which He has ordained) in the ordinary exercise of His providence, at times He "intervenes" in a more specific way in nature and history. In the forming of living beings from inorganic matter and in the working of miracles we see such dramatic interventions. Are the revelations given by the prophets and the conversion of sinners also of this extranomic type? This is not so clear. But in the class of events called miraculous, God acts "immediately," rather than by the medium of natural laws and the permanent dispositions He has conferred upon substances. Orthodoxy is committed by the plain words of Christ to the view that certain of Christ's actions display the specific intervention of God in the created order, and are not explicable in terms of the usual laws of nature:

> When Jesus saw their faith, He said unto the sick of the palsy, Son, thy sins be forgiven thee. But there were certain of the scribes sitting there and reasoning in their hearts: Why doth this man thus speak blasphemies? Who can forgive sins but God only? And immediately when Jesus perceived in His spirit that they so reasoned within themselves, He said unto them: Why reason ye these things in your hearts? Whether is it easier, to say to the sick of the palsy, Thy sins be forgiven thee, or to say, Arise, and take up thy bed, and walk? But that ye may know that the Son of Man hath power on earth to forgive sins (He saith to the sick of the palsy): I say unto thee, Arise, and take up thy bed, and go thy way into thine house. And immediately he arose, took up the bed, and went forth before them all; insomuch that they were all amazed, and glorified God, saying, We never saw it on this fashion. (Mark 2:5-12)

> If I do not the works of My Father, believe Me not. But if I do, though ye believe not Me, believe the works; that ye may know and believe that the Father is in Me, and I in Him. (John 10: 37, 38)

Christianity is a historical religion. While its theology treats of the eternal and man's relationship to the eternal, it nevertheless makes empirical contact by virtue of its claim that revelation occurs in time, to specific men, at namable dates and places. The forming of the first human body from the dust was an *event* (i. e., it has a spatio-temporal locus in the created order), Jerusalem is a physical *place*, Pontius Pilate was a flesh-and-blood

177

Roman official in secular *history,* the crucifixion really *happened.* According to Scripture, certain episodes took place in empirical reality — the same empirical reality which the natural and social sciences take as their domain — which are of crucial religious significance. We need not here decide precisely which of these many events we are bound to receive as due to God's acting without mediate causes, in what we may call "the extraordinary manner." It is sufficient that at least *some* of them are revealed as being of this character. The most confounding of them all, the bodily resurrection of Jesus Christ, occupied a central place in the convictions of the little band of men and women who constituted the apostolic church. This means to the determinist that his thesis is repudiated: Christians claim that certain events occur in the natural order which are not explainable *by* the natural order. In terms of the more exact way of formulating determinism, Christianity gives a central importance to space-time events which it claims are not instantializations of universal causal laws. And it further insists that their *being* "exceptions" is one aspect of their revelatory character. If any such events did (and do) occur, then determinism as a general thesis about the world is empirically false. To the scientist who generalizes from determinism as a fruitful research policy (methodological determinism) to determinism as a universal empirical extrapolation (empirical determinism), and, a fortiori, to anyone who asserts it as an absolute philosophical presupposition (metaphysical determinism), these Christian allegations constitute a terrible offense. This is what we alluded to above as the "scientific" stumbling block.

Consider now the ethical stumbling block. According to the determinist, all the moral and spiritual activities of a person are events within the system of natural laws. He holds that when a man sins, his behavior is strictly determined; when he withstands temptation, this is likewise determined. When a man hears a sermon preached and is converted, this event finds its place in the inexorable chain of causality, stretching backward in time to the mysterious beginning of things (described prosaically as the "initial conditions of the cosmos"). If one hears the Gospel preached and rejects the offer of salvation, he was determined to do precisely this. Knowing what Omniscient Jones

178

would know about his ancestry, his childhood training, his college teachers, the chemical constitution of the fried eggs he had for breakfast, etc., his rejection of God's offer of forgiveness is predictable. Like everything which takes place in the world, that a person obdurately resists the church's proclamation is simply another instantialization of the laws of nature. That this predetermined unbelief should cast a man into outer darkness must inevitably appear to the consistent determinist very much as Calvin's *decretum horribile* does to the Lutheran. And, apart from the problem of grace, the determinist sees that the very *concept* of "sin" is tied to some notion of responsibility for one's action; in repudiating "freedom of the will," the Confessions mean something very specific, which they define for us. They surely do not mean to deny that a person is a "free moral agent" in one of the several philosophical senses of this phrase.

2. *Some Preliminary Warnings*

In approaching the determinism-freedom-responsibility cluster we must first of all be aware of the extreme complexity and elusiveness of these concepts. The words used have often been used equivocally, and insufficient care has sometimes been exerted in the framing of definitions. Certain inferences from one proposition to another, treated by scholars as "obvious," will not bear closer examination. As an example of what absurdities can arise from superficial treatment consider the following:

a. Luther denied free will in his polemic against Erasmus.

b. The logical contradictory of free will is determinism.

c. Therefore Luther asserted determinism.

If determinism is taken in (c) to mean what we have explained as "empirical determinism," such a conclusion is ridiculous. How far the usage of these terms has shifted over the centuries is suggested by the fact that perceptive Lutheran theologians regard the scientific determinist as an intellectual opponent, and the attitude is mutual. We must be careful therefore not to assume that when the same words appear in several contexts, they refer to the same concept. The meanings of such terms in a secular writing must at times be teased out, as is done in exegesis of doubtful Scripture passages, by a careful attention to the

179

context and with the working assumption that a proper interpretation will make the underlying consistency manifest.

Perhaps we should here re-emphasize the framework and goal of the present discussion, which might otherwise be misunderstood by both Christian and non-Christian readers (although in different ways). We are concerned to explicate the logical *relationships* that exist between the determinist thesis and the Christian doctrine of man. We are not attempting primarily to expound the latter in all its ramifications. Nor, since this is not a treatise of apologetics, will we make any effort to *establish* the doctrine. The truth of the Christian doctrine of man as revealed in Scripture and succinctly set forth in the Lutheran Confessions will be presupposed in what follows. The non-Christian reader should fix this procedural point firmly in mind as he reads; otherwise he will — quite understandably and, from the scientific standpoint, quite justifiably — find himself reacting to a speculative reconciliation with: "But why *do* that, when a simpler hypothesis would eliminate the whole problem?" Whatever rational case for the Christian system can be made on grounds of philosophy, natural theology, psychology, and history will not be discussed here. We must also recognize that the appearance of irresoluble contradictions between a well-supported scientific claim and Christian doctrine would, in itself, constitute rational inductive evidence against the latter. In that respect the resolution of paradoxes itself belongs in the area of apologetics.

Probably the easiest way for the non-Christian reader to approach our present discussion is to ask himself how he would proceed *if* he believed the doctrine of man to be very strongly supported by a qualitatively diverse and quantitatively weighty mass of other evidence and yet saw that difficulties arose in the area of human behavior-determinism. We are suggesting that he approach the system for present purposes as he would a ramified scientific theory, so strongly attested to by many independent lines of data that it would be abandoned with extreme reluctance, and having implications (flowing from its *core* tenets) which seem prima facie not to square with a restricted domain of data. In scientific cases of this sort we usually examine the alleged implications very critically to make sure that

180

the contradiction is genuine; if it is, the scientist may try to erect special *ad hoc* subtheories regarding the subdomain.[4] The Christian psychologist's conceptual task arises from his having accepted the Christian "theory," including a certain corpus of revealed statements about man. He takes it for granted that revelation cannot genuinely *contradict* any truth about man or the world which is discoverable by other means. If such appears to have happened, he must operate on the assumption that this is only an appearance. That being presupposed, he then seeks to resolve the contradiction. To this end he permits himself the use of speculative reason operating within the double constraints imposed by revelation and scientific facts.

If a conceptual resolution is effected, it is likely to have some consequences, i. e., the hypothesis does not remain completely *ad hoc*. If it has no terrestrial consequences, it is left as a speculative resolution. If a resolution cannot be effected, the problem is put on the shelf as a mystery, not solvable by the lights of nature or of grace but only in the light of glory. We do not expect the non-Christian reader to be pleased with this methodology or even to understand how anyone can unblushingly adopt it. We merely wish to make plain, for the sake of communication, the framework in which the discussion occurs. We are not testing the Christian "theory" T_c as to its conceptual power or parsimony. We are putting the question: "Taking T_c as true, what relationship exists between it and the psychologist's theory T_p?"

Christian readers have no doubt already bridled at the word "theory" as applied to their faith, and we turn next to a warning in their direction. It goes without saying that we are not here writing for purposes of edification or conversion. Our task is to relate two systems of concepts. Our theology does deal with concepts because our religion rests upon beliefs. (*Fiducia* presupposes *assensus*, although not implied by it.) The stumbling block experienced by determinists (whatever we Christians may guess as to some of its deeper motivations) is a conceptual stumbling block. We do not derogate from the faith in any way

---

[4] *Ad hoc* is a term of scientific reprobation; but the history of the advanced sciences is replete with fruitful hypotheses of this kind. The philosophical issues involved are too technical for treatment here.

by examining the logical implications which flow from a formal statement of it. Since the cognitive component of Christianity (theology) consists of a system of propositions, and since, as pointed out in Chapter II, this system makes a contact with space-time events and human experience at certain loci, the theological formulation of the faith is in these fundamental respects like a "theory." Both Christians and unbelievers seem at times to be unaware of this similarity, perhaps because they are (quite properly) impressed with the very important *differences* between theology and theories in science. First, there is a profound difference in the attitude taken by the Christian in the two kinds of "theories." Second, theology is conceptually "vaguer" than, say, theoretical physics; in part because it does not use mathematics, in part because it employs the mentalistic language and the categories of personhood as primary, and in part because our discursive knowledge of God is necessarily "analogical." Third, the conceptual network has numerous unfilled regions, the theological paradoxes and mysteries. Fourth, the degree of empirical confirmation is, from the scientific standpoint, relatively low. But these four are all differences of degree, in which theology and such poorly developed disciplines as psychoanalysis, history, and sociology are closer to each other than any of them is to physics. An atheist positivist colleague puts it: "Sure, there is such a thing as empirical theology; the point is that it's false."

Some may feel that what Luther likes to call "mere human speculation" is here being introduced by theologizing, in the manner of the scholastics, beyond what Scripture reveals. We sincerely believe that we have nowhere done this. The resolution of a contradiction is not an act of ὕβρις in which we mortals claim to have plumbed God's mysteries. To resolve a contradiction is to show what a certain collection of propositions does not contain, or imply, both *p* and *not-p*. In the present instance it happens that the collection is heterogeneous in origin, being taken partly from revelation, partly from current scientific theorizing, and partly from philosophical extrapolations of the latter to what has been aptly designated "inductive metaphysics." [5]

_____
5 By Professor Herbert Feigl.

It is true that we shall in the course of our discussion concoct certain *positive* hypotheses by way of resolution. But the Christian reader will note that, without exception, these positive theorizings are *in the scientific domain,* and not constructions of exegesis or speculative theology. For example, we consider certain hypotheses about the workings of the brain. No theological concepts are explicitly involved in those hypotheses. The relation *between* those hypotheses and the plain content or revelation (as summarized by the Confessions) is then examined; there need be nothing illegitimate about this analytical step. *Deus absconditus* is not searched by any of our speculations; rather we juxtapose the workings of *Deus revelatus* with some "scientific" speculations about the natural domain. This may be scientifically fruitless, but it is not unscriptural.

3. *Determinism and Materialism*

The idea that the natural world is orderly or lawful is not a peculiarly modern one. Those social scientists who assert that "modern science, by demonstrating the reign of natural law, has made belief in the miracles of historical religion impossible," are philosophically careless. In speaking of what science has "demonstrated," we must distinguish between empirical determinism and metaphysical determinism. Science cannot render the former more than highly probable; and science of course does not attempt, *qua* science, to say anything about the latter. An attenuated form of empirical determinism is not only compatible with belief in miracles, but a moment's careful thought shows that the very concept of a miracle presupposes belief in natural law. The remarks of Jesus quoted above, for example, would be simply senseless if made to people who lacked any idea of natural law, people who would therefore expect routinely that "anything might happen." [6] The Christian may be said to hold that empirical determinism is approximately true *but not quite;* and that the deviations from it are not random departures arising from the fundamental constitution of the created order but purposeful interventions by the Creator acting as *causa efficiens.*

Nevertheless it is a sociological fact that the rise of modern

---

6 Cornelius van Til, *The Defense of the Faith* (Philadelphia: Presbyterian and Reformed Publishing House, 1954), pp. 337; 262, 263; 334.

experimental science greatly strengthened and concretized the abstract idea of nature's lawfulness. The extension of prediction and control into domains which had been *in practice* perceived as enigmatic or capricious (e. g., bacterial disease) led to the confident expectation that, given sufficient time, the scientific method would elucidate all phenomena, i. e., formulate the underlying universal laws. It was further shown that the various domains of scientific study manifested a kind of conceptual hierarchy (reflecting an actual, physical compositional hierarchy), such that the laws of conglomerate systems could themselves be *derived* from the laws of their components, together with statements describing the arrangement of the conglomerate. Thus the digestive functions of the human intestine are largely explained by invoking the laws of two nonbiological sciences — chemistry and physics. Twenty-five years ago the properties of water were commonly said to be "emergent" (i. e., not explicable on the basis of properties of the hydrogen and oxygen which constitute it). Today a philosopher or theologian who uses this example merely displays his ignorance, since the advances in quantum chemistry and the theory of resonance have now shown that a very long list of the properties of water, including practically every one of its optical, thermal, chemical, and mechanical qualities, can be rigorously derived from laws of atomic structure and the mere definition of a water molecule as being hydrogen and oxygen atoms linked in a certain way.

The human body is made up of the same chemical elements as are found in animals and in inanimate nature. The human brain is a complex chemical system, consuming fuel, utilizing enzymes, storing up substances, manifesting electrical activity, and giving off waste products. Mechanical and chemical interference exert a marked influence upon its function (e. g., "the mind is not sober when the body is drunk"). A vast body of clinical and experimental evidence supports the view that whatever else he may be in addition, a human being is, among other things, a physical machine. The tremendous success of this approach, apparent to anyone who spends a day visiting classes in a medical school, understandably leads the non-Christian scientist to the hypothesis that this is *all* there is to man. He knows that the human person exhibits many amazing and puzzling powers which are not yet explainable in chemical terms. But he is not disturbed by this, because he knows that scientific progress is slow and that scientific answers to the hard questions may be generations or even centuries in coming. The living brain is, so far as we know, the most complicated system of interrelated parts that can be found in the whole physical universe. It may be the toughest scientific nut to crack; in which case it may very well be the last. So when the skeptical scientist hears talk of a nonmaterial agency or factor entering the causal order to "explain" how men come to write symphonies or create science or pray or make moral choices, such talk seems to him analogous to theorizing in 1500 that brownies curdle milk, merely because the science of organic chemistry had not yet developed, nor had anyone yet looked through a microscope at *Lactobacillus bulgaricus.*

Thus it has come to pass that there is an intimate connection between *materialism* and *determinism.* The culturally transmitted experience which has made many educated men into determinists is largely the experience of natural science. (The predictive and explanatory powers of the social sciences, except in rare selected areas, are as yet so feeble that they would by themselves be quite incapable of exerting this influence.) By dealing with material bodies and forces, and by a concentration on their objective, nonqualitative features (mass, length, velocity, electric charge, etc.), natural science has succeeded in erecting a truly magnificent conceptual structure. It is hard to imagine anyone gaining even a slight familiarity with this structure and not being deeply impressed by it, almost to the point of awe. That men, many of them illumined solely by the light of nature, have been able to learn this much about the created order is a testimony to how fearfully and wonderfully we are made.

For philosophical purposes, however, the usual connection between materialism and determinism must not stand unquestioned. When we subject these two theses to careful scrutiny, we see that they are logically independent and that their usual coexistence in the same minds is an accident of history. In order to show this, however, we shall have to clarify the notion of materialism. It is not possible, in the present state of philosophical analysis, to present a completely satisfactory formulation

185

of this doctrine. It is what Rudolf Carnap calls an *explicandum*[7] for which a rigorous explication has yet to be worked out. To make a start at explicating it, which we hope will be sufficient for our present purposes, we may consider the list of characteristics (found in treatises on physics) attributed to the several elementary particles out of which the known physical world is constituted. This list includes such entities as the electron, the proton, the meson, the neutron, and so forth. Numbers are associated with these entities indicating such characteristics (called "fundamental physical constants") as their mass, diameter, spin, electric charge, and half-life. In reading such a table there are two sorts of things which we would be very much surprised to find. If, in addition to the vertical columns headed "mass," "charge," etc., we found columns headed "intention" or "intellectual level" or "state of grace," we would know that the printer had scrambled some copy or that the author was making fun of us. Going horizontally, if we found that one of the *rows* of the table was labeled "angel," we would come to the same conclusion. Moral, cognitive, or volitional powers and states are not appropriately predicated of such entities as the electron; and properties such as mass, spin, or electric charge are not meaningfully predicated of angels.

As pointed out in Chapter VII, the materialist does not deny that beings exist of which we can meaningfully predicate such states as knowledge and intention. He knows as well as anyone else that there are "persons" or "minds" (although he prefers, especially if he is a psychologist, to avoid the latter terminology). He admits that he himself feels, thinks, and wills, whereas stones and plants do not. What he denies is that there are any beings possessing *only* mental attributes or powers, lacking the kinds of characteristics found among the fundamental physical entities and not composed of parts having such characteristics. The beings of which we can significantly assert such statements as: "X *ought* not to have done act A"; or "X *knows* that Columbus discovered America"; or "X *intends* to study archaeology," are,

---

7 "The Two Concepts of Probability," in *Readings in the Philosophy of Science*, ed. Herbert Feigl and May Brodbeck (New York: Appleton-Century-Crofts, Inc., 1953), p. 438.

according to the materialist thesis, always composite beings, made up of elementary components arranged or organized in certain physical configurations. These elementary entities, however, do not individually possess such powers as knowing, willing, or intending. Hence such mental, moral, or personal categories as "error," "duty," "fault," "purpose," "conception," or "rectitude" cannot be significantly applied in speaking about them. The materialist further holds that there is no insoluble mystery here. Even in the inorganic realm, composites and arrangements often have properties and powers not exhibited by their components or parts. "Timekeeping" is a real activity, not an illusion; that is, there are devices which do, as a matter of physical fact, "keep time." But their constituent parts do not, and cannot, keep time. Electronic computing machines solve equations; the punch-card machines used in military personnel work can be instructed to "search" the records for the names of all soldiers having a specified set of characteristics, such as being over six feet tall, blue-eyed, and speaking German fluently. Electrical and mechanical models have been constructed to display at an elementary level the basic behavioral phenomena of goal directedness, choice making, and learning from the consequences of their actions. To a materialist the difference between such a device and the human organism, while vast in its *degree*, does not seem to suggest a difference in *kind*. He therefore adopts as the most plausible working hypothesis the view that a human being is what he is by virtue of his special kind of brain (some fourteen *billion* nerve cells, interconnected with fantastic complexity). Crudely put, his position is that a man acts like a man instead of like an earthworm mainly because he has a tremendously more high-powered electrical computer inside his skull.

Suppose we distinguish between "fundamental" entities — the basic building blocks of the universe, out of which all things are made — and "composite" entities, these latter being conglomerates or configurations of the primary entities. Then the thesis of materialist monism can best be stated negatively, as follows: *None of the fundamental entities have any moral, mental, or personal attributes or powers.* This view, while rarely stated explicitly, is the unworded view of most educated non-Christians in the West; and a little casual conversation also

187

shows it to be the implicit world picture of many, perhaps most, educated liberal Protestants. It is probably no exaggeration to say that the impact of science in our day has made the solid majority of Americans, most of whom have never had any interest in philosophy, into solidly convinced crypto-materialists.

From what has been said it is obvious why determinism and materialism have an affinity. They both grew out of the successes of natural science, and the most striking results of applying the determinist research policy have occurred in those domains (e. g., physics) where the entities and events studied can be described exhaustively without recourse to mental, personal, or axiological categories. In fact, one of the necessary steps in the development of a scientific physics consisted precisely in the ruthless liquidation of all such categories from scientific discourse. Concepts such as the "perfect geometric figure (circle)" or the "natural end of substance X" were a hindrance to the pre-Galilean physicist.

Nevertheless we must emphasize that there is no logical necessity linking determinism with materialism. One can dichotomize those world theories which recognize matter as real into materialism versus dualism; and one can also dichotomize on the determinism-indeterminism question, this second division cutting across the first. We then have four possibilities, namely:

a. All the fundamental entities are material, and they instantialize strict universal laws. (Deterministic materialism)

b. All the fundamental entities are material, but the "laws" they instantialize are statistical. (Indeterministic materialism)

c. The fundamental entities include both material and mental kinds, and they instantialize strict universal laws. (Deterministic dualism)

d. The fundamental entities include both material and mental kinds, and the laws they instantialize are statistical. (Indeterministic dualism)

Actually, all four of these world pictures have found proponents in the history of secular psychology and philosophy.

188

The first is the "classical materialism" of eighteenth-century philosophy and of many Victorian physical scientists. The second is the predominant view of contemporary physicists. The third is found in many psychologists of the "classical" (introspective) period (e. g., Wundt, Titchener) and is also represented by those contemporary workers who, while giving a dualist interpretation to the telepathy experiments, firmly expect to find lawfulness in this domain. The fourth combination would be represented by most "vitalists" and by a tiny minority of American psychologists (McDougall). Since dualism in some form is already presupposed by anyone accepting Christian revelation (e. g., an angel belongs to the created order and at times acts upon its material entities), the orthodox Christian world view must be either (c) or (d). Which of these two is compatible with revelation, or are they both? The examination of this difficult question will occupy the remainder of the chapter.

4. *Determinism and Revelation: Conversion as a Specimen Problem*

In order to concretize the discussion, let us return to the case of Saul's conversion. The Christian holds this experience to have been a revelation. That is, God here acted as *causa efficiens* to produce in Saul the latter's subjective sounds and sights; and further, the effect which these had upon Saul was what God, in His providence, intended for Saul's personal conversion, the completion of revelation, and the growth of the church. Note that the account in Acts does not purport to tell us anything about the physics or physiology of the situation. St. Luke, though a physician, is not apparently interested in discussing this question. *God does it,* and whether or not the microevents in Saul's brain are instantializations of God's "universal" modes of activity is not an important question to the narrator. Sometimes the instantialization question is treated by Scripture as important (as in the preceding quotes of Jesus' words from Mark 2 and John 10), when works or signs are to be received by the observers as credentials. But in Acts 9 no such reference is made.[8]

---

[8] It is doubtful whether the question that we are putting would have been fully understandable, in the form we have given it, to the first-century

189

Confining ourselves to the brain physiology (i. e., simply ignoring, but not denying, the existence or causal role of any hypothetical mental or spiritual substance), three possibilities regarding the brain events present themselves:

A. Probably the first hypothesis which most physiologically minded Christians would construct regarding Saul's conversion would be that a sort of "minor miracle" occurred in Saul's brain. That is, while Saul's muscle action and blood chemistry may have proceeded in accordance with the usual physical laws, Omniscient Jones would have discerned at least a minuscule "departure," an "exception," a "violation" of deterministic laws in the finer details of Saul's brain processes. From a perfect knowledge of the physical state of Saul's brain at the instant before the subjective light appeared to him, one could not have predicted the immediately subsequent state. Certain neurons should (normally) have discharged, but didn't; others, which shouldn't have, did. This reconstruction of Saul's brain process we shall refer to as the *cerebral-miracle theory*.

B. A second possibility also exists. As was mentioned above, contemporary theoretical physics is indeterministic, holding that certain events at the level of the fundamental particles, or involving energy transactions of this order of magnitude, are in principle unpredictable.[9] Some physicists, physiologists, and psychologists [10, 11, 12, 13, 14, 15] are of the opinion that what is

---

Jew; since in his frame of reference the living God is constantly at work in ordinary events with a concreteness which the modern mind, even the modern Christian mind, rarely *feels*. But the idea of a miracle was, of course, available to Jewish thought, as the Old Testament and the reactions of the Jews to Jesus' works clearly demonstrate. The formulation in terms of *brain* events (rather than as activities and dispositions of the *whole man, Saul*), is what renders our discussion peculiarly modern.

[9] See n. 30 below.

[10] Niels Bohr, *Atomic Theory and the Description of Nature* (New York: Macmillan, 1934), pp. 116—119.

[11] John C. Eccles, "Hypotheses Relating to the Brain-Mind Problem," *Nature*, CLXVIII (July 1951), 53—57.

[12] John C. Eccles, *The Neurophysiological Basis of Mind* (Oxford: Oxford University Press, 1953), pp. 271—286.

[13] Arthur S. Eddington, *The Philosophy of Physical Science* (Cambridge: Cambridge University Press, 1939), pp. 179—184. See also his earlier works cited therein: *The Nature of the Physical World* (New York:

known in physics as "quantum indeterminacy" may be a significant factor in nervous activity; others deny this.[16] In particular, it has been suggested by the former group that a suitable patterning and chaining of neuronal circuits could easily bring about a physical situation of instability, in which the outcomes of one, or a few, quantum-indeterminate events would cumulate systematically to determine a large-scale behavior effect (a process called *Verstärkung* by its proponents). Applying this reasoning to the present case, one can hypothesize that Saul's previous experiences (plus, if it pleases the materialist to emphasize it, the fried eggs he had for breakfast) had put his brain, at the instant prior to the light experience, in what we may call a "conversion-indeterminate state." That is, considering the millions of local electrochemical states at the loci where the end buttons of certain neurons synapsed upon others, and given whatever momentary intracellular molecular motions affect the reactivity of these local regions, Omniscient Jones would be able to identify a subset of these local situations as quantum-indeterminate. Combinatorial analysis of the entire neuronal pattern would show the shifting or nonshifting of Saul's brain into the converted state depended upon the *pattern selection* of the quantum-indeterminate events to happen or not happen. Certain patterned selections of these unpredictable local quantum events would "throw" the whole system to conversion; others would throw it to obduracy. No deterministically based prediction could be made, even from a complete knowledge of the momentary situation; since, if contemporary physics is correct, these small-scale events are not predictable in principle. This second speculative hypothesis about Saul's conversion (note carefully, only about the *physiology* of his conversion!) may be appropriately called the *indeterminate brain-state theory*. (For

Macmillan, 1929), pp. 310—315; and *New Pathways in Science* (New York: Macmillan, 1935), pp. 86—91.

14 Pascual Jordan, *Science and the Course of History* (New Haven: Yale University Press, 1955), pp. 108—113.

15 Ivan D. London, "Quantum Biology and Psychology," *Journal of General Psychology*, XLVI (1932), 123—149.

16 Erwin Schroedinger, *Science and Humanism* (Cambridge: Cambridge University Press, 1951), pp. 58—64.

a somewhat more detailed examination of this theory and criticisms of it, see footnote 31.)

C. Finally, we have the view which materialist determinists would find most congenial, that one endowed with unlimited calculational powers *could* have predicted the event in its (physiological) entirety from an exhaustive knowledge of the momentary physical circumstances, because every microevent instantializes physical laws. Let this view be designated the *determinate brain-state theory.*

We shall now examine each of these speculative formulations in the light of Scripture and the Confessions. We shall not, of course, expect any of them to be found in revelation or even to be positively supported there. The question we put about each theory is the more modest one: Is the theory *consistent* with revelation? It must be kept constantly in mind in considering these three conceptions that *we are examining only the brain physiology.* If more is read into each account than the words say, theological pseudo problems will arise. For example, the sentence, *"When* Saul was converted, *there occurred* a patterned selection of indeterminate brain events," must not be read as, *"The Holy Spirit selected* the pattern of outcomes for the indeterminate critical neurones" — a formulation which is obviously not equivalent and which could perhaps have Calvinist implications (i. e., irresistible grace).

Theory (A), the cerebral-miracle theory, is the one most evidently compatible with revelation. According to this hypothesis, when Saul is converted he is *changed,* and the change is not only unpredictable from what went before, but is (for Omniscient Jones) a change actually *counter* to what would be expected. There is no conceivable source of antecedent knowledge of this event. The whole man Saul is changed, and in that partial description of Saul which is a physiologist's account of Saul's brain immediately preceding his conversion, we find statements denoting particular (dated) electrochemical events and states which, if substituted in the network of natural laws, would yield a misprediction of the subsequent state. Whatever the Christian dualist may hold, or the materialist deny, regarding a change in some nonmaterial state or substance composing

192

Saul's being, both will insist that the conversion, and Saul's state following it, must include certain cerebral events. After all, we see that Saul speaks and moves differently immediately after his conversion; speaking and moving are bodily events, produced by muscular action; muscles are controlled by the brain. To deny that a man's brain is changed in some respects when he undergoes conversion would be scientifically absurd (and also redolent of Manichaeism, Docetism, and Apollinarianism). However, the theory under consideration asserts that these cerebral events are anomalous, unique, cut off causally from the past, literally a new beginning. From knowing what Saul was, Omniscient Jones could not foresee what Paul would be; on the contrary, he would mispredict Saul to go on breathing fire and slaughter against the church. Not only was there no "merit" or "readiness" or "willingness" in Saul by which the change could be foreseen;[17] there was nothing else either — including the fried eggs — which would imply the outcome. The statements of Scripture concerning grace and regeneration seem readily reconciled with this cerebral-miracle theory. And if we go beyond the strict logical implications to the overtones and associated ideas, it appears that the cerebral-miracle theory is the most thoroughly congenial to the Christian notion of pure grace. (E. g., "The wind bloweth where it listeth, and thou hearest the sound thereof but canst not tell whence it cometh and whither it goeth: so is everyone that is born of the Spirit," John 3:8.)

At first glance, then, there appears to be no contradiction between the cerebral-miracle theory and the theology of grace. Nevertheless one has the uneasy feeling that all is not quite well. For one thing, perhaps some consequences can be derived from the theory which are crypto-Calvinistic in nature; consequences which are implicit in it although not apparent prima facie. Lutheranism repudiates the Calvinist doctrine of irresistible grace, one of Calvinism's "Five Points." "Can man, then, resist the power of God? He could not if God worked conversion immediately, in His uncovered majesty. He can when God operates through the means of His Word. . . . Here both Calvinists and synergists deviate from Scripture. From the false premise

---

[17] All three hypotheses allow this, so important to Lutherans.

193

of the irresistibility of grace, Calvinism argues against the universality of grace, asserting that whatever God earnestly intends must in every case actually occur." [18]

Suppose that the proposition "Saul [the man, the *person*] is converted at time *t*" can be translated (i. e., rendered *without residue*) as "The physical configuration C [here we describe or locate Saul's body unambiguously] underwent a change at *t* from state S_1 to state S_2." The states S_1 and S_2, and the change from one to the other, are in turn exhaustively rendered by a conjunction of statements concerning the microevents. If we take the cerebral-miracle theory to say that each microevent is wrought by God's will, then the conjunction of them is wrought by God's will. Would such a microaction of God's will be "resistible," in the sense imposed by Scripture as explicated in the Confessions? It is hard to see how this could be. Nor does the familiar distinction between God's *active* and *permissive* will help us out of the difficulty. It makes sense to say that Pilate condemns Christ by God's permissive will; but what kind of sense would it make to say that a certain nerve cell in Saul's brain fires "by God's permissive will"? Does this mean "by chance"? This is an expression which *we* have not used, but some would argue that we imply it. If we do, we can hardly assert with the Confessions that he who resists God's action (through the means of the Word) is condemned "by his own fault." Since the identical problem occurs in connection with the remaining two hypotheses regarding brain activity, we shall postpone further discussion of this crucial question until they have been examined.

Candidate (B), the indeterminate brain-state theory, presents a more complicated analytic problem. It gives somewhat less of an offense to the physiologist, since it merely takes conceptual advantage of an element of unpredictability within the physical order; if we may so speak, it begins with a scientifically formulated looseness or "play" in the machine, and the special action constituting conversion does not extend beyond the statistical limits of that natural "play." The categories which are relevant

[18] Francis Pieper, *Christian Dogmatics*, trans. Theo. Engelder et al. (St. Louis: Concordia Publishing House, 1951), II, 464, 465.

to understanding the outcome are, to be sure, nonphysiological categories. That is, selection of *which* of the quantum-indeterminate neurons will be fired is a selection with reference to a religiously specified outcome. (Here we have, by the way, a rare kind of event: a *gestalt*-operation of a fundamental kind.) There is, however, an important difference between

(1) A physical event not *derivable* from the laws and initial conditions, but *compatible* with them; and

(2) A physical event *incompatible* with the laws and initial conditions.

Only case (2) is a miracle in the strict sense. Case (1) is merely a physiologically inexplicable bit of goal-directedness. Furthermore, since the non-Christian physiologist refuses to accept revelation, he need not even be offended by the goal-directedness, since he sees none in the outcome. While he can say nothing in his scientific capacity which *conflicts* with the Christian interpretation, he of course finds it a scientifically superfluous addition. All he knows is that Saul's brain was in a quantum-indeterminate state and that one of the many possible "chance" selections of firing patterns eventuated.[19]

The acceptability of the indeterminate-brain-state theory from the Christian point of view is not easily decidable. The systematic selection of a patterned subset of indeterminate neuronal events could result in a converted brain only if the preceding state were of a physically appropriate character. The physiological constraints imposed by this condition are not open to discussion, because no exact knowledge exists about the brain at this level of micro-detail. We must therefore put the question in general terms. Consider the following statements, which would constitute a slightly elaborated form of the indeterminate-brain-state theory, as generalized beyond Saul to all conversions that have occurred, or will occur, in the church's history:

---

[19] An interesting problem, which we cannot examine here, is whether a preclassification of all possible selections into two classes, those having "conversion" as an outcome and those leaving Saul in his unregenerate state, would permit a calculation showing that conversion was an extremely improbable event; hence leading, by virtue of an outcome-relevant "pattern" being discernible in the unlikely joint event, to an inductive argument for some teleological agency having "made the selection." (See Appendix E)

(1) Each conversion is effected, in respect of its brain physiology, by the systematic selection of a subset of quantum-indeterminate microevents from the whole class of physically possible selections, such that the actual firing pattern results in the gross outcome, "converted brain."

(2) No violations of the laws of brain physiology, chemistry, or physics occur, since the selections are in every instance made available by the "play" in the system which the momentary physical situation allows on a quantum-indeterminacy basis.

(3) There are, at any time, at least *some* brains in the world whose momentary states are such that no possible selective patterning of the available indeterminate events would result in a converted brain state.

What this means, put more briefly (but less exactly), is that there are persons whose physical brain state is such that they could not be converted *without* a cerebral miracle and that, in fact, no conversions ever take place in brains which are in that condition. Cerebral miracles, on this view, do not occur; when people are converted, it always comes about by their brains *first* being brought to a physical state in which there exists at least one patterned selection of the available indeterminate microevents which would effectuate conversion. No statement is made about the nature of the concatenated circumstances which lead up to such a state, except that — since cerebral miracles are expressly ruled out — these antecedent circumstances must all instantialize the laws of physics and physiology.

Of course, "psychological" factors are also included in this description of the instantaneous microstate. The physical basis of habits, expectancies, and state variables *is* the brain state, and the characterization of the brain state could be formulated by Omniscient Jones in either the physiological or psychological language. These two languages are not inconsistent; rather they describe the same events at different levels of analysis.

Suppose that an unbeliever reads in the newspaper that a new church organ is being dedicated, and he visits the church, actuated by musical motives. While there, he hears, willy-nilly, a brief dedicatory serman preached on the worship of God through music. On the drive home he "chances" (Christians would say, "in God's providence") to pass the scene of an automobile accident and is turned to thoughts of death. As a result he dusts off his grandfather's Bible and reads a few pages. He is unconvinced and antagonistic, but decides that "the preacher seemed like a sincere fellow," and so he goes to church the following Sunday. Suppose that the long-term outcome of this sequence of experiences and actions is that he becomes converted.

None of these events, as described, is outside the ken of the psychologist or physiologist. *Whatever else* may have been going on — and we are not prejudging that question — the reading of printed pages, the hearing of a sermon, and the sight of a dead body are physiological occurrences. Their inner impact occurs in a living brain; their initiating causes are light rays and sound waves emanating from external objects. They are examples of what our Lutheran dogmaticians call "secondary causes." The Christian has no interest in denying their reality or their causal influence; to do so would be ridiculous. If a pastor did not think that the brains in his listeners' heads were being physically influenced by the sound waves produced in his larynx, he would have no reason to design a church with good acoustics, nor would he be concerned with whether or not the congregation slept through his sermon.

Although the Christian who gives a little thought to the physical character of the Word read or preached will find nothing unscriptural in statement (1) of the indeterminate-state theory, statements (2) and (3) may rouse his doctrinal suspicions. Do these negative statements amount to saying that there are people whom God *could not* convert, at least for the time being, because their brains are in states which allow of no event selections of the necessary kind? For example, Saul had been reading and arguing about the Christian Church, had presumably been praying as a good Pharisee would, had witnessed the stoning of Saint Stephen, and so on. In the language of our Chapter V, certain habits, expectancies, cathexes, and perceptions had been set up in him. More importantly, certain state variables (motives and emotions) had been activated and hooked up to Saul's habits in definite ways. We have repeatedly alluded to the hypothetical fried eggs he ate for breakfast. We do this not in any spirit of

197

levity, and such an allusion neither besmirches sacred things nor pokes fun at the materialist. Body chemistry is very important in determining the state of the brain, and battles have no doubt been lost because of failings on the part of a field marshal's cook. So the fried eggs are part of the intricate concatenation of causes which converge on the Damascus road to put Saul — brainwise — where he is. Now let us suppose for a moment that, had everything else in Saul's immediate and remote past been just as it was *but the fried eggs had been lacking,* the brain state would have been subtly altered so that no available selection of indeterminate events would suffice to yield a converted brain. To the brain physiologist such a supposition has nothing against it and is quite compatible with scientific knowledge. The question is, Would statements (2) and (3) of the indeterminate-state theory commit us as Christians to the (heretical) view that God *could not,* then and there, have effected Saul's conversion?

Such an impression would reveal a superficial understanding of these statements. They do not make any mention whatever of *possibility,* of what the Lord *could* do. Statement (2) asserts that (in respect to their physiology) all actual, realized conversions occur without cerebral miracles, by the "throwing" of indeterminate events in a suitably configurated pattern. Statement (3) might erroneously be taken as meaning that persons whose brains are in a determinate state "could not" be converted. But it says nothing of the sort. All it says is that *if* they were to be converted at the moment in question, a cerebral miracle *would* have to occur; since their local micro-indeterminacies do not present any possible pattern selection which would cumulate to "converted brain." This is merely a descriptive statement about actual brain states. By saying that "some persons could not be converted at certain moments in their life histories *unless* God chose to perform a cerebral miracle," one does not really limit God at all, any more than He is limited when we say, "Under certain circumstances of disease, the person will die unless God performs a miracle; God 'cannot' make him survive otherwise." The word "cannot" which occurs in this statement is the "cannot" of logical contradiction; it "limits" God only in the trivial

198

sense that statements like "God cannot make the past not to have been" [20] or "God, being holy, cannot do evil" "limit" Him.

The term "cannot" has several meanings, determined by the several meanings of the logically more fundamental word "possible." Contemporary logicians are accustomed to distinguish the following three meanings of "possible":

(1) Logical possibility: This means "consistent formally and definitionally." Thus it is logically possible that the sun suddenly should cease to exist, without leaving any trace; or an atheist become converted without hearing the Word; or a physical object travel faster than light. The only entities or events which are logically *im*possible are those which violate the laws of logic [21] or which contradict the definitions of words. For a bachelor and his paramour to beget a legitimate child is logically impossible, given the meanings of the terms "bachelor," "paramour," and "legitimate." One way of putting this is to say that the logically impossible is meaningless. We cannot, strictly speaking, *convey* the logically impossible in a statement; because the statement violates the rules of our very language and hence says nothing. Wittgenstein writes: "It used to be said that God could create everything, except what was contrary to the laws of logic. The truth is, we could not *say* of an 'unlogical' world how it would look. To present in language anything which 'contradicts logic' is as impossible as in geometry to present by its coordinates a figure which contradicts the laws of space; or to give the coordinates of a point which does not exist. We could present spatially an atomic fact which contradicted the laws of physics, but not one which contradicted the laws of geometry." [22]

(2) Causal possibility: This means "consistent with the accepted framework of causal laws." That the sun should vanish without a trace would violate the laws of physics; as would the (logically possible) notion of an object exceeding the velocity

<hr>

[20] Thomas Aquinas, *Summa theologica*, I, Q. 25, a. 4, in *Basic Writings of St. Thomas Aquinas*, ed. Anton C. Pegis (New York: Random House, 1945), I, 265, 266.

[21] "Logic" here means *logic*, not "reason," "science," "good sense," "plausibility," or "what everybody knows."

[22] Ludwig Wittgenstein, *Tractatus logico-philosophicus* (London: Kegan Paul, 1933), p. 43.

199

of light, which is inconsistent with the postulates of relativity theory. That an atheist should be converted without the Word is not self-contradictory, and therefore such an event is logically possible; but it is incompatible with the *ordo salutis* which the Lord has established. So causal possibility is a more restrictive notion than logical possibility. Any event which is causally possible is logically possible, but not conversely. When we say that an event is not logically possible, we are in effect saying that a statement of it cannot even be *formulated* consistently. Its causal impossibility is a trivial consequence of its logical impossibility.

What we have designated "causal possibility" is usually referred to in the technical literature as *physical* possibility, because most analytic logicians happen to be materialists in their ontology. No violence is done to the concept by extending it as we have done. The basic idea is that this second kind of possibility is judged within the frame of causal laws, which are universal statements of synthetic nature. In a nonmaterialist framework the entities would include mental or spiritual substances, but if there were exceptionless generalizations which could correctly be asserted regarding these, such laws would be comparable to the physical laws customarily given as examples. According to revelation, all conversions are effected by means of the Word. The Holy Spirit never converts without the Gospel. Therefore a conversion in the absence of the Gospel, while logically possible (i. e., not self-contradictory or beyond God's powers), nevertheless is causally impossible, being excluded by the *ordo salutis* which God has ordained.

(3) Technical possibility: This concept has also been called "practical" possibility. It means that human beings could, either now or in the future, actually achieve certain results. It is difficult to exclude anything as technically impossible once it is known to be causally possible; the advances in technology are so dramatic and unforeseeable that even scientists have often been refuted after claiming confidently that something "will never be done." A classic example is that of Comte, who held that man could never ascertain the chemical constitution of the stars. This seemed a very sure thing at the time he said it, since chemical constitution was "obviously" investigable only by chem-

ical analysis, and the stars were permanently unavailable for the chemists' manipulation. The idea that man could infer chemical constitution from the character of emitted light did not occur to Comte; but modern spectroscopy uses this method. As a result we know the relative proportions of the various elements in certain stars with higher accuracy than we do that of our own earth.

Discussions as to what *could* happen or as to whether something *has to* happen (or "must" happen, or happens "of necessity"); and discussions making use of such words as "inconceivable" or "impossible" are often clouded by a failure to distinguish among these meanings of possibility. The free will controversy, for example, has been badly infected by linguistic confusions in respect to "possibility."

Returning to the question whether our indeterminate-state theory is heretical, we can reformulate it as follows: There are some individuals whose conversion at a given moment in time is *physiologically impossible*. This merely says that the person's momentary brain state is such that an instantaneous shift to a converted brain state would involve a violation of the causal universals which constitute the physiologist's law frame. To say of an event that it is "physiologically impossible" *means* no more than this; the adverb "physiologically," or a similar adverb modifying the term "impossible" by reference to a specified scientific domain, has as its function to inform the reader that a certain frame of causal laws is presupposed. So when we say: "To convert Saul on the Damascus road was physiologically possible for God," we are merely saying: "God could convert Saul, including the change in Saul's brain to a converted brain, without effecting any brain event which would fall outside the laws of brain physiology which He has ordained." And if we say: "For Pilate to have been converted at Jesus' trial was physiologically impossible," we are saying merely that if God at that time were to have put Pilate's brain into the converted state, this would necessarily have involved an exception to the laws of physiology (i. e., a cerebral miracle). This, obviously, God *could* do, *if* He so willed; even an atheist will readily admit that once the idea of theism is granted, "possible" and "physiologically possible" are not the same thing.

The second part of the indeterminate-state theory merely denies that God *in fact* has ever chosen to convert in this way. It asserts that all actual conversions are accomplished by first bringing the brain into a "convertible" state, without the suspension of any physiological laws. Once in that state, the subsequent state is (physically) indeterminate. After that convertible state has been reached, there then occurs a "selection" of a pattern of quantum-indeterminate events such that their cumulative outcome is a converted brain. The "preparation" of the brain by a suitable combination of preconversion experiences is not conversion; nor is this preparation any kind of merit or prevenient grace. The Lutheran reader need not suspect a crypto-Pelagian or synergistic element in what we have said. The brain categories involved are not theological or moral; and no hypothesis is made, or implied, as to any relationship between these disparate sets of categories. The experiences which bring an individual to a certain state, while he is still unregenerate, are part of God's providence.

The music-loving atheist in our example was motivated to go to church because he wanted to hear an organ recital. In pointing out this obvious fact we are surely not suggesting anything like preconversion merit; yet no one would wish to deny that the musical motivation was, in this man's case, a factor in the chain of causality leading to his hearing of the Word. If the sermon had been in German, he would not have understood it. That he understood it in English was possible because he *learned* English as a child — a process which we all assume occurred in accordance with physiological laws. The events which brought it about that this particular man sat where he did and understood the words are part of the order of nature; they instantialize the laws of chemistry, physiology, and psychology. For the Christian, to say this is not equivalent to saying, "God had nothing to do with it." *Everything that happens* falls within the scope of God's providence; everything that happens is by God's active or permissive will.

Suppose someone then asks: "At what point in your brain theory do you cease to treat of God's general providence (in accordance with which everything happens) and begin to speak of the specific action of the Third Person of the Trinity in conversion?" One who asks this question has moved from a speculative psychophysiology of how the *brain* is converted to speculative theology; the Scriptural theologian will quite properly refuse to consider this question, since no hint of the answer is to be found in Scripture. How, for example, the specific converting action of the Holy Spirit is involved, in the selection of indeterminate outcomes and the preceding "natural" development relegated to God's general providence, cannot be inferred from revelation. Consider, for example: "No man can come to Me except the Father which hath sent Me draw him" (John 6:44). The allocation of the components of conversion to the Persons of the Trinity, especially when components of the converted individual are analytically separated and different points in time are considered, is a task which is beyond our powers. Revelation having said nothing about it, nor implying anything with deductive necessity, we do not attempt to pass the limits of knowledge but desist from probing at this point. What has been made clear, we hope, is that the indeterminate-brain-state theory can be put alongside the cerebral-miracle theory as compatible with revelation.

We now turn to the third and last theory of conversion, the determinate-brain-state theory. According to this formulation, the cerebral events participating in conversion are, without exception, instantializations of physiological laws. (The strict determinist psychologist would have to hold either that the indeterminacy of theoretical physics is illusory; or, as he would more probably prefer to go along with the physicist's brand of physics, he might argue that the objects and energies involved in neuronal activity are beyond the range of magnitudes where quantum uncertainty plays a significant role, involving the combination of so many elementary events that the "practical certainty" of macroevents obtains). We shall neglect the theoretical niceties which grow out of the relation between an indeterminist physics and a "practically determinist" psychophysiology, and simply refer to the latter as determinist. This is justifiable for present purposes, because if conversion represented merely an extremely improbable event (such as a hard-boiled egg spontaneously unboiling itself), the probabilities would be so minute that no sinner would ever have been converted since the world began.

Is the determinate-brain-state theory consistent with revelation? To answer this question is far more difficult than in the cases of the cerebral-miracle theory or the indeterminate-brain-state theory. In fact, we have not been able to arrive at an answer to it, although we lean to the negative; but it appears to us to be an open question. The most that we can offer is a brief discussion of some of the relevant considerations. We know of no clear passages in Scripture which enable us to deal with the question. As was pointed out above, the modern way of formulating it would have accorded poorly with the forms of Jewish (or, to a lesser degree, Greek) thought. It is not natural to speak about such categories as sin, grace, conversion, etc., in the language of microevents. It is Saul, the person, the whole man, to whom something happens. And the microstate formulation has to be put with great care, lest we commit what the British logicians call a "category mistake." [23] Thus, to speak of one of Saul's brain cells as being converted would be nonsense, not only to St. John but also to the contemporary logician. Conversion is a category which applies to *persons*, not to nerve cells. An atheist materialist logician, even though he would reject conversion as a supernatural event, would be as insistent upon this as we are; and on the same logical grounds he would reject a statement such as, "Eisenhower's brain cells are Republican." This is a senseless utterance, immediately perceived as such by both Republicans and Democrats.

With this warning against category mistakes, we ask: Are the statements of Scripture attributing the conversion of an individual to the Holy Spirit compatible with an assertion that the microevents which occur in his brain at the time of conversion are instantializations of universal causal laws? Note that this formulation does not speak at all of such concepts as "inevitability" or "fatalism." These concepts are not sufficiently precise to be used as analytic tools, and in addition they have numerous noncognitive overtones which arouse irrelevant feelings in the thinker. Since such words contribute nothing positive to a rigorous analysis of our conceptions, they should be sedulously

---

[23] Gilbert Ryle, *The Concept of Mind* (London: Hutchinson's University Library, 1949), pp. 16—18.

avoided. The reader is urged to conceive the determinate-brain-state theory as meaning neither more nor less than what it says: that when a conversion is examined at the microphysiological level of brain events, these events instantialize universal causal laws.

Would the *total* event of theological interest — the conversion of the *person* — be attributable to God's activity if this were so? Surely it would, since, within a theistic frame, the universal laws are simply statements (by us) of modes of action to which the living God in His providence consistently adheres. God's will, theologically speaking, is not any more at work in a miracle than in an occurrence which instantializes physical laws; although, *epistemologically speaking,* we (quite properly) see the former as a "clearer" exhibition of the divine power. If Saul is moved, God moves him. If a microanalysis of Saul's brain events finds no cerebral miracles, the events do not thereby become classifiable as independent of God's will. (We must again remind the non-Christian reader that our task here is to deal with the *consistency* problem, not to raise the issue of confirmability of the theistic frame. Confining our attention solely to the physiology of conversion, it would be impossible, on the determinate-brain-state theory, to distinguish empirically between a theistic and a naturalistic account. This is not true of the other two theories, as will be shown in the concluding section of this chapter.)

At this point the uncomfortable thought occurs that one has proved too much. "If Saul is moved, God moves him" is an acceptable formulation of revelation. The Calvinist doctrine of irresistible grace cannot be derived, without the use of some further implicit premises, from the assertion that God's action is a necessary condition for conversion. But the determinate-brain-state theory has a suspicious look about it. Such familiar theological statements as: "Man does not prepare himself for conversion," or: "Man does not 'co-operate' in his conversion," do not entail, according to Lutheran teaching, "Grace is irresistible," (which we deny). Does the determinate-brain-state theory somehow imply irresistible grace?

This question arose earlier, when we were considering the cerebral-miracle theory; and it could have been raised also with respect to the indeterminate-brain-state theory. In the former case, we might say (or imply): "God converts by suspending the microlaws"; in the latter: "God converts by selecting an appropriate pattern of firing among the critically located cells which are 'physically available,' i. e., in the indeterminate state." If the reader turns back to the preceding discussion of these two theories, he will find that we very carefully avoided any such locutions as these. We spoke in impersonal terms, using passive-voice or intransitive verbs, saying things like "A pattern selection *occurs*," where it would perhaps have seemed more natural to say, "God selects a pattern."

We employ this noncommittal language for two reasons. First, statements such as "God selects the firing pattern" fall outside the scope of our task, which is to examine the compatibility of three theories of brain function during conversion with revelation. The statements we made in the course of our discussion of the three theories were physiologically meaningful (although, of course, not technologically testable). Strictly speaking, the discussion was scientific discourse, even though its content would not be pleasing to an atheist physiologist. Whereas statements about what God does are not admissible in the scientific language.

Secondly, we stated at the outset that our speculative activity would be speculative as to science, but not as to theology. One does not need revelation to formulate the three brain theories; these could be arrived at purely by logical analysis of the physical situation. Every microevent that takes place in a brain falls under one of three headings: It instantializes a universal causal law; it constitutes an "exception" to a near-universal causal law (i. e., a generalization of physics which holds *everywhere except* where the microevents involved, not individually or locally distinguishable in other respects, are part of the activity of living brains); or it is of quantum order and hence is physically indeterminate (i. e., no causal law applies). These are the available possibilities, and they could be listed by anyone knowing logic and physics, even if he were totally ignorant of both brain function and theology. On the other hand, to formulate sentences about God's action on the end buttons of neurons is to engage in speculative theology, which we have no desire to do.

Confining ourselves to what revelation says or clearly implies, we ask, Can any of the three theories, if further elaborated, be excluded theologically? This is an extremely difficult question. We are inclined to think that if a monistic metaphysics were combined with any of the three, fatalism or Calvinism would be implied. But we are not certain even of this much. The determinate-brain-state theory, as it would be held by a materialist, could probably be shown to contradict the Confessions. The cerebral-miracle theory, if interpreted as "God suspends the laws," and if taken within a materialist frame, would appear to render grace irresistible. The indeterminate-brain-state theory has the same fate if we go on to say that God makes the selections.

But, of course, we need not go on to say this. Consider the following statement: "The selection of quantum-indeterminate microevents, while each is *locally* unpredictable, exhibits statistically a systematic character by virtue of its *gestalt* relation to the molar outcome 'conversion' (i. e., the *patterning* of the microoutcomes is discernible as teleological when we permit ourselves the use of suitable categories falling outside the physiological language)." At first blush it does seem that this statement entails a disjunction of the following three statements:

a. The selection operation has a creature as its *causa efficiens* (examples would be the individual's substantive soul or a demon).

b. The selection operation has God as its *causa efficiens*.

c. The selection operation is "by chance."

Will the alleged entailment of this disjunction bear searching scrutiny? The basis of the entailment seems to be an assumption somewhat as follows: Everything that happens, happens either by chance or by God's action or by the action of a created agency. Is this an analytic truth? If not, what kind of statement is it? How can (c) be accepted when the statistical teleology is presupposed? The analysis of these problems is beyond the scope of this book and involves, among other things, the philosophical problems of "emergence." [24]

---

[24] Paul E. Meehl and Wilfred Sellars, "The Concept of Emergence," in *Minnesota Studies in Philosophy of Science*, ed. Herbert Feigl and M. Scriven (Minneapolis: University of Minnesota Press, 1956), I, 239—252.

Here the ontological dualism question forces itself upon our attention. The dualist would say that the usual, personal-language statement about Saul's conversion cannot be fully translated into a conjunction of statements, however complicated, about the microevents in Saul's brain. Specifically, he would argue that the name "Saul" designates a psychophysical unity which includes mental events, energies, or substances not reducible without residue to the brain events. The brain events occur, but some other events occur also. These latter events cannot be exhaustively described in the language of the cerebral events, although there may be universal psychophysical laws which make it possible to infer one kind of event from the other. Let us adopt the word "soul" (in one of its several meanings) to designate the noncerebral entity whose inclusion is required to complete the picture. Since revelation has already made the soul available in our armamentarium of concepts, it is perhaps permissible to reflect briefly upon the place it might find in these theories. For expository purposes we shall consider the soul within the framework of the determinate-brain-state theory. If introduction of the dualistic concept can square *this* theory with revelation, the other two theories will be very unlikely to pose an insoluble problem.

With the addition of this new ingredient to the determinate-brain-state theory, the original statement "Saul, the person, is converted at t" analyzes — this time without residue — into two statements, one couched in brain language, the other in soul language. We say, "The person Saul is converted at t" *means*

P. "Saul's brain state changed at t from state S_1 to state S_2" *and*

Q. "Saul's soul state changed at t from state S'_1 to State S'_2."

These two statements are different, i. e., they are about different events. Contentwise they are nonequivalent (although it may be that in the *ordo salutis* they *empirically* imply one another). The logical situation here is quite different from that which obtains between the microphysiological and the psychological languages, given a materialist ontology. In that framework, "Jones is angry" and "Jones has brain state A" are different ways of expressing the same facts. The conjunction of the present two statements P and Q is not redundant, but is required for a complete translation of "The person Saul is converted at t."

At the present stage of knowledge the dualist is forced to take the soul as an unanalyzed unity, exhibiting, to be sure, distinguishable dispositions, but not having known "parts" or "components." (In some Greek and medieval thought, this "unity" or "indivisibility" of the soul is given great importance and is used as an argument for immortality; but these are philosophical speculations without support in revelation. Lutherans are quite free to consider the soul as itself complex.) On a dualist analysis, "could" Saul — the whole man, the psychophysiological system — have resisted God's converting activity? This resistance would be an action of Saul's soul, occurring by God's permissive will; whereas the continuance of Saul's brain in the unconverted state would be an instantialization of universal physical laws. Since the doctrine of election, *even as interpreted by synergists and Arminians,* attributes to God at least foreknowledge [25] of conversion, the theoretical requirement imposed is that God so arranges the initial conditions of the physical order that the events in Saul's brain at t are instantializations of universal physical statements. This is necessary; because if the whole person, the psychophysical unity, is to be different in behavior *dispositions* after conversion, the postconversion brain state must be distinguishable from the (unrealized) brain state which *would have* obtained if Saul had resisted. As was pointed out above, after conversion Saul speaks and gestures differently. Saul's larynx and hands are controlled by his brain, and since we are assuming the determinate-state position, the dualist addition must not result in a departure of microevents from the physical laws. God, having ordained Saul's conversion "before the foun-

---

25 More rigorously, "eternal knowledge"; "foreknowledge" is anthropomorphic in a misleading way, because it calls to mind the epistemic situation of a knower who "knows" discursively or prophetically before he knows directly, a distinction not applicable to God, who does not exist in time, does not experience the phenomenal flux, and hence does not "come upon" events "previously anticipated." In Christian theology, time itself, like space and motion, is part of the created order. This is why, as St. Augustine made clear, the question "What was God doing before He made the world?" is devoid of cognitive content.

dation of the world" (Eph. 1:4), must, on this analysis, have so set the initial physical conditions of the cosmos that the events in Saul's brain at time t put it in the "converted" state necessary to yield a total psychophysiological system having the dispositions of a converted person. This assumption is not Calvinistic, because we insist on the basis of Scripture that grace is resistible. What is conversion on this analysis? It is a composite event, expressed by the two propositions P (concerning Saul's brain) and Q (concerning his soul). The conjunction $P.Q = C$ ($=$ conversion). Since logically the falsification of a conjunction is entailed by the falsification of one of the conjuncts, if God's grace does not operate irresistibly to realize Q, then it does not operate irresistibly to realize C. Hence grace is resistible, even though P is wholly determined by God's action. That P and Q are always true (or false) together is not an analytic consequence of their meanings but is a contingent fact of the *ordo salutis*. The philosophically oriented reader will recognize here elements of the doctrine called *occasionalism*, the relation of which to such concepts as secondary causes, providence, and the scientific idea of causal necessity is far beyond the scope of this book.

In terms of the traditional philosophical solutions of the mind-body problem, what has just been suggested falls under the heading of *psychophysical parallelism*. Although a correspondence exists between the sequence of soul states and the sequence of brain states, the latter series is internally predictable. From the physical causal laws alone, successive states of the brain are predictable; the co-ordinated soul state is, causally speaking, a supernumerary. A *psychophysical interactionist* position might also be formulated which would be deterministic; but in that case the series of brain events would not be internally self-explained. If the soul acts as *causa efficiens* with respect to brain events, complete determinism cannot hold within the physical law frame. Hence from the physiologist's point of view, the soul as *causa efficiens* implies that the determinate-brain-state theory is false. The cerebral-miracle theory or the indeterminate-brain-state theory squares nicely with interactionism, of course; the substantive soul being the miracle worker in the first and the pattern selector in the second. "Mind" as selector of physically indeterminate brain events is discussed by Eccles in the works cited.[26, 27] On such an analysis the locus of the theological mystery is transferred wholly to the action of God upon the substantive soul. The quantum-indeterminate brain events are selected by the soul, and the paradox of resistible grace and unconditional election lies wholly outside of physiology.

Some have argued that parallelism and interactionism cannot be theoretically distinguished; because, if the parallelist system is lawful, an invariable brain-mind correlation and succession will exist, making it impossible to find an instance of a $brain_1 \rightarrow brain_2$ sequence which is not attended by a corresponding $mind_1 \rightarrow mind_2$ sequence. Since all occurrences of the $brain_2$ state are immediately preceded by the same brain-mind *pattern*, the latter is the precondition (hence, efficient cause) of the former. Such an analysis ignores the important question of *derivability*. If the laws of physics and chemistry suffice to derive (i. e., by microevent causal laws) the subsequent brain state from its immediate predecessor, the preceding mind state is a supernumerary, causally speaking. This would lead us to parallelism or epiphenomenalism. Whereas, if such a microderivation is impossible, the succession of brain states is not causally self-contained, and the determinate-brain-state theory must be rejected in favor of interactionism.

We do not feel it profitable to pursue the analysis further in this place. Recent clarifications achieved by analytic philosophy may turn out to be of considerable use to the theologian who concerns himself with secular theories of the mind-body relationship. The "mind-body problem," which Schopenhauer rightly called *der Weltknoten* (at which all the great puzzles of secular philosophy somehow find a common nexus), can hardly fail to be of theological interest when the joint bearing of revelation and natural knowledge upon our view of man is under investigation. An incisive, thoroughly informed, and fair-minded treatment of the history and present status of the mind-body problem in secular philosophy has been recently written by the materialist Feigl, whose paper also includes an excellent bibliography.[28]

---

26 Loc. cit. See n. 11 above.

27 Neurophys., pp. 278, 279. See n. 12 above.

28 Herbert Feigl, "The 'Mental' and the 'Physical,'" in *Minnesota Studies in Philosophy of Science* (see n. 24 above), II (1958), pp. 370—497.

While our stated purpose was to examine consistency questions, the preceding discussion does raise some interesting issues regarding the scientific status of the three theories. "Confirmability" in contemporary scientific philosophy does not mean the actual ability to carry out an experiment (i. e., the technical possibility defined above), but merely that the formulation has some implications, even if only probabilistic, for statements in the intersubjective observation language.[29] It is worth pointing out that the first two theories examined both have theoretical confirmability in this scientific sense. The cerebral-miracle theory implies that when individuals are converted, the (usually sufficient) description of a microstate at t does not permit a derivation of the postconversion state. Since the subsequent dispositions of the individual are direct outcomes of the new microstate, it is in each case theoretically possible to examine the large (but finite) set of configurations which could have arisen had some one of the alternative patterns of individually indistinguishable micromiracles occurred instead of the patterning that did in fact occur. Suppose, for example, that the physical character of these component cerebral miracles is the failure of a nerve cell to discharge when it "ought to"; and suppose that a purely random patterning of such micromiracles in individual brains would not, in general, result in the formation of converted brain states. Statistical considerations (too technical to enter upon here) would justify the inductive inference that a teleologically *selective* process was at work, determining the pattern of micromiracles within each brain *so as to* leave it in the converted state.

The same can obviously be said, *mutatis mutandis,* of the indeterminate-brain-state theory. Here no suspensions of microlaws are involved, but the individually indeterminate microevent is seen as part of a *Gestalt* which is teleological in its macrooutcome. The teleology could be statistically manifested by a nonrandomness of firing patterns discernible in the entire class of conversion events.

---

[29] Rudolf Carnap's latest version of the "meaning-criterion" is even broader than that and would permit statements having no observational consequences. See his "The Methodological Character of Theoretical Concepts," ibid., I (1956), pp. 38—76.

Summarizing, we have examined three speculative theories regarding brain activity during conversion with respect to their compatibility with the theology of grace, taking an individual's conversion as a specimen for analysis. Two of them — the cerebral-miracle theory and the indeterminate-brain-state theory — were judged to be compatible with the theological system, quite apart from considerations of ontological dualism. Each of these theories is also empirical in the customary scientific sense, having statistical implications for brain function. The third theory, that of strict physical determinism, was deemed compatible with Christian doctrine provided that an ontological mind-body dualism is also maintained, but probably (although not certainly) leading to Calvinism otherwise. The third theory was judged, unlike the other two, to be nonempirical, if the empirical observation basis is confined to brain events and revelation is excluded from the empirical class.

It is likely that a satisfactory solution of the core problem of determinism and grace would show the way to a solution of most, if not all, of the other theological difficulties engendered by scientific determinism as a philosophical thesis.[30, 31]

---

[30] We are quite aware that the physical-indeterminacy conception, which has prevailed now for over 30 years, is susceptible of alternative ontological interpretations. A minority of theoretical physicists (including, however, such distinguished workers as Einstein and Planck) hold that the events *in themselves* must be deterministic, but that we have not yet succeeded in penetrating to a level of analysis which enables us to predict individual elementary physical events. In opposition to this view, the majority of physicists argue that since unpredictability is not a mere "technical" difficulty but is a theoretically derivable consequence of fundamental physical laws, such determinism is an act of faith without scientific value. Since probability expressions occur in the *object-language* formulation of those fundamental postulates which implicitly define the elementary physical entities and processes, contemporary physicists are not looking for laws and methods to enable prediction of elementary physical events, and most of them confidently expect that none such will ever be found. From the scientific point of view, the assertion that an event is determined "in itself" but is *theoretically* unpredictable is of very dubious meaning. It seems therefore appropriate to say that modern physics is, with regard to the "rock bottom" events which constitute the world, not deterministic in either the methodological or empirical senses of Chapter III; and that physicists as a group are not metaphysical determinists either. If an individual psychologist or physicist nevertheless espouses metaphysical determinism, he does so on philosophical grounds or as an act of faith. In so

213

doing he does not *contradict* physical theory, but he surely derives no support from it either.

31 It is of interest to ask whether any independent evidence exists with regard to the speculations in this chapter regarding micro-indeterminacy and brain function. It might be supposed that the present primitive state of our scientific knowledge of brain function obviously precludes the possibility of any such evidence being available; if we do not know much about the structure and laws of the brain, how could we fruitfully raise the question of whether these laws are deterministic? This *ignoramus* is admittedly plausible. Nevertheless it is too strong, as we shall now show briefly. The experiments which have been performed on precognitive telepathy (see, for instance, S. G. Soal and F. Bateman, *Modern Experiments in Telepathy* [New Haven: Yale University Press, 1954]) suffice to render the determinate-brain-state theory unlikely, *even though we know little of the microdetails of brain function.* How is this possible?

In precognitive telepathy, a person guesses the character of events which have not yet taken place, and concerning which he has no information providing a basis for inference, to a degree not explainable as "chance" or "coincidence." The experiments are carried out in such a manner that these "foreseen" events are unpredictable as a series (i. e., the sequence of characters which they exhibit is random, being made so by such artificial means as random number tables). These events are known to a second person, but not until after the subject, the "seer," has recorded his guess. A simple example would be a situation in which the telepathic "sensitive," the percipient, is in London and the "sender" (called technically the *agent*) is in Antwerp. They work by synchronized watches. At two-second intervals the agent flips a coin and records the outcome of this random event (i. e., is it heads or tails?). Two seconds *earlier* the percipient in London has recorded his guess. In the long run, if there is no causal connection between the percipient's call and the result of the actual coin toss, approximately 50 per cent of the calls should be "correct." There exist exact mathematical methods of determining whether the observed percentage of correct calls (= hits) is significantly in excess of the theoretical value. It turns out that some gifted individuals are able to perform this feat, which suggests modes of brain-to-brain (or mind-to-mind) communication of a kind not provided for by present-day physiological theory. When the telepathic transmission is "precognitive," so that the percipient's call antedates the target event, the phenomenon raises fundamental questions for physics as well, since it bears upon the nature of time and causality.

Now if the brain state of the percipient were strictly determined by the chain of physical causality stretching into the past, the "matching" of his guesses with the (not-yet-occurred) event would have to be explained by some sort of "presetting of the cosmos," such that the occurrences to be matched, whose causal ancestry is largely nonoverlapping (and with respect to the character being predicted, is entirely nonoverlapping) will be in correspondence. (Needless to say, the notion of such a cosmic presetting is anathema to atheist materialists.) The alternatives are: (1) A cerebral miracle occurs, or (2) The brain's activity is partly indeterminate. If we exclude miracles, the existence of precognitive telepathy may therefore be taken as evidence for either a cosmic presetting or for some degree

214

of cerebral indeterminacy. Now the experiments show that the precognitive effect fails when the agent is not (subsequently) permitted to know the random event, although the chain of causality leading up to the event itself is as usual. This renders the cosmic presetting theory very unplausible. It is therefore possible to say that some scientific evidence exists which runs counter to the determinate-brain-state theory and supports an indeterminate theory.

It is sometimes stated that the fact of quantum indeterminacy cannot provide a theoretical locus for the operation of mentalistic or teleological agencies, because if the physical system is responsive to the "selective" action of any such factors, at least a minimal distortion must be discernible in the frequencies. Putting it crudely, the physical-indeterminacy condition says that the micro-event happens by "pure chance," but then the subsequent introduction of a selection operation such as Eccles' implicitly denies this by postulating a "purposive" influence. Hence, in the long run, the operation of any such agencies should be manifested in a departure from the frequencies specified by physical theory (i. e., the quantum event will *not* be strictly indeterminate after all). For a discussion of this objection see Appendix E.

215

IX. Valid and Displaced Guilt, and Their Relation to Psychological Health and Spiritual Condition

IN CHAPTER II we asserted that whatever clinical forms it may take, anxiety has as its root source the sinner's knowledge that he is in a state of rebellion against, and consequent alienation from, his Creator. Tillich's threefold anxiety of condemnation, of meaninglessness, and of death are manifestations of this root anxiety. If man were in the proper relationship to God, he would not feel condemned (either by God, his fellows, or himself); he would derive the richest, truest, and most satisfying meanings, because in all things he would be God-oriented;[1] and he would not be under the curse of death. By this we do not mean that man's sense of alienation and condemnation is necessarily *worded* or *imaged*; in some men it is, in others not. We know from both revelation and secular psychology that the mental (the purposive and cognitive) is not coterminous with the *conscious* (the "aware," the worded, the introspectible, the reportable). Laboratory experiments and clinical investigation show that there are nonreportable processes, states, and "structures" in the human person which exhibit many of the properties and causal relations traditionally recognized as defining the "mental"; whence arises the scientific practice of using a mentalistic language (or derivations therefrom) in speaking of these

---

[1] "Thou hast made us for Thyself, O Lord; and our hearts can find no peace until they rest in Thee." — St. Augustine.

processes, in spite of their nonreportability. (For a brief but remarkably sophisticated methodological analysis of this question see Freud.[2])

So we do not mean to assert, what is obviously not true, that every man who experiences the anxiety of death reports verbally, "I am afraid of God"; or that the person who is still haunted with guilt feelings after 500 hours on the psychoanalytic couch is able to tell us: "I am an unworthy, condemnable person because I sin." What we do mean to say is this: First, the phenomenal experience and the associated behavior dispositions called "anxiety" (of which guilt feeling is a special subcase, intricately fused with other components) would not exist if a man were in the proper relationship to his God; and, secondly, that at *some level*, in *some sense*, the root character of this primal dread is perceived, internally represented, "known" (*pace* logicians!), even by the natural man.[3] Full clarity has not yet been reached among logicians and psychologists as to the exact sense in which such verbs as "know," "sense," "intend," "expect," "want," "believe," "realize," are to be taken when applied to the nonreported events within human organisms (or animals, for discussion of which see the classic work of E. C. Tolman [4]). That such quasi-mentalistic language can be used under suitable restrictions and precautions is a conclusion widely held, on quite distinct grounds, by contemporary scholars in three secular disciplines: psychiatry, experimental (human and animal) psychology, and analytic philosophy. There are many unsolved problems here, and they are being vigorously attacked by workers in the fields named. The resolution of conceptual difficulties, some of them extremely great, will gradually be achieved by a combination of philosophical analysis, laboratory experimentation, and clinical experience. For the present we shall employ the mentalistic language without further apology or quotation marks, knowing

[2] "The Unconscious," Collected Papers, IV (London: Hogarth Press, 1948), pp. 98—104.

[3] Cornelius Van Til, The Defense of the Faith (Philadelphia: Presbyterian and Reformed Publishing Company, 1954), pp. 111, 112; 165, 166; 259, 260; 325, 326; and passim.

[4] Purposive Behavior in Animals and Men (New York: Century Company, 1932), passim.

that the rigorous methodological explication of its use here, as in psychiatry, psychology, and philosophy, is an unfinished task for workers in these fields.

It is sometimes tempting for the Christian to introduce the idea of this root fear, and its correlative root knowledge of God, in apologetics with atheists. One hears Christians say to non-Christians: "You really *do* believe in God, deep down inside; only you won't admit it." There are few apologetic moves more likely to infuriate the unbeliever than this one. Tactically speaking, it should be sedulously avoided; it has no more merit than the premature interpretation of a clumsy psychotherapist. Suppose, for example, that a college student comes to a counselor with the complaint that he seems to have trouble with his professors every time he talks to them. After the first fifteen minutes of interviewing, the counselor perceives the familiar syndrome of father-figure hostility. But he does not then and there tell the student: "You felt rebellious to your father; unconsciously you even hated him, wished to conquer him, even at times to mutilate or kill him. Now you see all males in authority as your father, and you carry the old fight out repeatedly. You cannot talk to professors because you are always unconsciously talking to papa; and this makes you both frightened and angry. The professor perceives this reaction, and he therefore doesn't like you either, especially if he is himself insecure. That is your problem. Go and sin no more." The counselor knows that, for the one case in a hundred who can accept this kind of interpretation and use it (they *do* occur), there are ninety-nine who cannot. Such interpretations are characteristically met by one of two reactions. Either the client remains completely untouched, as if he heard the words but they had no meaning for him; or else he becomes disturbed and angry, mobilizes his defenses, and rejects the counselor. He cannot and will not accept what is said to him.

The atheist who is loftily informed by a Christian that he "really" believes in God usually has the same reaction. The natural man wears colored spectacles, and they are cemented to his eyes; to tell him that he really believes in God and recognizes his own sin would be as if Freud informed a Viennese burgher in the second analytic session that he had an Oedipus complex (i. e., an unconscious wish to murder his father and have sexual

218

intercourse with his mother).[5] In this respect the Christian should ordinarily adopt the same policy toward the unbeliever that the psychoanalyst does toward his patient. The psychoanalyst does not have contempt for his patient, and he does not pat himself on the back thinking: "I see the light, unlike this poor deluded neurotic lying there." His inner attitude is rather: "Like everyone else, I am motivated by unconscious forces and utilize defensive mechanisms. But I have, by virtue of a decent heredity, the kindness of life to me, and a personal analysis achieved a modicum of health; also I have had the advantage of formal training by experienced and learned men. Hence I can perceive connections in this suffering person's behavior which he cannot perceive by himself." Ideally this is said without either pride or false humility. Similarly the Christian should think to himself: "I am a sinner, moved to faith by the Holy Spirit and in no way to my credit. The scales have fallen from my eyes so that I can consciously, verbally report the awareness of God and of my sinful condition, which this unfortunate one cannot as yet do." To see this, and to say it within oneself, is one thing; to assert it bluntly to the other is quite a different matter.

It is perhaps worth remarking that the indirect manifestations of the natural man's hidden knowledge of God, and of his own sinful alienation, are perhaps in some respects even more striking at an obvious behavioral level than the (psychologically analogous) indirect manifestations of pride and sexuality which Freud detailed. Two examples of this tendency will suffice. The first is the very common, if not quite universal, tendency of adult converts to say that they "always dimly believed, or felt dogged by a compulsion to belief, but denied, fought against, or simply failed to label it. I sort of felt God was there at the very moments I was proving His nonexistence." The frequency and intensity of this postconversion retrospection is remarkable. The same phenomenon is not typically observed with changes in political, social, or scientific views. The unbeliever, of course, may attribute this report to biased retrospection; and this explanation cannot be scientifically refuted on present evidence. The convert

<hr>

[5] *The Interpretation of Dreams. Standard Edition of the Complete Psychological Works of Sigmund Freud* (London: Hogarth Press, 1953), IV 255—266.

simply finds it subjectively impossible to accept retrospectively. There is little that the convert can say to the atheist who accuses him of biased retrospection in the matter of his unregenerate knowledge of God. If the convert has experienced other major shifts in opinion, he knows that a comparable retrospection is lacking there. He remembers entertaining cognitive doubts about, say, his former socialism before he abandoned it; or being made anxious and irritable by hostile critics of the Culbertson bridge system while he was still using it and defending it. He knows, of course, that people deceive themselves and that he is not immune from this human failing. He tells himself all this, but it doesn't help. The scales have fallen from his eyes so that he now *recalls clearly* what was in some sense not clear at the time (no contradiction, to the psychologist!): that all the while he "felt" or "knew" that God was there and that he was both rebelling against Him and running away from Him. With socialism or Culbertson he may have had ripples of insecurity and cognitive conflicts when confronted by counterevidence; but he would quickly reject a retrospective suggestion that he had, in any strong sense, "disbelieved" these systems all the while. Whereas the now-admitted existence and sovereignty of God he recognizes, and vividly, as *something known all along.* Here, by the way, we see a similarity to the experience of insight in psychotherapy. A kind of report likely to be heard from a successfully treated neurotic (especially one who had exaggerated expectations from reading Freud as to what would be unearthed in the way of traumatic memories) is that the therapy has, among other things, enabled him to *word* bits of truth about himself or others which he "really knew all along."

A second phenomenon, also interpreted by the Christian retrospectively as a manifestation of a distorted and darkened but inescapable knowledge of God, is the peculiar manner in which most unbelievers treat the Gospel and the church. Jesus' assertion that "he who is not with Me is against Me" is psychologically reflected in the fact that neutral feeling toward the church's proclamation is exceedingly rare. The typical unbeliever characteristically exhibits an anger, a resentment, or a facetiousness when confronted with the Christian claims. He is not merely unconvinced himself; he finds it irritating that others are convinced. He feels an impulse to disrupt them or to poke fun at them or to refute them. Courtesy and natural kindliness frequently suffice to cover this spontaneous reaction, and in some circles the contact with doctrinal Christianity is so slight that the hostile appears at first to be lacking. For such persons, in such culturally selected groups, the matter is so much a dead issue that there is no occasion for taking it into account in any way. But the disposition is there nevertheless, as one can easily verify by introducing the Christian claims, even in a most innocuous manner. It is remarkable how many atheists exhibit a kind of self-conscious ὕβρις toward the God they do not believe in. They manage to convey an unmistakable quality of being angry with God, of saying no to Him, in the context of questioning His very existence. And this inadequately introspected feeling is also reported retrospectively by many converts, sometimes being recalled with extraordinary vividness.

To return to our main theme of valid guilt, we have been suggesting that man's objective sinful and alienated relation to God, with its attendant effects upon his relation to his fellows, gives rise to a psychological state of valid guilt. The sinner "knows," in some attenuated sense of the word, that he is evil. He knows that his impulses are dangerous and condemnable. Even on purely rational or empirical grounds, he has reason to be afraid. Thus he automatically projects his own aggressive and egocentric feelings to the outer world, a mechanism found by the psychoanalytic method to be present very early in life, and before the child even has any words with which he could formulate it. "I have murderous and self-aggrandizing wishes; so do the others, and therefore I am in danger." It is almost as if the most unsophisticated human child somehow dimly perceived the kind of thing of which Freud wrote so powerfully in his most pessimistic book:

> The bit of truth behind all this — one so eagerly denied — is that men are not gentle, friendly creatures wishing for love, who simply defend themselves if they are attacked, but that a powerful measure of desire for aggression has to be reckoned as part of their instinctual endowment. The result is that their neighbor is to them not only a possible helper or sexual object, but also a temptation to them to gratify their aggressiveness on him, to exploit his capacity for work without recompense, to use him

sexually without his consent, to seize his possessions, to humiliate him, to cause him pain, to torture and to kill him. *Homo homini lupus.* Who has the courage to dispute it in the face of all the evidence in his own life and in history? This aggressive cruelty usually lies in wait for some provocation, or else it steps into the service of some other purpose, the aim of which might as well have been achieved by milder measures. In circumstances that favor it, when those forces in the mind which ordinarily inhibit it cease to operate, it also manifests itself spontaneously and reveals men as savage beasts to whom the thought of sparing their own kind is alien. Anyone who calls to mind the atrocities of the early migrations, of the invasion by the Huns or by the so-called Mongols under Jenghiz Khan and Tamurlane, of the Sack of Jerusalem by the pious Crusaders, even indeed the horrors of the last World War, will have to bow his head humbly before the truth of this view of man.[6]

Consider the case of a neurotic whose symptom arises from a repressed hostile impulse. Suppose that he feels uncharitable toward his employer. He does not will the employer's good; he covets the employer's money and status; he resists his authority; he lusts after his pretty wife. All this may be conscious in varying degrees. At a deeper level, not worded or imaged, he hates the employer; he may unconsciously wish for the employer's death. In all these respects he sins actually, and by virtue of these impulses and the egocentric disposition from which they spring, he is in a state of objective guilt, theologically speaking. If he were not a sinner, or if he could, *per impossibile,* become utterly sanctified in the flesh, he would not have such thoughts and impulses. It is therefore literally correct to say that he develops a neurotic problem because of sin. If he did not have sin, if he were in the proper relation to God, he would not be in the condition he is in. Thus, if he feared, loved, and trusted in God above all things,[7] he would not set such inordinate value upon the employer's money. If his ego were not *incurvatus in se,* he would not experience the employer's status as a threat to his own pride.

---

6 *Civilization and Its Discontents* (London: Hogarth Press, 1953), pp. 85—86.

7 " 'Thou shalt have no other gods before Me.' What does this mean? We should fear, love, and trust in God above all things." *Luther's Small Catechism,* Section I.

222

While our patient may be able to report verbally that he resents the boss in this way or that, he does not recognize the full depth and pervasiveness of his hostility. He will be found saying, for instance, "I don't wish the old goat any bad luck, of course; but if . . .," whereas all the while he is unconsciously wishing for his death. This attitude engenders guilt feeling (a psychological concept, to be distinguished from the theological concept of *guilt*). What would we say of him, speaking theologically? We would say that he is, in fact, guilty; guiltier than he knows. So it is not surprising that he feels guilty; it is, after all, quite fitting that I should feel guilty about wishing to kill a man because his position piques my pride and I am sexually attracted to his wife.

But our patient has managed by various defensive stratagems to conceal the death wish and to obscure the full magnitude of the hatred which gives rise to it. He feels extremely guilty, but the feeling is detached from the original idea — the psychoanalyst says *displaced* — and appears in consciousness in the company of a different idea. Perhaps the patient cannot drive his automobile because he is haunted by the idea that he has run over someone without knowing it. He has made a shady deal with himself, he has a neurotic symptom. The guilt feeling is "valid" in the sense of being appropriate to the wish. But it is not manifested in the company of this idea, being attached instead to the automobile driving.

The aim of the psychotherapist is to break this neurotic connection. It is obviously not the psychotherapist's aim to make the patient into a real murderer, to encourage him to "act out" his murderous wishes. The psychotherapist has the aim of restoring the person's psychological integrity. The patient has engaged in a stratagem (albeit an unworded, automatic one) by means of which he succeeds in hiding from a bit of self-knowledge. The therapist tries to restore his self-knowledge. Insofar as the patient wants to kill his boss, he is a sinner; insofar as he disguises this wish and its attendant guilt by the automobile symptom, he is a neurotic. It would be a mistake to ask: "Is the poor fellow a sinner, or is he just neurotic?" He is both, and simultaneously. If he were not a sinner, he would not be a neurotic. Yet the psychotherapist is not thereby committed as part of *his* task to "curing sin," a function which is beyond his province and powers. If sin had not entered the world, there would be no neurosis. But not all sinners are neurotics. Putting it crudely, the secular therapist's job is to help a neurotic sinner become a "healthy" one, where we understand by health (roughly) that degree of competence, gratification, and freedom from symptoms which is normal in our society.

The non-Christian reader must remember in this connection the dispositional character of sin, especially as emphasized in the Lutheran conception. In saying that if there were no sin there would be no neurosis, we do not confine the idea of sin to concrete "actual sins." For example, when a person puts his trust in a huge bank account, making it the source of his security, he exhibits sin. The Catechism exposits the First Commandment as "We should fear, love, and trust in God above all things." St. Paul writes: "Whatsoever is not of faith is sin." So that a man who puts his trust and founds his security in a bank account, to that extent has an idol and is not trusting in God above all things. "Ye cannot serve God and mammon" (Matt. 6:24; cf. Luke 12: 16-21). He may not be stealing from the till or fudging on his income tax, but his misplaced trust testifies to his sinful condition and would not be possible if he really "trusted in God above all things." What we corrupted human beings allow as civil righteousness is, theologically speaking, far below the inner and outer perfection demanded by God's Law. "Ye shall be holy; for I, the Lord, your God, am holy" (Lev. 19:2). "Be ye therefore perfect, even as your Father which is in heaven is perfect" (Matt. 5:48). "Whosoever shall keep the whole Law and yet offend in one point, he is guilty of all" (James 2:10). "There is not a just man upon earth that doeth good and sinneth not" (Eccl. 7:20). "We are all as an unclean thing, and all our righteousnesses are as filthy rags" (Is. 64:6). "If we say that we have no sin, we deceive ourselves, and the truth is not in us" (1 John 1:8). "No man is justified by the Law in the sight of God" (Gal. 3:11). "So likewise ye, when ye shall have done all those things which are commanded you, say, We are unprofitable servants; we have done that which was our duty to do." (Luke 17:10)

This brief comment on sin is necessary because it seems clear that not every neurosis involves such specific (actual) sins as

224

wishing for another's death. Consider a neurotic who has not so much guilt feeling as "insecurity," feelings of rejection or inferiority, and the like. Many therapists have the impression that the contemporary neurotic suffers more from a kind of disarticulation of his interpersonal relations than from internal conflicts; that, so to say, his trouble is less with his own unacceptable impulses than with his relations to other people. These distinctions are matters of current dispute, and there are competent defenders of each position (including those who emphasize that a person cannot relate adequately to others unless he has come to terms with himself). However, the relation between sin and neurosis described above would be affected only in nonessential details by the outcome of this controversy, because a sinless person would not experience the kinds of interpersonal difficulty described either. If a neurotic is chronically "insecure" in relating to others, it is because his way of perceiving them and his motives respecting them are sin-tainted. How, for example, can he be perpetually anxious about his status in their eyes, unless he is status-oriented? How can he be distrustful of the intentions of others and unable to accept their love unless his own love is somehow defective? How can he get into trouble over his competitive strivings unless his orientation to common tasks is infected with fear and egocentricity? How can a person be overdriven by tension-producing values if he loves the Lord with all his mind and soul and his neighbor as himself (Matt. 22:37-39)? We are all so accustomed to garden-variety, respectable sinfulness that it is only by a great effort of thought that we can visualize the true connection of sin and neurosis. Yet psychotherapists are aware of these connections without using theological words; and the most convinced atheist therapist will not be found disagreeing with 1 John 4:18: "Perfect love casteth out fear."

Throughout the preceding discussion we have implicitly accepted the view of neurosis which is almost universally held by practitioners. There is disagreement as to the relative importance of various drives (e. g., sex, aggression, prestige) in producing neurosis, and also as to the exact causal sequences leading to the formation of neurotic symptoms and character traits; yet there is a basic assumption which cuts across these disagreements, consisting essentially of the notion that neuroses have their origin in the tension-reducing, pain-avoiding, gratification-seeking mechanisms of our mental apparatus. That is, the neurotic is one who is, unskillfully and unconsciously to be sure, *seeking* something or *avoiding* something (usually both at once, in a kind of compromise). A neurotic symptom seeks pleasure, or gets attention, or wards off anxiety, or avoids anticipated rebuff, or preserves the image one has of himself, or controls other people, or atones for guilt, or something of the kind. A neurosis has an *aim*, according to the received doctrine of secular psychotherapy. Almost all theorists and practitioners hold this view, and there is a good deal of evidence to support it. Therefore, at the risk of a somewhat dogmatic presentation in as nontechnical manner as possible, we have accepted this postulate in its generalized form.

In concluding this section, however, we must mention the existence of an important minority opinion; because the criticism of this minority, unlike the special disagreements within the majority group, would invalidate most of the development just presented. There are a few workers who deny that all neuroses are "goal-directed," and who believe that at least some of them are due to rather simple, nonpurposive conditionings of emotional habits. For example, a person may become phobic about automobiles because of a particular traumatic experience. Cases of this kind are reported, but their theoretical interpretation remains controversial. If it should be the case that some neurotic individuals suffer from a combination of "overly susceptible nervous constitution" plus an unfortunate series of traumatic incidents, in which their motivations and self-images play no significant part, then such neuroses would have no intimate relation to sin. The neurotic structure would then be like a kind of foreign body, not really growing out of the soil of the personality or maintained by reason of that personality's characteristics. The therapeutic task would be one of suitable "emotional reconditioning," and such tactics are used by practitioners holding this view. A similar qualification upon our analysis would be required if, as some psychiatrists believe, certain of the major mental disorders (e. g., schizophrenia, manic-depressive psychosis) have their primary causation in anatomical or chemical abnormalities, possibly on a hereditary basis. The chief difference between the schizophrenic and the "healthy sinner" would then lie in the schizophrenic's disordered brain metabolism or his peculiar nervous constitution. Like the healthy person, he has drives of lust, power, pride, hatred, envy, and so on. But his being *diseased* is due to a "nonpsychological" factor (although the disease leads to these drives being manifested in the special distorted forms known as schizophrenia). The relation of sin to neurotic suffering would, on these views, be not appreciably different from that between sin and cancer or a broken leg, discussion of which is obviously beyond the scope of this book.

Returning to our major interpretation, we imagine the reader asking with concern: "What, then, is the goal of the psychotherapist? Does he not wish to help his patient to become a 'whole person,' to 'fulfill his destiny,' or 'attain to his natural and proper end,' or however you wish to put it? And how can this be done apart from God? You say that neurotic guilt is displaced from unconscious impulses, and you admit that the content of these impulses is of such a nature that the person is objectively guilty. Suppose that the psychotherapist does succeed in uncovering these dark secrets and elucidating their multifarious psychological connections. What then? Does he *leave* the patient in this state?"

This line of questioning takes us to the heart of the difference between the Christian pastor's aim and the secular therapist's aim. There are fundamental differences in orientation which irenic intentions must not be allowed to obscure. These *differences* are not, however, *contradictions*. The relationship between pastoral and therapeutic aims is extremely complex and will someday require a volume devoted entirely to it. Oversimplified analyses are commonly offered, and what we can present suffers from the same defect to some degree. However, the centrality of this question requires that we present our best thinking about it, even at the risk of some superficiality.

To begin with, there is a noncontroversial overlap between pastoral and therapeutic aims which is theologically neutral. The pastor and the secular therapist are both committed to the alleviation of suffering and the improvement of interpersonal relations; they share an admittedly vague (but pragmatically orientative) goal which we may call "health." An atheist psychologist

227

and a psychologically untrained pastor could readily agree that to have a paralyzed arm or to be chronically afraid of people are, taken in themselves, undesirable conditions, and that, *ceteris paribus*, it is desirable to alleviate them. Their convergence here is on the same basis that Christians and non-Christians unite to build a community hospital. Christians do not teach that only those of the household of faith should be the object of good works or that missionary activity is the only manifestation of love. To set a broken bone or to feed a hungry person is a charitable action and directed to good ends; so also is psychological healing. Just as we do not reject the work of a medical missionary who administers penicillin to a zealous Moslem, so we do not reject the healing activity of a therapist who alleviates the neurotic suffering of an atheist or a Jew. Correspondingly, a Christian should not reject or fear the healing efforts of a non-Christian therapist. The healing impulse and the desire to meet well the responsibilities of one's calling are well-nigh universal human phenomena, classified by the Lutheran Confessions under "civil righteousness" (i. e., moral impulses and conduct attainable without divine grace and often quite sufficient for a humanly acceptable and even praiseworthy conducting of our affairs). The efficacy of a psychological healer does not depend upon his own religious condition, except insofar as his general mode of relating to others reflects his spiritual state. But this kind of influence is also found, of course, in the practice of other callings.

It is clear, then, that pastor and psychotherapist share the goal of "health" for the suffering individual. Let us next inquire into the relation which exists between health and a person's spiritual condition. Can a person be healthy, *in the ordinary medical and sociological senses of this word,* and be spiritually dead? This is a deep question, and we dare not dogmatize about it. But it appears reasonably clear to us that the answer is affirmative. Consider a human being who is free of medical symptoms; who experiences no more frequent or intense anxiety than most people do (and experiences it in "appropriate" contexts); who is able to work productively and enjoyably, having an output not too far below his potential; who experiences gratification in his social, affectional, and sexual life; and who is accepted and liked by those around him. Such a person is surely healthy insofar as medical and social criteria define that word. In saying this, we are not slavishly accepting "adjustment" as the highest goal of life or assuming that to have pleasure and get along with others is the ideal human condition. All that we are saying is that such a person is healthy as this word is customarily used. It is obvious to any but the most parochial mind that a man can be a Christian, Jew, Buddhist, agnostic, or fire worshiper and still be healthy in this garden-variety sense. One can readily find unbelievers who are healthy, Christians who are unhealthy, and the other way round, if he applies these criteria. Freud, when asked to define mental health, said simply, "*Lieben und arbeiten*"; needless to say, by *lieben* Freud, an atheist, did not mean to include the love of God.

It is true that by taking as a baseline the anxiety experienced "appropriately" by most people, we have implicitly settled for a standard of health which is a good deal lower than that of Paradise. There is, of course, a theological sense in which all men are radically "sick," and it is true that modern secularized man has largely lost an appreciation of this dreadful fact. The language of sickness is therefore appropriately used in certain contexts, as an aid in conveying the full meaning of our fallen and corrupted state to the blasé. But in such contexts we have modified the ordinary semantics of "health" for a special evangelical purpose. The word "health" as employed by physicians, insurance actuaries, hygienists, and common men obviously does *not* mean the pristine health of Adam; and it would be merely obscurantist to discuss the aims of psychotherapy as if that were the word's normal meaning. It would be like saying that all children with an IQ of 130 are mentally defective, since they necessarily manifest a darkening of intellect and corruption of understanding consequent upon the Fall! Suppose we were to quarrel with public-health statistics on the theological ground that all adults are "physically sick," since all at the very least are undergoing the progressive decline of powers, the appearance of minor infirmities, and the irreversible processes of aging, which end in death!

Enough has been said to indicate why we adopt the verbal usage of "health" to mean something distinguishable from the individual's spiritual state. Now the goal of the psychotherapist, which goal he tacitly or openly agrees upon in entering into the therapeutic relationship with his client, is health in this sense. This is why the client seeks help; this is what the therapist has been trained to do; this is the basis of the contract between them. The therapist is not in the missionary business; he is not even in the business of trying to increase the client's civil righteousness (although that often follows as a consequence of successful therapy). The client doesn't come to a psychotherapist saying, "I want to get right with God," or "I want to be a more sanctified person." (If he does come with these as his real aims, the secular therapist ought not, and in fact would not, enter into a treatment relationship with him.) He comes because of his psychosomatic headaches, or his sexual impotence, or his attacks of irrational fear, or his inhibition from productive work. He comes because he recognizes himself to be *unhealthy* or *unhappy* in the familiar sense of these words. The professional commitment of the psychotherapist is to help the patient to become healthier and happier. To enter (surreptitiously or openly) into a missionarylike relationship with the client is as inappropriate as it would be for a Christian plumber to spend his paid-by-the-hour time in passing out tracts to the various members of an atheist household. In fact the cryptomissionary therapist is even less defensible, because the plumber merely consumes additional time without thereby interfering with the plumbing repair once he gets to it; whereas the health-oriented task of the therapist would ordinarily be hampered by the introduction of religious issues.

We see that the psychotherapist (whether Christian or unbeliever) has the aim to restore health and earthly happiness. He works within realistic limits, knowing that the capacities of his client and the possibilities of the reality situation cannot be transcended by therapeutic intervention. He cannot make a stupid college student into a brilliant physicist; he cannot reform the unco-operative, alcoholic, adulterous husband of a depressed patient; he cannot make a thoroughly self-centered individual into a saint. There are aspects of adult personality which are relatively unmodifiable, no matter how skilled the therapist or how co-operative the patient. For example, almost no psychotherapists entertain the idea of enabling a chronic

230

alcoholic, a psychopathic personality, a severe schizoid type, or a confirmed, overt homosexual invert to be "just like everybody else." That is, even the goal of earthly health is frequently set at a very modest level.

A fortiori, the therapist has no illusions that he can make a client "good," even in the sense of civil righteousness. To the extent that "bad" behavior is itself a derivative of the neurotic conflict, it will often be ameliorated. For example, it seems that some persons — especially conflicted adolescents — perform actions which are objectively evil because they have a deep neurotic need to be punished, which springs from an unconscious sense of guilt. The patient has repressed an incestuous or aggressive wish, for which he feels guilty. Guilt feeling having in the past been assuaged by "taking one's medicine," he unconsciously arranges to get caught at something for which he will be punished. This delinquent action is in such a case neurotically motivated; hence a successful psychotherapeutic effort would remove (or at least reduce) the probability of its repetition. The "bad" behavior would have been alleviated by essentially nonmoral tactics.

Many forms of unacceptable behavior derive at least part of their motivation from similar neurotic sources. By contrast, many spontaneous "good" impulses are blocked by neurotic fears and defensive tactics. Such impulses as co-operation, laughter, sympathy, human interest, workmanship, intellectual curiosity, group identification, and love (amorous, filial, parental) are part of the equipment of the natural man. He does not need special supernatural grace to be moved to like people, to help them, to be interested in them, to take pride in his work, to obey the law, and the like. This is the other side of the coin from the *homo homini lupus* stressed above in the Freud quotation. Both are accurate accounts of human nature. Man is a strange mixture, as everyone knows. There is nothing contradictory about saying that in each of us there can be discerned traces of both glutton and ascetic, helper and exploiter, hero and murderer.

The nature of neurosis is such that while the rejected impulses express themselves indirectly as neurotic symptoms and traits, meantime the struggle against these impulses, and the frustration produced by the symptoms and traits, results in the formation

231

of rigid defensive structures and coping mechanisms. These defensive systems in their turn usually impede the expression and mature elaboration of *positive* impulses, so that a vicious circle is set up in which the neurotic is deprived of acceptance by others and gratification of his normal needs, becomes thereby resentful and fearful, handles these feelings by ineffective devices (e. g., withdrawal, physical complaints, arrogance, overfriendliness), which further block his gratifications and make him more distasteful to others. An interruption of this vicious circle, whether by accidents of life or psychotherapy, brings the self-healing and positive tendencies back into play. For this reason, successful psychotherapy may make a patient "morally better" even though that is not its avowed aim. If I attack others because I fear them, and cannot love them because I unconsciously expect my love to be rejected, the lifting of such fear and expectation will reduce my need to attack and "free up" my (natural) impulses to love. All this can (and does) take place within the framework of the natural man's dispositions and powers.

But aren't there people who are exploitive or competitive or crooked or adulterous for nonneurotic reasons? There certainly are. Does psychotherapy "inadvertently" make these people socially or ethically better? This is not claimed by most psychotherapists, and we know of no clinical or statistical evidence to support such a claim were it made. Most practitioners know of individual instances in which patients became more able to express their sexual, aggressive, or prideful impulses after a course of psychotherapy. Why should we expect it to be otherwise in such cases? Suppose that a man is a pickpocket and develops a severe tremor and disco-ordination of the hand; such a pickpocket suffers a severe occupational disability! He is treated by a neurologist for his defect of health and is thereby enabled to return to his nefarious livelihood. The physician, acting in accord with the responsibilities of his secular calling, has restored the man to his organic integrity. The patient is still a crook; as it happens, he is a more effective crook than before he was treated. But to reform crooks is not the physician's business. Similarly the psychotherapist's task is to heal neurotics, not to convert sinners or even to reform scoundrels.

It has been observed, although rarely, that certain patients who have undergone a prolonged classical analysis (see Chapter VI) become somewhat more bumptious and inconsiderate afterwards. As one psychotherapist put it: "He used to make himself uncomfortable; now he makes others uncomfortable." How are we to conceptualize such a development? The theoretical question regarding such a patient is: *Why* was he behaving more considerately before treatment? We can be pretty sure that he was not "kind" to other people because of objective ethical considerations (duty); nor was he motivated by spontaneous human sympathy or identification with them; spontaneous sympathy and conscious ethical thinking are not neurotic and are not attacked by psychotherapy. Our patient was presumably "nice to people" before therapy, not out of duty or from love, but because *he was neurotically afraid not to be "nice."* He would very much like to have said to his brother, "Thou fool" (Matt. 5:22); he didn't really consider it ethically wrong to do so, and he didn't feel loving impulses. He was afraid of retaliation and rejection if he should give vent to an aggressive impulse. The psychoanalysis unravels and desensitizes these unrealistic fears; he comes to realize that one does not drop out of the universe merely because he speaks cruelly to a subordinate or acts arrogantly toward a salesgirl. His restraints against such actions were neither dutiful nor loving, but merely timid. His timidity having been lessened by the psychoanalysis, he now behaves as he wanted to all along.

The point we are trying to make here can perhaps best be illustrated by an anecdote told among psychotherapists; it is told as a funny story, but it expresses a profound truth which professional workers freely recognize. It seems that there was once a young psychiatrist who had entered upon a personal psychoanalysis for professional reasons (called a "didactic analysis"). After several weeks he came in one day, lay down on the couch, and after a moment's embarrassed silence spoke thus: "I must say that I am feeling a little doubtful these days about this whole business of being analyzed. You know that Dr. Schafskopf has recently joined our staff here. Well, Schafskopf is a graduate of one of the best analytic institutes in the world. He was analyzed for 300 hours by the renowned Dr. Krankheit, and then he had another 100 hours in Vienna with Freud himself. He has surely had excellent training, and we consider him the best-qualified man on our staff. Yet look at him! He borrows money from the nurses and doesn't pay them back; he pokes fun at the social workers if they miss a diagnosis; he comes late for his appointments if he feels sleepy in the morning; he goes after other doctors' wives at the staff parties. I ask myself, why am I paying you $20 an hour to be analyzed? Look at the way this fellow Schafskopf behaves — it's terrible. I don't want to get like that. What has analysis done for *him*, I'd like to know? It's a big fake, if you ask me!" The analyst, after listening sympathetically to this outburst, replied with classical analytic calm: "Ja, so it is; but let me tell you something. In Vienna we had a good saying, it goes like this: 'You have a swine; you analyze him; then you have an analyzed swine.'"

This leads us to enter a *caveat* whose importance cannot be overestimated. There is grave danger of linking "sinfulness" with neuroticism in a way which is theologically unsound, scientifically absurd, and harmful to the cure of souls. Accepting the analysis we have offered, there is a correct sense in which we can say that the neurotic suffers because of sin. But this statement can also be taken in an incorrect sense. *We dare not interpret it to mean that the neurotic differs from the healthy in respect of his sinfulness.* The neurotic has the same inordinate drives as the healthy; there are no uniquely "neurotic motives." The *difference between* the neurotic and the healthy lies in the ineffective and self-defeating tactics by which the former unconsciously attempts to cope with his drives (i. e., to gratify them or to defend against them). Healthy people are sinners; if Christians, still sinners — *simul justus et peccator*. If a healthy Christian is tempted to think of his neurotic brother as more sinful than himself, he is thinking as the Pharisee thought about the publican (Luke 18: 9-14). The essential point involved can be summarized thus: The origin of neurosis in our common sinful dispositions is a *qualitative* truth; whereas to infer something about a person's "degree of sinfulness" (or degree of sanctification) from the state of his mental health presupposes a *quantitative* relation. It also presupposes that no part is played in the neurosis by counter-forces or by the accidents of human life. Both of these pre-

234

suppositions are false, and they are not implied by our analysis. It is perfectly possible that Jones carries within him more hostility than Smith, even though Smith suffers from a compulsion neurosis arising from his hostility whereas Jones does not. Furthermore, this reversed relation may exist if Jones is an atheist and Smith is a Christian. It may be that the unconscious hostility with which Smith, the neurotic Christian, struggles is quantitatively greater; it may be attached to persons whose relation to Smith renders it more frightening; it may be defended against by different mechanisms. These are quantitative matters which involve relationships of vast complexity within the personality structure.

But, it may be asked, surely *if* Smith were a more sanctified Christian than he is, he would not have his hostility? Does not his neurosis suggest that he has progressed very little in the Christian struggle, even though he is weak in faith? We believe that this line of thought is very dangerous. If it were possible to become entirely free of sinful dispositions in the present life, such a person would (if our analysis is correct) be free of neurosis. But Scripture and the Confessions make clear that this is impossible. (In this respect, Lutherans should be less prone to the error under discussion than either Romanists or the holiness groups, both of whom tend to foster exaggerated ideas as to the possibilities of "sinlessness" in the regenerate.) The most sanctified Christian may very well carry within him unconscious lusts, fears, or hatreds more than sufficient to create and maintain a neurosis, provided that the other relevant conditions in his life situation and his psychological organization are adverse in their pattern and intensity. (1 Cor. 10:13 cannot be applied in contradiction to this, because that passage treats not of unconscious motivations but of temptations to actual sins.)

We are not suggesting that conversion and sanctification have no effect upon behavior, a view which has been previously excluded in Chapter VII. If a neurotic becomes converted, he will be a different neurotic afterwards. More often than not, his psychiatric condition will improve — a phenomenon recognized as frequent by many unbelieving psychotherapists. But his conversion may, under certain circumstances, aggravate his neurosis. Suppose that he carried a volcano of unconscious hostility against his more successful competitors. This he formerly "siphoned off" by means of a large number of petty verbal attacks and subtle machinations against their interests. After his conversion, things change. On the one hand the hostility becomes less volcanic; he becomes more capable of experiencing charitable impulses toward them, his drive to complete is reduced, he takes a less frantic and foolish view of success and worldly goods. These changes have a tendency to improve his psychiatric condition. But, on the other side, he also begins to inhibit *consciously* some of his previous aggressive outlets. The partial gratification he had previously permitted himself now becomes the focus of a moral struggle. He had also engaged in unethical business dealings which greatly aided his efforts to compete, and these he now repudiates. What will be the result? It is clear that whether his neurosis is ameliorated or worsened will depend not upon the theological genuineness of his conversion but upon the *quantitative* interplay among the factors mentioned. The drastic reduction in both his objective "success" and his outlet via indirect attacks upon the more successful may quite possibly increase the total frustration load which he sustains, and thereby intensify his neurotic defensive mechanisms, in spite of the fact that there has been a reduction in the aggressive and competitive strivings. Formerly he was an atheist with a steam boiler of competitive rage and numerous (sinful) safety valves. Now he is a Christian with a reduced head of steam but also without the safety valves. There is no theological basis for predicting the quantitative outcome. To say that a genuine faith will *assist* him in mastering even the neurosis itself is one thing; to maintain that it must enable him to *overcome* it is another, without Scriptural warrant. We might as well argue that a bereaved Christian must be weak in the faith because he weeps, since his departed is now with the blessed and will shortly be reunited with him for eternity. In terms of an ideal of perfect faith and utter sanctification, to be sure, such faith is "weak." In this sense we are all of weak faith. "And lest I should be exalted above measure through the abundance of the revelations, there was given to me a thorn in the flesh, the messenger of Satan to buffet me, lest I should be exalted above measure. For this thing I besought the Lord thrice that it might depart from me. And He said unto

236

me, My grace is sufficient for thee; for My strength is made perfect in weakness. Most gladly therefore will I rather glory in my infirmities, that the power of Christ may rest upon me." (2 Cor. 12:7-9)

One last question must be considered before we bring this section to a close. It is not strictly a question about guilt, but it arises so directly from the preceding exposition that we shall consider it briefly at this place. Granted that the therapeutic process aims at the improvement of natural health rather than the salvation of souls or even the cultivation of civil righteousness, still it does aim to reduce the rigid system of self-deceptions and to facilitate a confrontation with self. Does it thereby have something in common with the preaching of the Law? What is the relation between the self-confrontation which says, "I am a sinner," and that which merely says, "I have murderous impulses"? Can these be utterly unrelated? Or consider the fact that some neurotics exhibit a passionate atheism as part of their character defense (just as some neurotic Christians become over-pietistic, pharisaical, fanatical, or divisive — all in the guise of Christian life and doctrine). Suppose that the "antichurch" neurotic reactions of such an atheist were to become alleviated with the help of a psychotherapist. If, subsequently, this ex-patient is converted, has the psychotherapist (who may himself be an unbeliever, even a zealous one in personal life) played a role in the patient's conversion? Where does such a situation find its place in the theology of grace? If we say that a person's antireligious feelings were removed by secular psychotherapy, thus making him "accessible" to the church's proclamation, isn't this treading on very dangerous ground from the theological point of view?

We think not. (Incidentally, we are not aware of any evidence indicating a tendency of successful therapy to be followed by religious conversion.) Obviously "freedom from rigid anti-religious attitudes" is not even equatable with "proreligious" attitudes, to say nothing of faith. To say that a person becomes "accessible" after a reduction in antireligious rigidities is not synergistic, unless we hold that a pastor's courteous treatment of truth seekers is synergistic. Suppose a man comes to seek personal instruction, telling the pastor that he doubts the existence of God. If the pastor were to reply gruffly: " 'The fool hath said in his heart, There is no God.' If you do not believe, you will be damned." No one would justify such behavior. Why not? Because the odds are 95 to 100 that the seeker would be repelled by it. "Not the right approach," we would all agree. The common-sense recognition that the emotional states aroused in a listener may block his reception of the Word is surely not per se synergistic.

Scripture does not reveal to us the intricacies of conversion or the precise relations between the general providence of God and the specific action of the Holy Spirit in conversion. An itinerant preacher intends to go to Town X, but misreads the map and instead finds himself at Town Y, where a man is converted listening to his preaching. Humanly speaking, we speak of an "accident," we say that it was "fortunate" (Lat. *fortuna*= chance, luck) for him who was thereby converted. But for theists there is no such category, theologically speaking. God *could* convert a person entirely apart from the written or spoken word; we do not attempt to "limit God" when we accept by His revelation the generalization that, in fact, conversion is always worked in conjunction with the Word (in some form). Similarly, God *could* convert the rigidly atheistic neurotic immediately, and, in fact, this happens at times to such people. In other cases, apparently, the neurosis is softened up first, whereupon an intermediate stage of "receptive seeking" develops. Seeking therapeutic help (for nonreligious reasons) and receiving it are preconversion events which take place under the aegis of Providence; at what exact point in time the specific action of the Holy Spirit in conversion is superimposed upon general Providence we cannot know. With this carefully formulated understanding of the words, and keeping within the bounds of knowledge set by revelation, it seems appropriate to say that a person may, under certain circumstances, be rendered more accessible to conversion as a result of successful psychotherapy. It seems obvious that the same considerations, *mutatis mutandis,* can be advanced to show that successful psychotherapy may sometimes contribute to a person's falling away.

238

X. Faith and Personality

IT IS INCONCEIVABLE that the behavioral phenomena, conscious and unconscious, noted separately by psychology and theology, should be unrelated. Man cannot behave theologically at one time and psychologically at another. What he says about his faith in God, his steady church attendance, his struggle to work as a truly Christian tradesman — all these are also psychological activities and have psychological meaning. What makes a man choose the job he does or want to kill his father — these are not only questions for psychology but have theological implications also.

The purpose of this chapter is to demonstrate some of the significant interrelations between psychological and theological observations about man. We want to show how these observations are mutually reinforcing, how the concepts of one field enlighten those of the other, how the significance of the observations differs radically. Since we cannot hope to handle all the questions, we will treat selected issues in a series of separate observations, all of which are related to the general thesis.

The concept of conflict is common to psychology and theology. Our purpose is not to develop a complete theory of conflict but to organize our discussion around it, since it is a concept highly significant to both fields. It is therefore at the point of need and conflict that this discussion begins.

Man's Needs

Psychology and Christian theology are concerned about the needs of man. Both observe that man does not possess all that

239

he wants, that his needs are sizable in number and complex, and that he often experiences great difficulty in satisfying his needs. In fact, man will often go to absurd lengths to take care of the demand that some need creates, as in the case of the neurotic who is compelled to check over and over whether he has locked the door. This behavior serves to quiet the voice of anxiety for the moment.

Man will work for objects that have acquired significance. It is not necessary to give him a loaf of bread at the end of the day; a pay check will do. He may store up a substantial quantity of the intrinsically worthless bits of paper called money because to him they symbolize security. Needs bring forth diverse kinds of behavior with varying degrees of effectiveness.

It would do little good to enumerate these needs. Psychologists would include such examples as hunger, thirst, sex, love, sympathetic evaluation of one's efforts, and feeling of worthiness. Theologians would name, among others, the need to love and be loved, to be reconciled to God, assurance about the future, eternal life, and understanding another's behavior.

Need and Conflict

If man could satisfy his needs, man could live a happy life. Yet, as both disciplines again observe, barriers of every description block satisfaction, inevitably producing the conflict that in some instances provides man with character-building difficulties, but in many other instances leaves him hurt, bloody, chagrined, and defeated.

Conflict occurs for various reasons. At times an individual cannot discern which of several goals offers the most satisfaction for a given need. If he wants to serve people, he can study their behavior and set up certain hypotheses that in time may contribute to community welfare, or he can minister to their spiritual needs, exhorting, advising, teaching on the basis of God's Word.

Conflict may revolve about the means to a desired end. An individual may be undecided about which course of action will effect a given result. If a college student wants to break into a social group, he will have to decide whether the best stratagem is to make friends with Joe, who is already a member in good standing, or to let the word leak out to the group that since he is quite accomplished on the piano, he could add something desirable to future gatherings.

Furthermore, conflict may occur when the various elements in need of satisfaction are obscure to the individual involved. He may not discern clearly the nature of his need or the way to go about taking care of it. A man who has lived with his parents all his life may feel the need to get away. Perhaps the father is domineering and generally antagonistic. Yet the son feels uneasy about packing his bags and leaving home; he becomes nervous and anxious at the very thought. It isn't until someone helps him see that he resents the position his mother has taken toward the father-son relation that the barrier is removed and he can leave home with a clear conscience.

In each case conflict occurs whenever an individual is prevented from taking the course of action that will contribute optimally to the fulfillment of a given need. Although objectively no barrier exists, the individual still will be thwarted if he perceives its existence subjectively. An alcoholic who believes that God cannot love anyone who drinks intemperately will find it difficult to get himself to church. The recognition of conflict is basic to an understanding of human behavior. It is as essential for the clergyman as for the psychotherapist to understand its importance.

Conflict with God

While the non-Christian psychologist and the Christian theologian would agree that conflict is fundamentally important to an understanding of human behavior, they would disagree on the significance and character of conflict.

The disagreement stems from the different foci of the two disciplines. Psychology is concerned about man as he relates to other men, to himself, to ideas, to experiences, to moral demands, and to God. This description appears so obvious as to become almost a truism. Yet it needs reiteration because, in talking about psychology and religion side by side, some theologians make the mistake of trying to fit God's creature into psychology's framework. By this maneuver man is made the central figure, who uses the satellite God (not too differently from the way he uses

241

other resources) to help him achieve certain goals, such as personality integration. James H. Vanderveldt and Robert P. Odenwald are quite explicit about the problem: "They [some authors] oppose humanistic to authoritarian religion, and in their eyes humanistic religion means that each individual takes the place of supreme importance, each one becoming his own god. The cultivation of his own personality, his self-realization, the development of his own strength and powers, is the objective of this kind of religion. . . . Fromm adds still more to the confusion by saying that his humanistic religion is also theistic, when he actually means by 'God' not a person, not a really existing being, but a symbol of man's powers." [1]

That the focus of psychology is man makes more than a schematic difference. There is a practical result in the way therapy is conducted. The psychiatrist attempts to arrive at what is good for the individual according to his own personality structure, environment, perceptions, and need organization. The psychotherapist, insofar as he is psychotherapist and not a moralist or Christian, is not interested in applying any kind of absolute standard by which to reorient the individual. What is good for one client may not be good for the next. What is good one time may not be good on another occasion. If a non-Christian therapist is concerned about his client's moral orientation, it is not because he thinks the client ought to be moral as such, but because he needs a certain amount of rectitude to get along efficiently with his fellows or to feel worthy and right as a person. The therapist would consider the patient's orientation to God from the angle of its negative or positive contribution to his client's mental growth.

While non-Christian psychologists are anthropocentric, theology is theocentric. Theology focuses on God and on man in relation to God. Man cannot take God or leave Him as man wishes, without consequence. The creatureliness of man implies a relation to God or intended relation to God. Man was created to worship and serve God, not God to serve man, although He has done this in His work of redemption.

The criterion by which the theologian works is revealed, and

---

[1] *Psychiatry and Catholicism* (New York: McGraw-Hill, 1952), p. 181.

it is unchanging. The measuring stick which theology applies to man is not man-determined but God-determined. What is morally good for man remains constant. Again a practical implication involves the application of this theocentric orientation to counseling. The pastoral counselor not only feels that he must apply the ordinances of God to the counselee but is certain that this course will be most helpful for the client.

Yet it would be an error to leave any impression that the intended theocentric orientation leaves man at the mercy of a capricious God. God is Love, and love characterizes His relation to man. Perfect obedience to God's will would result in the optimum personality integration.

Ordinarily what is best for the Christian theologically is best for him psychologically. By way of illustration: Occasionally a client will report that his therapist suggests that he shake himself loose from a sexual inhibition by cohabiting with a prostitute. The danger, though, of the resulting conscious and unconscious guilt accusations can be more serious than the original inhibition, to say nothing of the offense to God. The end cannot justify the means.

The excessively scrupulous individual is a special case, in which there appears to be variance between psychologically and theologically sound behavior. Melanchthon examined himself continually to make certain that he had discovered every sin. His conscience was excessively severe. But Luther is reported to have told him finally that he should go out and sin heartily and well. While Luther's suggested therapy may sound blasphemous, actually an overly severe conscience diverts attention from God and must be corrected, a difficult task calling for potent remedies. To tell a scrupulous individual "to sin for all you are worth" is meant as a piece of "uproarious chaffing," [2] not as an encouragement to actual sin.

Under certain circumstances, however, moral behavior may have deleterious effects psychologically. The case of the neurotic discussed toward the close of Chapter IX serves as an illustration. Giving up certain outlets that after conversion were seen as sin-

---

[2] Roland H. Bainton, *Here I Stand* (New York: Abingdon-Cokesbury, 1950), p. 226.

ful, the neurotic may face increased frustration and be forced to make greater use of substitute, comparatively ineffectual mechanisms for his defense.

Similarly, immoral behavior may under certain circumstances have healthy psychological effects. For example, suppose a neurotic is unable to get along with his employer because his employer arouses in him unconscious hostilities toward his father. Such a person may "tell off" his father after having opened up this topic in psychotherapy to the point that his defenses are less rigidly organized. He may do this in a way which is unquestionably a violation of the Fourth Commandment.[3] Yet the release of bottled-up rage and — more important — the learning experience that it is possible to stand up to an authority figure without catastrophe, may initiate a further series of actions and changes which "snowball" in the direction of adjustment. And these changes may be ethically neutral or favorable. Our patient may have been ineffective in group discussions with the other company executives whenever his employer was present, because he *unconsciously* translated as follows: "I am being strong, intelligent, and effective in the presence of the boss" = "I am competing with a father figure and outshining him" = "I am killing my father." This (by no means uncommon) equation made the patient anxious, so that his speech and gesture in such executive meetings was timid, clumsy, and incapable of conveying the real merit of his ideas to the group. This in turn resulted in the employer's underestimating him and making inadequate use of his talents, thus building up frustration and aggression in the patient. An attack upon the *real* father could under proper quantitative conditions "free up" the patient in his business relations long enough for him to speak effectively in a few executive sessions. These are further learning experiences, since his effective behavior is not punished by the boss but greeted with pleasant surprise. He counters an argument by the boss and carries his point; after the meeting the boss claps him on the shoulder and says, "George, you sure did a good job today!" The snowball is rolling, and in the direction of greater health.

In each of these cases the total interplay of factors must be

---

[3] Lutheran numbering. Fifth in the Reformed system.

evaluated. The converted neurotic does not only *lose* psychologically. He may also *gain* from lessened competitive struggle, for example, as he re-evaluates the importance of worldly goods and as he perceives his own status and role in a different way. The frustrated employee may begin to feel guilty about how he "told his father off." The net gain or loss in either case would depend on an evaluation of the actual individual case. We are interested here in pointing out the complexities in the relationship between theologically and psychologically sound behavior.

The different foci of psychology and religion lead psychologists and theologians to different doctrinal and practical conclusions about man. Some of these differences we have just discussed, but the area in which the two disciplines diverge most sharply is in the understanding of the nature and significance of conflict in general and of the nature and significance of man's conflict with God specifically.

When a psychotherapist works with a patient who in some way evidences disturbance in his religious life, i. e., he says that he has committed the unpardonable sin or that he is hostile to God, the psychotherapist becomes interested in how the patient's perception of his God and his God's laws affects his personality. What part does this particular conflict play in his total experiential world? For example, the expressed conflict with God may be symptomatic of another conflict, such as father hostility. It may be so severe as to require resolution through appropriate therapy — as the psychotherapist perceives the problem.

However, as far as theology is concerned, man's conflict with God is a fundamental disturbance signaling a break in the intended orientation of man to God. Since God is meant to be the focus of man's life and is the source of his creation and well-being, conflict threatens the very existence of human beings.

Man Versus God

Theology interprets history in the light of man's basic conflict with God. The story of man contains threads of love, sacrifice, and concern, but these threads are overshadowed by strong patterns of violence and hostility, fear and inability of man to live amicably with other men.

Psychological observation has pointed up the intricate interweaving of love and hostility, guilt, and fear in personality. Freud conceptualizes primitive pleasure seeking and destructive impulses in the id. Adler talked about the aggressive drive to excel and the compensations to which man feels himself forced when he cannot dominate his parents, siblings, business associates, and friends. Negative impulses, which often override inclinations to co-operate, understand, and appreciate, are implanted deeply in personality structure. Therefore they stubbornly resist change and correction.

While schools of psychology would differ on the nature, origin, and meaning of antisocial, primitive, aggressive, hurtful impulses in the personality structure, none would deny their existence as a significant threat to an individual's well-being. While the theologian describes the propensities of man toward sin, no one appreciates more than the psychotherapist how significantly these propensities are intertwined in the very structure of personality. God supplies the meaning to these phenomena in Rom. 3:9-18 (RSV):

> What then? Are we Jews any better off? No, not at all; for I have already charged that all men, both Jews and Greeks, are under the power of sin, as it is written: None is righteous, no, not one; no one understands, no one seeks for God. All have turned aside, together they have gone wrong; no one does good, not even one. Their throat is an open grave, they use their tongues to deceive. The venom of asps is under their lips. Their mouth is full of curses and bitterness. Their feet are swift to shed blood, in their paths are ruin and misery, and the way of peace they do not know. There is no fear of God before their eyes.

Nature of the Conflict

We have described three sources of conflict — identifying the most rewarding situation, selecting the operation required to achieve the goal, and understanding the elements in the conflict — realizing that these are closely intertwined in reality. Man's conflict with God involves him in all three categories.

In effect man substitutes goals in his rebellion so that his needs lead him to himself, rather than to God, for satisfaction. Man not only sees himself as capable of meeting all needs, i. e., he could act as the instrument, but as the end in himself. This is basically what sin is. Man pre-empts God's position. "No one seeks for God. . . . There is no fear of God before their eyes." (Rom. 3:11, 18, RSV)

If the satisfaction of the needs of man is man, then necessarily man chooses the wrong operation to reach his goal. Man resists the means of grace and strives to take care of his wants in his own way. These ways are as numerous as men themselves. The methods are all ungodly, since they stem from man's rebellious self-assignment to God's throne.

Man projects his guilt and blames someone else for his evil thoughts and activity. Using the mechanism of reaction formation, he tries desperately to protect a child that he doesn't love, for, if anything happened to the child, the guilt would be unbearable. And yet he passes on to the child the idea that his parent rejects him. He overcomes his timidity by becoming the fake life of the party, and the hypocrisy alienates the very people with whom he wants to be friends.

Man's confusion would be comical if it were not so tragic. But the consequences of the fact that "all have turned aside" are that "no one does good, not even one. Their throat is an open grave, they use their tongues to deceive. . . . Their feet are swift to shed blood, in their paths are ruin and misery, and the way of peace they do not know." (Rom. 3:13, 15-17, RSV)

The relation of conflict with God to the third source of conflict will be explicated below.

The Conflict with God Dynamically

There are several immediate consequences of man's conflict with God that effect basic changes in personality. One such consequence is guilt. Guilt, a feeling that is unique to man, results when he perceives that he has done something that he ought not to have done. Man, not escaping the feeling that he ought to be related to God, finds that actually he is in revolt against God. Scripture attributes this feeling to the natural knowledge of God "written in their hearts" and to the voice of conscience "accusing and excusing them" (Rom. 2:15). Undoubtedly the knowledge of God is reinforced from any number of sources — the testimony of the Scriptures, parents, teachers, reasoning from nature, threats to well-being.

247

The feeling is sharper in some individuals; less keenly felt in others. But there is some evidence from outside theology — and certainly from the Word of God itself — that the feeling of guilt before God is common to all men. This guilt feeling exists at a basic personality level and pervades much of the activity at the more conscious levels.

An atheist may deny the existence of objective guilt corresponding to such guilt feeling; yet certain situations may activate it and cause a defensive reaction. This is exemplified by the therapist who found that he could not establish a good working relation with his client. The therapist, an atheist, felt that he was accepting the religious feelings of the Christian client. However, at a point in the series of interviews, he discovered that he actually was not permissive about these feelings, but unconsciously was giving clues that evidenced his hostility. Had he felt free from guilt, he would not have had to react defensively. While an atheist may lay the source of such guilt at another door, the Christian sees in its persistence evidence of ineradicable real guilt before (the real) God.

A second consequence of man's rebellion against God is fear arising from the perception that man thereby has taken on himself a task of vast dimensions far beyond his ability to control. Some of the threats he finds he can handle. If he is hungry, he can work hard enough and long enough to earn something to eat. He can persuade someone to love him, although the relationship doesn't turn out to be entirely without its frictions and disappointments.

He cannot, however, begin to cope with the really significant threats. He cannot stave off death. If he reconciles himself to biological death, he cannot adjust to the possibility of a judgment. He cannot prevent change in the relationships he loves; nor can he escape all the persecutions to which his own personality bares him. Freud and other psychiatrists, particularly those of the analytic persuasion, have described the inexorable character of some of these threats.

Fear and guilt, two immediate consequences of the conflict with God, cannot be denied, and yet they are so fearfully disturbing that man cannot live with them. One way out is to repress these feelings and to hold them at an unconscious level.

Thus the unpleasant components, as well as the reality of the conflict itself, are banished from immediate awareness.

Repression of the conflict elements thus blurs the true situation. Man appears to catch himself in the webs of the third category of conflict, the conflict that is difficult to solve because the important factors cannot be discerned easily, if at all.

Repression, however, does not eliminate either the conflict or its resultant guilt and fear. Psychology shows that unconscious material does not lie dormant, but insistently seeks readmission to consciousness, appearing in the form of what are known as *derivatives*. Various situations serve to rouse the repressed experiences, re-creating the anxiety that led to repression in the first place and forcing the individual to some kind of maneuver that will serve to defend him from the reactivated fears and guilt.

A pastor called on a former member of the church who had renounced God, the church, and religion in general. He now claimed that God did not exist and that the church was autocratic. His reasons for denying the existence of God were based on material he had obtained from attending two lectures on evolution, and the claims about the church stemmed from an instance in which he had been seriously disciplined in the fifth grade of a church school. Obviously he had devised two transparent — and probably not wholly satisfactory to him — rationalizations to defend himself from a conscience accusing him on the basis of knowledge he had relegated to the unconscious.

Conflict and Hostility

At an unconscious level (or perhaps even consciously) man undoubtedly blames himself for the predicament into which his rebellion against God has led him. The overwhelming threats to existence are someone's responsibility. One could feel that logically he is not to blame, since unavoidably he is the victim of original sin. Yet, if he argues this way, it is more a rationalization than cold logic, since empirically it is observable that man does accept responsibility for his sin, although he makes every effort to project the blame.

The most plausible object to which responsibility might be attributed is God, who could have prevented the catastrophe by an act of will. But even the thought of accusing God compounds the guilt because it patently violates the conception of God.

As in many situations individuals displace feelings upon an innocent party, so here man may choose, unconsciously, to displace blame and hostility, attributing it to a convenient object, such as parent, child, pastor, the church, or government. Thus man makes himself more difficult to live with.

Resistance and Defense Mechanisms

Man must set up defenses against the results of his rebellion. The previous section gives an example of how such a defense works. What man concocts for this purpose is highly varied, complex, and ingenious. It focuses attention on problems far from the genuine ones, misleading not only casual observers but ordinarily the individual himself.

One of the most complex defense mechanisms is idolatry. If, for example, a Mahayana Buddhist worships his god, he is building a clever structure based on a modicum of truth. He is motivated by the knowledge that God *is*, but the god that he manufactures is just that — self-manufactured — for the purpose of quieting anxiety and guilt. It makes no difference that his ideas are highly evolved, that his motivation is apparently honest, and that he talks about religious matters. Again a conception of God is being used by man for his own ends.

Man's defenses drive him farther from God, but the natural man does not want it any other way. He has no desire to accept God. Turning to God is impossible if man has to initiate it.

An analogy might be drawn between the resistance of man to God and the resistance of the client to therapy. Every therapist and many pastoral counselors are aware that no simple explanation or exhortation will effect any degree of change in a client if the client's problem is at all serious. Therapy involves laying bare some of the most painful experiences an individual has suffered in his lifetime. The client resists this with all his effort, but at the same time feels that he must face them if he is to get help. Therapy is a taxing process because it involves drastically changing patterns of life that the individual has come to rely on, as unsatisfactory as they are. It often involves nothing less than a reorientation of sweeping proportions.

Conversion and the Natural Man

In conversion the deepest-lying structures of personality are violently shaken. Conversion involves the whole man. Through the means of grace the Holy Spirit overcomes the resistance of man and grants him the faith whereby he knows God and believes in Him. The old life is overthrown with its loves, devices, and motives, and a new life is created, completely reoriented — different knowledge, different motivations, different goal.

Since through Christ man's sin is forgiven and since through faith man shares God's life, faith removes the basic guilt and anxiety which are immediate consequences of man's rebellion.

While the Scriptures teach that conversion is complete in the instant that it is accomplished, they also declare that the Christian retains his former disposition to go his own way and to disobey God's will. It is astonishing that the Christian cannot escape the persuasive voice, "I can do it myself." But he cannot, and he continues to maintain a dual motivational system. Immoral activity is prompted by the defiant self-interest that perceives this course as most satisfying, even though his new knowledge of God points out, sometimes rather feebly, that this is a violation of God's will, a will imposed for the good of man, for his happiness, and for peace with himself and others. Moral activity results from the response of the Christian to God's love and, insofar as it is thus motivated, is unselfish and good before God. Yet even the most charitable acts are tainted by the selfish interests still a part of man's make-up.

Thus, during his life, the Christian still must contend with his unregenerate drives. On the one hand, faith banishes guilt and anxiety. On the other hand, his self-centered inclinations create guilt and anxiety. Experientially it is difficult, if not impossible, to separate the one state from the other. While John Smith is conscious of carrying out some altruistic activity purely in response to his faith in God, in the next split second he is bothered by the fact that there are strong selfish overtones to the anticipation with which he looks forward to the gratitude of the humble recipients of his good favor.

251

Motivation in Natural Man

Theology distinguishes between the righteousness of the Christian and that of the unbeliever, calling the latter civil righteousness. Civil righteousness refers to the natural desire to help one's associates, to serve man through an esteemed profession, and to contribute to harmony in the various communities. God wills such activity out of His concern for the welfare of all His creatures. Thus God may use even natural religion to help create good will.

Therefore, on a purely phenomenal level, both Christians and non-Christians produce good and evil works, though the dynamics of the two kinds of lives are qualitatively different. Christ's condemnation of the Pharisees, who gloried in their self-righteousness, applies here: "The tax collectors and the harlots go into the kingdom of God before you." (Matt. 21:31, RSV)

Experiential Correlates of Christian Growth

Sanctification refers to the Christian's life after conversion. In sanctification the Holy Spirit operates through the means of grace to sustain and nurture the faith begun at the point of conversion. Strengthening the will to resist the blandishments of the old rebellious desires is one aspect of this work.

The sanctifying work of God, however, is not analogous to operating a puppet. Prompted by his unregenerate impulses, the Christian may refuse to expose himself to the Word. He can misinterpret or deny the truth of what he hears. He can choose, consciously or unconsciously, to counter God's will with his own godless activity. In these ways he limits his growth in the knowledge of God and in righteousness.

These considerations, however, do not rule out the possibility that God, operating through what theologians call secondary causes, often directs the Christian life according to certain observable principles or "laws" of behavior. Nor does theology rule out the possibility that the Christian, resisting God's will according to his old nature, acts according to principles or "laws" of behavior (the laws in the second case not necessarily contradictory to those in the first case; e. g., the laws of learning could describe the behavior in both instances).

Sunday schools, chaplaincies, and religious television programs are all based in part on the observation that there are relationships between various facets of Christian experience. Keeping in mind the conditions under which these associations exist, the church can capitalize on them by employing scientific methods to investigate the circumstances which are correlated with, for example, desirable religious attitudes. God wants man to use the wisdom with which he is endowed by his Creator. (An obvious warning is that no scientific method will ever measure faith. Science can measure only what an individual says his faith is like.)

Substantial correlations, for example, have been obtained between the religious viewpoint of parents and their children's consciousness of God's influence on conduct as they reached their college years. Thus it would be possible to state the probability (but only a probability) that a child whose parents held a certain religious viewpoint as measured by a psychological scale, would feel his conduct highly influenced by God as an adult.

Pastors often hear parents object to sending their children to Sunday school on the grounds that the children will be unfairly restricted in deciding about religion later in life. Research shows the fallacy of the argument. An overwhelming percentage of children who do not go to Sunday school are negatively disposed toward religion as they become adults, whereas, if the argument held, they would be neutral in their religious attitudes at that age.

Negative Emotional Conditioning

Hospital chaplains meet patients who have been disappointed in almost every interpersonal relation they ever attempted. Perhaps orphaned and feeling rejected by a series of foster parents, they were turned out at an early age, only to find the world cruelly competitive. Bitter experiences taught that no one really cared. They generalize their feeling: "No one can be trusted," to include God. An experience which they interpret to mean that God is unloving or doesn't care can seriously challenge the very validity of their faith.

The question of the relation between the will of the new man

253

and the desires of the old — sorely aggravated by such suffering — becomes a very practical one here. The chaplain senses that he must cut through the hostility and independence to help this man in his faith. This means doing something about the influence of experiences, past and present, which reasonably the patient interprets as threats to himself.

The chaplain's tool is the Word of God. Yet it would be folly immediately to sermonize on the Christian's obligation to turn the other cheek! As guided by the Holy Spirit, he may find the best approach initially is to encourage the patient to talk about his feelings. The venting of emotion may take the wind out of the unregenerate sails. Getting the hostility out in the open may reduce its potency and help the individual see himself more clearly in the light of God's Law. Through the Gospel the chaplain reassures him of God's grace in Christ.

Frustration and Sin

An individual's sin can be better understood in the light of the psychological dynamics at play. Frustration can so upset the balance that the individual is led to the most serious offenses, perhaps confessing afterwards that he didn't know what possessed him. He wasn't himself.

If we ask ourselves what drives a man to the sin of intense jealousy, the answer — though, of course, not all of it — ordinarily can be found in a significant frustration revealed by the case history. He may have been prevented from developing the social skills with which the object of his jealousy is well gifted. He may be unhappy in his vocation, but finds it difficult to change jobs.

We cannot answer the theological question raised here, nor can we discuss the problem at any length. The Scriptures speak of two kinds of temptation: a temptation for evil which originates with Satan and a temptation for good which God originates to strengthen faith. The reader is referred to Richard R. Caemmerer's discussion of temptation from the theological point of view.[4]

------

[4] "Temptation" in *The Abiding Word*, ed. Theodore Laetsch (St. Louis: Concordia Publishing House, 1946), II, 171.

What is the genesis of the strange and crippling religious feelings often observed in the mentally ill? Many psychiatrists suspect that the church produces such feelings by preaching sin and the consequences of sin. One religious writer acknowledges the attack thus: "The depth psychotherapists have made one of the most trenchant criticisms of religion by empirically describing the various concealment and defense devices whereby the sick person defends himself from reality." [5]

There are three possible sources from which religious symptomatology might spring:

1. From faithful adherence to the doctrines of the Scriptures; i. e., the Word of God makes mentally upsetting demands or assertions.

2. From the church's or an individual's formulation of Scriptural teaching. Some teaching creates unhealthy attitudes which lead to breakdown, or aggravates existing defects which otherwise would not be handicapping.

3. Individuals break down for other reasons. The religious content serves some useful purpose in the economy of the disease.

1. From Adherence to the Doctrines of the Scriptures

How closely do the religious concepts of the mentally ill correspond with the teaching of the Holy Scriptures? Those with Messianic delusions, those who feel they have committed the unpardonable sin, and those with pathological consciences serve as three cases in point.

Those suffering from the Messianic delusion profess a calling to a special mission. They are sent by God to warn the world of an attack by the international armies, and they are to gather forces and lead them in holy war. Or they are to work their supernatural magic to save the lives of designated individuals. Obviously this thinking represents in name only the concept of the Messiah in the Old and the New Testament. Both testaments point to Jesus of Nazareth as the one Messiah, who is

---

[5] Wayne E. Oates, *Religious Factors in Mental Illness* (New York: Association Press, 1955), p. 31.

sacrificed in atonement for the sins of the world. The task assigned to the faithful is to proclaim the Gospel of the Messiah. On the other hand, the Messianic ideas of the mentally ill individual are self-centered and egotistical. He points to himself as having the special designation. His task has anything but spiritual quality. There is no reality basis; he is the only one who shares the concern.

Also the psychiatrist sees many patients who believe that they have committed the unpardonable sin. They say they cannot pray; they cannot communicate with God; they will not be saved. The Scriptures teach that those who consistently, perversely, and blasphemously reject the clear witness of the Holy Spirit in the means of grace are those who commit the unpardonable sin. It does not occur in the unregenerate or in those who turn away from God out of fear. God is not the cause, nor — as some erroneously teach — is this sin a result of predestination to damnation. When asked why they think they are guilty of the unforgivable sin, these sick people may reply that they remember misbehaving in Sunday school or entertaining an immoral thought during a worship service. Thus objectively their sin does not fit the description. The very fact of their concern indicates that they are not rejecting God; and God would never reject them.

The overscrupulous patient, as another example, constantly fears that he will commit sin — even in carrying out some morally neutral activity. He never ceases searching his soul to discover a previously hidden fault. He doubts even his own confession and hence questions his salvation. However, God does not expect that we can know all of our sin. By inspiration the psalmist cries: "Who can understand his errors? Cleanse Thou me from secret faults" (Psalm 19:12). And God does cleanse from all faults. "But ye are washed, but ye are sanctified, but ye are justified in the name of the Lord Jesus and by the Spirit of our God." (1 Cor. 6:11)

In each of these cases an obvious discrepancy exists between the Scriptural concept and the delusion of the patient. The divergence represents a qualitative difference and is so striking that no one could argue that religious symptomatology consists of a direct application of revelation itself. The only other possible source is in the perversion resulting from the interference of "the devil, the world, and our flesh."

2. From a Particular Formulation of Doctrine

Denominational groups may represent the Word of God in such a way as to produce or aggravate mental defect. One would tend to be most suspicious of those sects which generally are considered to diverge most sharply from the main stream of Christian thought. Certain characteristics of the Holiness bodies, for example, raise questions about the denominations' impact on the emotional life of the practicing members.

The doctrine of these groups varies from one to another, but one finds the following points emphasized rather generally: A. Belief in the Triune God, Father, Son, and Holy Ghost. B. Divine inspiration of the Bible. C. The natural depravity of man. D. Salvation through faith in Jesus. E. Conversion through rebirth by the Holy Spirit. F. Perfectionism, worked through a second act of grace in which all inbred sin is removed; sin does not originate in the sanctified but from external sources. G. Baptism by the Holy Spirit, distinct from conversion; an esoteric, ecstatic, highly mystical experience; evidence of such a baptism lies in the ability to speak with tongues and possession of other charismatic gifts. H. Faith healing.

To teach that sin no longer comes from within the individual once he has been sanctified creates a serious disparity between what one is supposed to believe and the clear voice of conscience. Experience makes it utterly impossible honestly to deny the sinful desires that still exist in the flesh after conversion and which the Scriptures recognize. Daily contrition and repentance are necessary, but the Holiness member who feels the need for this must doubt his own sanctification.

Bizarre attitudes and strange actions of the individual actually may be validated by the Holiness groups as expressions of charismatic gifts, whereas in reality these symptoms should be treated as signs of incipient psychosis. Anton T. Boisen reports that the first case assigned to him as a social worker at the Boston Psychopathic Hospital was that of a Portuguese cook. He had been observed thrusting up his hands in a peculiar manner on a crowded street corner. When he explained to the police that he had been baptized by the Holy Spirit and that the Holy Spirit was responsible for his strange actions, he was promptly hospitalized.[6]

Yet when Boisen in his capacity as a social worker reported that the group to which this Portuguese cook belonged not only approved of but valued such manifestations and that he was in good standing with the group, the cook was promptly released. As long as the belief is shared by others, psychiatrists may have doubts, but committal is not in order.

The case of the Portuguese cook gives the tenor of Boisen's conclusions after investigating the rise of Pentecostal groups in the stress period of 1930–35. With regard to the effect of the emotional experiences attributed to these sects, he writes: [7]

Among those who join the Pentecostal cults and pass through such experiences there are, as we might suppose, some who become mentally disordered. I myself have dealt with a number of these. However, the amount of actual disturbance which is attributed to them is much exaggerated. In my recent study of the Holy Rollers, I took the occasion to examine the new admissions in the mental hospital which was serving in a region in which these groups were especially active. I was surprised at the relatively small number of cases in which the influence of these sects had been clearly a causal factor. Out of 249 new admissions in a six months' period there were only 15 which could be considered at all. Closer study indicated that in these cases the disturbance was due to an accumulation of unsolved personal problems, and the influence of these sects, where it did appear, was never more than an upsetting factor.

We await more research on this question before attempting definite answers. In the research just referred to, Boisen's own history as a mental patient and his gropings in religion may have biased his observations. Yet his investigations, as well as good scientific sense, urge caution in generalizing about the effect even of the most unusual denominational beliefs and practices on mental stability. It is entirely possible that in periods of social stress — from a purely psychological point of view — cultism draws people together and develops a strange but effective group

---

[6] *Religion in Crisis and Custom* (New York: Harper, 1955), p. 88.
[7] Ibid., pp. 87, 88.

support for each of the members that may protect him from the violent pressures that otherwise would lead to a breakdown.

It is more likely that parents or individual teachers within a denomination twist Scriptural concepts to the detriment of those who come under their influence rather than that denominational emphases as such are to blame. It would not be at all surprising, for example, to find that when a father uses religion as a club ("If you don't do this, God will punish you"), the child pictures God as little else than a punishing God to be feared — and avoided if at all possible.

It is also impossible for a minister or other religious teacher to bury his own personality needs when he steps before a group to transmit the Word of God. If he should be depressed, have guilt feelings, and feel the need to be punished, he may picture a threatening God and lack conviction in speaking of the redemption. Some pastors try to handle personality needs by becoming heresy hunters. If they lay this burden on the consciences of their parishioners, the parishioners may be seriously disturbed about the validity of their doctrine, or they may adopt the same attitudes as the pastor's and thus behave in just as inadequate a way.

There are theories of personality which describe how concepts of God could be heavily biased by parental and other authority-figure attitudes, but there is little data which would pin down the exact character of this influence on religious belief, and how the change in religious belief itself might work negatively on emotional health. Yet if religion is going to generate unhealthy attitudes, it is in just this way that it is most likely to be done, i. e., through the perversions of individuals who find something in religion to bolster an inadequacy in personality. In theological language, sin limits our understanding and causes us to misunderstand. Fear and guilt may seriously distort the concept of God which is taught to others. This concept may aggravate a weakness in another's personality and work hardship on his emotional stability.

3. Religious Content as a Defense

Finally, the hypothesis most effective in explaining the genesis of religious symptomatology in mental illness is that the individual is primarily responsible for his religious attitudes and that his religious feelings serve some useful purpose in the economy of the disease.

A case Karl A. Menninger cites is useful in describing how an individual uses religion and finally finds that no orthodox religion can satisfy her needs:

Let us take, for example, the religious history of Mrs. Henderson. She was an aristocratic girl, whose father was a government official of some prominence whose duties prevented his giving any attention whatever to his daughter. This is a point of great psychological significance in what is to follow. Accordingly she was educated in private boarding-schools, since he felt that her mother, a nervous irritable woman, was a deleterious influence upon the child.

The patient was married when she was only eighteen years old to a young man who had not quite finished his training in law school. She had a fashionable wedding and she and her husband and the two children that were soon born to them lived in a city in Ohio, where her husband developed a good practice.

She had been reared in the Methodist church and for some time continued to work in it. For reasons not very clear to anyone she suddenly decided that the Protestant Episcopal Church was more nearly in accord with her religious concepts and she transferred her membership. She became very active in the work of that church, attended all the services and all of the regular and irregular meetings, never omitting Holy Communion when it was offered. She spent long hours reading and discussing religious matters.

After seven or eight years, during which time she had established herself as one of the pillars of that church, she decided that she should again change faiths and insisted upon joining the Catholic Church.

[A period of two years elapses.]

At this time she had declared herself to be a member of the "invisible church" and announced it as her mission to destroy all Catholics. She felt herself to be the head of the "eternal triangle," which she described as God the Father, the Son, and the Holy Ghost. She also thought herself to be a supernatural teacher or a nun in disguise. Such convictions were announced by her going to the church, kneeling in front of the altar, letting her hair down about her shoulders, and remaining there for several hours weeping and praying; she then returned home, knelt before her husband, and announced: "Unto us a child is born; unto us a son is

260

given," explaining this statement by saying that she was Virgin Mary and was soon to have a child by immaculate conception.[8]

In this case, Mrs. Henderson was anything but encouraged by the profession and practice of her church. On her own initiative she sought out other churches. It was her growing insatiable need that was leading her to seek more mystical experiences, not the mystical experiences that were creating additional demands — and emotional instability. In this connection, Oates observes that the sicker the person becomes, the more literally and legalistically he tends to interpret religious symbolism.[9]

Religious content almost invariably can be described as helping the individual — in a strange way, to be sure, but nonetheless making a contribution. The phenomenon of prepsychotic turning to religion illustrates this point. In sheer desperation a certain percentage of prepsychotics — Oates found it to be 10 per cent in a sample of 68 cases [10] — will turn to religion in a frantic, last-ditch attempt to save themselves. While before there has been no or little interest in religion, it now becomes an obsession. There is a fundamental difference between this turning to religion and conversion. In conversion man looks to God as his Savior and Lord, but the prepsychotic wants to "use" God for his own purposes. The former God initiates, the latter man.

In the same study mentioned above, Oates found that 20 per cent of the patients studied were described by psychiatrists and chaplain alike as simply "clothing" psychotic conditions with religious ideas. There was little prepsychotic religious concern. The patients were picking up religious ideas from other patients or from the chaplain and were using them just as "chatter," to get approval or to make an impression.

We can see that the Messianic delusion can be explained as a defense against feelings of defeat. "I believe I'm great. I believe it strongly. I am great." Delusions are defects of belief. The intellect operates with those premises and facts which are attractive emotionally. Usually the reasoning is strong. The deluded like to argue and build up a foolproof exposition of their

---

8 *The Human Mind* (New York: Alfred A. Knopf, 1946), p. 464.
9 Page 104 (see n. 5 above).
10 Ibid., p. 6.

case. The argument reinforces the belief. Everyone suffers from delusions to some degree. In the case of the psychotic the circumstances are so emotionally charged that the delusion must be extremely grandiose. The role of Messiah is second only to God.

We would suspect that the patients who insist that they have committed the unpardonable sin and the patients who are excessively scrupulous have not been burdened with guilt of God's or the church's making, but that they are burdened with personal guilt so terrifying that they adopt the method of self-punishment, self-condemnation, and searching out faults where there are no faults, to assuage that guilt. The real guilt is unknowable to consciousness through any method short of intensive psychotherapy. In scrupulosity, for example, the actual guilt may center in hostility toward a parent.

In slightly over 50 per cent of his cases, Oates found no evidence of any prepsychotic religious concern, despite the fact that his sample was taken from a region in and around Kentucky, where the percentage of religious people exceeds the national average. If the genesis of negative bizarre religious feelings lies primarily in external sources, specifically the church or attitudes taught by leaders in the church or by parents using religion as a threat, one would expect more religious people than nonreligious people to get sick. In this small study apparently more nonreligious people were getting sick than religious.

The question of the source of religious content in mental illness concerns both clergymen and psychiatrists. Psychiatrists must work with the attitudes and feelings of their patients and must understand the role of religion in generating these feelings. Clergymen understand that individuals may seize on religion to gratify selfish, ego-centered goals, rather than surrender themselves to the lordship of Christ. The clergyman is interested in how the individual members of his flock are faring spiritually and emotionally. Using religion to bolster an emotionally unhealthy idea is as much a danger signal to the clergyman as it is to the psychiatrist, perhaps even more so since the individual's salvation is involved as well as his mental health.

Easy generalizations are impossible. The patient must be

understood as a unique individual. The resources of religion and psychiatry must provide their unique applications to that individual.

Accountability in Mental Illness

To what extent are the mentally ill accountable to God? Their self-centered inclinations, outspoken hostility, cursing and swearing, ascendance to the eminence of God Himself, openly immoral sexual behavior — how are these to be interpreted theologically?

The Scriptures are clear that behavior stems either from the old Adam, i. e., the unregenerate nature of man, or from the new man, reborn to life in Christ. The source of the abusive, egotistical, sensual behavior of the mentally ill is certainly not the latter. It is entirely believable that it is the former. "Now the works of the flesh are plain: immorality, impurity, licentiousness, idolatry, sorcery, enmity, strife, jealousy, anger, selfishness, dissension, party spirit, envy, drunkenness, carousing, and the like" (Gal. 5:19-21, RSV). Since the apostle is speaking of man in general, it follows that one cannot exclude the mentally ill from this behavior description.

Furthermore, in certain cases an illness can be traced to a particular sin. Syphilitic infection can lead to paresis, with disorientation, degeneration, and delusion. Alcoholics can show definite psychotic syndromes. Other less obvious examples might be adduced to demonstrate a causal link between mental illness and sin, both original and actual.

As far as mental illness is the result of sin, man is responsible to God. If abnormal behavior follows from emotional upset, it is hard to see how that fact changes the picture of accountability.[11] As we have pointed out before, sin and emotional conditioning are inextricably linked in normal behavior, but the explanation offers no excuse. God could not look away when Saul

---

[11] If illness is due to a hereditary organic defect of the brain, such as in Huntington's chorea, from which an individual may become a paranoid psychotic, it would seem that the principle of accountability would apply inasmuch as man is responsible for sin, with its degenerative effects and resulting aberrant behavior. But this must be understood in the light of God's grace and His will that all men come to Him and receive His blessing. As we will say later on, man cannot judge. This applies here also.

with an evil spirit sought to pin David against the wall with a spear.

Yet observation of patients gives one a different perspective. Often the mentally ill just do not appear responsible for their actions. If one studies the etiology of the diseases, he is impressed by the weight of evidence for conditioning of emotional response. Previous experiences weigh heavily in personality malfunction. Indulgent overprotection by mothers leaves children selfish and demanding without regard for the rights of others. They cannot stand normal frustrations of life, must have their own way, lack good manners and social insight, and turn out sloppy work even when they have adequate ability. Such weak personalities are prone to mental illness.

Accidents create the most clear-cut cases of environment impinging on the individual's life with minimal responsibility. How can one hold the individual who has suffered brain damage through an automobile accident responsible for his subsequent bizarre, pathological behavior?

Understanding, reasoning, and retention enter into the problem of accountability. For extended periods of time many patients will not respond to auditory or visual stimulation. There is little reason to believe that they know what is being said to them or that, if they know, they can relate it to reality.

However, the Word of God is communicated through the ordinary sense channels. God does not work directly, but indirectly through the means of grace to establish and maintain faith. The problem is obvious. It has different ramifications for the Christian psychotic than for the non-Christian psychotic.

Obviously the question of accountability is complex, and the answer, if there were one, would plumb the depth of the wisdom of God. The Scriptures give no explicit answer. However, within the context of the revealed will of God and in the light of modern psychological insights, some principles can be formulated.

1. The psychoses and most fully developed neuroses are to be considered illness. To a substantial degree there is no difference between these syndromes and the more physical ones. The same organism is involved in both, weakened by sin and prone to disability, with the same physicochemical structure operating in both physical and mental abnormalities. The organism's

unique emotional conditioning plays into the history and prognosis of any kind of disturbance.

2. The approach of the church to the physically sick applies also to the mentally ill. While man cannot escape responsibility for the sin that directly or indirectly has led to a disability, he has no grounds for feeling that God has deserted him. In fact, God promises health to the faithful. "And because you hearken to these ordinances . . . you shall be blessed above all people. . . . And the Lord will take away from you all sickness" (Deut. 7: 12-15, RSV). Jesus Himself healed the hundreds of people brought to Him from dawn to evening. This was a fatiguing task that He certainly would not have undertaken if He did not earnestly want His creatures healthy.

It is obviously not God's purpose to drive people away from Him through sickness. As a matter of fact, illness often has just the opposite effect. Many a patient has entered a period of convalescence with the attitude: "Why did this happen to me? This confirms the position I've felt for a long time: going to church and everything associated with church is a waste of time. God ought to be partial to those who do the most for Him." However, as the patient ponders the matter, he begins to lower his defenses, finally reaching the point where he can admit the smugness of his pre-illness attitude and can turn in healthy humility to God's grace. Experiences connected with illness have strengthened a weak faith.

There is no reason to believe that God does not use mental illness as He uses other sickness — to serve His own good purposes.

It seems reasonable that two factors could operate to strengthen faith in God. First, at various stages of the illness, therapy, and recovery, the fear of the concomitant strange and uncontrollable emotional experiences could turn an individual to whatever resource he could find for comfort and assurance. The Christian would think of God as the ultimate Refuge.

Secondly, in the course of therapy, the individual presumably grows in self-understanding. As he goes into treatment, the hateful, hostile, bitter patient could not easily worship God. Negative feelings even may be projected on to God. Individuals who cannot love others find it difficult to love God. If therapy alleviates symptoms and uncovers causes, then some of the barriers to a close, meaningful relationship with God should also be removed. In theological language self-examination may help an individual understand his sin. If such understanding leads to repentance, faith is strengthened.

While we do not know why God permits His people to be afflicted with mental illness, this is fundamentally a specific instance of the more general question: Why any sort of illness? The Scriptures answer: "But when we are judged by the Lord, we are chastened so that we may not be condemned along with the world" (1 Cor. 11:32, RSV). "It was not that this man sinned, or his parents, but that the works of God might be made manifest in him" (John 9:3, RSV). While we do not fully understand the answer, we feel that it applies to the mentally ill as well as to the physically ill, perhaps even more so.

3. We have not answered directly the question of theological attitude toward abnormal behavior that descriptively is sinful. To arrive at a point of view, it is necessary to realize that behavior of normal and abnormal alike falls along a continuum with no qualitative difference or definite line of division separating the two. While there are normal people and there are abnormal, the two groups shade into each other.

Thus the theologian must look at abnormal behavior as dynamically but not qualitatively different. The sin of the normal person may be kept in check by a functioning superego. In the normal, sin arises as thoughts, impulses, urges that are ordinarily controlled in one way or another. They may be conquered. They may be allowed expression in a way that is "normal," i. e., socially approved.

With weak control of his emotions, the abnormal individual, on the other hand, may not be able to shape, redirect, or contain his impulses. His sin is different only in its form and mode of expression.

The abnormal individual is not more culpable than the normal. He is expressing in more violent form feelings and attitudes which normal people also feel but which have not destroyed their faith. The fact that the abnormal seems to go farther in expression of similar ideas does not necessarily mean that his faith is destroyed thereby. If abnormal behavior is symptomatic of illness, the abnormal condition must be viewed with the sympathy and mercy with which God Himself approaches sickness. The sin must be understood in the light of the sickness, and the sickness in the light of God's purposes for His creatures.

4. The individual that is so separated from reality that no one can communicate with him raises a special problem. In these instances the pastoral approach is based on the assumption that the faith held by the patient before the illness survives the illness, even though the conscious awareness of it may be clouded and confused with a tangle of unrealistic thoughts and emotions.

SUGGESTED READINGS

Bergsten, Göte. *Pastoral Psychology* (New York: Macmillan, 1951).

May, Rollo. *The Meaning of Anxiety* (New York: Ronald Press, 1950).

Outler, Albert C. *Psychotherapy and the Christian Message* (New York: Harper and Brothers, 1954).

XI. Pastoral Counseling and the Means of Grace

Interviewing by Pastors

COUNSELING provides the pastor with a most obvious opportunity to make use of the knowledge and skills of psychiatry and psychology. Yet he finds it difficult to relate the insights of secular therapy to religious counseling because of the radically different context. Questions involve the difference in the role of the pastor and the role of the therapist. Furthermore, counseling is fundamentally a skill. Even if the skill is much the same for both religious and secular counselors, the matter of how to get training raises an obstacle to using these techniques.

This section considers two sources of difficulty in relating psychological and psychiatric knowledge to pastoral counseling. One involves practical problems that commonly arise when pastors undertake counseling. The other involves conflicts with counseling theory, since the pastoral counselor uses the Word of God.

No attempt is made here to survey the relationship comprehensively, nor is this section meant to be a systematic manual on pastoral counseling.

In a current brochure issued by a newly organized Mental Health Association there is a statement: "The minister, the priest and the rabbi are among the first to be consulted by those in emotional difficulties." This is a generalization which I am sure would be challenged by many of the clergy as well as by psychiatrists and others who treat persons with emotional problems.

There is also a tendency for persons who give advice in newspaper and magazine columns to refer persons with problems to their spiritual advisers, apparently being unaware that a large proportion of the population is unchurched and would have no idea where to go if so inclined.

The first question that arises is: "Should people with or without church connections consult pastors concerning their personal (or emotional) problems?" In former times, in small communities, when the pastor was one of the few educated men in the community, he was consulted about many problems — finances, health, family, and personal problems. At that time also he was not as much burdened with organizational and administrative duties. It still seems to many church people, however, that the pastor should be the first to be consulted, if only for help in being sent to the proper person who can help them work out their problems.

Why, then, do many people with problems fail to come to their pastors for help? Direct inquiry of the people themselves brings out many factors. Some say that they have no idea the pastor is interested in anything except having them come to church. Some do not feel they know him personally. Others feel they know him too well personally or socially to tell him their innermost thoughts. Some feel he is too busy to devote any amount of time to any one individual. Some feel guilty because they have been given the impression that real Christians have no problems. Others feel that the pastor will be unable to help them because of the problems in his own personal life that he has apparently been unable to solve. Still others have some question as to whether the fact of counseling and its content will be confidential. There is still another question. Should pastors actively encourage their parishioners to come to them for help with personal problems? Most pastors, some because of real interest in counseling, some out of a sense of responsibility, will automatically answer yes. However, it is important for them to examine themselves in the light of the factors which have been brought up and their knowledge of themselves, insofar as they have insight into their own feelings, before giving an answer. Some pastors will feel that their position as leader of the church automatically places them in a position where they can help solve problems. Others may have to admit to themselves that they are uneasy at the idea of being presented with problems. Up to the present time their training has not equipped them to evaluate people and problems objectively. Much of it cannot be obtained from reading books on the subject of counseling, since counseling is a very personal interaction, in which the personality and true feelings of the counselor and counselee play the important part.

Probably the most difficult aspect of interviewing persons who come for help with personal problems is the ability to remain objective. This is obviously much easier for the therapist, who sees such a person on a purely professional basis and has no bias based on knowledge of the person socially or in other areas. The person seeking help can get sympathy, adverse criticism, and amateur advice from family and friends and probably has already done so. These people have undoubtedly tried to help, but their help has been biased by their own feelings which have become involved. A wife complains of her husband's neglect, and the pastor has difficulty in accepting this, since he may know the same man as a regular churchgoer, active and helpful in church activities. However, he must see this same person from the point of view of his wife, whose frame of reference is an entirely different one. A young girl may complain of neglect on the part of her mother, who to the pastor, up to this time, has been a model person because of her interest in church and community activities. These activities may actually fulfill some need of hers but may be responsible for the feeling of neglect on the part of her family.

Another factor which cannot be overlooked is the feelings of the pastor himself. The pastor's life is not without its problems. A study indicates, for instance, that pastors' marriages percentagewise are no happier than those of the general population. His children are just as likely to present problems as those of nonclergymen. If the person presenting himself has problems which are similar to some which are bothering the pastor, it may be difficult, if not impossible, to be objective and to help that person.

The pastor or any counselor interviewing a person with problems must be a good listener. Frequently the mere process of being able to pour one's troubles out to an objective person (called technically ventilation or catharsis) will give relief from the tension connected with the problems. One should be neither oversympathetic nor critical but merely recognize the fact that there is a problem and that it will take time to explore all the various factors involved. A question or comment which interrupts the train of thought can confuse or irritate the person speaking and often lose valuable information or associations. One should keep in mind also the importance of watching for associations in the thought process. If the person, for instance, mentions some problem and then goes on to mention his mother, one can assume that the mother is involved, in some way which may not be obvious at first. This "association of ideas," as it is called by therapists, can be recognized every day in the thinking of everyone. A subject may be under discussion in a group, and suddenly someone mentions something seemingly entirely unrelated. Actually it is a thought which has come to him through a series of ideas set off by something in the conversation.

We have endeavored to point out that mental and emotional illnesses and their symptoms are beyond the control of the patient, just as are the causes and symptoms of most physical illnesses. It is important to remember this in dealing with these people, as they often present symptoms or ideas which are unacceptable or exhibit unjustified hostility or resentment and complaints. It is important not to adopt a critical or punitive attitude toward these symptoms, since it will either spoil the relationship we are trying to establish or increase the guilt, which may be one of the basic factors in the problem, and thus intensify the symptoms. Many persons consulting pastors complain that the pastors adopt a punitive attitude when the persons themselves feel helpless about their problems. Thus all their negative feelings become exaggerated. It is just as valid to present to the person a God who is an understanding and forgiving Father as it is to present one who is just and punishes sin.

Another important factor in helping people with their problems is to establish early their security in the confidentiality of the interviews and the material they bring out. It is very difficult at best for many persons to admit their difficulties, and they are certainly inhibited in some cases by the fear that they may be discussed with others. This type of interview should be considered as private as the confessional. In a survey of persons, some of whom were psychiatric patients and others who were questioned casually as to their attitude should problems arise, it becomes noticeable that one of the chief reasons that they would not consult their pastor was that they would not want word of their troubles to get around. One made the remark: "I went to school with his wife, and I could never look her in the face again, because I'm sure he tells her everything." Even discussing an interesting case and attempting to disguise the persons involved can sometimes lead to disaster. We all know that the arm of coincidence is a long one, and untold damage can be done when there is gossip, both to the person involved and to the pastor.

It is also important to know when not to counsel. One of the purposes of this book is to give pastors some understanding of emotional problems and mental illness. When the person coming for counseling does not respond, when there is deterioration of his personality, when the diagnosis is in doubt, or when danger is suggested (e. g., the person threatens suicide or harm to someone) — in these instances the pastor would be well advised to seek the aid of someone who has the specific professional training to deal with the problem. The pastor should not hesitate to discuss the case, from his own point of view, with the therapist.

When the counselee's attitude indicates that there is a lack of rapport, or when it is impossible for the pastor to devote sufficient time and thought to the counselee and his problem, it is better not to begin counseling. Many people tell secular therapists that they resented the pastor giving them a half hour, a few platitudes, a final verse of Scripture, and then acting as if he had solved the whole problem.

Pastoral Counseling and the Means of Grace

Pastoral counseling is a practical situation which raises theoretical questions. The questions arise from a dual obligation facing pastors. The pastor must remain true to his theological convictions, but at the same time he cannot ignore the insights of secular psychotherapists. In applying psychological insights to his own counseling, the pastoral counselor therefore faces critical issues involving (1) the approach to the counselee, (2) the capabilities of the counselee, and (3) goals.

272

According to sound psychological principle, effective counseling is nonjudgmental. The counselor accepts the counselee, is ready to listen, and demonstrates a capacity for understanding. If he fails to accept the counselee, the empathic relationship necessary to real communication is precluded. A counselor who suggests through subtle mannerism or attitude that he condemns the counselee destroys his own effectiveness.

However, to accept is not to condone hostile, loveless behavior. The counselor does not love the counselee because of his poor behavior — or because of his good behavior. He is accepted in spite of his inadequacies and deviations.

The nonjudgmental theory should strike a responsive chord in the pastoral counselor. He finds that Christ did not reject the Samaritan woman, although He certainly did not approve of her marital life. Quite the opposite, He offered her the Water of Life. Secular acceptance does not go as deeply, in fact, as the pastoral relation where one sinner in need of God's grace confronts on the same plane another sinner aware of his need for God's grace. The severity of the transgression makes no difference in the common need of utter dependence on God.

While the pastor can support the nonjudmental approach wholeheartedly, he encounters difficulty with other aspects of the theory of permissiveness. The permissive counselor, beyond creating the accepting atmosphere, allows the counselee to proceed with the unraveling of his problem in his own way and at his own speed. When the counselee is satisfied that he understands his problem and can cope with the difficulties that still stand in his way, the counselor is also satisfied. The emphasis, though varying in degree from theory to theory, is on the counselee's ability to solve his own problem. The counselor's degree of direction ranges from deliberate nondirection to oblique suggestions and leading questions, at the most. He rarely tells the counselee what to do.

Can a pastoral counselor be a permissive counselor? The answer is complex.

He cannot be if it means that he cannot evaluate on the basis of God's Law. God's Law rightly understood and applied is the

273

only theologically valid way to evaluate behavior. What God asks of the Christian is sound also psychologically. It is essential that the counselee see the implications of his behavior for his whole life — his faith *and* his health. "Godliness is of value in every way, as it holds promise for the present life and also for the life to come." (1 Tim. 4:8, RSV)

The difficulty is that secular counselors have serious reservations about the authoritarian approach in any form, and these reservations are considerably heightened when it is a moral demand that is being brought to bear on the counselee's problem. The feeling is that the counseling relationship is to help the counselee get away from the threatening situations of his life — and that religion and God's Law in particular may be highly threatening to him.

However, that religion is a threat is an unwarranted generalization. The intensity of feeling among some secular counselors about this matter ordinarily can be linked to several instances in their experience in which God's Law has been misunderstood or misapplied, perhaps because of the pastoral counselor's own imperfections. These instances, however, do not negate the principle, or need, of applying the Law.

Of course, while holding the necessity of teaching the Law, no pastor would deny the need to understand himself more fully and to learn from the Holy Spirit more devotedly to minimize the hurtful influences which he himself may introduce into the counseling relationship. Nor would any pastor deny the need to study with every theological and psychological means available how the pastoral counselor may bring the parishioner the most effective help.

In practice even secular therapists may abandon permissiveness if they feel strongly that a given course of action is not advisable. In bringing their concern to the attention of the counselee, they may urge that several other choices be considered. The most client-centered therapist is free to express misgivings if he feels them deeply. (Of course, his purpose is far different from the pastoral counselor's; the therapist wants to prevent his unspoken feeling from arousing resistance.)

To illustrate how the thinking of two counselors, one a pastor, might differ on this point, a counselee might decide as one ex-

274

pression of his new freedom that he will go home and "tell his parents off," that is, express directly deep hostilities that he has harbored for a long time. In this particular instance (others, though similar, might differ) the pastoral counselor questions this course. Though arrived at by the counselee through the therapeutic process, it is not morally justifiable. While a secular counselor might be inclined to let the counselee go ahead — in fact, by virtue of his theoretical orientation would feel that he should not stop him — the pastoral counselor would be constrained to interject the point of God's will and to state that point emphatically if the counselee seemed resolved to disregard it.

Can the pastoral counselor be permissive? The answer is also yes. He can be through his interest in getting the counselee to solve his own problem with the minimum of interference. How far this can be done is not only an unresolved issue for pastoral counseling; it is a matter of debate in secular counseling as well. But most psychotherapists and counselors would agree that the more the counselee can do on his own, the more responsible he becomes, and the more likely he is to be able to handle his own problems in the future.

Hence the pastor will listen and be less ready to talk, especially in the earlier sessions. He will rely as far as possible on the Christian's own understanding of God's will to enlighten his concerns and to shape his solutions. We are not minimizing the pastor's role here, but emphasizing that he may use less direct methods to accomplish his unique goals — and accomplish them more effectively.

Of interest at this point are the findings of psychotherapeutic research that outcomes generally reflect the restrictions imposed by parental, social, self, and religious regulation. Decisions are not destructive and dangerous, but positive and constructive. Psychotherapy tends to free patients from guilt and resentment so that they can act with more freedom and responsibility.

For example, the individual who previously has not contributed to the group but has been rigid and self-centered during counseling may change dramatically. He becomes more cooperative, participates, and is more healthfully altruistic. One student who up to the point of the interview had steadily lost interest in his academic studies and had spent the previous eve-

275

ning drinking and looking for sympathy from tavern patrons anxiously began telling his story to the counselor. As he went on, he relaxed and finally on his own said: "I know what to do. First I'll take this to God. Until now I've felt too unworthy to pray about this — or even to pray. Then I'm going to see my professors. I feel that I can really stick to a study program now." It is doubtful that the outcome would have produced the obvious satisfaction if the counselor himself had laid out for the student these very same suggestions.

Permissive counseling leads to a truer picture of self because defenses are shown up for what they are — covers for guilt, pride, and hostility. In therapy the Law may penetrate man's protective bulwarks. After the Law convinces man of his sin, the Gospel can show him his Savior.

Can the pastoral counselor be permissive? The evidence of implicit directions might be cited to support the affirmative. During counseling attitudes are transmitted in an indirect way by the mannerisms, speech, and perceived role of the counselor. How this is done is not clear. But it is important for pastoral counseling because the permissive pastoral counselor may be passing on certain values in a subtle, yet highly effective manner. For example, there is some evidence that during therapy moral values change to resemble more closely the therapist's.

To summarize, there is no question in the mind of the theologian about the necessity or desirability of bringing God's Law to bear on the problem raised during the counseling. How to do this most effectively is an open question. The theories of secular counseling, supported in part by empirical confirmation, suggest that often the Law can be effectively applied within the framework of permissive counseling. Here the counselee in effect preaches the Law to himself — finding in the warmth and strength of the counseling relationship that he can look at his problem — at himself — more objectively and more helpfully.

Self-Capabilities and the Grace of God

The theoretical issues also revolve about the doctrine of self-capability held by psychology in apparent contradiction to the doctrine of sin and grace in theology.

By the doctrine of self-capability we refer to the explicit

statements of the client-centered school, after which much of current thinking in pastoral counseling is patterned. Man has within himself a positive force which leads him to constructive, positive growth. We also refer to formulations of some of the analytic schools which state that human resources can supply all that man either needs or wants to achieve.

Undeniably, psychology has helped people back to health and has shown what destroys and what promotes satisfactory solutions to some of man's personality problems. Man has certain capabilities for growth. The Rogerian group claims they are innate. God not only provides these basic strengths but ordains psychology as a resource for developing them.

When these strengths and resources are declared *all* that man needs, psychological formulations conflict with the Christian doctrine of man. Client-centered therapy with its emphasis on self-actualization does not approach an adequate explanation of those phenomena of human personality that are manifestations of man's sinful state. While some of the other schools of psychotherapy recognize more clearly the negative motivations of man, they naturally are not aware of, nor do they concern themselves with, theological insights into the nature of sin or what is necessary to shake the hold of sin in human life.

Overcoming sin is a task totally beyond the capability of man. It is a work of the Holy Spirit. It is a work which God originates and which He carries through. Only through the conversion accomplished by God can man know God in the sense that he is in a living, saving, empathic relationship with Him.

Conversion is not a direct process. A man is not converted by virtue of the counseling relation, the therapeutic results of counseling, or the fact that the counselor is a minister. Rather the knowledge of God is conveyed by the Word of God and the Sacraments. It is only when the Word of God or the Sacraments are present that the ultimate goal of human beings can be achieved and the benefits of God's grace applied to the immediate need.

The practical result of this differing point of view concerning man's capabilities is that the means of grace must become a part of the counseling. They are not just dragged into the relation because the pastor thinks he should bring them in. They are not used as a magic formula to dissolve the problem. It is not that the pastor will offer platitudes with the words "God" and "have faith" in them. But the revelation of God must underlie the whole approach. What the counselee says must be understood in the light of the Word. Whatever solutions are arrived at must be drawn in one way or another from the Word.

The Word may be communicated to the counselee in any number of ways; for example, quoted or paraphrased. It is conceivable that as counseling proceeds, the counselee himself will bring it into the counseling as he recalls a Sunday school lesson, a sermon, or a familiar passage. After running the gamut of defensive reactions, one hospital patient said to the chaplain, after a long pause: "All right, I know that I'm not as good as I pretend to be. I'm a sinner, and I need God just like everybody else." The conversation went on about the forgiveness of sin offered to man through the redemptive work of Jesus.

It might be possible to distinguish several levels of counseling, of which only the more serious would need to involve the fundamental questions of sin and grace. In other words, some questions could be cleared up by secular and religious counselors alike without reference to the Christian life. While undoubtedly secular therapists can handle even serious problems without such a reference, the pastoral counselor's experience would indicate that the assurance of God's grace and mercy is helpful in every problem. It is helpful from both theological and psychological points of view.

Goals of Counseling

What approach to counseling one follows depends on what one expects counseling to accomplish. Many psychologists feel that the goal of counseling is self-awareness. Experiences previously not admissible must be consciously perceived. Hostilities and resentments must be voiced. Restricting attitudes must be understood. One must become more aware of his motivations.

The issue for pastoral counseling revolves about the question of whether self-awareness can be considered an adequate outcome for therapy.

As described above, self-awareness seems highly desirable theologically. Some concomitants appear good in themselves. Getting rid of hostility is an example. Some appear to open up the personality for ministering with the means of grace. Thus self-awareness is a desirable goal, and the pastor will want to assure himself that his counseling approach is such that it leads to self-awareness. In this he gives all credit to the secular psychotherapist.

But to the pastoral counselor self-awareness cannot be considered an adequate goal. The individual who vents hostility must see that the hostility in the first place was not justified. Even if he had just cause, hostility is still not right, but evidence of his sin. To bottle up hostility and maintain a meek, pious demeanor so that people remark on his goodness makes the situation no better in God's sight. In fact, the individual is likely to express that hostility — perhaps against someone else — in irritating but subtle ways. The whole arrangement leaves the individual uncomfortable because of his dim awareness that it is all wrong. To see how subtle and devastating his sin was should lead him all the more to seek God and His righteousness. The pastoral counselor is responsible for showing him the meaning of his behavior in the light of God's counsel. Only then can the individual be properly counseled and completely helped — and only then can the pastoral counselor be totally satisfied with his counseling.

Resolving the Issues

In practice pastoral counselors have attempted to resolve the issues raised by apparent discrepancies between the tenets of secular psychotherapy and Christian doctrine in one of the following ways:

1. Sometimes pastors ignore psychological insights. They may feel that the secular world has nothing to contribute to the spiritual. Or they may believe that the trial-and-error process has led them to a satisfactory counseling method. The method thus arrived at often hurts more people than it helps by being overly dogmatic, authoritarian, and guilt-provoking. The counselor may fire the furnaces of hell in the face of the individual who comes to find forgiveness of sin.

2. Some pastoral counselors try to be theological and psychological, one at a time as it seems appropriate, without attempting a real integration. As one religious educator put it: "What psy-

chology says makes a lot of sense to me, but I'm not sure that I can quite fit it into my theological framework, with the result that I'm uneasy."

3. In some theological orientations no conflict arises. In liberal Protestantism, if the salvation of man is equivalent to his taking an effective and creative place in society, there psychotherapy could be considered a most helpful tool in liberating man from negative attitudes and allowing him to become his own natural helpful self. In reading much of the current literature on pastoral counseling one gets the impression that mental health is equated with morality and therefore either one may be considered the goal of the church. The grace of God seems to be equivalent to the blessing of God on healthy interpersonal relationships. Progress in therapy is evidence of the operation of God's grace, conveyed by the empathic counseling relationship.

4. Some make a distinction between counseling and teaching. Many counselors suggest that counseling does not provide answers for problems, but creates freedom and ability to solve problems. Thus in the counseling phase the soil is prepared; in the teaching phase the seed is planted. In the teaching phase the counselor takes a more direct role; in the case of pastoral counseling he introduces the means of grace. After going through the counseling phase, the counselee presumably would be more receptive to the counselor's suggestions. If the counselor had been didactic from the start, the counselee would more likely raise his defenses.

There are two recommendations for this approach. One is that this method is valid theoretically, within the limitations of our present knowledge of psychology and our understanding of the pastor's role. The second is that in practice pastoral counseling which proceeds along these lines often is found to be fruitful.

5. Pastoral counseling theory is in its infancy. Its development depends to some extent on the progress made in secular counseling, where a thousand questions are still unanswered. Some believe that psychiatry itself must tear down most of the old structure and start again from the beginning to try to arrive at a more precise, meaningful understanding of human dynamics.

Moreover, pastoral counseling has a multitude of its own

questions to consider. What is different because the counselor is a minister? What problems can be handled by the pastoral counselor? Does the pastor have a helpful contribution to make at certain stages of psychotherapy? In what way does the pastor communicate his theological concerns?

The ultimate approach will take account of the more precise knowledge of psychology, but also will be formed to its own requirements, to take care of its own tasks and make use of its own resources.

Confession, Absolution, and Catharsis

Private confession to a pastor involves a specific type of counseling situation.

Confession is always an expression of guilt over transgression of the will of God. The substance of the confession may include definite sins of which the individual is aware as well as an admission of his state of rebellion against God. It always includes an expression of faith in Jesus Christ.

Confession is followed by the act of absolving, performed by the pastor by virtue of the authority invested in him by God. "And when He had said this, He breathed on them and said to them: 'Receive the Holy Spirit. If you forgive the sins of any, they are forgiven; if you retain the sins of any, they are retained'" (John 20:22, 23, RSV). "Truly, I say to you, whatever you bind on earth shall be bound in heaven, and whatever you loose on earth shall be loosed in heaven" (Matt. 18:18, RSV). The pastor with the express authority of Jesus Christ assures the confessing individual of the forgiveness of God. In the worship service this formula is used: "Upon this your confession, I, by virtue of my office as a called and ordained servant of the Word, announce the grace of God unto all of you, and in the stead and by the command of my Lord Jesus Christ I forgive you all your sins in the name of the Father and of the Son and of the Holy Ghost."

It is evident that there are profound spiritual and psychological results from confession and absolution. God Himself removes all the sinner's guilt and forgives as well as cancels the trespass. Far from compounding guilt, the church offers the resource of God's grace for complete removal.

281

In the church, confession can take a number of forms. It may occur in corporate worship. It may occur between the individual and God without an intermediary. Or it may occur in the counseling relationship as the individual pours out his heart to the pastor. It is this last case which is most similar to catharsis, and we restrict our comments to this instance.

Confession in Relation to Catharsis

Catharsis refers to a therapeutic situation in which the patient vents his feelings in an emotional way. His thoughts may ramble, but the feeling is that just being able to talk it out helps considerably. After the catharsis the counselee reports that a load has been removed, that he is more relaxed, and that he is grateful for the opportunity to have poured out his innermost thoughts. Thus there are definite therapeutic benefits accruing to him in the process itself.

Confession is similar to catharsis in that it also involves outpouring of intense feelings. There is a sympathetic listener who is perceived as someone who can help with the problem. As "just being able to talk about it" gives catharsis its therapeutic value, so unburdening to a pastor in itself is helpful to a parishioner.

Yet the spiritual implications make the differences larger than the similarities. For example, catharsis can occur for a number of reasons, only one of which is guilt feelings. Perhaps an individual has been oppressed beyond his endurance. He has contained his feelings within himself as long as he can, and at last must yield to the internal pressures. It is possible that some guilt will be discovered as therapy progresses, but this is not the impulse for the catharsis.

Furthermore the role of the pastor by the very nature of his office is vastly different from that of a secular counselor. A counselee may bring his guilt to either counselor, but his choice is determined by what he expects of the counselor. Depending on the individual, his expectation will make it more difficult or less difficult to come to the pastor to confess. He may expect the pastor to be condemnatory, or he may expect understanding and particularly absolution.

The most important difference — quite evident, but necessary to point out because some have misunderstood it — is that confession is not an end in itself. Catharsis may be, but confession involves the very relation of man to God. Confession is followed by absolution, in which God alleviates the anxiety of guilt with assurance that the offense has been forgiven. Faith makes absolution meaningful and salutary.

The Pastoral Role in Confession

There are contributions which psychology has made to an understanding of catharsis which profitably may be used to understand the process of confession also.

Catharsis is thwarted if the counselee picks up any cue that he is rejected because of what he says. If the counselor is a pastor, the counselee's sensitivity to rejection is increased because the pastor represents God and morality. Many an individual has reported that the pastor pictured the horrible hellish consequences of his confessed sin and so thoroughly upset the counselee that it was impossible to proceed. The pastor may have mouthed some healing words, too, but the individual was in no mood to listen.

Such a feeling of rejection can occur partly because the pastor feels an obligation to verbalize the Law before applying the Gospel. It is correct that Law and Gospel both must be used in pastoral counseling. But psychological insights make it clear that when an individual confesses to a pastor, the Law has already worked. The individual may not be totally conscious of the Law at first — nor of all its implications — but one can be assured that the fact he is there at all is due to some painfully accusing experience. One cannot lay down a blanket rule, but it should be evident that it is not necessary to make use of the Law to reinforce a feeling of sinfulness and unworthiness that is already bitterly acute.

The Psychology of Temptation

A practical problem that pastoral counselors often face is how to handle those who have fallen to temptation. Here again psychology provides some insight. Psychologists have pointed out that religious people have paid little attention to ways of handling the problem of temptation beyond picturing its terrible consequences. But to scare a person is only to make the tempta-

283

tion more alluring. The more one dwells on its evils, the more strongly is the temptation reinforced — and thus the more difficult it becomes to destroy its force. Psychology offers two suggestions. Since temptation is heightened by environmental circumstances, counseling should aim to change the relevant conditions. This may involve a shift in vocation, direction in the use of leisure — whatever is indicated by the individual problem. Secondly, attention should be directed away from the temptation. If one covets a low-slung sports car, it is not helpful to spend time thinking of low-slung sports cars and how evil it is to want one that badly.

To be most helpful, a confessional situation may require more than listening and pronouncing absolution. Uncovering the underlying dynamics is also important to effect a change in behavior.

A young woman confessed that she had broken the Seventh Commandment* by pilfering ribbons and socks from a dime store. She was obviously contrite about the transgression, and the pastor assured her of God's understanding and gracious forgiveness. In a few weeks she was back in the study to confess that she had stolen again, this time a few cents from her mother's purse. Again absolution was pronounced. When not too many days after this the girl again came in tears, the pastor began looking more deeply. Professional help was called in to assist the girl. Serious deficiencies in her home life were uncovered. It became apparent that she had unexpressed misgivings about whether God had actually forgiven her after her previous confessions. While she had repented of the sin that she knew, she recognized her inability to straighten herself out; this feeling created internal doubts about her confession. As these feelings were brought out and she began to understand them, the urge to steal waned — and the absolution was accepted and believed.

The more an individual understands himself (understands himself as sinner), the more ready he is for the forgiving grace of God. If he is not sure that he understands his problem, he cannot consciously and unconsciously feel easy about God for-

---

* Lutheran numbering; eighth in the Reformed system.

284

giving him. If he does not understand himself, he will find it difficult to change his behavior. A sympathetic pastoral counselor will help him through the necessary soul searching but not a cataloguing or search for sins. This process does not supplant the work of the Holy Spirit in any way. It may be through this, as the means of grace are used, that the Holy Spirit works to strengthen faith and bring the assurance of God's mercy.

The counselee-pastor relationship may need to continue beyond the absolution into a phase in which the pastor helps the counselee see himself in the light of "the whole counsel of God." The length of this phase and the exact approach depend on the individual's faith. However, the essential elements include both Law and Gospel. The function of the Law is to show how blind the wisdom of self-dependency is and how it may lead into wholly unsatisfactory and hurtful directions; of the Gospel, to show the solution of the problem through faith in Jesus.

XII. Salutary Interaction Processes in the Christian Parish

The Basis for Christian Interaction

MODERN SOCIOLOGY and social psychology have with increasing frequency and persistence pointed out the importance of man as a social being. In the extensive literature which applies to man as an interacting member of the human family, frequent reference is made to the dynamics of group interaction, group therapy, the sociodrama, the psychodrama, and the impact of culture on the behavior of the individual. Protocols of interaction, controlled experiments, and descriptive theory have been resorted to in order to gain a better understanding of the principles underlying human interaction and to arrive at effective techniques for making human relationships serve educational, administrative, therapeutic, and prophylactic purposes.

Interpersonal life and face-to-face group action are manifestly inherent in Christian faith and life. This aspect of the life of the Christian finds its roots in man's earliest history. God said of Adam: "It is not good that the man should be alone; I will make him an help meet for him" (Gen. 2:18). He commanded Adam and Eve to be fruitful. Thus the human family, which has so strikingly been made a part of modern psychoanalytic thought, came into being. From then on the Old Testament record teems with incidents of human interaction involving love and affection, sibling rivalry, father dominance, mother anxiety, and intertribal conflict. In due time specific provisions for interaction were placed under the Mosaic Law and Levitic regulations, administered by prophets, priests, judges, and kings.

In setting the standards for human relationships, the Savior referred His hearers to the law of the prophets. Matthew records the touchstone of the Savior's provision for human interaction in the following dramatic scene (Matt. 22:35-40): "Then one of them, which was a lawyer, asked Him a question, tempting Him, and saying, Master, which is the great commandment of the Law? Jesus said unto him: Thou shalt love the Lord, thy God, with all thy heart and with all thy soul and with all thy mind. This is the first and great commandment. And the second is like unto it, Thou shalt love thy neighbor as thyself. On these two commandments hang all the Law and the Prophets."

The Law was applied by the Savior, and His disciples as well, to parents, husbands, wives, children, servants, the poor in spirit, them that mourn, the merciful, the pure in heart, the meek, bishops, deacons, and many more.

The spirit and tone of the Scriptural approach to interpersonal life may be summarized in the words of Paul (Eph. 4:31, 32): "Let all bitterness and wrath and anger and clamor and evil speaking be put away from you, with all malice; and be ye kind one to another, tenderhearted, forgiving one another, even as God for Christ's sake hath forgiven you."

The Need for Complementary Christian Interaction

Modern man is in need of both: complementary and worthwhile activities, and relationships free from hostile and contentious strife. This need grows out of the very nature and culture of our modern-day society. The person working on a restricted job in the assembly line is likely to have many individual and social needs which remain unfulfilled as far as his vocation is concerned. Compared with the earlier craftsman who designed, created, and marketed his product, the man in the assembly line is in danger of becoming a rebellious human automaton. The professional or technical worker, too, has arrived at a hedged-in position. He must remain relatively ignorant in many areas in order to attain competence in one.

Modern man faces a second dilemma, to which M. F. Ashley Montagu so poignantly directs attention, namely, the social ap-

287

plication of the evolutionary "survival of the fittest" concept.[1] The pervasive influence of the survival-of-the-fittest concept has no doubt had a devastating influence on the relation of man to man. Montagu proposes that human relations on a co-operative basis should be a fourth "R" in education.

A third difficulty which man in our society faces is that as a worker in government, industry, business, finance, and commerce he must often compromise his conscience in order to save face and to maintain status. It does not require an oversize imaginative mind to project the many situations in which this may happen. Not the least is in the pursuit of the sciences by the believing Christian.

That the many leisure-time activities in which people engage may have a complementary value and a tension-reduction effect is observable. People appear content and happy when they pursue their hobbies and voluntary interests. As such these activities no doubt have a constructive purpose in addition to having a drainage function.

The spontaneous efforts and movements in various areas of culture to provide man with a richer life individually and satisfying human relationships, as well as the scientific, technological, and how-to-do-it literature, demonstrate a conscious sensitiveness on the part of our generation to do something about the void in human beings. What could be more appropriate, then, that Christian congregations, preaching and teaching the message of grace in the Savior and urging individuals to live in accordance with God's love, deliberately and with forethought foster a parish life (a) which provides the individual with most worthy activities, and (b) which provides for interpersonal relationships on the basis of Christian love and fellowship?

The Quality of the Parish Milieu and Christian Interaction

The dynamics of interaction in group life are modified by the satisfaction or dissatisfaction which the persons derive from their participation as individuals. And if the action of the group is to have more than incidental and chance values, it must give evidence of some action or movement based on consensus or agree-

---

[1] *On Being Human* (New York: Henry Schuman, 1950).

ment. Not only the planned agenda, but what has been called the "hidden agenda" enters into the process of group life.

The hidden agenda element is likely to enter forcefully into the interpersonal milieu in a society in which free speech and the power of decision are exercised by the individual with little restraint. An eyewitness of such a group in action may find that one or more members are engaging in a display of emotions which clearly indicates attempts to solve their own personality difficulties. When some members of the group resort to individual problem-solving ways of interaction, others who are more concerned with the forward movement of the group as a whole may then resort to counterpunches. And they, too, begin to show the lurking weaknesses and conflicts in their own personalities. In such an event the group arrives at a point of crisis which could be disruptive for individual problem solving as well as for common action. It might also lead to a feeling of guilt with apologies and result in a constructive forward movement. The latter is not likely to happen, however, unless the individuals can submerge their own problem-solving attempts to the common cause. They might, of course, see the apology route as a way of saving face.

When an individual resorts to deviant or at least odd conduct as a member of a group, it cannot at once be assumed that he does not have an appreciation of the common cause. It is more likely that his previous life has left him with overwhelming unresolved conflicts, to which he reacts with pugnacity and hostility. For "some indeed preach Christ even of envy and strife." (Phil. 1:15)

On the other hand, it cannot be assumed that because a person is a colorless hanger-on or middling, he has no individual hidden agenda. This may be the person who reveals his dependence or unwillingness to take on responsibility by saying: "Pastor, you tell us what to do. You know best." If the pastor then does tell him what to do, he may harbor an inner resentment for being forced to do something which he did not want to do in the first place.

Behind the group milieu the answer to interaction processes must finally be sought in the role which the individuals consciously or unconsciously play on the premise of their own life plans. Knowing this, those charged with the responsibility of leadership may modify their own plan of interaction on a constructive if not a therapeutic level. It cannot be assumed, however, that in each case the leader will know the full answer, for that would require psychoanalytic techniques or intensive group-therapy skills, for which neither the pastor nor other parish leaders should be made responsible.

From the previous discussion of the nature and difficulties underlying human interaction, it is but a logical next step to ask: What kind of leadership is required to attain a salutary parish milieu? The answer to this question must go beyond the consideration of the quality of leadership, important as that is, to the question: What position and status do the members of the parish occupy in the interpersonal relationships? For leadership is not a function in isolation.

Fortunately Scripture gives us a clear and comprehensive answer to both questions.

Regarding leadership the Bible makes repeated references to the exacting qualities required of leaders, especially of bishops and deacons (cf. 1 Tim. 3:1-13). In modern language we would say that a pastor as well as other parish leaders should possess a considerable emotional maturity or, at a minimum, be ready to strive for it. That we must allow for growth and not expect primordial perfection is clear when Paul says to Titus (Titus 3:3, 4): "For we ourselves also were sometime foolish, disobedient, deceived, serving divers lusts and pleasures, living in malice and envy, hateful, and hating one another. But after that the kindness and love of God, our Savior, toward man appeared."

In a salutary Christian parish milieu we would expect the leaders to have a clear conception of the reason for the very existence of the parish and to subordinate their own personal desires to the attainment of the final purpose for which the parish exists. In other words, individual hostility, quick tempers, personal-status seeking, the urge to dominate, sensitivity because of a lingering childhood intolerance, and whatever other emotional conflicts are present, will not stand in the way of the message of God's saving grace in Christ for sinful man. In the words of Paul (Phil. 4:12, 13): "I know both how to be abased, and I know how to abound; everywhere and in all things I am instructed both to be full and to be hungry, both to abound and to suffer need. I can do all things through Christ, which strengtheneth me."

Effective leadership does not begin with what the leader does but with what he is. In the language of sociodrama one would ask: What are the ingredients of the role he is playing?

Turning now to the question pertaining to the position and status of the members of the parish, it is the equality of all before God which should characterize the individual and group attitude. The grace of God is inclusive, not only within the parish but also beyond it to all people. Equality applies to all in whatever station of life they may be. It carries with it the privilege to communicate with God directly without the intervention of another person and to interpret all things, including the Bible, according to the dictates of the individual's conscience.

The status of the members of the parish is in addition strengthened and fortified by the priesthood of all believers. As Peter states it (1 Peter 2:9): "But ye are a chosen generation, a royal priesthood, an holy nation, a peculiar people, that ye should show forth the praises of Him who hath called you out of darkness into His marvelous light."

Peter does not only designate the believers as the royal priesthood but also shows the purpose, "that ye should show forth the praises of Him who hath called you out of darkness into His marvelous light."

The parish is, of course, not a disarrayed organism in which everybody does everything. "For as we have many members in one body, and all members have not the same office; so we, being many, are one body in Christ, and everyone members one of another" (Rom. 12:4, 5). The actual structural arrangement of the modern parish will leave room for many gifts and talents and for individual skills and preferences. But it will not do so on the premise of priority, privilege, and an assumed role of superiority or inferiority, at the expense of the Christian's duties, privileges, and rights. It will rather do so on the basis of the principal purpose for which the parish exists and in keeping with the individual's needs, fitness, and educability.

While we may say that the parish with its integrated activities in the Christian Church of today fosters therapeutic and mental health values, this does not imply that it should aim first of all to be a therapeutic agency. The first purpose of the Christian parish is to administer the means of grace. Out of its first purpose, nevertheless, follows the consequent aim to promote a Christian life in all of its aspects.

Referring more specifically to interpersonal and group life, Paul says (1 Thess. 5:11): "Wherefore comfort yourselves together, and edify one another, even as also ye do."

We gain further insight into the therapeutic nature of Christian interaction from James' admonition (James 5:16): "Confess your faults one to another, and pray one for another that ye may be healed. The effectual, fervent prayer of a righteous man availeth much."

Turning now to the scientific and technological view of human interaction, we may say, first of all, that ordinarily it is not advisable for anyone or any group within the parish to engage in direct intensive group therapy. We may, nevertheless, learn from such therapy [2] that group activity and individual counseling are complementary as an approach to instruction, guidance, and administration. We may also learn from the technical aspects of group therapy that permissiveness, within limits, is necessary to arrive at a deeper understanding of the feelings and emotions of the individual or the group. But permissiveness on the part of the counselor or leader is not the same as indifference or license. It is regarded as a tentative moment from which the leader as well as the group move to an improved position. If the group takes the lead toward an improved position under its own power, so much the better. The counselor can then follow up with the mirror technique in that he clarifies and reflects back to the group the action or the position which it has taken. A counselor thus serves as a sounding post rather than a hitching post. Within limits he may be per-

---

[2] George R. Bach, *Intensive Group Psychotherapy* (New York: Ronald Press, 1954).

missive as long as he demonstrates interest, warmth, and concern for the group agenda. But there is no room for coldness and indifference.

To be permissive does not mean to be completely nondirective. False premises are not passed by without being challenged. Observation of a group in action which proceeds on false premises without anyone calling attention to them is not an edifying experience. The Christian pastor, counselor, teacher, and leader will seek opportunity to apply Scripture and to use prayer when called for. Such a use of Scripture calls for versatility, much more so than its use in previously planned admonitions.

A second point of interest from the psychology of group dynamics is related to the question whether leadership should be leader-centered or group-centered. If the purpose is to elicit group interaction, to give opportunity for the release of pent-up feelings and to arrive at a consensus in group movements, it is clear that leadership should be group-centered. Group-centered leadership does not exclude free communication of pertinent information on the part of the leader, provided the information is not given in such a way that it forecloses interaction and the seeking of a common solution by the group. A persuasive person who overwhelms the group with an array of incontrovertible facts is not necessarily a dynamic leader. He is more likely to be a person with a hidden agenda.

Where an interested permissiveness and a group-centered leadership prevails functionally in youth groups, adult instruction, Bible classes, and confirmation instruction, one would look for doubts, misgivings, uncertainties, and even hostilities and resentments to come to the surface, which would remain repressed and hidden in an autocratic, leader-centered situation. The fact that they remain repressed does not mean that they do not exist, nor that they will not influence the future thought and action of the individual harboring them.

A third point of interest to the group leader in the Christian parish concerns the question of authoritarianism and autocracy in leadership. The statement that in every man lurks the tyrant appears to be more than a half-truth. Observation and analysis of autocratic leaders in action leads one to the conclusion that more often than not they are acting on the basis of their own uncertainties and hostilities. Their interest in the group situation serves them as an occasion to attempt a solution to their personal problem in their own way.

What effect does autocratic leadership have on the group dynamics? In the White and Lippitt study [3] the effect of autocratic leadership was what one would expect. Autocratic leadership tends to incite interpersonal conflict and hostility, discontent, scapegoat finding, destructive behavior, and leader-dependent action. In an autocratic atmosphere the group members tend to avoid taking on responsibility for their conduct, remaining self-centered with little or no attempt at developing a "we" feeling. The same study indicated that under democratic leadership the groups tended toward a friendly, independent, and group-minded conduct. The members generally maintained a high interest throughout the study. Even such an irresistible leader as Paul declares (1 Cor. 4:21): "What will ye? Shall I come unto you with a rod or in love and in the spirit of meekness?"

What values do we seek in Christian interpersonal relationships? It is clear that we are not seeking opportunities for the tyrant within us to exercise compulsion, nor the elaboration of our hidden agenda, nor evasion by verbalized sugar-coating, nor survival of the fittest, but an inner peace and harmony in serving God, and a charitable attitude toward man.

SUGGESTED READINGS

Cartwright, Dorwin, and Alvin Zander. *Group Dynamics.* Evanston, Ill.: Row, Peterson and Company, 1953.

Haiman, Franklyn Saul. *Group Leadership and Democratic Action.* Boston: Houghton Mifflin, 1951.

Montagu, M. F. Ashley. *On Being Human.* New York: Henry Schuman, 1950.

Thelen, Herbert A. *Dynamics of Groups at Work.* Chicago: University of Chicago Press, 1954.

---

[3] Dorwin Cartwright and Alvin Zander, *Group Dynamics* (Evanston, Ill.: Row, Peterson & Co., 1953), pp. 585—611.

XIII. Retrospect

We have endeavored in the preceding chapters to achieve three aims: (1) to explain Christian doctrine to non-Christian psychotherapists; (2) to explain psychology and psychiatry to pastors; (3) to examine critically some of the relationships existing between these two systems of concepts. As stated in the introductory chapter, our assigned task was not that of writing a handbook, manual, or textbook of pastoral counseling. Nor was it to produce a treatise of apologetics. Least of all was it to "prove" that "religion" and psychiatry are striving to do the same things and are in blissful harmony in all important respects. We have conceived our task partly as elementary exposition, and partly as the delineation of some important problems awaiting solution.

We began our treatment with an exposition of the Christian view of man, specifically that held within confessional Lutheranism. It was set forth there that man's root difficulty lies in his alienation from God and the consequent guilt, fear, inordinate impulse life, corruption of fellow feeling, and darkening of intellect. From there we moved to a consideration of the basic concepts of contemporary psychological science, beginning with three rock-bottom ideas: *determinism, materialist monism,* and the *intersubjective confirmability* criterion for admissibility of propositions. We continued with a condensed presentation of what is known today about man's biological nature, and how this nature is further shaped by the processes of learning through life experiences. The products of this learning which are of particular concern to the pastoral counselor were then sketched out: mental mechanisms, the unconscious, and the chief syndromes into which aberrant behavior is classified.

Having before us the Christian doctrine of man and the psychologists' picture of him, we next made an inquiry into what relations exist between the two. It was pointed out that conflict arises from several distinguishable causes. Sometimes the conflict is based upon semantic confusions, as when the same word (e. g., "guilt") means one thing to a theologian and another to a psychologist. Sometimes, but rarely, it is a matter of pastor and psychotherapist having conflicting aims in their practical work; more commonly, each attributes aims to the other which vaguely resemble his own but disagrees about the other's means of trying to achieve them. Then there are open questions, both theological and scientific, which the disputants erroneously perceive as closed and then interpret the "answers" in an oversimplified way, which brings them into apparent conflict with oversimplified formulations from the other discipline. There are theological mysteries which are unashamedly called such by the church, but which the non-Christian psychotherapist quite understandably looks upon as mere obscurantism. (Science has many unsolved problems; but it has no "mysteries" in the sense of the church.) Finally, we pointed out the existence of genuine disagreements, in which the clarification of concepts, rather than resulting in convergence, makes it painfully obvious that a head-on collision has occurred. Ontological dualism, in some form, seems to be inextricably woven into Christian doctrine and is explicitly denied in the world picture shared by the vast majority of psychologists and psychiatrists. We saw that some of these *real* disagreements are potentially resolvable by further empirical evidence (e. g., in the matter of dualism, evidence from such special phenomena as clairvoyance or precognition, which many non-Christian thinkers take to support the idea of nonmaterial forces or entities). As Christians, the authors, of course, anticipate confidently that if a permanent resolution occurs at this empirical level, it will be in harmony with revelation — a "promissory note" kind of attitude, which we do not expect our non-Christian readers to share.

In spite of these various possibilities for resolution of conflict, we concluded the discussion of kinds of relations by emphasizing

296

that at least a few of the real differences are radical in nature and not, so far as one can see, resoluble by either conceptual clarification or the gathering of further factual data. The defining property of a Christian is faith, and whatever else faith means, it means a commitment which is to at least some degree non-rational (we did not say *ir*rational!). If one imposed the same standards of clarity and evidential support upon his religious thinking that he does in practicing good science, and if his strength of conviction were proportional to the evidence, he could not be a Christian. We tried to make clear, however, that this is not tantamount to saying: "A Christian who is also a scientist must somewhere contradict himself." That cannot be, in the long run, if Christianity and science are both true. We have insisted that there are no propositions *within the corpus of verified scientific knowledge* which contradict Christian doctrines. (Modernists continue to make reference to the "contradictions," but they are extraordinarily elusive.) The conflict is not a substantive one; it is methodological and philosophical.

A little careful thought will suffice to convince an inquiring and disinterested reader that frictions between the actual content of scientific knowledge and the Christian picture set forth in Chapter II are very hard to exhibit. If the reader doubts this, he may test it by a very simple experiment. Let him examine a textbook or treatise on psychology, being careful to distinguish between established scientific facts (or well-supported theories) and the obiter dicta about life and "things in general" which some social scientists permit themselves. (Thus: "The IQ's of children from professional homes are 15–20 points higher than those of laborers' children" is a scientific fact; "modern sociology shows us that everything is relative" is not, although it may appear in a context which suggests that it is.) Having written down a score or more of scientific facts and laws, let him then confront each of them with some succinct formulation of Christian doctrine, such as the Nicene Creed, asking each time, "Are these propositions incompatible?" He will find that the logical situation is quite different from that which obtains when one juxtaposes Mrs. Eddy's writings with a textbook on bacteriology!

If, however, we mean by a "consistent scientist" one who thinks through all cognitive questions, adopts all value orienta-

297

tions, and makes all important decisions in the same way — the scientific way — then, to be sure, a scientist could not be a Christian. The "scientific attitude" and the "religious attitude" cannot coexist with respect to the same subject matter. This admission, however, is neither surprising nor damaging. Christianity has never made the claim that faith is a scientific act, and it is not clear why anyone would feel impelled to make such a claim for all of his beliefs and actions. Since the Catechism explicitly teaches that one *cannot* come to faith by one's own strength or reason, it should not come as a shock to anyone that a similar conclusion is reached by cold epistemological analysis! Since the Christian faith amounts in its cognitive aspect to an *overbelief* (i. e., "beyond" what science can show) rather than a *contradiction* (i. e., "against" what science shows), the radical conflict need not be reflected in any such pragmatic consequence as a pastor's inability to use the psychiatrist's services. The technical tools of psychotherapy are justified within a framework of psychological concepts which the Christian pastor *can* accept; it is only if the (rare) psychotherapist uses tools (e. g., antireligious propaganda) which work counter to the Christian overbeliefs that a pragmatic conflict arises.

The next chapters were then devoted to a detailed and speculative inquiry into two representative problems, one practical and the other theoretical. In treating the practical problem — that of the relation between valid and displaced guilt — we offered as a formulation that both normals and neurotics have *objective* guilt and objective reason to be afraid; both experience *guilt feeling* and anxiety; but the neurotic experiences more of both, and he deals with his guilt and dread by the use of ineffective and self-damaging (unconscious) methods. The usual outcomes of employing these distorted methods for handling conflictful impulses are social disarticulation, subjective dissatisfaction, loss of efficiency, distortion of reality, characterological quirks, and sometimes medical symptoms. The aim of secular psychotherapy is to undo these distorting tactics and thus to alleviate their unhealthy consequences. This procedure does not address itself to the objective guilt, which is a moral, forensic, and theological category rather than a psychological one.

The specimen theoretical problem — that of determinism —

was chosen because it is one of the core concepts which psychologists think of as running counter to Christian teachings; also because it involves philosophical issues and methods and provides thereby a good illustration of the kind of analytic method which we believe should be applied to the whole area with which this book treats. Taking the conversion of Saul as an example, we examined the three logically exhaustive alternatives for a scientific theory of the *physical* aspect of this event. Two of these — the cerebral-miracle theory and the indeterminate-brain-state theory — were found to be both consistent with revelation and scientifically meaningful according to the empiricist meaning criterion. The third, that of strict materialist determinism, was held to be doubtfully consistent with revelation as understood by Lutherans, having possible Calvinistic implications. It was suggested that the addition of ontological dualism (to which Christian orthodoxy already commits us anyhow) to the strict materialist determinism of the third theory would render the third theory acceptable. However, this enlarged third theory, unlike the first two, does not seem to be scientifically admissible if the confirmability criterion of meaning is imposed.

We then returned to practical problems in the final two chapters. In discussing pastoral counseling and the means of grace, we saw that in the counseling relationship it is necessary for the pastor to suspend *momentarily* his task of expounding the Law in favor of an attitude of maximum uncriticalness and receptivity. By adopting this inquiring and accepting role in the initial stages of interviewing, he maximizes the probability of eliciting feelings and information about the parishioner and his problem. This is particularly important when the real problem (whether psychiatric or religious) is not the problem which the parishioner initially presents, because too early an active intervention may prevent the underlying difficulty from emerging into the discussion. It was pointed out that the pastor himself may react with anxiety or resentment to the material being presented; hence an adequate psychiatric adjustment among pastors is important. Some specific difficulties and tactics in interviewing were briefly discussed. Finally, some of the forces at work in group interaction among Christians were analyzed in terms of group dynamics, with particular reference to the adverse influence of neurotic drives and "hidden agenda" within a congregation, and the positive values of healthy group relations for the development of Christian life.

A pastor totally untrained in the technical tools of counseling developed by psychologists and psychiatrists will not, as a result of reading this book, be appreciably more skilled in understanding an individual's dynamics or in his actual interview tactics. (One does not become skilled as an interviewer by reading books, any more than mere reading makes a watchmaker or a surgeon. But it's a good place to start.) Such a pastor will perhaps be better able than previously to spot a classical sociopath or forestall a suicide in an involutional depression, especially if he studies the references cited in Chapter VI. If the general *flavor* of psychological thinking has been conveyed, the pastor may find himself taking a new orientation to his pastoral work. The problem of referrals and subsequent co-operation with psychiatrists and psychologists should be eased somewhat by understanding the secular aims of the workers in these callings.

Above all, doctrinal issues have been emphasized throughout, in the hope that the anti-Christian spirit of the prevailing scientific humanism may be disentangled in the pastor's thinking from the technical know-how which psychological practitioners possess. The first step in improving the relations between two groups is usually to facilitate communication. A pastor who really absorbs the psychological, psychiatric, and philosophical sections of this book will, we believe, find his doctrinal anxieties allayed and his semantics clarified. In fact, he will be a good deal clearer in the head about the logical relations between Christian doctrine and psychological concepts than most psychotherapists.

The non-Christian psychotherapist who reads this book will not have become convinced of the Christian claims. But we hope that the fair-minded among them have experienced some attrition in the common attitude that Christian theology is "refuted" by our scientific knowledge of the human mind and that Christians preserve their beliefs by the simple expedient of remaining systematically uninformed. The Christian doctrine of man is properly understood by the unbelieving psychologist as *going beyond* the corpus of scientific statements rather than *contradicting* any scientific statements. When a psychotherapist treats

300

a Christian patient, he need not fear that the doctrinal ideas of his patient will "get in the way" of psychological understanding. The patient — at least, the Lutheran patient — is not bound to receive any religious beliefs that stand in contradiction to the basic beliefs underlying psychotherapy (unconscious motives, conflict, defense mechanisms, displaced guilt, the special importance of hostile and erotic wishes in symptom formation, etc.). The patient may *think* that his religious beliefs contradict some of these ideas; if so, he is either theologically misinformed, or he is using his religion in the service of the resistance. In such cases the closest co-operation, including even some doctrinal discussion, between the psychotherapist and the patient's pastor is necessary. They should be perceived by the patient in the roles of "backing each other up," not of competing for the patient's allegiance or of offering him two opposed roads to the same kind of salvation.

Of course, pastors will usually have dealings with non-Christian psychotherapists who have not read this book, and conversely. There is no hiding the fact that *some* psychotherapists subtly sabotage the patient's religious beliefs and devotional practices (a tiny minority even doing this more actively); similarly there are pastors who believe that the works of secular psychotherapy are of the devil and who find themselves personally made angry and anxious by the entry of these concepts into thought. A book such as this may alleviate such cases, although the motivations leading to missionary atheism among therapists and psychiatry phobia among pastors are probably neurotic in character and not, therefore, amenable to rational argument.

We close with a special plea to readers who have technical competence and scholarly interests. We believe — and this would be expected in a committee set up by "the Missourians" — that the theoretical issues raised here are of extreme importance. Nothing is gained by glossing over difficulties or tactfully avoiding mention of real differences. The widespread interest in the pastoral counseling movement, the numerous interdisciplinary conferences which have been held between clergy and psychiatrists, the increasing number of pastors who seek such special

301

training from the few sources available, indicate a rapidly growing *rapprochement*. A Christian who reads between the lines of current non-Christian writing on personality and healing is tempted to say to himself: "Aha — they're coming around, but *they don't know it yet!*" And there is some reality basis for this reaction. One has the impression, however, that things are going a bit too smoothly between some people who *should* be disagreeing, at least here and there. Some real difficulties have been repressed or, in other cases, have been reserved for the "hidden agenda." In the long run, as we all know, this kind of *rapprochement* cannot succeed. While the daily, practical co-operation of psychotherapists and pastors is improving, there is a need for hard-headed, rigorous analysis of the conceptual relations involved. Psychology and psychiatry are complex (and primitively developed) sciences; theology is complex and, by its very nature, full of obscurity and mystery. It can be assumed that the conceptual relations that arise when these two are brought together will have a high order of complexity.

The locus of their contact involves still a third discipline — analytic philosophy — which is a life study in its own right. Co-operative work among scholars technically competent in theology, psychology, and philosophy will be necessary for a solution of the theoretical problems posed. It will take more than mutual good will and a few clichés. Unfortunately psychologists and psychiatrists are almost universally ignorant of technical theology, even in its rudiments. (In this respect, by the way, the church need not feel defensive about "parochialism"; there are many more pastors who know at least a little scientific psychology than there are psychologists who know, or show any willingness to learn, an iota of theology.) Theologians often know some psychology, but usually of a special kind. Real competence in analytic philosophy is hard to find in either group. We hope that the unsolved problems presented in this book will motivate confessional Lutheran theologians to inform themselves about the technical development of philosophical analysis over the last half century and that a few philosophically oriented psychologists will take the trouble to find out in some detail what Christian theology actually says — whether they come to believe

302

it or not. Only through high-level research collaboration among such technically trained persons can the theoretical base for a solid, honest, and permanent *rapprochement* be established.

SUGGESTED READINGS

Ayer, Alfred J. *The Problem of Knowledge.* New York: St. Martin's Press, 1956.

Feigl, Herbert. "Some Major Issues and Developments in the Philosophy of Science of Logical Empiricism," in *Minnesota Studies in the Philosophy of Science,* I: *The Foundations of Science and the Concepts of Psychology and Psychoanalysis* (Minneapolis: University of Minnesota Press, 1956), pp. 3-37.

Feigl, Herbert, and W. S. Sellars. *Readings in Philosophical Analysis.* New York: Appleton-Century-Crofts, 1949.

Mitchell, Basil, ed. *Faith and Logic.* London: Allen and Unwin, 1957.

Pap, Arthur. *Elements of Analytic Philosophy.* New York: Macmillan, 1949.

Russell, Bertrand. *An Inquiry into Meaning and Truth.* New York: W. W. Norton and Co., 1940.

Appendix A. Faith Healing

NOT ALL THE CURRENT stir about faith healing is coming from the sects and the splinter-group sensationalists. Some sober analyses, carefully done by creditable people, are coming off the presses. Beyond this, some of the old, established church bodies are taking a second look. The Church of England and the Presbyterian Church, U. S., have established commissions to answer some of the questions about faith healing.

Faith healing is related to the question of this symposium, since it involves both theological and psychological dimensions. Furthermore, psychologists and church people are likely to take radically different positions. In one survey prepared for a class in psychology by a Lutheran clergyman, the instructor praised the careful research but placed large red question marks by even the most cautiously drawn evidence and restrained conclusions.

The best analyses made today follow a discernible pattern. An investigation of the claims of such people as Oral Roberts and such sects as Christian Science and New Thought leads the author of these analyses to discount almost all the advertised successes. Most of the public healers sift their cases ahead of time in one way or another and work only with those most likely to respond. According to Boggs, only a small percentage is actually cured; the others are quickly shunted aside.* The reporting in the official organs is heavily biased. Nothing remotely resembling a systematic follow-up occurs. For every positive

---

* Wade H. Boggs, Jr., *Faith Healing and the Christian Faith* (Richmond: John Knox, 1955), pp. 20—35.

304

testimonial that gets printed undoubtedly there are many more that are not, even though the heartily disappointed people would like nothing better than to have their say.

The published analyses then go on to consider cases more carefully controlled. The Lourdes Shrine is the best example. Checks are made by medical doctors, including skeptics, as well as the church itself, and there are follow-ups. Under the standards which the Roman Church has set up, forty-nine cases out of the hundreds of thousands who have visited the shrine thus far have been declared miraculous cures. Whether the standards are such as to eliminate all possibilities other than a miracle is a matter of dispute on theoretical grounds for the skeptical observer — and probably always will be.

Admittedly the percentage is small, but still the hard core of difficult cases remains to be explained. The doubters say: "If we knew enough about the human being, we could describe the healing process in these cases also." Some religious writers agree.

The rabid enthusiasts headline these cures, as well as hundreds of others they have accomplished, as hard-and-fast proof of "faith healing."

A more careful theological approach points out that these forty-nine cures may have been miracles, or they may have been occurrences of low probability. Or they may have been preternatural but nonmiraculous occurrences comparable to clairvoyance, the effects arising under the special psychological circumstances attendant at Lourdes (e. g., mass prayer). We are not referring here to "suggestion" or other factors of group psychology. We mean paranormal mind-body interactions which obey their own laws and are not, therefore, miraculous. (See the discussion in Chapter VIII.)

The studies now coming to our attention go on to describe Jesus' healing ministry as it throws light on the controversy. Those authors who previously have declared that there is no such thing as faith healing as it is commonly understood bolster their position by explaining the signs and miracles, meant to accredit the Gospel, only as natural phenomena. They were accomplished by a man with far deeper spiritual insight than any of us possess, are wonderful to behold, and are highly significant — but they are not miracles.

The Lutheran Church acknowledges that there are miracles — acts admitting of no natural explanation, in which the predictable did not occur.

This conviction bears on the question of faith healing. Theologically it proves that God has healed people through miracles in the past. If God deigned to use this method at one time, there is no reason to believe that He would not use it again. As a matter of fact, He has used it, in post-Ascension days, through the apostles. While there is no explicit statement in the Scriptures to indicate that He wills this gift to His church for all the New Testament era, neither is there any statement that He does not. Beyond this argument we must say this: To deny that God can perform miracles in contemporary life would limit God, but God is omnipotent.

The debate continues largely because the issues have been confused. Generally the first question asked is the obvious one: "Is there such a thing as faith healing?" But this question precludes a clear answer because it is not the fundamental question. It suggests a division of spiritual healing versus all other kinds of healing, whereas the important *fundamentum dividendi* is direct versus indirect cures.

By *direct* cures we mean miracles as described above in the discussion of Jesus' ministry. We have said that there is no theological basis for denying this kind of divine healing in the contemporary world. On the other hand, nontheistic scientists deny miracles on ideological grounds. Experimentally the question could be answered only if science actually had its Omniscient Jones. We will never reach the point where the behavioral sciences can answer with certainty the question of miracles through experimentation.

By *indirect* cures we imply the use of medicines, psychotherapy, surgery, medical doctors, psychotherapists, and all of the other physical, psychological, and human agencies employed to heal people.

In the list of means we include prayer. While the main function of prayer is praise and petition, there is the incidental consequence: God uses the psychological effects of the prayer itself as part of the answer to prayer. People are helped through the act of praying itself. We also include the suggestion of the

306

frenetic faith healer, the laying on of hands, group singing, and music as other possible means which God may choose to employ — and undoubtedly has chosen to employ. We need not exclude the water and shrines about which great expectations have been aroused in certain people. God uses Christian and non-Christian alike to bring health to His creatures. He may work through an orthodox Christian faith healer as well as an unorthodox one.

The important thing to remember is that God is always the primary Cause in restoring health. Medicine, music, mutterings — these are secondary causes employed according to the will of God.

Direct healing is not restricted to faith healing, but can occur in medical work and psychotherapy as well. To put spiritual healing in a separate category is valid only if the *fundamentum dividendi* is the observable agent. One could then get the following categorizations: medical, psychological, spiritual; or, medical doctors, psychotherapists, clergymen; or medicine, suggestion, and prayer.

Actually in all three categories the same organism is being acted upon; the same over-all laws of behavior and physiology apply. When we speak of faith healing, we ordinarily are talking about processes now classified as psychological. There is no basis in psychology or in theology for conceiving of a third separate system, the spiritual, with its own laws. This concept, however, is often implicit in discussions of faith healing.

This discussion of faith healing does not depreciate religious healing. It is meant to offer another viewpoint. In the final analysis, as far as the Christian is concerned, any act of healing is a manifestation of the loving concern of God. However, we would not encourage the church to undertake faith healing, i. e., conduct services primarily for the benefit of the sick, suggesting that through the medium of the worship people will be made whole. This is not the main function of the church. The church's responsibility toward the sick is (1) prayer for recovery, according to God's will, (2) direction to sound medical and psychiatric resources, (3) teaching of helpful attitudes toward health, medicine, and the cross of pain and poor health on the basis of faith in Christ.

To summarize, faith healing involves the prior question of direct healing. Debate over this point with the scientific world is fruitless. It would be helpful to all concerned to realize that spiritual healing ordinarily is explainable on purely psychological grounds. This does not mean that God has not worked the cure. For this reason it makes little difference to the consecrated Christian whether a cure is direct or indirect. To the Christian the debate becomes not only fruitless but also pointless.

Appendix B. The Problem of Conscience in Pastoral Counseling and Psychotherapy

THE MEANING of the word *conscience* has historically passed through changes and shifts of emphasis. These meanings have gone from the concept of conscience as being an innate sense of right and wrong or "reflex" in human beings, not educable or influenced by experience, to the other extreme of its being purely a product of man's sociological environment, its value being utilitarian with little reference to absolute moral and ethical standards. It is understandable therefore that discussions of the involvements of conscience may be endless because the discussants are not talking about the same thing.

Modern psychology and psychiatry, deriving their points of view from the observation of behavior and believing in the modifiability of human conduct, would find the "reflex" connotation unacceptable. Even the baby's burp is modifiable, as we know.

Apparently an active conscience is more than knowledge and information with a mild oughtness or ought-not-ness appendage. A number of studies have shown a low correlation between knowing and conduct. Because a child is told that stealing is wrong — he may even recite it — does not necessarily mean that he will not steal. In an active or "strong" conscience we would look for an emotionalized conviction.

It appears that those social scientists who believe conscience is no more than the impelling force which emerges from societal utility without reference to set moral standards and individual responsibility are treading on dangerous ground. When there is no reference to divine Law or to moral and civic laws derived from it, the watering down of the conscience of men is imminent because of man's perverted nature. What is to prevent the individual from making use of all of the legal loopholes or acting upon the I-must-not-get-caught level of conduct? If he plays the role of a tycoon, he may even take pride because he came out best in the battle for survival of the fittest. If there still is a small inner accusing voice left in him, he can squelch it by the everybody-does-it cliché.

The whole problem of conscience is somewhat difficult to place in the behavioral sciences. It appears that Freud likewise had difficulties in fitting the superego, which he defined as conscience, into his analytic theory (cf. *Outlines of Psychoanalysis*, 1940, tr. 1949). In his trio of id, ego, and superego, the ego, having the task of self-preservation and being mainly intellective and executive, carried the banner for keeping the individual personality in balance. The ego was to keep the illogical, pleasure-seeking, and destructive id in check while at the same time doing battle against the inroads of an accusing superego. The chief function of the superego was the "limitation of satisfactions." In the treatment of the neurosis where the ego had been weakened, the therapist joined hands with it to support it and to strengthen it. The superego, according to Freud, comes from the cultural past, especially as transmitted by the parents, and follows the dissolution of the Oedipus complex. Freud was right, of course, in his inferences from observation that the forces and energies within man and their relationships to others are in a state of conflict and turmoil. In recent psychological and psychiatric thought the attention given to guilt feelings in man's repertory of problems is associated with an incorrigible and pleasure-seeking id coming in conflict with the superego. It was but logical that the ego, the preserver of safety, governed by the reality principle, and being intellective, should become the analyst's chief ally.

The Christian knows well enough what troubles the conscience may cause man. In Lutheran literature the very expression "terrors of conscience" testifies to this. He cannot, however, accept a limitation which makes out of conscience a reflex or an independent automatic mechanism, nor one which holds that the voice of conscience always functions correctly, nor one which makes it solely a product of social experience or leaves little room for individual responsibility. Nor can he agree that the answer to the problems caused by conscience and feelings of guilt can be solved solely on an intellective level based on self-preservation without reference to divine Law.

When the statement appears in religious literature: "Conscience never errs," or, "Conscience is the voice of God," the writer separates the standard by which the action is judged from the inescapable feeling of necessity to apply the judgment to specific situations. The definition of conscience in this sense is based on Rom. 2:14, 15, which states that the Law written in the hearts of the Gentiles, together with their conscience, leads their thoughts to accuse or excuse one another. Conscience, then, presupposes knowledge of a moral law followed by an interpretation, which is then applied to action planned or already taken or under way. The implication evidently is that man's intellectual understanding of the moral principle may be false or incomplete, that his interpretation of the rightness or wrongness may be faulty, but once the judgment has been made, the action of conscience as to its application is the same without modification in every human being.

If we grant that the function of conscience may be restricted as indicated, it still makes such statements as "conscience never errs" easily subject to abuse. A person may refuse to take action or to permit others to do so, such as having people of different colors in the same church, for example, because he maintains his conscience forbids him.

Conscience can thus be used (better abused) as an instrument of domination over others. But it has been stated repeatedly in this volume that man's responsibility to God and to his fellow man is an individual matter. If, then, his responsibility is individual, his right to judge the oughtness and ought-not-ness of an action must also be individual. Specifically, should our conscience be governed by another man's conscience? Paul says (1 Cor. 10:29): "Conscience, I say, not thine own but of the other; for why is my liberty judged of another man's conscience?" Our answer to the foregoing question is an unqualified no. Where we do not have a distinct divine law which is applicable to a situation, the Christian may at times not exercise his individual prerogative because of the weakness of conscience of a fellow Christian. But this is an entirely different matter from saying that his conscience is under the control of the conscience of another person.

Regardless of the precise limitation which is definitively placed upon the concept of conscience, its functional existence presupposes an inborn tendency to seek out right and wrong, a standard or law which applies to the action, and a decision of the moral validity of the action. In his perfect state man could not possibly have had a bad or an accusing conscience. For his will and life were in complete agreement with God's will. Moreover, he had a complete and infallible knowledge of God's Law, and his moral judgment was inerrant. Thus an excusing or accusing voice within him was unknown to man. With man's rebellious act against God's will, fear in the presence of God came into his nature (Gen. 3:9, 10). The moral voice of conscience is inborn in every human being since Adam, but his knowledge of divine Law has been blurred, his moral judgment has been beclouded by a rebellious will which is not in accord with God's will, his self-knowledge has been distorted by conscious and unconscious mechanisms of deceit so that he cannot even confront himself objectively. As the psalmist says it: "But who can discern his errors? Clear Thou me from hidden faults." (Ps. 19:12, RSV)

Man retains his responsibility before God, and his conscience has become his master for his moral conduct. Because of his sinfulness and perverseness the standard for his conduct has become insecure. "And for this cause God shall send them strong delusion, that they should believe a lie." (2 Thess. 2:11)

Man's guilt has brought uncertainty and anxiety into his life. "And thy life shall hang in doubt before thee; and thou shalt fear day and night, and shalt have none assurance of thy life. In the morning thou shalt say, Would God it were even! And at even thou shalt say, Would God it were morning! for the fear of

312

thine heart wherewith thou shalt fear and for the sight of thine eyes which thou shalt see." (Deut. 28:66, 67)

When the Christian speaks of a bad or accusing conscience, there appears to be some agreement or at minimum an association with the "guilt feeling" which psychological or psychiatric interviews bring to light in human behavior. The analyst, having once determined the presence of an overwhelming feeling of guilt, may find along with it a system of anxiety-laden behavior. The uncovering of such an anomaly is obviously of vital interest to the psychotherapist as well as to the pastor for further treatment of the case. (See Chapters IX and XI.)

Although he may have a high regard for the skill of the therapist and the therapeutic results attained, the Christian counselor's interest is more than supplementary. It is intrinsic, and he would not rest until the counselee had, under the guidance of the Holy Spirit, given evidence of his acceptance of the forgiveness of sins for Jesus' sake and had arrived at a willing acceptance of, and a security in, a loving God. Whether the pastor, in his use of Word and Sacrament, would depend on the usual congregational channels, that is, the divine service, announcement for Communion, confession and absolution, and Holy Communion, or whether he will in addition make use of private confession and absolution and private pastoral interviews, depends on need and circumstance. The patient's active participation in public worship and group life is in itself a favorable indication. If the pastor makes use of private pastoral interviews, which would of course be voluntary on the patient's part, he will naturally be cautious not to open old wounds by unnecessary probing. It is self-understood that the pastor will pray with the patient as the occasion arises and otherwise bring his own prayers to the Throne of Grace for the healing of the afflicted conscience.

It is likewise self-understood that not every question of conscience should be regarded as having a neurotic or psychotic source. Ordinarily when an individual has a question to which he seeks an answer, the usual two-way interview may be sufficient to come to an acceptable position, which can then become the basis for action. The difficulty arises when a person cannot, despite his good intentions, accept a revision of his doubt of con-

313

science because of unmanageable emotional factors in his personality make-up. In that case it may be expected that a single conference, humanly speaking, will be ineffective, and the principles of counseling, displaced guilt, etc., discussed elsewhere in this volume, are relevant.[1, 2]

---

[1] The purpose of the present discussion is to point out the immediate relationship in matters of troubled consciences and guilt feelings. An understanding of the agreements and conflicts involved may presumably be helpful in a working out of the practical problems between the psychotherapist and the pastor to the advantage of the patient. For a fuller discussion of the involvements of conscience the reader will find ample literature elsewhere.

[2] (Meehl): *Conscience and social learning.* Paul's expression about the Law being written on men's hearts (the heathen included) is sometimes taken to mean that the specific content of moral propositions is independent of the individual's experiences and is "innate" in some such sense as the instinctive patterns of insect behavior are innate. Atheist social scientists sometimes poke fun at what they take to be the Christian doctrine of conscience. They point out that cultural anthropology attests to the wide variation in ethical concepts (*not*, by the way, so very wide in basic respects) and that the existence of a person's "conscience" presupposes his having other expectancies, habits, and perceptions which depend upon interpersonal experiences for their very formation. To experience a feeling of "obligation," or to grasp such concepts as "equity" or "justice" or "stealing," a person must have available certain prior concepts and expectancies (e. g., "person," "mine," "his"). These concepts are themselves of a high order of psychological complexity, and their development requires literally thousands of acts and experiences by the growing infant and child. Paul may be taken to deny all this, as if learning about people and their possibilities for interaction had no causal connection with the existence of conscience. Such a reading of the text is, of course, preposterous. If a human being were kept alive by artificial means until adulthood, never having observed another living creature, he would simply have no conceptual equipment regarding interpersonal relations. The sacred writers were not feeble-minded, and they had observed the growth and training of children. But Paul did not envisage such science-fiction experiments as maintaining a person's life while preventing all human interaction. He takes the human being as he is actually found — a social being who *has* experienced interpersonal relations in the very process of surviving biologically to adulthood.

The conscience of the heathen is imperfect as to the *content* of the Law, as the dogmaticians indicate in their concept of an "erring conscience." (Francis Pieper, *Christian Dogmatics* [St. Louis: Concordia Publishing House, 1950], I, 532.) In speaking of the Law written on men's hearts, Paul is primarily concerned to distinguish this Law from the *explicit, revealed* Law, i. e., "the Law" *(Torah)*, which was given through Moses to the chosen. As so often happens, the unbeliever and the Christian here suffer a breakdown of communication because they are talking about categories framed for completely different purposes. The *theologically* important distinction

314

is between the revealed Law and an (imperfect) set of norms which can be discerned among those who have not had cultural contact with the revelation as such. This is the distinction with which Paul is concerned; he is not interested in the (scientifically important) question of "innate" versus "learned" behavior. But when the contemporary psychologist comes across an expression such as "written on men's hearts" (especially if he ignores the other Scriptural texts, with whose assistance this must be interpreted), he naturally thinks in terms of the scientific issue which interests him, i. e., the innate-versus-acquired dichotomy. So he assumes that Paul is committed to the notion that all cultures have the same moral ideas, which is patently false. (Paul, being a cultivated and traveled Hellenized Jew, did not need a course in cultural anthropology to teach him that Romans, Jews, and Greeks differed markedly in the content of their moral ideas!) And the psychologist may take Paul to mean that growing up with other humans around has nothing to do with the formation of a conscience, since "written on men's hearts" he reads as "inborn."

It is an interesting question whether such a notion as "equity" requires to be specifically taught by precept and example, as some tacitly assume. Given the previous formation of normal perceptions (e. g., there are other people, who act and talk like oneself; there are five loaves of bread to go around, and there are six hungry people), does one need to be *taught* by an older culture transmitter to form an ethical idea? No one knows the answer to this scientific question. It seems unavoidable to say that *some* human being must have formed it spontaneously or received it by revelation, since otherwise it would never have arisen. Whether the formation of certain basic ethical concepts takes place solely by cultural transmission or by a subtle admixture of this process with spontaneous insightful developments once the preparatory concepts become formed, makes little difference theologically. Either would be an adequate scientific reconstruction of Paul's "Law written on men's hearts."

One might ask by way of analogy: "Is the science of arithmetic written on men's minds?" In the sense of a memorized multiplication table, clearly not. Yet, could a person of normal intelligence survive to adulthood without inevitably developing the rudiments of arithmetical thinking? The experience of daily life, even if the culture scrupulously sheltered him from all contact with formal arithmetical symbols, would give rise to notions of "adding," "taking away," "more than," and the like. Man, as an organism with certain perceptual-cognitive powers, inevitably *develops* at least a crude arithmetic when exposed to the physical fact of numerosity. A Christian historian of mathematics does not assert that the multiplication table came by a divine revelation, yet it is evident that the dispositions and powers implanted in man's nature by the Creator are such that arithmetic has, in fact, come into being. Man is an "arithmetizing animal," the squid is not, the chimpanzee is to some extent. Man is also a moralizing animal, the only one there is.

315

Appendix C. The Dualism Problem

MAN'S PRE-EMINENT POSITION in the world in which he lives cannot be explained in terms of his biological nature alone. Even the most careful scrutiny of his gross structure, his neural equipment, or the composition of his body cells leaves many questions unanswered. Yet man cannot live or function in this world without a living biological self.

From earliest times man has speculated about a mental or spiritual entity as separate from his body. In mythology this immaterial something appeared in the form of Psyche, a beautiful goddess who consorted with men. In Plato's *Phaedo* it appeared in the form of a psyche, or soul, a superior entelechy, which was imprisoned in an inferior body. The soul, according to Plato, came into a glorified state when it left the limitations and impurities of the body.

As time went on, many speculations and meanings were associated with the concept "soul" and the related concept "spirit." The *Oxford English Dictionary* (1933) gives twenty-five definitions and uses of the word *soul*, twenty-three of the word *spirit*, and thirty of the word *body*.

Out of this surge of meanings, philosophy and more recently science turned more and more to the analysis of the biological nature of man for more precise answers to the riddle of life. Anthropology became engrossed in the evolutionary ancestors of man to explain his mentality and culture. To the psychologist, engaged in objective and empirical study of behavior, the concept of soul appeared speculative, and so today the word has all but disappeared from the psychological literature.

316

In fact, science, especially biology and psychology, became impatient with the use of the concept soul. Dualism, it was felt, was confusing to science, and if we would but push our search far enough, we would find our answers in the biological nature of man.

The foregoing point is illustrated by a recent publication in which the author attempts to show that mental life, spirit, values, beauty, and the soul are all inherent in the human self-regulated cell. The living organism is thought of as "a magician of nature." The direction appeared to be from cell to psyche and not from psyche to cell.[1]

Meanwhile, because of the newer disciplines, the believing Christian has become involved in several problems. He has observed that science has achieved an impressive record in the study of the human body and its functions in human behavior. He has appreciated particularly that scientific effort has often led to biological, physical, and psychological knowledge which helps to prolong life and to ease the pains of life. He is concerned about the relation of science and its inferences to his position as based on the Bible and doctrines drawn from the Bible.

To begin with, he believes that God is the Creator and that he (man) is the creature. According to Genesis, moreover, God created man's body and then "breathed into his nostrils the breath of life; and man became a living soul" (Gen. 2:7; 1 Cor. 15:45). The Revised Standard Version renders the Genesis text: "Then the Lord God formed man of dust from the ground and breathed into his nostrils the breath of life; and man became a living being." Though the RSV does not use the word *soul*, it still records that life came to the body by an act of creation. Henceforth, after the fall of man, the Bible speaks frequently of death as a separation of the soul (or ghost) from the body (Gen. 35:18; Matt. 27:50; Luke 12:20). But death is not thought of as annihilation, since the soul is immortal; and although the body is corrupted in death, soul and body will be reunited in resurrection.

---

[1] Edmund W. Sinnott, *The Biology of the Spirit* (New York: The Viking Press, 1955).

317

Although the word *soul* is used hundreds of times in the Bible in a number of meanings, and the word *spirit* as well, it is interesting to note that Luther thought of the soul first of all as the life of the body, operating through it, pervading it, and making itself known through it. He took issue with the idea that the soul emanates from the body, and he ascribes this confusion to Aristotle.[2]

The interpretation of soul in our current language is at times confusing. Its meaning in Scripture must follow a fundamental rule of interpretation, namely, to define the word in terms of the immediate context as well as in keeping with the total frame of Scripture.

The Genesis account states that man was created in the image of God. The question now arises, What became of soul and body when man fell into sin? That is, Did the soul remain pure while the body became evil?

In the answer to this question there appears a fundamental difference between Hellenistic philosophy and the teachings of Scripture. While Hellenistic thought brought a distinct dualism to bear on the question, Jesus and Paul, in keeping with Scripture, did not. Throughout the Bible man is spoken of as one responsible being, who by nature, because of original sin, is in a depraved state. "The soul that sinneth, it shall die" (Ezek. 18:4) was the verdict of the prophet. The body is spoken of as "the temple of the Holy Ghost" (1 Cor. 6:19). That the fall of man corrupted both body and soul is attested to repeatedly in the Lutheran Confessions.[3] But that the saving grace of God applies to the entire being is equally clear.

Man is not now a soul and then again a body. Man is a single being, a self, an I, or a you. Scientifically man's integrated nature becomes apparent in the study of the emotions. The individual receives a message from a loved one or bad news, or he tells a lie. Automatically, in normal circumstances, his heart beats faster or slower, his breathing amplitude and rate change, adren-

---

[2] Martin Luther, *Sämmtliche Schriften* (St. Louis: Concordia Publishing House, 1910), XXXIII, 1663 f.

[3] Cf. *Concordia Triglotta* (St. Louis: Concordia Publishing House, 1921), pp. 43, 111, 477, 863.

alin may be discharged into the blood stream. These and other events are then spoken of as psychosomatic. But man remains one being.

There are naturally a number of questions about the nature of the soul which come to the inquiring mind: Is the soul as such rational? When does the soul come into existence? What is the state of the soul between death and resurrection? The student of religion will make his answers to the proposed questions guarded and cautious, for Holy Writ makes but scant reference to them. And to interpret by inference may lead to speculation which is helpful neither to science nor to religion.

To the foregoing statement we make one exception in the belief that with death the soul of the redeemed child of God enters a state of bliss and is at peace with its Maker. Whether the soul of the condemned may be in a benumbed condition, as Luther thought might be the case, we do not know.

A brief reference to the word *spirit* as used in Holy Writ seems necessary, since its use is at times interpreted as indicating that man is a tripartite being, having body, soul, and spirit. Spirit, as used in Scripture, must, of course, also be interpreted in terms of its immediate context as well as within the frame of Scripture. Frequently the word means Holy Spirit, or Holy Ghost. In several instances it refers to angels. At times it is used synonymously with soul. Beyond these meanings the word is used over and over in the sense of what might be termed the operational content and direction of man's thoughts, words, and actions. Spirit, then, is a fruit, an outcome of the individual's life and experience. It is a reaction to stimuli in the light of one's past experience. Thus the Bible speaks of the spirit of wisdom, understanding, love, grief, falsehood, envy, prophecy.

If spirit is regarded as a functional outcome rather than a separate structural entity, the difficult and troublesome trichotomy theory becomes entirely unnecessary. One difficulty of interpreting certain Bible texts divisively is that we arrive at a number of entities: body, soul, spirit, mind, heart, and strength (cf., e. g., Heb. 4:12; Matt. 22:37; Mark 12:30). If they are interpreted, however, as descriptive terms to include the whole man, the entire being, we arrive, as previously, at a unitary being. "And the very God of peace sanctify you wholly; and I pray God your whole spirit and soul and body be preserved blameless unto the coming of our Lord Jesus Christ" (1 Thess. 5:23) illustrates the point.

Whether in the original state of purity and holiness or after having been tainted by sin, the body is and remains an essential entity in human nature, through which and in which soul and spirit are manifested.

A brief reference to the use of the word *mind* seems to be called for at this point. We find it in the Bible, but less often than the words *soul* and *spirit*. In modern use the word has become a synecdochical catch-all for almost everything psychic, intellectual, emotional, and whatnot. It may be regarded as a term which describes an aspect of the behavioral content, such as memory, consciousness, unconsciousness, knowledge, will, and feeling. Its use has become so broad that it may serve the person who believes that man has a soul as well as the one who does not. For definitive purposes the word has all but lost its value.

In a number of instances the Bible speaks of carnal desires and desires of the flesh. On the surface it might appear as if the desires of the flesh were pitted against the desires of a more noble spirit. On closer examination we find a different situation to prevail. In Gal. 5:17-26, for example, Paul lists idolatry, witchcraft, hatred, variance, emulations, wrath, strife, seditions, heresies, and envyings with adultery, fornication, uncleanness, and lasciviousness. The meaning of flesh here evidently goes beyond the biological connotation. Paul then adds: "But the fruit of the Spirit is love, joy, peace, long-suffering, gentleness, goodness, faith, meekness, temperance; against such there is no law." It is obvious that Paul is here speaking of the work of the Holy Ghost in man and not of man's natural spirit or soul. The use of the words *flesh* and *carnal* lies near for descriptive language because it is in the body in which the evil desires are felt and manifested to others.

The Christian's view of man embraces the entire being. Insofar as the Christian is in agreement with the concepts of science, he considers it in full harmony with his belief to use the techniques and instruments developed by science for the welfare of man as long as they are not contrary to divine law. The Christian theologian understands that the approach to human welfare may be mainly biological in some cases, while in others it may be principally psychological and psychiatric. That in individual cases there may be and frequently is a combination of the two approaches is self-evident. While freely and thankfully acknowledging the contribution of science to human welfare, the Christian doctrine of man as set forth in this report does not yield anything whatsoever in its inherent interest in man's spiritual and religious needs.

Appendix D. Differential Psychology

BECAUSE OF limitations of space we have been forced in this volume to confine our discussion to those branches of psychological science which have the most intimate theoretical bearing upon the Christian doctrine of man. Some of the most highly developed and socially useful aspects of the professional psychologist's work have therefore been omitted from consideration. As examples we might mention the psychophysiology of the sense organs, the psychology of motor skills, the *applied* psychology of learning as practiced in the field of education, psycholinguistics and communication theory, public-opinion polling, and the new interdisciplinary field known as *biomechanics,* which brings together knowledge from engineering, physiology, and psychology to solve problems posed by "the man in the machine" (e. g., supersonic flight). School systems, government agencies, the Armed Forces, and private industry are all making steadily increasing use of the services of professional psychologists.[1]

One of the most important and technologically advanced fields of applied psychology is that generally referred to as *differential psychology* (or the "psychology of individual differences"). That human beings differ widely among themselves with regard to almost all attributes one can name is in itself a matter of common observation and was known to the ancients.

---

[1] Kenneth E. Clark, *America's Psychologists* (Washington, D. C.: American Psychological Association, Inc., 1957), passim.

The practical problem to which this everyday fact gives rise is that we often have need of determining accurately the behavior dispositions of an individual in a conveniently short observational period or at a time prior to the real-life situation in which these dispositions will be important. One of the earliest recorded examples of differential psychology is to be found in the Book of Judges, where we read of Gideon's performing military selection by the use of a certain "minor" item of behavior, i. e., how a soldier drank water from a stream. (Judg. 7:2-8)

Differential psychology studies the facts of human variability from several points of view. The characteristics studied are diverse and include capacities (e. g., intelligence), school achievement (e. g., spelling), social patterns (e. g., dominance), psychopathology (e. g., schizophrenic tendency), attitudes (e. g., radicalism), interests (e. g., vocational bent), special defects (e. g., color blindness), motor skills (e. g., driving ability), and value orientation (e. g., religiosity). The methods utilized in studying these domains also vary and include psychological tests, ratings by others, self-ratings, and work samples. In addition, the influence of such factors as heredity, social class, school experience, parental attitudes, race, religion, sex, physical condition, geography, and chronological age upon individual differences have all been studied, some of these in great detail. Another important concern of the differential psychologist is "mental organization," by which is meant how certain traits are related statistically and causally, how many basic "factors" must be postulated to account for the observed patterns of individual differences, how and for what reasons a single person's dispositions fluctuate over time, and so forth. While these questions are studied chiefly for their theoretical interest, they also have an indirect bearing upon applied psychology, because they influence our methods of test construction and job analysis.

Probably the single aspect of differential psychology which stands out in the educated person's mind is the "psychological test." To many people — including some clergymen — the psychological test is a mysterious gadget which is a combination of wizardry and fraud. It seems that very few people are able to adopt an objective attitude toward these devices, but instead either accept them uncritically as infallible or else reject them out of hand as worthless.

The first thing to see about psychological tests is that they are not *in principle* different from the more familiar methods by which we try to assess the behavior dispositions of other persons. If we are faced with the task of picking a man to do a certain job, and it is important that we pick the best man, all of the nonrandom means by which we can proceed fall under two broad rubrics. We either make use of *samples* of the disposition, from whatever source (including our own deliberate, prearranged sampling); or, if no adequate sample is available to us, we employ indirect *signs* of the disposition.

If you observe a man surreptitiously pocketing money from his employer's till, you are not likely to hire him as your cashier. You have "sampled" his behavior with regard to other people's money, and if this is all the evidence you have to go on, it is bad business to trust him with yours.

But suppose that you had never sampled a prospective employee's honesty; you might still have reasons for questioning it. You learn that he is a bigamist, that he takes drugs, and that he has several times been incarcerated for assault and battery. These facts are "signs" which might lead you to distrust him in money matters. A sign, unlike a sample, does not itself exemplify the behavior disposition which it is desired to predict. Rather a sign is behavior of *one* kind which bears upon the probability that a disposition of *another* kind exists.[2]

A psychological test, no matter how complex the apparatus utilized or how high-powered the statistical formulas applied, is at bottom nothing more than a sign or a sample or a mixture of the two. A psychological test differs from our informal methods of sampling and sign seeking chiefly in four respects:

1. Standard procedure of obtaining and observing the behavior.

---

[2] For simplicity we have referred to dispositions as being "present" or "absent." Actually one of the fundamental findings of differential psychology is that practically all dispositions exist in varying *degrees*, so that the more precise formulation of signs and samples is expressed in quantitative symbolism.

2. Immediate recording of the behavior (or behavior product).

3. Objective classifying of the responses ("scoring").

4. Comparison of the score with some reference point, such as other comparable individuals, the previous level of the subject himself, or the test score associated with a specified degree of the disposition being assessed, in case the test is a sign and not a sample ("norms").

It is obvious that some of what we see referred to in the popular press (or even, alas, by a few poorly trained or irresponsible psychologists) as "psychological tests" are nothing of the kind, since they do not possess these defining properties.

A vast body of technical knowledge exists regarding the construction and use of psychological tests. Experience in industry, education, and especially of the two world wars, has demonstrated beyond any doubt that psychological tests can be made to have very respectable accuracy and extremely great practical usefulness. It is not too strong a statement to say that anyone who asserts today that "you cannot test a person's intelligence" or that "human judgment is better than any test" is merely displaying his ignorance. The psychological test is here to stay; and it will stay, not because businessmen and Army officers (both of whom tend to be quite practical and hard-headed) are fond of psychologists but because the psychological test has conclusively demonstrated that it works.

It should be pointed out, however, that different tests vary widely in their validity and that this variation depends largely upon the differences among those domains of behavior for which tests have been devised. For example, we now have very powerful tests of intelligence, of certain special abilities and achievements, and of vocational interests. Tests of "personality" traits, on the other hand, are in a much less satisfactory state of development. It must even be admitted that, in the popular field of clinical psychology, numerous "tests" are in widespread use which are of very doubtful accuracy, so far as can be judged from an objective perusal of the research literature.

It seems to disturb some people to find that psychological tests are being used to "foretell a person's future." Probably the underlying animus involved in this common reaction — which sometimes exhibits an extraordinary intensity in people otherwise quite rational — is the dislike which we all have of being "predictable."[3] If a test can forecast what I will do, it almost seems that I am an automaton, lacking any genuine choices, a victim of fate (or of the all-seeing psychologist!).

It helps to alleviate this needless distress to remind oneself that tests (again, like informal samples and signs) predict only *probabilistically*. Nevertheless, it is unwise, in most ordinary situations, to guide our conduct in opposition to high probabilities when such exist. The degree of accuracy which a test should have in order to justify its use depends upon the entire economic and moral context and cannot be decided solely on the basis of statistical considerations.[4, 5] For example, in certain military or industrial situations the use of a test to select and eliminate people may be justified even if the test has a rather low validity. If we know in advance that we can accept only one fourth of the enlisted men who apply for a certain kind of special training, any improvement in selection over what we could achieve by picking every fourth man at random is worth having. Since it costs over $25,000 to train a single soldier, and since human life is at stake in his subsequent military performance, the elimination of even five or ten per cent of unsuitable applicants is both ethically and financially defensible almost regardless of how many potentially "good bets" are also rejected in the process.

In military and industrial situations the primary object of concern is the institution rather than the individual. No one has a "right" to be a bombardier or radar operator, and we have no hesitancy in rejecting a large number of applicants who *would* have succeeded if by so doing we get rid of even a small number of failures. On the other hand, when a psychological test

3 Bertrand Russell, "On the Notion of Cause, with Applications to the Freewill Problem," in *Our Knowledge of the External World* (New York: W. W. Norton and Co., 1929), pp. 247, 248.

4 Irwin D. J. Bross, *Design for Decision* (New York: Macmillan, 1953), p. 24.

5 Lee J. Cronbach and Goldine C. Gleser, *Psychological Tests and Personnel Decisions* (Urbana: University of Illinois Press, 1957).

is used in a context where the welfare of the *individual* is of primary concern, then the situation becomes quite different. The psychologist who is forced to use highly fallible tests for purposes of *guidance* and *treatment* is in a more difficult spot than he who is concerned with problems of *selection*. Various opinions exist as to how tests may best be used in the guidance situation, but neither the technological nor the moral (and political?) problems involved here have as yet received satisfactory solutions. It is generally agreed that the vocational counselor or psychotherapist should *not* make flat predictions to his client (e. g., "You shouldn't go to engineering school because your tests show that you will flunk out"); but just how directively test probabilities should be utilized, even when carefully fitted into the total picture, is a matter of current dispute. One has the impression that applied psychologists are becoming increasingly concerned with problems which fall under the formerly respectable heading of *casuistry*, but the philosophical and ethical sophistication of most psychologists does not permit them to attack these issues at a very high level.

SUGGESTED READINGS

Anastasi, Anne. *Psychological Testing*. New York: Macmillan, 1954.

Anastasi, Anne, and John P. Foley. *Differential Psychology*, Revised edition. New York: Macmillan, 1949.

Cattell, Raymond B. *Personality*. New York: McGraw-Hill, 1950.

Cronbach, Lee J. *Essentials of Psychological Testing*. New York: Harper, 1949.

Meehl, Paul E. *Clinical Versus Statistical Prediction*. Minneapolis: University of Minnesota Press, 1954.

Tyler, Leona E. *The Psychology of Human Differences*, Second edition. New York: Appleton-Century-Crofts, Inc., 1956.

Appendix E. Indeterminacy
and Teleological Constraints

THE OBJECTION that any kind of teleological selection operation acting upon quantum-uncertain brain events would necessarily constrain their statistical distribution and thus lead to a contradiction of the indeterminacy assumption surely seems plausible. It is, however, fallacious, and in a rather interesting way. An analysis of the mistake involved highlights an important characteristic of contemporary materialist thought in the matter of a hidden assumption which is usually unquestioned. We shall therefore take a little time to analyze the mistake and the implicit presupposition which gives rise to it.

For simplicity, and to avoid theological speculations, let us take the precognitive telepathy experiments as our empirical context. We assume that *usually* the percipient's calls are physically determinate; e. g., unless a suspension of the laws of nature occurs, at his 23d call he will guess "heads," because his brain at the moment of this call is in a definite "head-calling" state. This determining state is itself a function of both external and internal factors, not the least of which is the physical residue of his immediately preceding call pattern. (Human guessing is not random, and a person cannot even make it so voluntarily. Mathematical analysis of a long sequence of any kind of human guessing behavior invariably reveals at least some degree of internal order. For example, the incidence of long "runs" of repeated calls is typically reduced below the theoretical expectation. When a person has called "heads" twice in a row, he is very unlikely to call heads a third time; whereas the *chance* probability of another H is still ½.) The determinate character of the great preponderance of calls seems to be the simplest explanation for the relatively low extrachance accuracy displayed even by good sensitives. That is, most of the time the brain state is such that no selection of local quantum-uncertain outcomes exists which would throw the system to a call matching the target. It is only when the "ordinary" (nontelepathic) psychophysiological determiners have momentarily put the brain in a delicately balanced state between a hit call and a miss call that the telepathic influence, whatever its nature, is able to operate within the "play" of the system.

According to Eccles' theory, from time to time a brain state arises which is not call-determinate from the physical point of view. This is because certain cells occupy critical roles in determining the activity of very large numbers of other cells by virtue of their position in the neural network, and the firing of these cells may on occasion be quantum-indeterminate. (The idea of critical cells is by no means purely speculative; it is suggested by presently available direct observations on the microanatomy of the cerebral cortex.) This implies that a suitably selected pattern of firing imposed upon the indeterminate critical cells could "throw" the whole system in the direction of calling heads or tails (Jordan's *Verstärkung*). The selector agency (Eccles' *mind*) patterns the indeterminate events in such a way that the call matches the target (i. e., the percipient scores a "hit"). Does such an account impose constraints upon the local microevents which would violate the quantum-indeterminate postulate?

In the telepathic experiments the answer is no, but for a trivial reason. The target series being matched is itself random; hence the call series can be random even though it is nonrandom *with respect to the target series*. Even if the percipient were able to perform perfectly, the brain-state sequence would necessarily be random (both in its internal order and with respect to external stimuli), because it would be isomorphic with a target series that is *ex hypothesi* random in each of these respects. There is, of course, no mathematical contradiction involved in the notion of two sequences being random (1) internally and (2) with respect to other external sequences, and yet correlating to any specified degree, including perfectly, with one another. The random se-

329

quence of *ace-up* (and its negation) produced by throwing a die repeatedly is isomorphic with that of *six-down*, since the opposite sides of a die total seven. Such an analysis does not, however, apply to situations in which the target series is "rigged" in some way, as has also been tried in these experiments, with success.

The consistency of target-following with quantum uncertainty in this special case provides us with a bit of insight which can now be generalized to less trivial situations. We have seen that the term "random" is an incomplete expression; a precise formulation must specify randomness *with respect to* something, either internal or external. The structure of the statistical situation is this: A class of *occasions* must first be specified on a rational basis, prior to examining their individual outcomes; for example, the sequence of calls by a telepath defines a class of occasions, the outcome of each occasion being a "hit" or a "miss" depending upon its correspondence with the temporally associated target event. When we speak of the indeterminacy condition's being imposed upon the microevent, precisely what does this mean in terms of such occasion sequences?

To concretize matters, let us assume with Eccles that the physical locus of indeterminacy is at the point where an individual end-button synapses upon the surface of the next neuron in a particular network, this neuron being "critical" in call-determination. Actually the necessary and sufficient condition for its activation would normally be a *disjunction* of *patterns* of end-button events, since the discharge of a neuron seems to depend upon the occurrence of a suitable number, placement, and timing of local disturbances produced by multiple end-button stimulation over its surface. But this complication does not affect the logic of our argument, as will become apparent in the course of its development.

The first and most obvious respect in which the end-button event must be indeterminate is that its occurrence must not instantialize a deterministic physical law formulable in terms of the local (i. e., immediately neighboring) conditions. This requirement is easily satisfied, provided that these local conditions are themselves random with respect to the target. There is no theoretical or experimental reason for assuming that the local

330

conditions are systematically related to the target, whether the latter is random or nonrandom.

Another formulation of local indeterminacy would be that the relative frequency of local outcomes of a certain kind should converge to some theoretical probability number, as, say, ½, and that the sequence of these outcomes should be random internally. To make sense of this demand, we have to specify the reference class of *occasions* within which the calculation of *outcomes* would be carried out by Omniscient Jones. When we try to set up such a reference class, we see immediately that there is something odd about the conceptual situation. As Eccles points out, any brain cell belongs to many different networks, and, correspondingly, any behavior or perception can be mediated by alternative patterns of cell activation. It is mathematically possible, for instance, that two calls of "heads" involve the activation of entirely nonoverlapping neuron sets (although this is not neurologically probable). Suppose we define the occasion class as "all occasions (regardless of locus) in which the synaptic distance and energy conditions momentarily present at the end-button are such that on the basis of physical theory the local outcome would be considered quantum-indeterminate and the theoretical probability of local outcome *plus* would be exactly ½." Thus we consider the class of all such occasions in all individuals' brains. It is obvious that the frequency of outcome *plus* could converge to ½ in this heterogeneous class even though all of the brains in question were those of telepathic sensitives. Outcome *plus*, the local microevent at the end-button, need not be correlated with the target series in any way, in order for the percipient's *calls* to be so correlated. Sometimes it happens that a correct call can occur if a certain cell is activated at a given instant; at other times the same call depends upon the same cell's remaining unactivated. Even in the case of two successive calls involving activation of the same critical cell, it is possible that the first necessitates local outcome *plus* and the second requires *minus*, the facilitating or inhibiting effect being dependent upon the precise time- and space-relationships among the activations of other end-buttons synapsing on the critical cell.

The reason for this paradox lies in the *gestalt* property of a "hit." The non-gestalted physical categories which are sufficient

331

to characterize the local end-button situation and its outcome are simply insufficient to identify a call. The percipient's call "heads" is not something co-ordinated to a particular neuron (or, a fortiori, to a quantum-indeterminate event at one of the 100 or so end-buttons synapsing upon the cell body of a particular neuron). In fact, the call "heads" as a *behavioral* event is not even co-ordinated to a specific system of cells or chain of cells; rather there are (literally) thousands of alternative activation patterns, each of which utilizes cells which are also activated in the course of quite different and unrelated behavior (such as playing the piano). To say that end-button *b* on cell 27,436 in area 9 "hits" would involve the same kind of category mistake as to say that one of Eisenhower's end-buttons is Republican or that one of Arius' brain cells thinks heretically. It is not a cell which thinks, it is a brain.

The call "heads" occurs when one of the huge (but finite) set of cell-activation patterns occurs which is effective in producing this symbolic response. Suppose that the target series is biased so that 60 per cent of the time the target is "heads." Suppose that the percipient is infallible so that 60 per cent of his calls must also be heads. Further, suppose that the target sequence is internally systematic, exhibiting invariable runs of six heads followed by four tails and then repeating the cycle. Does this constrain the sequence of outcomes at a particular end-button away from ½? (We do not suggest any direct relation between the two probabilities, of course. The situation is far too complicated for that.) Not necessarily. It will constrain certain correlations *among* end-button outcomes; that is, a team of 100 end-buttons which in a nonsensitive would behave independently may act in a patterned manner so as to activate a critical cell in the case of a sensitive. This can happen without any single button's deviating from the theoretical value ½. Many different neural patterns can be constructed to yield such an outcome; the more complex the network and the more elements involved, the easier it is.

One oversimplified example will suffice to demonstrate the anatomical possibility. Imagine a critical cell upon which synapse end-buttons from six preceding cells, these contact points being arranged in an approximately circular pattern upon the critical cell's surface. Suppose the reactivity of the critical cell to be such that it will fire whenever two or more *adjacent* end-buttons are near-simultaneously activated so as to produce local disturbances over contiguous regions. Holding the activation-probability of each quantum-uncertain end-button event rigidly fixed (say, $p = \frac{1}{2}$), one can alter the frequency with which the critical cell is discharged by manipulating the location pattern of these local activations. One can, for example, determine the critical cell to fire *every time*, by assuring that at least two adjacent end-buttons are activated on every critical occasion. As the other extreme, the critical cell can be prevented from *ever* firing, by alternating between local activation patterns 1-3-5 and 2-4-6, whereby no adjacent surface regions are ever disturbed simultaneously (but each end-button is still being activated half the time). By suitable juggling of activation patterns, all intermediate firing frequencies between these extreme values of 0 and 1 can be imposed upon the critical cell. (The idea of a strictly circular arrangement is merely schematic; the essential feature is that certain formal relationships be reflected in the physical configuration as closeness, relative position, sequence, and the like.) The reader familiar with neurophysiology will not need to be told that such simple systems as this exhibit a very low order of complexity in comparison with the actual microstructure of the brain. This simple example suffices to demonstrate the mathematico-anatomical point of interest, which is that systematic alterations in the firing probability of a critical cell could be achieved through pattern selectivity of the individual quantum-indeterminate events at the stimulating end-buttons, without necessitating any distortion, however slight, of the theoretical statistics for any single button.

A third consideration is even more damaging to the criticism, and in fact deprives it of all meaning. In the preceding discussion we used as our example the telepathic experiment. In this artificial situation one dealt with a defined target *series*, which could be rigged so as to exhibit departures from randomness. The theoretical problem arose because the brain events were required to "follow" this nonrandom target. In the case of a person's conversion, however, the situation is quite different. To the question "What is the sequence of occasions whose theoretical probability and internal randomness is to be preserved?" no meaningful answer can be given. A particular end-button may play its role by acting, another by not acting, on a critical occasion. Consider an end-button whose quantum-uncertain result was "plus" at that momentous instant on the road to Damascus; alongside of it is one which was "minus." To what occasion class do we assign these in calculating a probability? Do they both go into the same reference class? If not, why not? There simply *is* no reference class which makes statistical sense. Each of these end-buttons has, furthermore, participated in a long series of macroevents of a completely nonreligious character. For example, the last time end-button X was in a quantum-uncertain state, it reacted *plus;* the response to which this local outcome "contributed" was part of a movement sequence in the course of Saul's activity as a tentmaker. Let us suppose that the macroevent — conversion — happened only once to the man in question. A sequence consisting of all occasions on which a particular end-button of Saul's brain was in the quantum-indeterminate state will reveal no internal order and no correlation with anything else.

One might suppose that a departure from "chance" could be demonstrated by setting up the class of all occasions on which *anyone's* conversion occurred. But this will not get us anywhere, because in order for a conversion to occur, *some* of the quantum-indeterminate events have to be *plus* and others *minus.* Suppose we try, "The reference class of occasions is defined by all of all those local (i. e., end-button) situations in which a quantum-indeterminate outcome, if *plus,* would lead to conversion; if *minus,* to nonconversion." Here it looks as though we begin to get somewhere, although there is a gross oversimplification involved in ignoring the fact of alternative patterns, none of which is necessary but any one of which is sufficient for conversion.

Let us examine the oddly constituted class defined by this complex criterion. We first define a class of macro-occasions, each occupying some suitably small time interval, upon which there existed at least one physically possible pattern of outcomes to the quantum-uncertain microevents which would have eventuated in conversion. We collect all of the microsituations on all of the macro-occasions for all of the brains that have existed on the earth since Pentecost. (This is admittedly a nonsensical proceeding, but what else can be done when such a question is put?) From the premise that the selection of patterns in certain instances was teleological, can it be inferred that the incidence of *plus* micro-outcomes in this class deviates from the expected? We see no way in which this could be inferred. There is not the slightest neurophysiological reason for thinking that *plus* outcomes favor conversion. (Suppose that they did. Are we told by Scripture that "more people get converted than would 'by chance' "? Hardly. Such a statement is without religious meaning.)

Of course, if empirical evidence of God's activity apart from revelation is to be available at the microlevel, *some* extrachance effect will be discernible. But it need not be detectable by a preponderance of *plus* outcomes, nor by a nonrandom sequence; it could be reflected in the disproportionate incidence of conversion-producing *configurations* (as will be explained below). In the class of microevents under study, no time series is involved. There is, of course, not the slightest reason for imagining that the sequence of quantum-uncertain occasions at an end-button which is *plus* at the time of conversion has been nonrandom previously.

The reader is no doubt saying, "But *something* systematic is going on; why is it so elusive?" Yes, there might be something "systematic" going on, although Scripture does not require us to believe so. Suppose that Omniscient Jones computes the probability of conversion on each occasion. The teleology could lie in the fact that, in the long run, these calculated probabilities were in error. More (or fewer?) physically *possible* conversions may be realized than would be expected by applying mathematics to the sets of alternative configural outcomes.

In what sense is this a departure from indeterminacy? From the standpoint of physics, the situation at each end-button re-mains "locally" indeterminate. That is, a complete physical knowledge of the synaptic region and its immediate neighborhood (including the momentary state of intracellular molecular motions, ion concentrations, the electric field, and the like) would render *plus* and *minus* outcomes equally probable, as was true of this end-button when Saul was last tent-making, and on the still earlier members of the series. The categories of the physicist or the physiologist do not enable any prediction to be made, because the selection operation for patterns is formulable only by reference to an end-result, i. e., teleologically. The teleological hypothesis is scientifically meaningful, because the incidence of systematic selection *patterns* (formulated by reference to outcome) is presumably beyond chance expectation. What is systematic, "nonchance," is a correlation of a complex kind among microevents. That correlation can be expressed only by reference to the *gestalt* and its behavioral outcome. No local microevent at an end-button has to be *plus* to convert Saul; and there is no antecedent basis for classifying an end-button outcome in Saul's brain along with one in Augustine's brain so as to establish a reference class of occasions. What must be done in order to exhibit the teleology is too complicated for thorough explication here. Essentially it amounts to this: We consider the class of *all* occasions in *all* brains at which there exists at least *one* selection of plus-and-minus configurations of the microevents which would, if realized, effect conversion. We then set up the disjunction of all the alternative patterns, i. e., those not sufficient to "throw" the system (by *Verstärkung*) to conversion. The teleology is then exhibited by showing that the incidence of favorable configurations within the total set of local outcome configurations is in excess of that computable by the assumption of independence. The situation is similar to one in which we toss the fourteen letters A, C, E, I, L, N, N, N, O, O, P, S, T, T into the air and they come down arranged as CONSTAN-TINOPLE.

The gestalted and teleological character of the postulated selection operation gives offense to the materialist, and it is probably his all-pervasive assumption that such emergent properties never arise which misleads him into making the objection we have been considering. In a nutshell, his unconscious reasoning would probably look like this: "You say that the event called conversion is not a matter of 'chance.' But this event is nothing but a complex of microevents, *each of these being either determined by its immediate neighborhood or else not determined in any way.* Hence the outcomes of these microevents cannot follow the laws of chance either, if your views are correct." He cannot imagine a teleological feature of a whole which is not a *physical consequence* of the constituent microsituations; in short, he cannot imagine a whole determining its parts, which is essentially what we have postulated. To predict the microevent at an individual end-button, one must ask, "What are the possible configurations of outcomes of the available indeterminate microsituations *which would bring about an over-all effect of a specified kind* (e. g., a telepathic hit, or the conversion of Saul)?" The prediction would have to be made by reference to (a) the neural pattern and (b) the future outcome. But this future outcome is precisely what we do not know, in the case of someone's conversion.* Even if we knew (e. g., supernaturally, as in prophecy) that a certain person would be converted at *t*, calculation of the micro-outcome utilizes information about end-buttons physically remote from the one under consideration. Such a procedure combines action at a distance and "unreduced" teleology, both of which are an intellectual offense to the materialist.

In conclusion, we have seen that the indeterminate-brain-state theory need not involve an implied deviation from its own original assumption of local quantum uncertainty. The first reason for this is that the local conditions of the critical cells will be random with respect to the specified molar outcome ("target"), so that the micro-outcomes (*plus* or *minus*) needful to combine with these conditions in generating that macro-outcome may be random also. Secondly, we saw that the brain's structural possibilities permit patterning effects in which the end result of a *Verstärkung* is attainable by any one of a set of properly configurated microresults, thus maintaining the random character of each sequence of microresults associated with a particular end-button. Thirdly, it was pointed out that in the case of such events as conversion, there is no physical basis by which a given micro-event can be grouped with others in the world in order to set up a reference class for which probabilities can be computed.

---

* In the precognitive telepathy case, we may know it under certain experimental setups, as when the target series is predetermined by a random number table. Here predictability obtains, via the teleological outcome-classification. If attention is confined to the end-button neighborhood, however, we still cannot predict.

SUGGESTED READINGS

In addition to references 2, 3, 6, 7, 10-16, and 29 of Chapter VIII, the following will be helpful to readers who wish to pursue the problem of determinism further.

Cassirer, Ernst. *Determinism and Indeterminism in Modern Physics.* New Haven: Yale University Press, 1956.

Eddington, Arthur S. *The Nature of the Physical World.* New York: Macmillan, 1929. Chapter XIV, especially pp. 306-315.

Feigl, Herbert. "Notes on Causality," in *Readings in the Philosophy of Science,* ed. Herbert Feigl and May Brodbeck. New York: Appleton-Century-Crofts, Inc., 1953, pp. 408-418.

Grünbaum, Adolf. "Causality and the Science of Human Behavior," ibid., pp. 766-778.

Russell, Bertrand. "On the Notion of Cause, with Applications to the Freewill Problem," in *Our Knowledge of the External World.* New York: W. W. Norton, 1929, pp. 247-256. Reprinted in *Readings in the Philosophy of Science,* pp. 387-407. See *Feigl* above.

Stebbing, Lizzie S. "Causality and Human Freedom," in *Philosophy and the Physicists.* London: Methuen and Co., Ltd., 1937, III, 141-242. Pages 141-155 also contain an excellent brief summary of the determinist-naturalist *Weltanschauung.*

THE MEMBERS OF THE SYMPOSIUM

PAUL E. MEEHL, Ph. D., Professor of Clinical Psychology, University of Minnesota Medical School. Dr. Meehl served as chairman of the Symposium Committee. B. A., University of Minnesota, *summa cum laude*, 1941; Ph. D., University of Minnesota, 1945, majoring in clinical psychology and minoring in neuropsychiatry. Took his clinical training in the Psychopathic Unit of the University of Minnesota Hospitals. Assistant Professor at Minnesota, 1945; Associate, 1948; Professor, 1952, holding concurrent appointments in the arts college and the medical school. Acting Chief Clinical Psychologist at the Minneapolis Veterans Hospital, 1947–1949. Clinical consultant at the same hospital to date. Co-author (with W. K. Estes and others) of *Modern Learning Theory* (1954). Member of the Minnesota Center for Philosophy of Science, 1953–1955, in undertaking a philosophical analysis of psychological concepts. Chairman of Department of Psychology, 1951–1957. Presently co-director of a $238,000 research project on diagnosis granted to the Division of Psychiatry by the Ford Foundation. President of the Midwestern Psychological Association in 1954. He is a Diplomate in the applied specialty of Clinical Psychology and is a member of the American Board of Examiners which grants these diplomas. His professional publications include over forty theoretical and experimental papers on statistics, philosophy of science, learning theory, animal behavior, psychodiagnostics, psychotherapy, and methodology of behavior prediction. Author of *Clinical Versus Statistical Prediction* (1954) and co-author of *Atlas for Clinical Use of the MMPI* (1951). Member of Sigma Xi and Phi Beta Kappa. In addition to research and teaching activities, he is a practicing psychotherapist and is engaged in the supervision of therapists in training.

H. RICHARD KLANN, B. D., Ph. D. Graduated from Concordia Seminary, St. Louis, Mo., 1938; B. D. in 1938; M. A., Washington University, St. Louis, 1939; missionary at large, Nashville, Tenn., 1940–1941; pastor, Carthage, Mo., 1941–1942; chaplain, Army of the United States, 1942–1946; Ph. D., Columbia University, 1951, where he did much of his graduate work under Dr. Paul Tillich and Dr. Reinhold Niebuhr, concentrating particularly on the field of Systematics and Christian ethics. Author of numerous articles, including "The Political Ethics of Martin Luther," published in *The Lutheran Scholar* (1957). Member of the editorial staff of the *American Lutheran*. Author of *We Believe and Confess* (1953), a text for religious instruction used by Lutheran campus pastors at secular colleges and universities. He has been campus pastor in the Greater New York area since 1946, continuing his research and writing.

ALFRED F. SCHMIEDING, M. A., LL. D. Graduated from Concordia Teachers College, Seward, Nebr., 1907. Ph. B., 1929, and M. A., University of Chicago, 1933; LL. D., Valparaiso University, 1952. Served as teacher, Zion Lutheran, Newton, Kans., 1907–1911; principal, Immanuel Lutheran, Mount Olive, Ill., 1911–1916; principal, Bethlehem Lutheran, Saginaw, Mich., 1916–1922. Joined the faculty of Concordia Teachers College, River Forest, Ill., 1922, where he is now Professor of Education and Psychology. He is the author of a number of books, including *The Language Curriculum for Lutheran Schools* (1932), *Teaching the Bible Story* (1935), *Reading in the Primary School* (1940), *Understanding the Child* (1945), *Sex in Childhood and Youth* (1953). In addition he has written many articles for *Lutheran Education* and other professional journals. Consulting psychologist at Dyslexia Memorial Institute, Chicago, since 1940; consultant in child guidance to child welfare agencies in Chicago. Member of Phi Beta Kappa, LEA, and the American Psychological Association.

KENNETH H. BREIMEIER, B. D., Ph. D. Graduated from Concordia Seminary, St. Louis, Mo., 1949; B. D., 1949; M. A., Washington University, St. Louis, 1948; instructor at Concordia Teachers College, River Forest, Ill., 1949–1950; assistant pastor at Grace Lutheran, River Forest, Ill., 1950–1952; Ph. D., Northwestern University, Evanston, Ill., 1952; pastor at Grace Lutheran, Northbrook, Ill., 1952–1954. Since 1954 he has been Assistant Professor of Pastoral Theology and Director of the Field Work Program at Concordia Seminary, St. Louis, Mo.

SOPHIE SCHROEDER SLOMAN. B. S. and M. D. from the University of Illinois College of Medicine. 1947–1950 Superintendent, Illinois Institute for Juvenile Research. At present Clinical Assistant Professor in Psychiatry, University of Illinois College of Medicine. She is a Fellow of the American Psychiatric Association, a Fellow of the American Orthopsychiatric Association, and a member of state and local medical societies. She is the author of a number of articles on child psychiatry.

Bibliography

Allport, Gordon W. *Personality*. New York, 1937.

Anastasi, Anne. *Psychological Testing*. New York, 1954.

Anastasi, Anne, and John P. Foley. *Differential Psychology*, revised edition. New York, 1949.

Aquinas, Thomas. *Summa theologica*, I, in *Basic Writings of St. Thomas Aquinas*, ed. Anton C. Pegis. New York, 1945.

Auden, W. H. *Kierkegaard* (The Living Thoughts Library, ed. Alfred O. Mendel). New York, 1952.

Ayer, Alfred J. *The Problem of Knowledge*. New York, 1956.

Bach, George R. *Intensive Group Psychotherapy*. New York, 1954.

Bainton, Roland H. *Here I Stand*. New York, 1950.

Barth, Karl. *Fides Quaerens Intellectum, Anselms Beweis der Existenz Gottes*. Munich, 1931.

Bergsten, Göte. *Pastoral Psychology*. New York, 1951.

Boggs, Wade H., Jr. *Faith Healing and the Christian Faith*. Richmond, 1955.

Bohr, Niels. *Atomic Theory and the Description of Nature*. New York, 1934.

Boisen, Anton T. *Religion in Crisis and Custom*. New York, 1955.

Bross, Irwin D. J. *Design for Decision*. New York, 1953.

Brown, James. *Subject and Object in Modern Theology*. New York, 1955.

Brown, Judson S. "Pleasure-Seeking Behavior and the Drive-Reduction Hypothesis," *Psychological Review*, 1955.

Brubacher, John S., ed. *Modern Philosophies of Education* (Fifty-fourth Yearbook of the National Society for the Study of Education). Chicago, 1955.

Bugelski, B. R. *The Psychology of Learning*. New York, 1956.

Burtt, Edwin A., ed. *The English Philosophers from Bacon to Mill*. New York, 1939.

Cannon, Walter B. *The Wisdom of the Body*. New York, 1939.

Carnap, Rudolf. *The Continuum of Inductive Methods*. Chicago, 1952.

Cartwright, Dorwin, and Alvin Zander. *Group Dynamics: Research and Theory*. Evanston, Ill., 1953.

Cassirer, Ernst. *Determinism and Indeterminism in Modern Physics*. New Haven, 1956.

Cattell, Raymond B. *Personality*. New York, 1950.

Clark, Kenneth E. *America's Psychologists*. Washington, D. C., 1957.

Clifford, W. K. *The Ethics of Belief*. London and New York, 1947.

Concordia Triglotta (The Symbolical Books of the Ev. Lutheran Church, German-Latin-English edition). St. Louis, 1921.

Cronbach, Lee J. *Essentials of Psychological Testing.* New York, 1949.

Cronbach, Lee J., and Goldine C. Gleser. *Psychological Tests and Personnel Decisions.* Urbana, Ill., 1957.

Dollard, John, and Neal E. Miller. *Personality and Psychotherapy.* New York, 1950.

Eccles, John C. "Hypotheses Relating to the Brain-Mind Problem," *Nature,* CLXVIII (July 1951).

————. *The Neurophysiological Basis of Mind.* Oxford, 1953.

Eddington, Arthur S. *The Nature of the Physical World.* New York, 1929.

————. *New Pathways in Science.* New York, 1935.

————. *The Philosophy of Physical Science.* Cambridge, 1939.

Feigl, Herbert, and May Brodbeck, eds. *Readings in the Philosophy of Science.* New York, 1953.

Feigl, Herbert, and M. Scriven, eds. *Minnesota Studies in Philosophy of Science.* Minneapolis, Vol. I, 1956; Vol. II, 1958.

Feigl, H., and W. S. Sellars, eds. *Readings in Philosophical Analysis.* New York, 1949.

Ferster, Charles B., and Burrhus F. Skinner. *Schedules of Reinforcement.* New York, 1957.

Flew, Antony, and Alasdair Macintyre, eds. *New Essays in Philosophical Theology.* New York, 1955.

Freud, Sigmund. *Civilization and Its Discontents.* London, 1953.

————. *Collected Papers,* I. London, 1950.

————. *Collected Papers,* IV. London, 1948.

————. *The Ego and the Id.* London, 1927.

————. *The Future of an Illusion,* trans. W. D. Robson-Scott (International Psychoanalytical Library, No. 15). London and New York, 1928.

————. *A General Introduction to Psychoanalysis.* New York, 1945.

————. *Inhibitions, Symptoms, and Anxiety.* London, 1948.

————. *The Interpretation of Dreams. Standard Edition of the Complete Psychological Works of Sigmund Freud,* IV. London, 1953.

————. *Outline of Psychoanalysis.* New York, 1949.

Fritz, John H. C. *Pastoral Theology.* St. Louis, 1932.

Fromm, Erich. *Escape from Freedom.* New York, 1941.

Haiman, Franklyn Saul. *Group Leadership and Democratic Action.* Boston, 1951.

Hall, Calvin S., and Gardner Lindzey. *Theories of Personality.* New York, 1957.

Harlow, Harry F. "Mice, Monkeys, Men, and Motives," *Psychological Review,* 1953.

Hayes, Cathy. *The Ape in Our House.* New York, 1951.

Hobart, R. E. "Free Will as Involving Determinisms and Inconceivable Without It," *Mind,* XLIII (1934).

Jordan, Pascual. *Science and the Course of History.* New Haven, 1955.

Josselyn, Irene M. *The Happy Child.* New York, 1955.

Kegley, Charles W., and Robert Bretall, eds. *The Theology of Reinhold Niebuhr* in *The Library of Living Theology*, II. New York, 1956.

Keller, Fred S., and William N. Schoenfeld. *Principles of Psychology*. New York, 1950.

Kierkegaard, Sören. *The Concept of Dread*, trans. Walter Lowrie. Princeton, 1946.

————. *Fear and Trembling: A Dialectical Lyric* (Doubleday Anchor Books). New York, 1954.

————. *The Sickness unto Death*. New York, 1954.

Klotz, John W. *Genes, Genesis, and Evolution*. St. Louis, 1955.

Kretschmer, Ernst. *Körperbau und Charakter*. Berlin, 1944.

Laetsch, Theodore, ed. *The Abiding Word*, II. St. Louis, 1946.

Levinson, Abraham. *The Mentally Retarded Child*. New York, 1952.

Levy, John, and Ruth Munroe. *The Happy Family*. New York, 1938.

London, Ivan D. "Quantum Biology and Psychology," *Journal of General Psychology*, XLVI (1932).

Luther, Martin. *Sämmtliche Schriften*, XXXIII. St. Louis, 1910.

————. *Selected Psalms I* (Luther's Works, vol. 12, American edition). St. Louis, 1955.

————. *Selected Psalms II* (Luther's Works, vol. 13, American edition). St. Louis, 1956.

————. *Small Catechism*. St. Louis, 1943.

————. *Works of Martin Luther*, vol. VI. Philadelphia, 1932.

McClelland, David C. *Personality*. New York, 1951.

McClelland, David C., and John W. Atkinson. *The Achievement Motive*. New York, 1953.

MacMurray, John. *The Boundaries of Science: A Study in the Philosophy of Psychology*. London, 1939.

Maslow, Abraham H., and Bela Mittelman. *Principles of Abnormal Psychology*, rev. ed. New York, 1951.

May, Rollo. *The Meaning of Anxiety*. New York, 1950.

Meehl, Paul E. *Clinical Versus Statistical Prediction*. Minneapolis, 1954.

Menninger, Karl A. *The Human Mind*. New York, 1946.

————. *Man Against Himself*. New York, 1938.

Miller, Neal E. "Learnable Drives and Rewards" in *Handbook of Experimental Psychology*, ed. S. S. Stevens. New York, 1951.

The Miracle of Growth. Urbana, Ill., 1950.

Mitchell, Basil, ed. *Faith and Logic*. London, 1957.

Montagu, M. F. Ashley. *An Introduction to Physical Anthropology*. Springfield, Ill., 1951.

————. *On Being Human*. New York, 1950.

Mowrer, O. H. *Learning Theory and Personality Dynamics*. New York, 1950.

Mueller, John T. *Christian Dogmatics: A Handbook of Doctrinal Theology for Pastors, Teachers, and Laymen*. St. Louis, 1934.

Munroe, Ruth. *Schools of Psychoanalytic Thought*. New York, 1955.

Murray, H. A. *Explorations in Personality*. New York, 1938.

Niebuhr, Reinhold. *Christian Realism and Political Problems*. New York, 1953.

Noyes, Arthur P. *Modern Clinical Psychiatry*, 4th ed. Baltimore, 1953.

Oates, Wayne E. *Religious Factors in Mental Illness*. New York, 1955.

Outler, Albert C. *Psychotherapy and the Christian Message*. New York, 1954.

Pap, Arthur. *Elements of Analytic Philosophy*. New York, 1949.

Perry, Ralph B. *General Theory of Value*. New York, 1926.

Pieper, Francis. *Christian Dogmatics*, trans. Theo. Engelder et al., 3 vols. St. Louis, 1950—53.

Pierce, C. A. *Conscience in the New Testament* in *Studies in Biblical Theology*, No. 15. Chicago, 1955.

Preston, George H. *Psychiatry for the Curious*. New York, 1940.

Reichenbach, Hans. *Experience and Prediction*. Chicago, 1938.

————. *The Rise of Scientific Philosophy*. Berkeley, 1951.

Robinson, John A. T. *The Body* in *Studies in Biblical Theology*, No. 5. Chicago, 1952.

Russell, Bertrand. *An Inquiry into Meaning and Truth*. New York, 1940.

Ryle, Gilbert. *The Concept of Mind*. London, 1949.

Sayers, Dorothy. *The Man Born to Be King*. New York, 1943.

Scharlemann, Martin H. "A Theology for Biblical Interpretation," *Concordia Theological Monthly*, XXIX (January 1958), 38—45.

Scheinfeld, Amram. *The New You and Heredity*. Philadelphia, 1950.

Schroedinger, Erwin. *Science and Humanism*. Cambridge, 1951.

Sheldon, W. H. *The Varieties of Temperament*. New York, 1942.

Sinnott, Edmund W. *The Biology of the Spirit*. New York, 1955.

Skinner, Burrhus F. *Science and Human Behavior*. New York, 1953.

Soal, S. G., and F. Bateman. *Modern Experiments in Telepathy*. New Haven, 1954.

Stebbing, Lizzie S. *Philosophy and the Physicists*, III. London, 1937.

Temple, William. *Nature, Man and God*. New York, 1953.

Thelen, Herbert A. *Dynamics of Groups at Work*. Chicago, 1954.

Tillich, Paul. *The Courage to Be*. New Haven, 1952.

————. *Systematic Theology*. Chicago, Vol. I, 1951; Vol. II, 1957.

Tolman, E. C. *Purposive Behavior in Animals and Men*. New York, 1932.

Tyler, Leona E. *The Psychology of Human Differences*, 2d ed. New York, 1956.

Van Til, Cornelius. *The Defense of the Faith*. Philadelphia, 1954.

Vanderveldt, James H., and Robert P. Odenwald. *Psychiatry and Catholicism*. New York, 1952.

White, Robert W. *The Abnormal Personality*, 2d ed. New York, 1956.

Whitehead, Alfred North. *Process and Reality*. New York, 1929.

Wittgenstein, Ludwig. *Tractatus logico-philosophicus*. London, 1933.

General Index

Absolution and catharsis 281—283
Accountability in mental illness 263 to 267
Achievement motive as drive 93
Activity as drive 92
Ad hoc hypothesis 181
Addiction 137
Adult and infant different 101 f
Aggression, Freud on instinct of 221 f
Alcoholism 137, 231, 263
  as escape from reality 90
Alexander, Samuel, evolutionary theory of 40
Allport, Gordon W. 95
Ambrose, St. 28
Angel 159, 189
Animal, man distinguished from 87—89, 99, 123 f
Anselm, St. 36
Anxiety 53—56, 120 f, 126, 216-218, 240, 248—251, 312; see also Guilt feeling
  bound 152
  existential or primary, needs Law and Gospel 56
  and God's baptismal covenant 71 f
  an important state variable 121 to 124
  in involutional reaction 136
  lessening of, and repression 142
  neurotic; see Neurotic anxiety
  overcome by Christian hope 66
  is part of normal life 122
  in psychoneurosis 136
  relieved by confession and forgiveness 68
  removed by faith 251
  seemingly lacking in sociopathic personality 137 f
Apollinarianism 193
Aristotle 36, 318
Arminianism 209
  and free will 58

Augustine 18, 172, 216
Autonomy, functional, theory of 113

Baptism, lifelong implications of 71 f
Behavior
  abnormal, theological attitude toward sinful 266 f
  importance of secondary reinforcers in everyday 112 f
  molding and activating of 101 to 130
  mostly the result of learning 104
  problems of children 138—142
  versus introspection as scientific evidence 86
Believing; see Faith; "I believe"
Bergson, Henri 173
Body
  dualism of mind and 5, 158 f, 316—321
  human, as physical machine 184 f
  protective and corrective devices and functions of 90
Boisen, Anton T., on psychological effects of Pentecostal denominations 257 f
Brain of man
  and conversion 189—215
  functional centers in 89
  makes life integrated and rational 88 f
  states of 198, 329

Caemmerer, Richard R. 254
Calvinism 207
  on free will 58
  on irresistible grace 193 f, 205
Carneades, dilemma of 36
Catatonic schizophrenia 135
Catharsis 271
  confession, absolution, and 281 to 283
Cathexis 114, 118, 122, 128, 197
  activated by state variable 124
  defined and illustrated 111—113

345

Curiosity
  as drive 92—95
  as state variable 116

Death and the soul 317, 319
Decretum horribile of Calvin 179
Defense, religious content as 259 to 262
Deficiency, mental 132 f
Delusion 134—136
  Messianic 255 f, 261 f
Depression
  in involutional reaction 136
  in manic-depressive reaction 135
  in psychoneurosis 136
  shock treatment for psychotic 146
Derivatives of unconscious material 249
Descartes, René 158
Determinism
  in Calvinism 58
  empirical 81 f, 176, 178; and metaphysical to be distinguished 183
  freedom and 41—48
  and human behavior 178 f
  and materialism 183—189
  metaphysical 81, 178, 213
  methodological 78—82, 178
  as principle of inquiry 45
  psychological 175
  and related problems 172—215
  and revelation 189—215
  scientific 4 f, 78—84, 213 f
  substantive 83 f
Deus absconditus 58, 183
Differentiation 110
Discrimination 125
Displacement 143 f
Docetism 193
Doctrine, particular formulation of, and mental defect 257—259
Dostoevski, Fëdor 36
Drives 115, 119, 124 f, 225 f
  biological reductionism of 86
  Christian and his 251
  in infant 101
  learned and unlearned 93—95
  and needs 89—95
  secondary 93
  as state variables 117 f

as tissue needs 91—95
viscerogenic and psychogenic 93
Dualism 5, 158 f, 208—211, 316 to 321
  deterministic and indeterministic 188 f

Eccles, John C. 210, 329—331
Election 151, 156 f, 174, 209—211
  a mystery 6
Elicitation 116, 118—120, 152
  self-production of, in man 123
Emergence 207, 336
Emotion 115, 119, 197, 253 f, 318 f
  as controlling state for habit 116
  as state variable 118
Empiricism 14—18, 161 f, 173, 208, 213
  and existence of God 25
* and historical Christianity 177 f
End-buttons of neurons 206
Environment
  and man's actions 45
  and problem child 140
  and temptation 284
Epiphenominalism 211
Escape 144
Eucharist; see Supper, Lord's
Evolution 40, 160 f
  Jesus not acme of 61
  of man 158
Excess of instinct 147 f
Expectancy 110 f, 114, 128, 196 f, 314
  activated by state variable 124
Experience, subjective, as evidence 86
Extinction 125
  of S.R. disposition or habit 107, 114 f
  of expectancies 111

Faith; see also "I believe"
  accommodation of Christian, and scientific method 34
  and contrary evidence 23 f, 35
  definition of 29 f
  God's guarantee changes hope into certainty of 75 f
  "in," not "that" 22—25, 34
  logic of 20—22
  and logical necessity 37

347

new creation lives by 70
and personality 239—267
removes basic guilt and anxiety
251
in risen Christ receives forgiveness 66
and scientific certainty 22—24
of scientist and of Christian 24
to 26
validated by God's activity 36
Faith healing 304—308
Fall of man into sin 57
Fatalism 45, 204, 207
Fear; *see also* Anxiety
in animals externally elicited 119 f
as state variable 116
Foreknowledge; *see also* Predictability
of God 46, 209
nonratiocinative 160
Feigl, Herbert 211
Flesh, desires of 320
Forgiveness 4, 151, 278, 281, 313
by faith in risen Christ 66
Free will 155 f, 179, 201
theological views on 58
Freedom 156, 174
and determinism 41—48
of man in creation 49 f
man's lack of spiritual 59
Freud, Sigmund 2 f, 5, 26, 43, 139,
147 f, 151, 153 f, 168—170,
173, 217—222, 229, 231, 248,
310
on aggressive instinct 221 f
on anxiety 54, 121
on determinism in psychiatry 83
Fromm, Erich 242
misjudges faith of Luther 70
Frustration and sin 254
Functions formulated by monists in
physico-chemical terms 84

Generalization 125
of expectancies 111
of stimulus equivalence 109 f,
113 f
Genes as carriers of heredity 96 f
Gestalt 106, 195, 207, 216, 331, 336
God; *see also* Word of God;
Theology

activity of, validates faith 36
as Author of truth 20
conflict with 241—250
concepts of, biased by parental
attitudes 259
empirical knowledge of 15
existence of 25
intervenes in nature and history
177
must confront man 18—20
providence of; *see* Providence
salvation only by grace of 58
not static, but active in world 62,
174
will of 49, 251
Gospel, Word of God as 11
Grace of God 11, 126, 157, 193,
204, 278; *see also* Means of
Grace
resistible or irresistible 157, 193 f,
205—207, 210 f
salvation only by 58
self-capabilities and 276—278
Guilt 5, 216—238, 312 f
expresses self in conscience 55
faith removes basic 251
objective 4
Guilt feeling 26, 124, 152 f, 216 to
238, 246—251, 275 f, 310, 313
in involutional reaction 136
lacking in sociopathic personality
137 f
of parents of mental defective 133
repressed into the unconscious
145

Habit 105—110, 114, 122, 196 f,
314
activation of, controlled by state
of organism 115 f
is disposition, stimulus-response
connection 105 f, 114 f
laws of 106
Hallucination 124, 134 f
Health
mental, goal of pastor and therapist 228—232
psychological, and guilt 216 to
239
Hebrephrenic schizophrenia 134 f

348

Heredity
  and individuality 95—100
  and man's actions 45
  and mental disorder 226
  and problem child 139 f
Hermeneutics 9—14
Hobbes, Thomas 36
Holy Spirit (Holy Ghost) 22, 28
  and conversion 29—32, 170 f, 202
  to 204, 251, 277, 285
  and sanctification 252
Homeostasis 89 f
Homo homini lupus 221 f, 231
Homosexuality 137, 231
Hope, Christian 75 f
Hormones affect appearance and behavior 102
Hostility, conflict and 249 f
Hume, David
  on freedom 46
  on miracles 64 f

"I believe" 27—33
Id and original sin 168—170
Identification 144
Idolatry a defense mechanism 250
Image of God, meaning of 38—40,
  49 f, 57
Incarnation of Christ proof of God's
  mercy 61 f
Independence of categories between
  psychology and theology 165
  to 168
Indeterminacy; see also Determi-
  nacy; Quantum indeterminacy
  and teleological constraints 328
  to 338
Induction 110
  of expectancies 111
Inductive method
  Reichenbach on 80
  of science 16 f
Inevitability 204
Infant
  needs, drives, reactions of 101
  difference between adult and
  101 f
Inhibition 243
Insomnia in involutional reaction
  136
Instantialization of law; see Laws

Integrity, aim of therapy is restora-
  tion of psychological 223
Intelligence tests 132 f
Interaction processes in parish 286
  to 294
Interactionism, psychophysical 210 f,
  305
Introspection as method in scientific
  psychology 86
Involutional reaction a type of psychosis 136

Jesus Christ 11—16, 26, 28—38,
  44 f, 70—73, 305
  as God 11, 15, 20, 22—24, 28,
  34 f, 38, 44, 60—63, 65 f, 71,
  75
  person and work of 59—66
  as Redeemer 11—13, 24, 26, 29
  to 32, 34—36, 56—67, 71, 75
  to 77

Kierkegaard, Sören, on anxiety 55
Kinsey, Alfred Charles 166
Knowledge of God 15—18

Law, Moral 4, 44—46
  application of, and pastoral counseling 273—276, 285
Laws
  of habit 106
  instantialization of 80 f, 128 f,
  176, 178 f, 196, 203—206, 209,
  330
  of learning 104 f, 252
  natural, and conversion 192 f; and
  miracles 183
  of psychiatric 83
  of psychology 175
  scientific 17, 79—81; are generalizations 175
Learning 103—130
  laws of 104 f, 252
  not limited to formal education
  103
  parameter 115
  process and mental mechanisms
  142
Leadership in parish interaction 290
  to 294

Motive 115, 197, 252
  as controlling state for habit 116
Murray, H. A., on distinction between viscerogenic and psychogenic drives 93
Mystery 157, 181—183
  of conversion 27 f
  of creation 37 f
  of person and work of Christ 59 to 66

Naturalism 159, 172—174
  logical empiricist 173 f
  strongest intellectual enemy of church 173
Necessity 156, 210
  defined 17
  not equated with coercion 129 f
  faith and logical 37
Needs
  and conflict 240 f
  drives and 89—95
  of infant 101
  of man 239 f
Nervous system of man makes life integrated and rational 88 f
Neurosis; see Psychoneurosis
Neurotic
  anxiety 55 f, 121, 142; may be relieved by self-knowledge 56
  guilt feeling 152—155
  introvert 123
  perceptions 126
  versus normal individual 122 f
New Thought 304
Nominalism 43
Normal
  not equated with licit 166 f
  individual versus the neurotic 122 f
  life, anxiety part and parcel of 122

Oates, Wayne E.
  on prepsychotic religious concern 262
  on religious content as defense 261
Occasionalism 210
Odenwald, Robert P. 242
Oedipus complex 218 f, 310

"Omniscient Jones" 176, 178 f, 190 to 193, 196, 306, 331, 335
Open questions in theology and science 155 f
Original sin; see Sin
Overeating as substitute for emotional needs 90
Overlap
  partial, between psychological and theological categories 168—171
  between pastoral and therapeutic aims 227 f

Paradox 157, 182
  of Jesus Christ 62
  of salvation by God's grace, damnation through man's own fault 32 f, 58
Parallelism, psychophysical 210 f
Paranoid
  schizophrenia 135
  reaction type of psychosis 135 f
Parents
  blamed for problem child 140
  of mental defective, guilt feeling of 133
Paresis 263
Parish, salutary interaction processes in 286—294
Pastor; see also Counseling, pastoral
  interviewing by 268—272
  personality needs of, affect parishioners 259
  psychiatric adjustment of, important 299
Patience to be joined to hope 76
Pelagian view of free will 58, 202
Perception 197, 314
  activated by state variable 124
  formation of 113 f
Perfectionism
  of Holiness denominations 257
  in involutional reaction 136
Permissiveness
  in pastoral counseling 273—276
  and problem child 140 f
Personality
  compulsive 136
  disintegration of, caused by guilt and anxiety 72
  faith and 239—267

relation of physique to 99
sociopathic 137 f
tests of traits of 325
Perversion of instinct 147 f
Philosophy 14
analytic 217, 302
presuppositions of psychologists in 78—86
speculative 10
Phobia as symptom of psychoneurosis 136 f
Phrenology discredited 99
Positivism
classical Vienna, refuted on ethics 129
logical 81 f
Possibility, meanings of term 199 to 201
Pragmatism, fatal weakness of 40
Prayer
benefits of 73—75
and faith healing 306 f
of pastor with counselee 313
Predictability 156, 213 f
of crime and delinquency 82 f
of human behavior 79 f, 179
and indeterminate brain-state theory of conversion 194
and synergism in conversion 157
Priesthood of believers 291
Progress, philosophical idea of 48 f
Projection 144
Providence and conversion 202 f, 210, 238
Psyche; see Soul
Psychiatric social worker 149
Psychiatrist 148
Psychiatry 217
misconceptions concerning 147
Psychoanalysis 146
Psychodynamics and psychopathology 131—149
Psychologists
American, are mostly atheists 81
clinical 149
defined 148 f
non-Christian, are anthropocentric 242
philosophical presuppositions of 78—86, 127
Psychology
differential 115, 322—327

experimental 217
noncontradictory relations between theology and 165—171
and theology, tensions between 107, 150—171, 241—245, 277
use of term 7
Psychoneurosis 220, 222, 231 f, 243 to 245, 264 f, 310
has aim, is goal-directed 226 f
and conversion 235—238
described 136 f
with insecurity feelings 225
from repressed hostility 222—224
without sin no 223—225
and the unconscious 145
Psychopath 122, 231
Psychopathology, psychodynamics and 131—149
Psychosis
and "charismatic gifts" of Holiness denominations 257 f
as illness 264 f
types of 133—136
Psychosomatic
events in emotions 318 f
illness as symptom of psychoneurosis 136
Psychotherapy 145 f
problem of conscience in 309 to 315
resistance of client to 250 f
use of term 7 f
Pursuit and confrontation 18—20

Quantum indeterminacy 190 f, 195 f, 207, 215, 329, 334
Rationalization 137 f, 143, 249
Reaction formation 144, 247
Reality
must be assumed 25
retreat from, in schizophrenia 134
Recovery, spontaneous, of habit 107
Reductionism, biological 86
Reflex
conscience as 309—311
in infant 101
Regeneration; see Conversion
Reinforcer 114, 125, 142
drive-reduction theory of 117 f
as necessary for forming habit 106 to 108

Spiritual truth, sinful man cannot understand nor willingly accept 57—59, 62

State
or inner condition controls habit 115 f
variables 116—126, 196

Stimulus 118
aversive 120
classes of, discriminated 110
definition of 106
equivalence, generalization of 109 f
neutral 111, 120
situation (S) 106

Stimulus-response connection (S.R) 106, 114, 116

Sublimation 143

Suicide, danger of
in involutional reaction 136
in manic-depressive psychosis 135

Superego
and conscience 169 f
id in conflict with 310

Supper, Lord's, as nurturing the new creation 72 f

Suppression 154
distinguished from repression 143

Surgery in mental illness 146 f

Symbolization 143

Synapsis of neuron end-buttons 330 to 334

Syndromes, psychotic 263 f

Synergism and conversion 157, 202, 209, 237 f

Telepathy 160, 214 f, 328—334

Temple, William, on freedom as self-determination 43

Temptation
psychology of 283 f
two kinds of 254

Tensions between psychology and theology 1—7, 147 f, 150—171, 174, 241—245, 277, 279—281

Terminology; see also Semantics
confusing because specialized 131 f
of psychology and theology non-overlapping 150

Test, psychological tests 323—327

Theology
modern, retreat of 10
noncontradictory relations between, and psychology 165 to 171
scope and method of 9—14
tensions between psychology and; see Tensions
and the three theories of conversion 207—211

Theory, Christianity as 181 f

Tillich, Paul, on forms of anxiety 54 f, 216

Titchener, Edward Bradford 189

Tolman, Edward Chace 217

Trauma 220, 226

Treatment, types of 145—148

Truth is unitary and objective 20 to 22

Unconscious, the 145

Variables, state; see State

Vanderveldt, James H. 242

Ventilation 271

Verstärkung 329, 336 f

Vinson, Frederic Moore, on absolutes 47

Whitehead, Alfred North, evolutionary theory of 40

Will
defined 49
free; see Free will
of God, active and permissive 194
of God and of man in creation 49
human, and conversion 30
of man under sin 56—59

Wittgenstein, Ludwig, on logic 199

Word of God
interpretation of 9—14
as communication 11—13
is consistent 13
as truth 14

Worry in involutional reaction 136

Wundt, Wilhelm 189

Index to Scripture Passages

356